CUBAN SPANISH DIALECTOLOGY

Recent titles in the Georgetown Studies in Spanish Linguistics series
JOHN M. LIPSKI, SERIES EDITOR

Subject Pronoun Expression in Spanish: A Cross-Dialectal Perspective
ANA M. CARVALHO, RAFAEL OROZCO, AND NAOMI LAPIDUS SHIN, EDITORS

Fonología generativa contemporánea de la lengua española, segunda edición
RAFAEL A. NÚÑEZ-CEDEÑO, SONIA COLINA, AND TRAVIS G. BRADLEY, EDITORS

Fundamentos y modelos del estudio pragmático y sociopragmático del español
SUSANA DE LOS HEROS AND MERCEDES NIÑO-MURCIA, EDITORS

Varieties of Spanish in the United States
JOHN M. LIPSKI

CUBAN SPANISH DIALECTOLOGY

VARIATION, CONTACT, AND CHANGE

Alejandro Cuza, Editor

GEORGETOWN UNIVERSITY PRESS
Washington, DC

Library of Congress Cataloging-in-Publication Data

Names: Cuza, Alejandro, editor.
Title: Cuban Spanish Dialectology : Variation, Contact, and Change / editor, Alejandro Cuza.
Other titles: Georgetown Studies in Spanish Linguistics.
Description: Washington, DC : Georgetown University Press, 2017. | Series: The Georgetown Studies in Spanish Linguistics series | Includes bibliographical references.
Identifiers: LCCN 2017002311 (print) | LCCN 2017006726 (ebook) | ISBN 9781626165106 (pb : alk. paper) | ISBN 9781626165090 (hc : alk. paper) | ISBN 9781626165113 (eb) |
Subjects: LCSH: Spanish language--Dialects--Cuba. | Sociolinguistics--Cuba.
Classification: LCC PC4854.C8 C83 2017 (print) | LCC PC4854.C8 (ebook) | DDC 467/.97291--dc23
LC record available at https://lccn.loc.gov/2017002311

♾ This book is printed on acid-free paper meeting the requirements of the American National Standard for Permanence in Paper for Printed Library Materials.

18 17 9 8 7 6 5 4 3 2
First printing

Printed in the United States of America

Cover design by Jim Keller

Contents

Illustrations

Figures

Tables

Foreword

ROBERT M. HAMMOND
Purdue University

DUE TO A MYRIAD of complex historical, political, geographic, and socioeconomic factors since 1492, the language of Spain has evolved into many diverse dialects and subdialects. However, even in 1492 the language of Spain was far from being a homogeneous entity, but rather, was already a variety of dialects stratified along different lines of political and religious demarcations. The Spanish of Granada, for example, was distinct from that of Madrid, Barcelona, or Bilbao. That stratification of Peninsular Spanish in 1492 and later has, in many important ways, contributed to the development of American Spanish dialects as they exist today. Clearly the initial influx of settlers from Southern Spain (i.e., Andalucía) into the Caribbean area shortly after Columbus's first voyage influenced the Spanish spoken in that area today. Another important factor that had an impact on many current dialect areas in the New World was the influence of the indigenous peoples inhabiting these different areas of America from 1492 to date. Many of the indigenous languages of America (e.g., Náhuatl in México, Guaraní in Paraguay, Quechua in Bolivia and Peru, and Taíno in the Caribbean basin) also have had various degrees of impact, albeit mostly lexical, on the dialects of Spanish spoken in these areas. In addition to the indigenous languages of America, the importation of numerous peoples and technologies has also had a profound influence, again mostly lexical, on the Spanish-speaking dialect areas of the New World.

The Spanish-speaking geographical zones of Cuba, Puerto Rico, the Dominican Republic, and Panama, along with the Atlantic coastal areas of Venezuela and Colombia and the remainder of the Spanish-speaking littoral areas of Central America as well as both the Caribbean and Pacific coastal regions of Mexico are generally classified as Caribbean Spanish dialects. Within the Spanish-speaking Caribbean zone, however, the Spanish of Cuba is quite different in many ways from the other Caribbean dialects of this region.

Even though Cuba has played important intellectual, linguistic, political, cultural, and socioeconomic roles in the Caribbean for many years, there is still a relative paucity of studies carried out on Cuban Spanish. While studies published on Cuban Spanish date back to the first half of the nineteenth century (e.g., Pichardo

1836), prior to the middle of the twentieth century, almost all of those studies were highly impressionistic in nature and most dealt with lexical observations. (See Almendros 1958 for an exception to this generalization.) Similarly, most studies published on Cuban Spanish in the second half of the twentieth and the first two decades of the twenty-first centuries have come from the US, although in more recent decades some important studies that deal with Cuban Spanish carried out by Cubans living in Cuba have emerged (e.g., Darias Concepción 2001; Choy-López 1985; Costa Sánchez 1987; Ruiz Hernández and Vitelio 1977). Along with the relative absence of scholarship done by Cuban scholars in Cuba, there is also a need for further research on the Cuban Spanish that is spoken in the larger Cuban communities in the US (e.g., the greater Miami, Florida, Tampa, Florida, and New York City areas as well as in several areas of California).

Despite the importance of Cuba in the Caribbean basin along with the large Cuban presence in the US, research on Cuban Spanish remains somewhat underdeveloped, and it has not received as much attention as other varieties of American Spanish, due to what are principally accidents of history, for example, the relative isolation of Cuban scholars from the rest of the academic world and the strong influence of several important scholars describing particular Spanish regions in the New World (e.g., Tomás Navarro Tomás on Puerto Rican Spanish, Luis Flórez and the Instituto Caro y Cuervo on Colombian Spanish, and Juan M. Lope-Blanch on the Spanish of Mexico). These three scholars have brought about what could be considered a disproportionate quantity of scholarship to have been published on the Spanish of these three countries. Another deficiency prevalent in research carried out on Cuban Spanish until quite recently has been a lack of the use of present-day methodologies and theoretical frameworks. These deficiencies, of course, are partly due to the fact that Cuba has been rather inaccessible, since January 1959, from the international community due to the official lack of diplomatic relations between Cuba and the US.

In his introduction to the current book, *Cuban Spanish Dialectology: Variation, Contact and Change*, referring to the lack of empirically based scholarship on Cuban Spanish, Alejandro Cuza writes that "The main goal of the volume is to fill this major gap in the literature," and, he continues, "to provide the reader with the most up-to-date and comprehensive compendium on Cuban Spanish research." It is my pleasure to report that the goals outlined by the editor of the current monograph have been very successfully attained.

In this manuscript, fourteen outstanding original essays are organized into four distinct divisions: *Phonological and phonetic variation*; *morphosyntactic approaches*; *lexical variation;* and *heritage language acquisition*. The three chapters in the first section deal with phonetic and phonological variation in Cuban Spanish. These chapters provide empirical data for further analysis and offer interesting outcomes that tend to reach different conclusions than those found in previous descriptions on Cuban Spanish.

The five chapters of the second component of the present monograph deal with morphosyntactic variation in Cuban Spanish, a topic that has also received little attention in the earlier literature. The first three chapters provide important new data and comparisons on subject pronoun expression by Cuban speakers residing on the island and Cubans living in contact with English in the US. They also provide some interesting conclusions on variables that influence outcomes. The last two chapters analyze the use of reduplicative *que* and variations in the choice of the verbs *ser* and *estar*.

The three chapters of the following section of the book are all based on analyses of empirical data and deal with lexical variation in Cuban Spanish. These chapters provide, in general, very different perspectives on factors that influence the Cuban Spanish lexicon as well as its influence on other varieties of Spanish. Among the principal factors discussed in these chapters are the use of Anglicisms in Cuban Spanish, based on written surveys by Cubans living in the Miami, Florida, area.

The final unit of *Cuban Spanish Dialectology: Variation, Contact and Change* presents novel research on the acquisition of Cuban Spanish among second- and third-generation heritage speakers born and raised in the US. A very important aspect of these three chapters is that they address heritage language acquisition of Spanish by speakers of Cuban ancestry.

There are many reasons why the current volume is an extremely valuable contribution to research on Cuban Spanish. First, each of the chapters of this book is structured following an up-to-date methodology and recent theoretical framework. Secondly, this manuscript provides the reader with many essays that open new avenues of research along with a great deal of data that can be utilized for further research. Furthermore, a unique characteristic of the present study on Cuban Spanish is that only three of its fourteen studies treat phonetic or phonological themes. This is unlike most of the previous research realized on Cuban Spanish, which deal almost exclusively with the sound system of this dialect (see, for example: Hammond and Resnick 1988; Guitart 1980; Terrell 1979; Alfaraz 2008; Haden and Matluck 1973; Ringer Uber 1986). Likewise, although there have been numerous prior lexical studies published concerning Cuban Spanish, very few were compiled following any type of scientific methodology and are little more than impressionistic observations. Additionally, some of the essays in this book compare the Cuban Spanish spoken in the US with the Spanish spoken in Cuba by monolingual speakers, a perspective often lacking in other volumes on Cuban Spanish. In a similar vein, chapters herein also provide comparisons between the Spanish spoken by different generations of Cubans residing in the US. This manuscript without a doubt will take its place as a highly informative and long-lasting research tool for students and scholars involved in Cuban Spanish as well as others with a more general interest in Hispanic dialectology, sociolinguistics, psycholinguistics, and language contact.

Acknowledgments

THIS PROJECT WOULD NOT have been possible without the gracious time and collaboration of many colleagues serving as anonymous reviewers, including Gabriela Alfaraz (Michigan State University), Meghan Armstrong (University of Massachusetts, Amherst), Jennifer Austin (Rutgers University), Joyce Bruhn de Garavito (University of Western Ontario), Eugenio Bustos (Universidad Complutense de Madrid), Richard Cameron (University of Illinois, Chicago), Manuel Díaz-Campos (Indiana University), Laura Domínguez (University of Southampton), Nydia Flores-Ferrán (Rutgers University), Melvin González-Rivera (Universidad de Puerto Rico, Mayagüez), Pedro Guijarro-Fuentes (Universidad de Islas Baleares), José Ignacio Hualde (University of Illinois, Urbana-Champaign), Daniel Olson (Purdue University), Ricardo Otheguy (Graduate Center, CUNY), Luis A. Ortiz López (Universidad de Puerto Rico, Río Piedras), Rafael Orozco (Louisiana State University), Ivan Ortega Santos (University of Memphis), Rocío Pérez-Tattam (Swansea University), Silvia Perpiñán (University of Western Ontario), Rajiv Rao (University of Wisconsin, Madison), Daniel Sáez Rivera (Universidad Complutense de Madrid), Michael Shelton (Occidental College), Sandro Sessarego (University of Texas at Austin), Eva-María Suárez Büdenbender (Shepherd University), Julio Villa-García (University of Manchester), and Erik Willis (Indiana University). To all of them I am extremely grateful. Furthermore, I am deeply appreciative of Robert Hammond for graciously agreeing to write the foreword for this volume. Robert Hammond's work and indefatigable dedication to Cuban Spanish research for the last forty years have impacted the field tremendously, and this project would have been incomplete without his contribution. Finally, I would like to express my profound gratitude to the series editor, John Lipski, and to the editorial staff at Georgetown University Press for their assistance and support.

Introduction: New Facets in Cuban Spanish Research

ALEJANDRO CUZA
Purdue University

THE PRESENT VOLUME SHOWCASES fourteen state-of-the-art studies on Cuban Spanish, the Spanish dialect spoken on the island of Cuba. Cuban Spanish differs from mainstream varieties by having specific phonological, syntactic, and lexical features stemming from the combination of several historical, geographical, political, and linguistic factors. The initial contact with pre-Colombian cultures and languages (e.g., the Arawak language and the Taíno culture), the contact with African languages brought by African slaves (e.g., the Yoruba language), and the massive immigration of Spaniards from the Canary Islands have all shaped the formation and evolution of what we today know as Cuban Spanish. This variety of Spanish is spoken by more than 11 million people currently living in Cuba, as well as by a large number of first-, second-, and third-generation Cubans residing abroad, crucially in the United States (US).

Cuban Spanish is part of the family of Caribbean Spanish dialects spoken in Puerto Rico, Dominican Republic, Panama, and the Atlantic coastal areas of Venezuela (e.g., Caracas) and Colombia (e.g., Cartagena, Barranquilla) (Lipski 1994). These dialects behave similarly in regards to phonological, lexical, and syntactic features, including most prominently the overuse of second-person subject pronoun *tú* (you) (e.g., *¿Qué tú quieres*? 'What do you want?'), aspiration and deletion of word-final /s/ (e.g., [*l****oh*** *niño∅*] instead of *los niños*, 'the children'), deletion of intervocalic /d/ (e.g., [*de∅o*] instead of ***dedo***, 'finger'), lateralization of final syllable /r/ (e.g., [*ta**l**de*] instead of ***tarde***, 'late') or the lack of subject-verb inversion in *wh*-questions (*¿Dónde* ***Betty compró*** *ese vestido?* instead of *¿Dónde* ***compró Betty*** *el vestido?* 'Where did Betty buy that dress?') (Choy-López 1986; Guitart 1976; Hammond and Resnick 1988; Lipski 1994, 2008; López-Morales 1970, 1992; Ordóñez and Olarrea 2006; Varela 1992).

Despite the existing similarities with other Caribbean Spanish dialects, Cuban Spanish is also quite different. For example, in contrast with Puerto Rican Spanish, the lateralization of /r/ in syllable-final or word-final position is stigmatized in Cuba, and is more common in the eastern part of the country (see Alfaraz 2008 for recent discussion). Furthermore, western Cuban Spanish (the Spanish spoken in the western provinces of Pinar del Río, Havana, and Matanzas) is particularly known for its assimilation of liquid /r/, as in [kad¬ne] instead of *carne* (meat) (e.g., Alfaraz 2007; Carlson, this volume; Guitart 1980). This is a distinctive feature of Havana Spanish not present in other Caribbean Spanish varieties or in other parts of Cuba. There is also notable variation within Cuba itself (phonologically and lexically) depending on geographical area—crucially western versus eastern dialectal zones—and external factors such as educational level, socioeconomic status, age, and gender. The linguistic and social status of Havana Spanish within Cuba has also led to speakers from other dialectal zones to incorporate this dialect when moving to Havana or emigrating out of the country. This is evident in many linguistic enclaves within the US (e.g., Miami) where many speakers from Oriente (eastern Cuba) end up adopting *el español habanero* to avoid mockery from fellow Cubans when saying something like *hallaca* instead of *tamal* (tamal) or the Arawak word *cutara* instead *chancleta* (flip flops).

Motivation for the Current Volume

Research on Cuban Spanish goes back as far as 1836 with the pioneering work of Esteban Pichardo (*Diccionario Provincial de Voces Cubanas,* Pichardo 1836). Since then, scholars have been fascinated with the linguistic analysis of Cuban Spanish, paving the way for landmark work, especially in regards to phonological and lexical variation (Choy-López 1986, 1988; Guitart 1976, 1980, 2004; Hammond 1976, 1986; López-Morales 1970, 1992; Solé 1982; Varela 1992). Most of this previous scholarship comes from the US, where over 2 million Cubans currently reside. Cuban immigration to the US dates back to late 1800s when thousands of Cubans immigrated to Tampa and Key West for cigar manufacturing. The number of Cubans in the US increased dramatically after the Cuban Revolution of 1959, when an estimated 546,945 Cubans entered the US between 1959 and 1970 (Lipski 2008; Portés and Bach 1985). This number increased significantly with the Mariel Boatlift of 1980 when 125,000 Cubans left the island. The Cuban population on American soil today represents the nation's third largest Hispanic group, making up 3.7 percent of the total Hispanic population in 2013 (Pew Research Center). Most Cuban Americans (1.2 million as of 2012) live in the Greater Miami area (Miami, Hialeah, and Fort Lauderdale). Other large Cuban enclaves are located in northeastern New Jersey (Union City, North Bergen, West New York) and in California.

Despite the large presence of Cuban immigrants in the US and its economic and political clout (García and Otheguy 1988; Lipski 2008), Cuban Spanish remains largely underexplored. It has not received as much attention as other varieties of Caribbean Spanish (e.g., Puerto Rican and Dominican), and there is little research on Cuban Spanish using current theoretical perspectives and methodological tools. This stems from the fact that Cuba has remained somewhat isolated from the international community due to more than half a century of severed relations between Cuba and the US.

The main goal of the volume is to fill this major gap in the literature and to provide the reader with the most up-to-date and comprehensive compendium on Cuban Spanish research. The fourteen empirical studies presented in this volume focus on Cuban Spanish from the island, as well as in contact with English in the US. This comes at a timely moment with the recent normalization of diplomatic ties between Cuba and the US, and a renewed interest in Cuban Spanish research. The specific dialectal features of Cuban Spanish and the sociodemographic characteristics of the Cuban community in the US (Pérez 1986; Portés and Bach, 1985) make it an ideal testing ground to evaluate not only specific linguistic aspects of this dialect (eg., morphosyntax, phonology), but also sociolinguistic aspects of language contact and change, intergenerational transmission, and heritage language development. The empirical studies in the current volume focus on these specific issues, connecting the dots between typical research in Spanish dialectology and interrelated fields.

Overview of the Volume

This volume brings together established and emerging scholars in Hispanic linguistics in a collection of fourteen studies examining various aspects of Cuban Spanish research on four core areas: *phonological and phonetic variation* (part I), *morphosyntactic approaches* (part II), *lexical variation* (part III), and *heritage language acquisition* (part IV). The book is directed at students and scholars interested in Hispanic linguistics in general, and Cuban Spanish dialectology specifically. It is a welcome addition to existing volumes on Latin-American Spanish dialectology (e.g., Alvar 1996; Hammond and Resnick 1988; Lipski 1994, 2008; Zamora and Guitart 1982) and could be used in courses on Spanish dialectology, Spanish sociolinguistics, introduction to Hispanic linguistics, Spanish in the US, and Spanish in contact. Faculty members could also use some of the chapters as supplemental readings for courses on the acquisition of Spanish morphosyntax as a heritage language. In what follows, I briefly discuss each part of the volume and its contribution.

Part I: Phonetic and Phonological Variation

Documenting phonetic and phonological variation in Cuban Spanish has been at the forefront of previous research in Cuban Spanish dialectology (Choy-López 1988; Figueroa Esteva, Choy-López, and Dohotaru 1990; Guitart 1976; Hammond 1976; Terrel 1982). The first part of this volume complements this previous work by providing recent empirical data and analyses on two seminal issues in Spanish phonetics and phonology: 1) the status of English and Spanish vowel systems in a language contact scenario, and 2) the phonetic nature of gemination in western Cuban Spanish. Furthermore, part I adds to previous work by presenting an empirical study on phonetic code-switching among Cuban American speakers, an area of research so far unexplored.

In chapter 1, Brandon Rogers and Scott Alvord undertake the study of Spanish and English vowels in the speech of Cubans in Miami. Specifically, the authors examine the role of crosslinguistic influence in the vowel system of Cuban immigrants. Results show a stable Spanish vowel system, impermeable to English influence regardless of language dominance. English vowels, on the other hand, did show some degree of variation and transfer from Spanish. These results have important implications for current work on the extent and directionality of phonological transfer in Spanish-English bilingual populations, and specifically on current research documenting the existence of a 'Miami accent' among Spanish-background native speakers of English. Shifting from a phonetic analysis of Cubans in Miami to Cubans on the island, Kristin M. Carlson presents an analysis of the phonetic nature of gemination in syllable-final, word-internal liquids (/l/ and /ɾ/) in Havana Cuban speech (chapter 2). Despite previous research showing gemination as a defining characteristic of western Cuba, Carlson demonstrates that the occurrence of partial and full gemination fell below chance.

Ann Aly closes the first part of this volume (chapter 3) by presenting a study on the suprasegmental and segmental properties of phonetic code-switching among early and late Spanish-English bilinguals in Miami using evidence from a semi-spontaneous corpus. The author shows that Miami-born simultaneous bilinguals are able to utilize the intonation of either English or Spanish when code-switching, while Cuban-born bilinguals tend to favor Spanish-like pitch accents. Aly also finds later peak alignment in code-switches among the Cuban-born group. In contrast with the results of Rogers and Alvord in chapter 1, Aly demonstrates strong correlations between the degree of switches, language dominance, and age of onset of bilingualism.

Part II: Morphosyntactic Variation

In contrast with the large number of studies examining phonetic and phonological variation in Cuban Spanish, there is only a handful of studies dealing with morphosyntactic variability (Alfaraz 2011; Cuza and Frank 2011, 2015; Dauphinais and Ortiz López 2016). Part II addresses this gap in the literature by presenting five empirical studies on this topic. The first three focus on subject pronoun expression and word order, and the last two focus on reduplicative *que* and copula *ser/estar*. Although subject pronoun expression in Spanish has been amply investigated (Camacho 2013; Cameron 1993; Carvalho, Orozco, and Lapidus Shin 2015; Otheguy and Zentella 2012), this part of the volume presents new data on subject pronoun expression from Cuban speakers on the island and in contact with English in the US.

In the first chapter (chapter 4), Daniel Erker, Eduardo Ho-Fernández, Ricardo Otheguy, and Naomi Lapidus Shin examine subject-verb word order (*Rosa llamó* versus *Llamó Rosa*, 'Rosa called') among first- and second-generation Cubans in New York. Results show a strong preference for preverbal position among the two groups. The authors argue that although the second-generation Cubans show higher rates of preverbal positioning, variable and factor hierarchies demonstrate considerable evidence of cross-generational continuity and similarity among the two generations. As discussed in other studies in this volume, there appears to be an overall level of morphosyntactic stability among second-generation Cubans in the US, against previous research documenting patterns of crosslinguistic influence in child and adult heritage speakers of Spanish (Cuza 2016; Montrul 2008; Montrul and Rodríguez Louro 2006).

In chapter 5, Gabriela Alfaraz discusses the variation of overt pronoun use over time in Cuban Spanish. The author examines the corpus of 8,305 tokens from fifty-seven Cuban speakers born between 1885 and 1970. A comparative analysis based on year of birth shows strong correlation between overt pronoun expression and person, number, and coreference across time. The author demonstrates that factors such as verb type, tense, mood, aspect, and polarity have lesser effects in overt pronoun variation over time.

Like the previous two studies, Luis Ortiz López, Ashlee Dauphinais, and Héctor Aponte Alequín present an analysis of the distribution of subject pronouns and subject-verb word order (chapter 6). In contrast with the corpus-based study presented by Alfaraz and the work with Cubans in New York presented by Erker and colleagues, Ortiz, Dauphinais, and Aponte Alequín analyze data collected in Havana using acceptability judgment questionnaires and semi-spontaneous data. The results show that semantic-pragmatic variables have the greatest effect on pronoun realization and word order.

Joshua Frank and Almeida Jacqueline Toribio (chapter 7) investigate the syntax of reduplicative *que* in the Spanish of Havana, an area of research so far unexplored (e.g., *Me pregunta que si gano (que) cómo voy a gastar el premio monetario*, 'S/he asks me that if I win, how will I spend the monetary prize'). Using a repetition task and a sentence completion measure, the authors find that the use of reduplicative *que* is dispreferred among monolingual speakers of Spanish. This leads the authors to argue that multiple complementizers are not licensed by the grammar of Cuban Spanish. This finding contrasts with what has been found in other varieties of Spanish (e.g., Peninsular Spanish, Colombian Spanish), where reduplicative *ques* are allowed (Frank 2016; Villa-García 2015).

Part II closes with a chapter by Manuel Díaz-Campos, Iraida Galarza, and Gibran Delgado-Díaz (chapter 8). The authors focus on a grammatical area so far underexplored in Cuban Spanish research, namely the potential linguistic and extralinguistic factors constraining the use of *ser* and *estar* among speakers from Havana. Furthermore, the authors compare Cuban Spanish with other varieties to reach a better understanding of the potential variation in [copula verb + adjective] strings under a grammaticalization perspective. Results show that the use of *estar* in Cuban Spanish was restricted by semantic (resultative state, adjective class) and pragmatic (frame of reference, experience with the referent) factors. However, it was found that age, gender, and socioeconomic class were not significant. Results also revealed that *estar* is conditioned by the same linguistic factors across dialects in the comparative analysis. The authors argue for a cross-dialectal prototypical meaning of *estar* in attributive contexts [temporally bounded, immediate, + comparative] and suggest that these copular constructions are stable, contrary to what has been stated in previous investigations.

Part III: Lexical Variation

Part III showcases three articles discussing linguistic and extralinguistic factors constraining lexical variation in Cuban Spanish. This part opens with a chapter by Andrew Lynch (chapter 9), in which the author addresses the issue of English-based lexical innovations among 130 Cubans residing in Miami. Lynch follows previous research to scrutinize loanwords, phonological calques, semantic calques, and phrasal calques, while controlling for several variables including immigration generation, educational level, community characteristics, bilingual proficiency, and language use patterns. Results show that the more proficient the speakers are in English, the less likely they are to adopt and accept English-influenced lexical innovations and to use loanwords. Lynch also demonstrates that phrasal and phonological calques are the most acceptable type of lexical innovation and the most widely diffused.

Related to the issue of English-influenced lexical innovations is the assumption that Cuban Spanish is quite different from Peninsular Spanish due to its large number of so-called anglicisms, when in fact this is just part of the story. This is precisely one of the main issues that Pascual Cantos-Gómez addresses in chapter 10. Specifically, Cantos-Gómez examines the structure and structuring of the lexical repertoires in both language varieties (lexical variability, growth, types, functional types/lemmas) according to their underlying mathematical properties. Furthermore, he provides up-to-date data on the visibility of both language varieties.

Keeping with the theme of lexical variation, Antoni Fernández Parera (chapter 11) examines the extent of lexical influences of Cuban Spanish on other varieties of Spanish in Miami, as well as language attitudes and perceptions toward this language variety. The author examines 129 second- and third-generation speakers, including Cubans, mixed-ethnicity Cubans, and non-Cubans. Results show that Cuban Spanish carries significantly less prestige than other varieties, such as Colombian or Argentinian. Furthermore, results demonstrate that the lexical influence of Cuban Spanish on other varieties spoken in Miami is not as substantial as people might think.

Part IV: Heritage Language Acquisition

The acquisition of Spanish as a heritage language in the US is an area of research that has attracted recent attention among acquisitionists and applied linguists, following the pioneering work of Guadalupe Valdés, Ana Roca, and Carmen Silva-Corvalán. Existing research, however, has focused primarily—if not exclusively—on the acquisition of Spanish among Mexican-background heritage speakers. Despite the large number of second- and third-generation Cuban Americans in the country, there is very little research examining the acquisition of Spanish among speakers of Cuban descent. We address this gap in the literature by presenting three studies investigating the acquisition of Cuban Spanish among second- and third-generation heritage speakers born and raised in the US.

Alejandro Cuza and José Camacho open this part of the volume (chapter 12) with a study on the acquisition of personal pronoun subjects with inanimate reference (e.g., *Ella solita suelta su agua*, 'It pours its own liquid'—*ella* here meaning the beef) among heritage speakers of Cuban Spanish. The authors investigate the grammar of Cuban heritage speakers residing in Miami and New Jersey via an acceptability judgment task, a preference task, and an elicited production task. Overall, results show that heritage speakers of Cuban Spanish have knowledge of this specific morphosyntactic property, despite their preference for null subjects, behaving similarly to native speakers. There is a generational continuity as far as this specific dialectal feature is concerned, corroborating the results of Erker and colleagues in chapter 4.

Diego Pascual y Cabo and Inmaculada Gómez Soler investigate the acquisition of dative experiencer predicates in Cuban heritage children (chapter 13). Results from an elicited imitation task show significant differences in the target production of *gustar*-like verbs versus non-*gustar*-like verbs among the bilingual children. This is evidenced in a high rate of omission of the dative marker –*a* in obligatory contexts and noncanonical verb agreement. The authors argue that the differences observed stem from cross-generational attrition as evidenced in the speech of the adult immigrant group.

Ana de Prada Pérez and Andrea Hernández close this final part of the volume (chapter 14) by presenting a thoughtful study on the effects of code-switching on *ser/estar* copula choice among Cuban heritage speakers living in Miami. The authors investigate two code-switching conditions: one with Spanish adjectives and one with English adjectives. Results from an acceptability judgment task reveal a strong distinction of the copulas with some adjectives, as well as a loss of distinction with other adjective types. Prada Pérez and Hernández conclude that there is a simplification in code-switching in order to alleviate the cognitive cost of processing two languages simultaneously.

Conclusions

This volume contributes to previous research in specific and substantial ways. It provides the reader with state-of-the-art research on Cuban Spanish linguistics in one compendium of empirical studies. Specifically, it offers new insights into seminal issues including the status of Spanish and English vowels in contact situations, liquid gemination in Spanish, the syntactic and phonetic status of code-switching utterances, subject pronoun expression and distribution, the syntax of multiple complementizer structures, copula *ser/estar* use, linguistic and extralinguistic approaches to lexical variation, and heritage language acquisition. Furthermore, these studies encompass data from both the island and the US, which makes the volume extremely relevant for current discussion pertaining to Cuban Spanish dialectology research, as well as language contact and change in general. The exceptional quality of the papers depicted in this volume and the presence of renowned experts and emerging scholars provide irrefutable proof of the vitality of Cuban Spanish research today, and a timely encouragement for future research.

References

Alfaraz, G. 2007. "Effects of Age and Gender on Liquid Assimilation in Cuban Spanish." In *Selected Proceedings of the Third Workshop on Spanish Sociolinguistics*, edited by J. Holmquist, A. Lorenzino, and L. Sayahi, 23–29. Somerville, MA: Cascadilla Proceedings Project.

———. 2008. "The Lateral Variant of (r) in Cuban Spanish." In *Selected Proceedings of the Fourth Workshop on Spanish Sociolinguistics*, edited by M. Westmoreland and J. A. Thomas, 36–42. Somerville, MA: Cascadilla Proceedings Project.

———. 2011. "Accusative Object Marking: A Change in Progress in Cuban Spanish?" *Spanish in Context* 8:213–34.

Alvar, M. 1996. *Manual de dialectología hispánica: El español de América*. Barcelona: Ariel, S.A.

Camacho, J. 2013. *Null Subjects*. Cambridge: Cambridge University Press.

Cameron, R. 1993. "Ambiguous Agreement, Functional Compensation, and Nonspecific *Tú* in the Spanish of San Juan, Puerto Rico, and Madrid, Spain." *Language Variation and Change* 5 (3): 305–34.

Carvalho, A., R. Orozco, and N. Lapidus Shin, eds. 2015. *Subject Pronoun Expression in Spanish: A Cross-Dialectal Perspective*. Washington, DC: Georgetown University Press.

Cuza, A. 2016. "The Status of Interrogative Subject-Verb Inversion in Spanish-English Bilingual Children." *Lingua* 180:124–38.

Cuza, A., L. Czerwionka, and D. Olson, eds. 2016. *Inquiries in Hispanic Linguistics: From Theory to Empirical Evidence*. Amsterdam: John Benjamins.

Cuza, A., and J. Frank. 2011. "Transfer Effects at the Syntax-Semantic Interface: The Case of Double-*Que* Questions in Heritage Spanish." *Heritage Language Journal* 8 (2): 66–89.

———. 2015. "On the Role of Experience and Age-Related Effects: Evidence from the Spanish CP." *Second Language Research* 30:3–28.

Choy-López, L. R. 1986. "Sistema fonético y sistema fonológico." *Neuphilologische Mitteilungen* 3:400–13.

———. 1988. "El consonantismo en el habla culta de la ciudad de La Habana y Santiago de Cuba." *Islas* 91:130–43.

Dauphinais, A., and L. Ortiz López. 2016. "Microvariation in the Null Subject Parameter: Word Order in Cuban Spanish." In Cuza, Czerwionka, and Olson, *Inquiries in Hispanic Linguistics*, 281–300.

Figueroa Esteva, M., L. R. Choy-López, and P. Dohotaru. 1990. "Para la caracterización fonológica del habla urbana actual de Cuba." *Revista Cubana de Ciencias Sociales* 24:20–34.

Frank, J. 2016. "On the Grammaticality of Recomplementation in Spanish." In Cuza, Czerwionka, and Olson, *Inquiries in Hispanic Linguistics*, 39–52.

García, O., and R. Otheguy. 1988. "The Language Situation of Cuban Americans." In *Language Diversity: Problem or Resource? A Social and Educational Perspective on Language Minorities in the United States*, edited by S. McKay and S.-L. C. Wong, 166–92. New York: Newbury House.

Guitart, J. 1976. *Markedness and a Cuban Dialect of Spanish*. Washington, DC: Georgetown University Press.

———. 1980. "Aspectos del consonantismo habanero: Reexamen descriptivo." In *Dialectología hispanoamericana: Estudios actuals*, edited by G. E. Scavnicky, 32-47. Washington, DC: Georgetown University Press.

———. 2004. "En torno a un cambio en la pronunciación del español de la Habana en el último tercio del siglo XX y sus posibles causas." *Lingua Americana* 14:9–20.

Hammond, R. 1976. *Some Theoretical Implications from Rapid Speech Phenomena in Miami-Cuban Spanish*. Unpublished doctoral dissertation, University of Florida.

———. 1986. "En torno a una regla global en la fonología del español de Cuba." In *Estudios sobre la fonología del español del Caribe*, edited by R. Nuñez-Cedeño, I. Páez Urdaneta, and J. Guitart, 31–39. Caracas: La Casa de Bello.

Hammond, R., and M. Resnick. 1988. *Studies in Caribbean Spanish Dialectology*. Washington, DC: Georgetown University Press.

Lipski, J. 1994. *Latin American Spanish*. New York: Longman Group Limited.

———. 1996. *El español de América*. Madrid: Cátedra.

———. 2008. "Cuban Spanish in the United States." In *Varieties of Spanish in the United States*, edited by J. Lipski, 98–115. Washington, DC: Georgetown University Press.

López-Morales, H. 1970. *Estudios sobre el español de Cuba*. New York: Las Américas Publishing Company.

———. 1992. *El español del caribe*. Madrid: Editorial MAPFRE.

Montrul, S. 2008. *Incomplete Acquisition in Bilingualism: Re-examining the Age Factor.* Amsterdam: John Benjamins.

Montrul, S., and C. Rodríguez Louro. 2006. "Beyond the Syntax of the Null Subject Parameter: A Look at the Discourse-Pragmatic Distribution of Null and Overt Subjects by L2 Learners of Spanish." In *The Acquisition of Syntax in Romance Languages*, edited by V. Torrens and L. Escobar, 401–18. Amsterdam: John Benjamins.

Otheguy, R., and A. C. Zentella. 2012. *Spanish in New York: Language Contact, Dialectal Leveling, and Structural Continuity*. New York: Oxford University Press.

Ordóñez, F., and A. Olarrea. 2006. "Microvariation in Caribbean/Non-Caribbean Spanish Interrogatives." *Probus* 18:59–96.

Pérez, L. 1986. "Cubans in the United States." *Annals of the American Academy of Political and Social Science* 487 (September): 126–37.

Pichardo, E. 1836. *Diccionario Provincial de Voces Cubanas*. Matanzas, Cub.: Imprenta de la Real Marina.

Portés, A., and R. Bach. 1985. *Latin Journey: Cuban and Mexican Immigrants in the United States*. London: University of California Press.

Solé, C. 1982. "Language Loyalty and Language Attitudes among Cuban-Americans." In *Bilingual Education for Hispanic Students in the United States*, edited by J. Fishman and G. Keller, 254–68. New York: Columbia University Teachers College Press.

Terrell, T. D. 1982. "Current Trends in the Investigation of Cuban and Puerto Rican Phonology." In *Spanish in the United States: Sociolinguistic Aspects*, edited by J. Amastae and L. Elías-Olivares, 47–70. Cambridge: Cambridge University Press.

Varela, B. 1992. *El español cubano-americano*. New York: Senda Nueva de Ediciones.

Villa-García, J. 2015. *The Syntax of Multiple* Que *Sentences in Spanish: Along the Left Periphery*. Amsterdam: John Benjamins.

Zamora, J., and J. Guitart. 1982. *Dialectología hispanoamericana: Teoría, descripción, historia*. Salamanca, Esp.: Ediciones Almar.

PART I

PHONOLOGICAL AND PHONETIC VARIATION

1

Miami Cuban Vowels

BRANDON M. A. ROGERS
Ball State University

SCOTT M. ALVORD
Brigham Young University

ONE OF THE MORE recent Spanish-speaking groups to arrive in the US are the Cubans living in Miami, Florida. The first waves of Cuban immigrants came to US soil between 1959 and 1962 as approximately 250,000 Cuban immigrants fled the communist Castro regime during the Cuban Revolution. Several more large waves of refugees came between 1973 and 1979 and in 1980 (López-Morales 2003). Consequently, Miami has become the first US city of more than 2,000,000 inhabitants that has a Spanish-speaking majority, and is often known as a truly bilingual city and referred to as the "Gateway to Latin America" (López-Morales 2003). Lynch (1999) states that bilinguals in Miami enjoy a higher status in the workplace than monolinguals of either English or Spanish, and Boswell (2000) observes that Miami Cubans enjoy a higher economic status than other Spanish-speakers in the US have enjoyed. He also asserts that "especially in Miami, Hispanics are empowered both economically and politically. Thus speaking Spanish is not associated with the stigma of poverty and social disaffection in Miami to the same degree that it is in many other large American cities" (Boswell 2000, 423).

As a result of this linguistic coexistence, English and Spanish are in constant, intense contact with one another in Miami. One consequence of this intense language contact situation are the reports of local linguistic norms. The Spanish spoken by this bilingual community has been well documented; for example, Varela (1974) and Otheguy and García (1988) analyze possible lexical and syntactic influences of English on Miami Cuban Spanish. Lynch (2000) studies possible English influence on Miami Cuban morphosyntax while Varela (1992) and Lynch (2009) focus on Miami Cuban Spanish phonology. Alvord (2010) examines Miami Cuban absolute interrogative intonation and the effect of contact with English and other varieties of Spanish spoken in Miami on the use of falling and rising interrogative patterns. Alvord and Rogers (2014) survey the Miami Cuban Spanish vowel systems.

However, the English spoken by Miami Cubans has been ignored in the literature. There are many anecdotes about a "Miami Accent" in the English spoken there; for example, Carter (2013) states that Miami English exhibits differences from general American English in the "pronunciation of vowels, intonation, stronger-sounding consonants, including the consonants 'L' and 'R,' and literal translations." Many people believe that a vowel system that has been influenced by Spanish may be the most important feature of Miami English. Nevertheless, no known studies exist that look at the possible Spanish influence on any aspect of Miami Cuban English. The current study examines the vowels produced by Miami Cuban bilingual speakers in order to describe their Spanish and English vowel systems, explore possible cross-linguistic influences, and to provide an initial consideration of Miami English vowel pronunciation.

The English and Spanish Vowel Systems

There are a great number of differences between the English and Spanish vowel systems, many of which have been documented in laboratory studies (e.g., Quilis and Esgueva 1983; Quilis 1999) and highlighted in many Spanish phonetics textbooks (e.g., Whitley 2002; Guitart 2004; Hualde 2005; among many others). One of the most obvious differences is the scope of each vowel system. General American English has ten vowels—/i, ɪ, ɛ, æ, ɑ, u, ʊ, o, ɔ, ʌ/ (Trudgill and Hannah 1982; Ladefoged 2006)—while general Spanish has only five: /i u e o a/.[1] The larger scope of the English system also undergoes much more variation than the Spanish system. For example, in syllable-final position, while Spanish vowels maintain their quality, in English diphthongization or off-gliding occurs (e.g. /e/ → [ei̯], /o/ → [ou̯]). Another well-known phenomenon is that of unstressed vowel reduction or centralization to a mid-central lax vowel, often referred to as schwa (Brown 1990).

Another notable difference between Spanish and English vowels is the realization of the high back vowel /u/. With specific regard to the American English high back vowel, Labov (2006) reports that 90 percent of native English speakers in the United States front /u/ to some extent. This fronting can be observed through measuring the second formant, which correlates with tongue position on the horizontal axis (i.e., from front to back of the oral cavity). These productions of /u/ are often described as having "i-coloring" and can overlap the vowel spaces traditionally occupied by the English high front tense /i/ and lax /ɪ/ vowels yielding pronunciations such as [t^{i}u] or [t^{ɪ}u] for the English word "two." Godinez and Maddieson (1985) compared the vowel productions of monolingual English speakers from Los Angeles with those of bilingual Chicanos, and found that the English productions of /u/ of the bilinguals were more backed than those of the monolingual English speakers. They explained this finding by citing possible influences of Spanish on the Chicano English /u/. In a more recent study, Fought (1999) examined the English of Chicano and Mexican American speech communities near Los Angeles, California. She found that speakers in both communities, despite being minority communities, fronted /u/

like their majority California English–speaking counterparts, showing that despite the influence of Spanish in their respective social circles, their English had been affected by a sound change that was associated with the majority speech community. Willis (2005) analyzed the vowels of a bilingual community in New Mexico and reported fronting of the Spanish /u/ by his speakers. While Willis makes no indication of the extent of English influence on the speakers of his study, based on the pervasiveness of /u/ fronting in American English, the possibility of /u/ fronting at the very least must be considered.

Until recently, the general assertion regarding the standard Spanish vowel system has been that it is relatively stable and exhibits little or no variation (e.g., Navarro Tomás 1977; Quilis and Esgueva 1983; Bradlow 1994). Several studies (e.g., Delattre 1969; Skelton 1969) cede that there is slight variation with the Spanish vowel system, specifically centralization of unstressed productions of the mid and low vowels, simultaneously observing that the most stable of the Spanish vowels was the high back vowel /u/, followed by the high front vowel /i/. More recently, Harmegnies and Poch-Olivé (1992) compared controlled and more spontaneous productions of the five Spanish vowels, and found a large amount of variation. Most of the variation they report occurred with unstressed mid and low vowels centralizing and reducing. Other studies report different types of vowel variations such as vowel deletion in Mexican Spanish (Lope-Blanch 1964), unstressed vowel reduction in Ecuadorian Spanish (Lipski 1990), and vowel devoicing in Andean Spanish (Hundley 1983; Delforge 2008). However, despite the studies that show different degrees of vowel variation and even a slight inherent tendency to centralize when unstressed, the general consensus continues to be that the Spanish vowel system is very stable, especially when compared to English.

Regarding English and Spanish vowels in contact, Godinez and Maddieson (1985) found that all of the contrasts (i.e., lax versus tense) present in the productions of monolingual English speakers from California were also present in the English vowel productions of bilingual Chicano speakers from East Los Angeles. However, they also report that in the Chicano productions the front vowels were more raised and fronted. Roeder (2010) studied the English vowels of Mexican Americans in Lansing, Michigan, and shows that their English vowel productions, with the exception of /æ/, all reflect the local norms of the Northern Cities Vowel Shift. Willis (2005), in his analysis of the Spanish vowels of a bilingual population in the North American Southwest, reports that along with fronting the Spanish /u/, his participants also fronted their productions of Spanish /a/ into the low front vowel space traditionally occupied by English /æ/.

With respect to Miami Cuban vowels, Varela's (1992) impressionistic study of Cuban American Spanish vowels concludes that there was evidence of unstressed vowel reduction to schwa, English vowels in the Cuban American Spanish vowel system (i.e., /o/ → [æ] or "extreme fronting"), and word-final off-gliding. She attributes all of these phenomena strictly to English influence on Cuban American Spanish. Alvord and Rogers (2014), in an acoustic study of Miami Cuban Spanish vowels, found no evidence of any English vowels in the Miami Cuban productions of Spanish vowels. Regarding the centralization of unstressed Spanish vowels, our results show a very strong tendency of the unstressed Spanish vowels, particularly the mid and low vowels, to centralize. Additionally, our results show no evidence of /u/ fronting in the Spanish of any of the three immigrant groups. They concluded that while language shift may be present in the Miami Cuban community, as previous studies have shown English transfer in the lexicon and morphosyntax of Miami Cuban Spanish, the phonology, particularly the vowel system, is resisting English transfer in bilingual speech.

Concerning Spanish influence on the Miami English vowel system, there are no known studies at the present time. If there were Spanish influence evident in the Miami Cuban English vowel system, several phenomena might be expected. First, due to the smaller five-vowel Spanish system, speakers might merge or have difficulty differentiating between English tense and lax vowels such as /i/ and /ɪ/ and /u/ and /ʊ/ along with other vowels that share close proximity in the English vowel space. Likewise, a hispanized English vowel space might show less overlap between vowels due to the tendency of Spanish to reduce and centralize much less than English (e.g., Skelton 1969). Finally, with specific regards to Alvord and Rogers's (2014) findings on Miami English /u/, it is possible that the fronting trend is absent in the English of Miami Cubans. In other words, the high stability of the Miami Cuban Spanish /u/ could limit the extent that it is fronted in the English of these bilingual speakers.

The current study seeks to examine the effects, if any, of Spanish on Miami Cuban English vowels and English on Miami Cuban Spanish vowels. Additionally, specific attention is given to the behavior of Miami Cuban English /u/. The following research questions guided the study:

1. Does the Miami Cuban Spanish vowel system show evidence of influence from English?
2. Does the Miami Cuban English vowel system show evidence of influence from Spanish, specifically in the production of tense or lax vowels, /u/, and /æ/?

Research Methodology

Speech samples from eleven Miami Cubans were taken in order to analyze both Spanish and English vowel productions. The following sections describe the participants, the elicitation devices, and the data analysis.

Elicitation Devices and Acoustic Measurements

Participants were recorded performing three different speech tasks in both English and Spanish: a word list, a story, and a sociolinguistic interview (Labov 1997). The recordings were made with a Marantz PMD 671 digital recorder at a recording rate of 44.1 kilohertz (kHz). Using Praat (Boersma and Weenink 2012), 4,634 English vowels were extracted from the three English tasks, and 9,125 vowels were extracted from the Spanish tasks. All vowels were marked for lexical stress because Spanish does not have discourse stress like English. Additionally, the first formant (F1) and second formant (F2) values were measured at the midpoint of each vowel. In all, eleven speakers were recorded. For the English data analysis, only ten speakers were analyzed because one of the speakers was not comfortable speaking English. To account for physiological differences in the participants, all vowels were normalized using Thomas and Kendall's (2007) NORM vowel normalization and plotting suite. The Nearey 1 method of normalization was chosen: F*n[V] = anti-log(log(Fn[V]) – mean(log(Fn)), in which F*n[V] is the normalized value for Fn[V], formant n of vowel V, and mean(log(Fn)) is the log-mean of all Fns for the specific speaker in question. The normalization process changes the nature of the unit of measure and is subsequently reported as 'normalized height' for the F1 and 'normalized advancement' for the F2 instead of other frequency units of measure (e.g., hertz).

Participants

The participants consisted of six male and five female Miami Cubans and were divided into three different immigrant groups based on Silva-Corvalán (1994). Those of the first group (G1, n = 3) were born in Cuba and immigrated to the US after the age of eleven; those speakers who made up the second group (G2, n = 5) were either born in Cuba and immigrated to the US before the age of six or were born in the US to at least one G1 parent; and finally, the third group (G3, n = 3) are those who were born to at least one G2 parent.

Statistical Analysis

After the formant values of each vowel were normalized, it was determined that for the particular data set the most appropriate statistical analysis would be a random effects model, specifically a mixed model analysis. A random effects model is normally used in instances where measurements are taken over time because it takes into account that some of the variation in the responses or data of the subjects will be random and not due to any particular factor: "The essential feature of a random effects model for longitudinal data is that there is natural heterogeneity across individuals in their responses over time and that this heterogeneity can be represented by an appropriate probability distribution" (Landau and Everitt 2004, 201). Although the current study is not a longitudinal study, the high number of repeated measurements of the participants' vowel formants acts similarly to a study of a more traditional longitudinal nature. The results show two major findings: (1) the Spanish vowel space produced by these bilingual speakers is very stable and exhibits no measurable influence from English vowels, and (2) the English vowels produced by the Miami Cuban informants show a great deal of variability in ways that are not always consistent with general American English vowels.

Miami Cuban Spanish Vowels

For all three immigrant groups, the Spanish vowel system was extremely stable in spite of the varying levels of English and Spanish dominance between groups. The overall patterns shown in figures 1.1–1.3 reveal a progressive change across the three groups in the shape of the vowel space from one that has more separation and less reduction and resembles the traditional shape of the Spanish vowel space (G1), to one that has slightly more overlap and reduction and resembles a more general American English–like vowel space (Groups 2 and 3). This is not necessarily surprising because the G1 participants are L2 English speakers. The examination of stressed and unstressed vowels revealed no statistically significant F1 differences for /a/, /e/, /i/, or /u/, or F2 differences for /a/, /e/, /i/, /o/, or /u/ in any of the three immigrant groups (table 1.1). While there was an overall significant effect for immigrant group for the F1 means of /o/ ($F(2, 8.710) = 4.383$, $p = 0.048$), there were no significant differences between any of the groups. A visual inspection of the vowel plots shows that G3 appeared to centralize the mid vowels, /e/ and /o/, more than G1 and G2. In spite of this movement of the mid vowels toward the center of the vowel space, no statistical differences were observed and there is no evidence of unstressed vowel reduction to schwa. It is very apparent that, even though Miami Cuban Spanish tends to reduce unstressed vowels, this process is much weaker than the reduction to schwa found in English (Delattre 1969).

Table 1.1. F1 and F2 means for /u/ and /ʊ/ by immigrant group

	/u/		/ʊ/	
	F1	**F2**	**F1**	**F2**
G1	0.780	0.668	1.046	0.607
G2	0.754	0.854	1.010	0.687
G3	0.778	0.978	0.988	0.776

Also of note, /u/ was very consistently produced in the high back region by all three groups with no i-coloring at all. In other words, there was no indication of English influence in any of the Spanish vowel spaces of any of the speakers. Figures 1.1–1.3 show the Spanish vowel spaces of all three groups and illustrate the similar shape and stability exhibited in all three groups.[2]

Miami Cuban English Vowels

The current section reports the findings on the English vowels produced by the Miami Cuban bilingual speakers. Each immigrant group is discussed and special attention is paid to the shape of the vowel space, the tense-lax distinction, /u/ fronting, and the production of the low front vowel /æ/.

English Vowel Space

Figures 1.4–1.6 show the overall English vowel spaces for the three immigrant groups. The ellipses show the extent of each vowel within the respective vowel spaces to two standard deviations. Traditional analyses of Spanish vowels have shown that there is little to no overlap of individual vowel spaces (e.g., Skelton 1969; Delattre 1969),

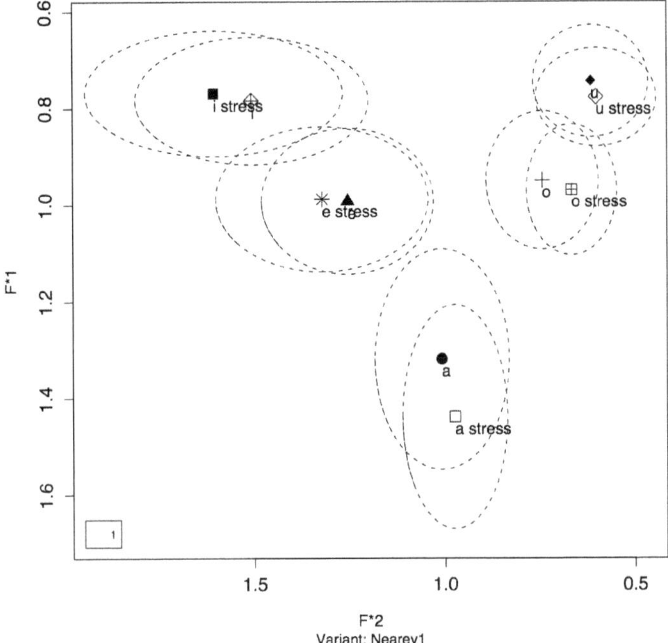

Figure 1.1. Group 1 Spanish vowel space

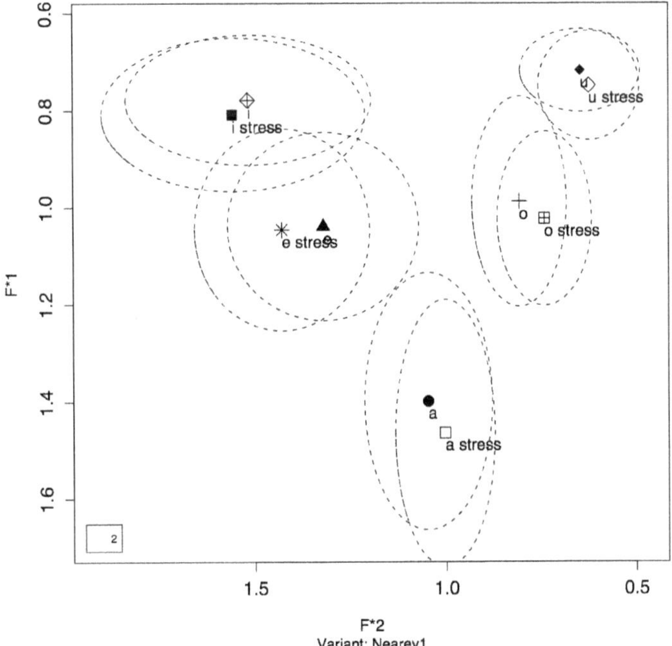

Figure 1.2. Group 2 Spanish vowel space

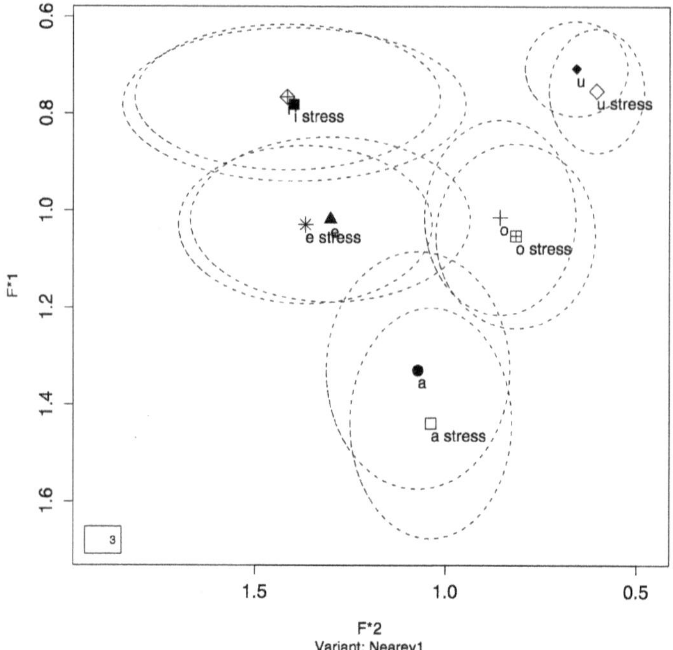

Figure 1.3. Group 3 Spanish vowel space

while the high levels of reduction in English cause a much greater degree of overlap of individual vowels (Delattre 1969; Brown 1990). As seen in figure 1.4, the shape of the English vowel space produced by members of the G1 group strongly resembles their Spanish vowel space (figure 1.1). However, with each progressive immigrant group the vowel spaces showed fewer similarities with the traditional shape of the Spanish vowel space.

Figures 1.4–1.6 show that all three groups produced both /ʌ/ and /ə/, despite their absence in Spanish. However, they also demonstrate that the G1 English vowel space has less overlap between vowels, resulting in a more Spanish-like vowel distribution, while the latter two generations' English vowel space is more English-like in its shape (i.e., more overlap of vowel space and reduction), as indicated by the ellipses.

Tense-Lax Distinction

One of the more notable trends seen in the first immigrant group's vowel space is the apparent merging of the high back lax vowel /ʊ/, into the high tense back vowel /u/. Figures 1.5 and 1.6 show that in subsequent immigrant groups this tense-lax merger did not occur. Table 1.2 illustrates the F1 and F2 means for all these two vowels by immigrant group.

Of all three groups, G1 had the lowest and most backed productions of the tense /u/ and the highest and most backed productions of the lax /ʊ/. Post hoc pairwise tests comparing the F1 values ($F(1, 56.638) = 2.483$, $p = 0.121$) and the F2 values

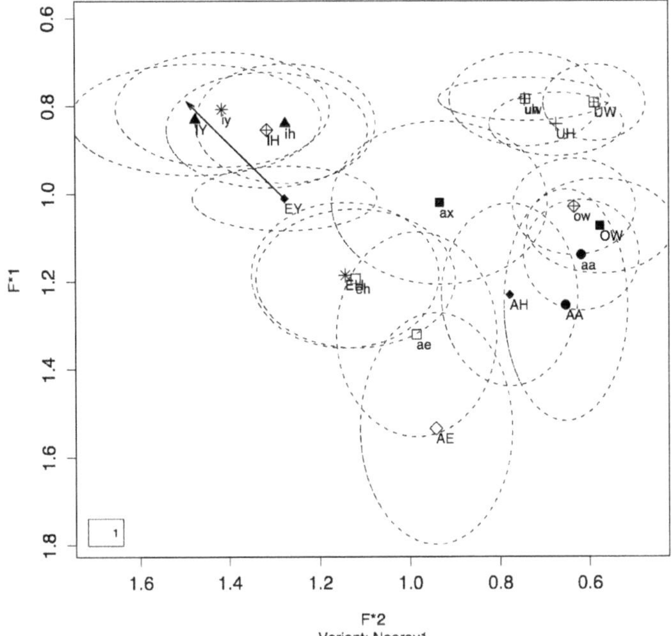

Figure 1.4. Group 1 English vowel space

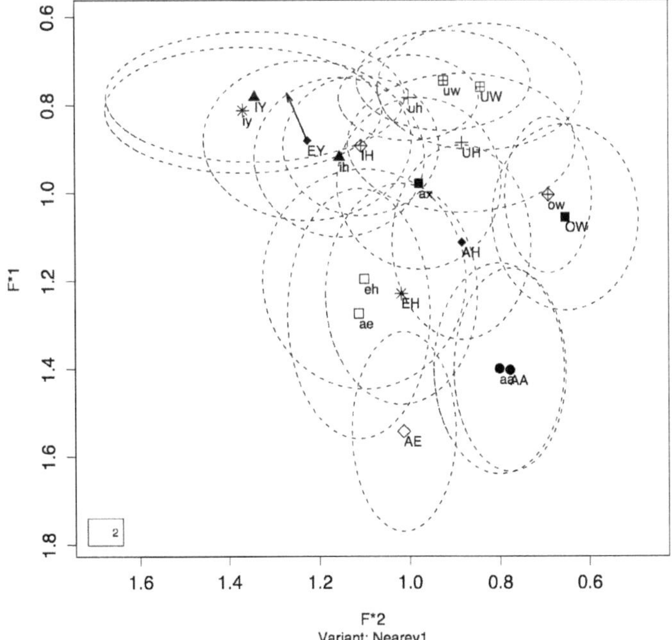

Figure 1.5. Group 2 English vowel space

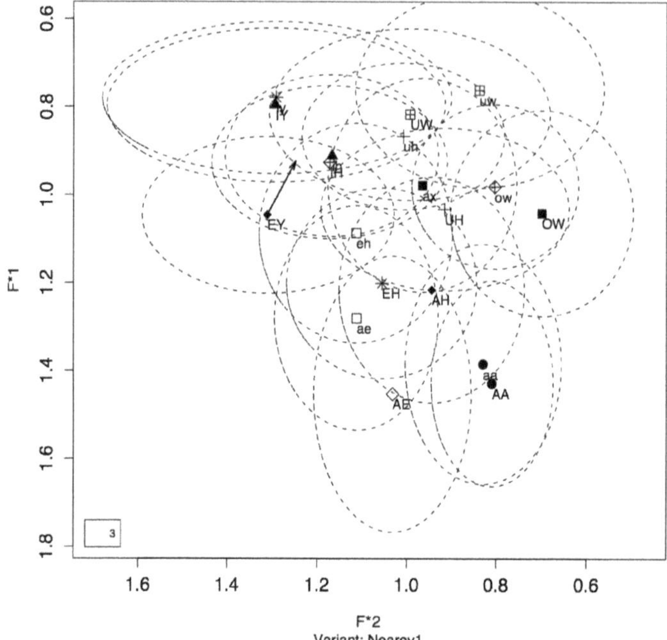

Figure 1.6. Group 3 English vowel space

Table 1.2. F1 and F2 means for /u/ and /ʊ/ by immigrant group

	/u/		/ʊ/	
	F1	F2	F1	F2
G1	0.780	0.668	1.046	0.607
G2	0.754	0.854	1.010	0.687
G3	0.778	0.978	0.988	0.776

($F(1, 56.012) = 1.118$, $p = 0.295$) of /u/ to those of /ʊ/ found no significant differences for G1. In other words, relative to both height and backness, both vowels were produced in the same region of the G1 vowel space, indicating the existence of a tense-lax merger of the English back vowels /u/ and /ʊ/ in the English of G1 speakers. Subsequent post hoc tests indicated that this merger did not occur in the G2 and G3 vowel spaces. The tendency of the G1 speakers to group the high tense and lax vowels fairly tightly suggests that they have difficulties acquiring the production of the general American English tense and lax distinction, which is absent in Spanish. The participants in the other groups, however, showed that they were able to produce the different tense and lax high vowels.

/u/ Fronting

While it was observed that the Miami Cuban Spanish /u/ was the most stable of all of the Spanish vowels produced and that there was no evidence of English influence on the Spanish /u/ of any of the three immigrant groups, the English vowel data show a gradual decrease of Spanish influence on the English /u/ in each subsequent group. Acoustically, a higher value of the second formant, or F2, indicates a more fronted vowel (i.e., the position of the tongue is closer to the front of the oral cavity when producing the vowel). Based on Labov's (2006) assertion regarding the North American English /u/, it might be expected that speakers with more English experience (i.e., G2 and G3) would produce higher F2 values for /u/ than speakers who are more Spanish dominant. This prediction was borne out in the data where it was observed that the overall F2 values for /u/ increased with each subsequent immigrant group, showing a gradual fronting of English /u/ as English dominance increases. Table 1.3 shows the overall F2 means for English /u/ by group.

Table 1.3. Overall group F2 means for English /u/

Group	Mean	Standard Deviation
1	0.659	0.066
2	0.852	0.043
3	1.024	0.055

However, Bonferroni post hoc pairwise tests (table 1.4), comparing the F2 means for each group, revealed that the only significant difference was between groups 1 and 3. The post hoc analysis shows that there is a significant difference in /u/ fronting between groups 1 and 3, while also confirming that group 2 produced English /u/ similarly to both groups. This finding corroborates the idea that English /u/ is fronted more by those who are more English dominant and less by those who are more Spanish dominant. Group 2, the most balanced of the groups in terms of their language use, produces English /u/ that is similar, or intermediate, to the other groups.

Table 1.4. Group pairwise comparisons of F2 for English /u/, $F(2,7.257) = 9.268$, $p < 0.05$

Group Pair	Mean Difference	Standard Deviation	Sig.	Post hoc
1 and 2	−0.193	0.078	n.s.	n.s.
1 and 3	−0.365	0.085	0.010	1 < 3
2 and 3	−0.172	0.068	n.s	n.s

Low Front Vowel /æ/ Shift

In both the first and third immigrant groups, the English low front lax vowel /æ/ shifted back into the low central region traditionally occupied by the Spanish low central vowel /a/. This resulted in words such as "fashion" and "cat," normally pronounced [fæˈ.ʃən] and [kætˈ] in standard North American English, being pronounced [faˈ.ʃən] and [katˈ]. Table 1.5 shows the overall normalized F1 and F2 means for /æ/ of each immigrant group.

Table 1.5. Normalized F1 and F2 means for /æ/ by group

Group	F1 Mean	Standard Deviation	F2 Mean	Standard Deviation
1	1.422	0.026	0.968	0.036
2	1.375	0.017	1.084	0.023
3	1.370	0.024	1.104	0.031

With regard to vowel height and backness, all three immigrant groups produced /æ/ similarly. While the ANOVA results showed a significant main effect for immigrant group ($F(2, 6.960) = 4.821$, $p = 0.049$), the results were barely significant. Bonferroni post hoc analyses reveal no differences between the three immigrant groups' productions of /æ/ for either F1 or F2, as seen in tables 1.6 and 1.7, meaning that for all intents and purposes the three groups produce English /æ/ the same.

Table 1.6. Immigrant group F1 pairwise comparisons for /æ/

Group Pair	F1 Mean Difference	Standard Deviation	Sig.	Post hoc
1 and 2	0.047	0.031	n.s.	n.s.
1 and 3	0.052	0.035	n.s.	n.s.
2 and 3	0.005	0.030	n.s.	n.s.

Table 1.7. Immigrant group F2 pairwise comparisons for /æ/

Group Pair	Mean Difference	Standard Deviation	Sig.	Post hoc
1 and 2	–0.116	0.042	n.s.	n.s.
1 and 3	–0.136	0.047	n.s.	n.s.
2 and 3	–0.020	0.038	n.s.	n.s.

A visual inspection of the English vowel space for the three groups (figures 1.4, 1.5, and 1.6) reveals that English /æ/ seems to be produced in the low central area of the vowel space typical of where the Spanish /a/ is produced. In order to determine whether English /æ/ was, in fact, produced in an area back in the low central space where Spanish /a/ is produced, post hoc tests were run comparing the F2 values of each immigrant group's productions of English /æ/ and Spanish /a/. G1 productions of Spanish /a/ were significantly more raised (F1) than their English productions of /æ/ ($F(1,1302.832) = 15.833$, $p<0.0001$). However, there were no significant differences between the F2 values of the G1 productions of each vowel ($F(1, 1303.986) = 1.231$, $p = 0.267$). In other words, while G1 Spanish /a/ was generally produced higher than G1 English /æ/, both vowels were produced in the same low central area normally occupied by Spanish /a/, as can be seen in figure 1.4.

This backward shift was also observed in the G3 productions of English /æ/, but not in those of G2. For the third immigrant group, post hoc tests indicated that there were no significant differences between either the F1 values ($F(1, 584.990) = 0.239$, $p = 0.625$) or the F2 values ($F(1, 584.770) = 3.28$, $p = 0.071$) of Spanish /a/ and English /æ/. However, the second immigrant group was found to have produced significant differences between Spanish /a/ and English /æ/ in F1 ($F(1, 1092.006) = 11.882$, $p < 0.05$) and F2 ($F(1, 1092.650) = 34.93$, $p < 0.0001$). Group 2 productions of the English low front lax vowel were both lower and more fronted than their productions of the Spanish low central vowel.

This backward shift of English /æ/ had somewhat of a domino effect in the vowel space of G1. With the low front lax vowel now in the low central space, the low back English vowel /ɑ/ shifted up and partially merged with the mid back vowel /oʊ/. This merger was evident in words such as "all," normally pronounced /ɑɫ/ in standard North American English, being produced as /ol/ by G1 speakers. A post hoc pairwise test comparing the F1 values ($F(1, 103.264) = 21.887$, $p < 0.0001$) of /ɑ/ to those of /oʊ/ indicated that there was a significant difference between the two vowels and that /oʊ/ was still significantly more raised than /ɑ/. However, a post hoc test comparing F2 values of each vowel ($F(1, 103.136) = 20.025$, $p = 0.158$) showed that there were no statistically significant differences between either vowel. Hence, while G1 productions of /ɑ/ were lower than /oʊ/, both were produced with more or less an equivalent amount of backness.

The domino effect observed in the first group was not observed in the vowel space produced by G3. Even though the /æ/ was produced as a low central vowel, the low back English /ɑ/ remained in the low back region and did not shift upward to the mid back region. The normalized F2 mean for the G3 productions, 1.104, was higher than that of G1 and therefore more fronted, but was still in the low central region of the vowel space. As a result, G3 productions of /æ/ had both low front and low back coloring at times, unlike the first group, whose overall /æ/ tokens had mostly low central coloring.

Discussion and Conclusions

There are two main findings to the present study. First, the Miami Cuban Spanish vowel system, as described in detail in Alvord and Rogers (2014), is very stable and it has maintained its Spanish-like quality in spite of a very intense language contact situation with English. This includes the vowels produced by English-dominant bilingual speakers in the third immigrant group. The second major finding is that the English vowels produced by Miami Cuban bilinguals exhibit a great deal of variation and there appears to be Spanish influence on certain aspects of the English system. The current section is organized by the research questions (RQs) followed by concluding remarks.

- **RQ#1:** Does the Miami Cuban Spanish vowel system show evidence of influence from English?

The Spanish data clearly show a vowel system that is stable across all three immigrant groups. The Spanish vowels produced reflect the Spanish norm as described in the literature and show no evidence of any English influence. This is significant because other bilingual groups in the US have been observed to produce Spanish vowels that resemble those from American English. For example, Willis (2005) observes that Spanish-English bilinguals produced a Spanish /a/ that was fronted toward the vowel space of English /æ/ and a Spanish /u/ that was fronted, following a process very common to standard American English. The Miami Cuban Spanish vowel system shows no evidence of a similar influence by English.

- **RQ#2:** Does the Miami Cuban English vowel system show evidence of influence from Spanish, specifically in the production of tense-lax vowels, /u/, and /æ/?

  Several patterns suggested Spanish influence on the English vowel system produced by the Miami Cuban informants. Not surprisingly, G1, who spoke English as an L2, showed the most Spanish influence in their English vowels. First, their English and Spanish vowel spaces had very similar shapes, and they appeared to reduce the number of vowels in their English system by partially merging /ɑ/ with /oʊ/ and /ʊ/ with /u/. Second, G1 also showed a tendency toward less unstressed vowel reduction in English than the subsequent two groups. This reflects tendencies observed in their production of Spanish vowels, suggesting that this phonological process has not been completely acquired in their L2. Similarly, the first immigrant group produced their English vowels with no discernable difference between the high tense and lax vowels, /u/ versus /ʊ/. This tendency was not observed in the other two groups, thus reflecting the greater level of English dominance in these two groups when compared to G1 (see, for example, Lynch, this volume).

Regarding the production of the high back vowel /u/, the results of the current study reveal, perhaps predictably, a gradual decreasing Spanish influence on the Miami Cuban English /u/. The first group spoke English as an L2 and therefore showed the most Spanish influence in their production of this phone. This observation is based on the relative lack of /u/ fronting produced by G1, which is considered characteristic of the English /u/ (see Labov 2006). The fronting of English /u/ was observed to gradually increase in the subsequent two immigrant groups, with the least amount of i-coloring in the /u/ produced by G1 and the most produced by G3, with the G2 productions being intermediate. Data from the current study suggest that /u/ fronting is a part of Miami English in general but that it is variable and that only the most English-dominant bilinguals produce /u/ with i-coloring.

Of all the patterns observed, the backward shift of the English low front lax vowel /æ/ into a lower central position was the strongest indication of Spanish influence on Miami Cuban English vowels. Unlike the previously discussed patterns, where only G1 produced English vowels with certain Spanish traits, the shift of /æ/ toward the low central region of the vowel space was observed, to some extent, for all three groups. The shift was most dramatic, however, for the G1 speakers for whom the backward shift of /æ/ created a chain shift. With the English /æ/ in the low central region, these G1 speakers raised their English productions of /ɑ/ into the mid back region and partially merged them with their productions of English /oʊ/. The overall lack of a low front lax vowel in the G1 English vowels combined with the raising or merger of /ɑ/ reflects the structure of their native Spanish system where there is only one low vowel /a/.

A notable finding of the current study is that all three groups produce a backed English /æ/. However, this backed production of /æ/ is only statistically significant for the first and third immigrant groups. This finding is somewhat unexpected because most of the vowel production patterns that can be linked to influence from Spanish are either only present in the productions of G1 (e.g., unstressed vowel reduction and tense-lax distinctions) or are gradually reduced through the subsequent immigrant groups (i.e., /u/ fronting). The fact that /æ/ is backed by the third group but not the second points to the possibility that this is a characteristic of Miami English. Carter (2013) hypothesizes that there are several areas where Miami English is perceived as differing from general American English. He states, "Miami English is a systematic, rule-governed variety of English with subtle structural influence from Spanish. It's spoken by native English speakers, mostly second-, third-, and fourth-generation Latinos, who learn it as their first-language variety." According to Carter, some of these Spanish influences are lexical and phonetic. With regard to the phonetic influences, he states that among these, there are some vowel differences between Miami English and general American English.

The similarity in the phonologies of the first and third immigrant groups is also not a unique observation in Miami. For example, Alvord (2010) observes that the first and third immigrant groups maintain the falling Cuban-style intonation pattern in absolute interrogative utterances. This phenomenon of the first and third groups patterning similarly, maintaining more Spanish-like features in their Spanish (i.e., intonation) or producing more Spanish-like features in their English vowel system (i.e., backing of /æ/) suggests a connection between these groups. Alvord (2010) hypothesizes that this tendency could be due to familial relationships and close proximity between the first and third immigrant groups. While the current study does not provide any definitive evidence that caretaker speech is responsible for the similarities between these two groups, it does add another linguistic trait that these two groups have in common. Future research in Miami should explore the role of caretaker speech on the third and fourth generations of Miami Cubans.

To summarize, the current study has shown that the Miami Cuban Spanish vowel system is retaining its Spanish character and shows no measurable influence from English. This finding contradicts the claims of Varela (1974, 1992). On the other hand, the Miami Cuban English vowel system shows a great deal of variability. This is mostly manifested in Spanish-like vowel phenomena in the speech of the first immigrant group, who are all L2 English speakers. However, a few trends were observed that are carried through all of the immigrant groups. The fronting of English /u/ is absent in the first group, intermediate in the second group, and actively present in the third group. Additional research on Miami English /u/ pronunciation should be carried out with more English-dominant speakers as well as monolingual English speakers in order to determine the extent of /u/ fronting in Miami and to explore the role that this vowel may play in the Miami accent (Carter 2013). The backward shift of the English vowel /æ/ seems to be a more promising phenomenon when exploring the vowel characteristics of a Miami accent. The current study provides the first examination of English vowel pronunciation in Miami and provides a starting point for future research on Miami English vowel production. While the current study did not analyze any speech of Miami Cuban speakers beyond the third immigrant group or any monolingual English speakers in Miami, the fact that the lower vowel shift continued into the third group is tentatively indicative of the possibility that Spanish has had an important influence on Miami English. In other words, with the status that Spanish has enjoyed in Miami over the last half-century, future research should examine the possible influence of Spanish on Miami English in general.

Notes

1. For evidence of an eight-vowel nonstandard variety of Spanish in Andalucía, see Villena Ponsoda (1987).
2. For more details, consult Alvord and Rogers (2014).

References

Alvord, S. M. 2010. "Variation in Miami-Cuban Interrogative Intonation." *Hispania* 93 (2): 235–55.

Alvord, S. M., and B. M. A. Rogers. 2014. "Miami-Cuban Spanish Vowels in Contact." *Sociolinguistic Studies* 8 (1): 139–70.

Boersma, P., and D. Weenink. 2012. "Praat: Doing Phonetics by Computer." Version 5.3.32. http://www.fon.hum.uva.nl/praat/.

Boswell, T. D. 2000. "Demographic Changes in Florida and Their Importance for Effective Educational Policies and Practices." In *Research on Spanish in the United States: Linguistic Issues and Challenges*, edited by A. Roca, 406–31. Somerville, MA: Cascadilla Press.

Bradlow, A. R. 1994. "A Comparative Acoustic Study of English and Spanish Vowels." *Journal of the Acoustical Society of America* 97:1916–24.

Brown, R. L. 1990. "A Maverick Vowel: The Notorious /ə/ (Schwa)." *Hispania* 73:1158–61.

Carter, P. M. 2013. "Sociolinguist Debunks Miami English Misconceptions." *FIU News*, July 13. http://news.fiu.edu/2013/10/sociolinguist-debunks-miami-english-misconceptions/68533.

Delattre, P. 1969. "An Acoustic and Articulatory Study of Vowel Reduction in Four Languages." *International Review of Applied Linguistics* 7:295–325.

Delforge, A. M. 2008. "Unstressed Vowel Reduction in Andean Spanish." In *Selected Proceedings of the 3rd Conference of Laboratory Approaches to Spanish Phonology*, edited by L. Colantini and J. Steele, 107–24. Somerville, MA: Cascadilla Press.

Fought, C. 1999. "A Majority Sound Change in a Minority Community: /u/-Fronting in Chicano English." *Journal of Sociolinguistics* 3:5–23.

Godinez, M., Jr., and I. Maddieson. 1985. "Vowel Differences between Chicano and General Californian English?" *International Journal of the Sociology of Language* 53:43–58.

Guitart, J. M. 2004. *Sonido y sentido: Teoría y práctica de la pronunciación del español*. Washington, DC: Georgetown University Press.

Harmegnies, B., and D. Poch-Olivé. 1992. "A Study of Style-Induced Vowel Variability: Laboratory versus Spontaneous Speech in Spanish." *Speech Communication* 11:429–37.

Hualde, J. I. 2005. *The Sounds of Spanish*. Cambridge, UK: Cambridge University Press.

Hundley, J. 1983. "Linguistic Variation in Peruvian Spanish: Unstressed Vowels and /s/." PhD diss., University of Minnesota.

Labov, W. 1997. "Some Further Steps in Narrative Analysis." *Journal of Narrative and Life History* 7:395–415

———. 2006. "Triggering Events." In *History of the English Language IV: Empirical and Analytical Advances in the Study of English Language Change*, edited by S. Fitzmaurice and D. Mincova, 11–54. Berlin: Mouton de Gruyter.

Ladefoged, P. 2006. *A Course in Phonetics*. Boston: Thomson Wadsworth.

Landau, S., and B. S. Everitt. 2004. *A Handbook of Statistical Analyses Using SPSS*. Boca Raton: Chapman & Hall/CRC Press LLC.

Lipski, J. M. 1990. "Aspects of Ecuadorian Vowel Reduction." *Hispanic Linguistics* 4:1–19.

Lope-Blanch, J. M. 1964. "En torno a las vocales caedizas del español mexicano." *Nueva revista de filología hispánica* 17:1–19.

López-Morales, H. 2003. *Los cubanos de Miami: Lengua y sociedad*. Miami: Ediciones Universal.

Lynch, A. 1999. "The Subjunctive in Miami-Cuban Spanish: Bilingualism, Contact, and Language Variation." PhD diss., University of Minnesota.

———. 2000. "Spanish-Speaking Miami in Sociolinguistic Perspective: Bilingualism, Recontact, and Language Maintenance among the Cuban-Origin Population." In *Research on Spanish in the United States: Linguistic and Challenges*, edited by A. Roca, 271–83. Somerville, MA: Cascadilla Press.

———. 2009. "A Sociolinguistic Analysis of Final /s/ in Miami Cuban Spanish." *Language Sciences* 31:767–90.

Navarro Tomás, T. 1999. *Manual de pronunciación española*. 27th ed. Madrid: Consejo Superior de Investigaciones Científicas, Instituto Miguel de Cervantes (Publicaciones de la Revista de Filología Española).

Otheguy, R., and O. García. 1988. "Diffusion of Lexical Innovations in the Spanish of Cuban Americans." In *Research Issues and Problems in United States Spanish: Latin American and Southwestern Varieties*, edited by J. L. Ornstein-Galicia, G. K. Green, and D. J. Bixler-Márquez, 203–42. Brownsville, TX: Pan American University at Brownsville, in cooperation with the University of Texas at El Paso.

Quilis, A. 1999. *Tratado de Fonología y Fonética Españolas*. Madrid: Gredos.

Quilis, A., and M. Esgueva. 1983. "Fonemas Vocálicos Españoles." In *Estudios de fonética*, edited by M. Escueva and M. Cantarero, 159–252. Madrid: Consejo Superior de Investigaciones Científicas Instituto Miguel de Cervantes.

Roeder, R. B. 2010. "Northern Cities Mexican American English: Vowel Production and Perception." *American Speech* 85 (2): 164–84.

Silva-Corvalán, C. 1994. *Language Contact and Change: Spanish in Los Angeles*. New York: Oxford University Press.

Skelton, R. B. 1969. "The Pattern of Spanish Vowels." *International Review of Applied Linguistics* 6:231–37.

Thomas, E. R., and T. Kendall. 2007. "NORM: The Vowel Normalization and Plotting Suite." http://lingtools.uoregon.edu/norm/.

Trudgill, P., and J. Hannah. 1982. *International English: A Guide to Varieties of Standard English*. London: Edward Arnold.

Varela, B. 1974. "La Influencia del Inglés en los Cubanos de Miami y Nueva Orleans." *Español actual* 26:16–25.

———. 1992. *El Español Cubano-Americano*. New York: Senda Nueva.

Villena Ponsoda, J. 1987. *Forma, Sustancia y Redundancia Contextual: El Caso del Español Andaluz*. Málaga: Universidad de Málaga.

Whitley, M. S. 2002. *Spanish/English Contrasts: A Course in Spanish Linguistics*. Washington, DC: Georgetown University Press.

Willis, E. W. 2005. "An Initial Examination of Southwest Spanish Vowels." *Southwest Journal of Linguistics* 24:1–14.

2

The Phonetic Output of Word-Internal, Post-nuclear /l/ and /ɾ/ Weakening in Havana Cuban Spanish

KRISTIN M. CARLSON
Thiel College

THE GEMINATION OR LENGTHENING of a consonantal segment that is positionally subsequent to the deletion of a syllable-final liquid has been repeated in the literature as a prominent and defining characteristic of western Cuban Spanish. Considering the geographic, demographic, and historical importance of Cuba vis-à-vis the dissemination of language and culture throughout the Hispanic Caribbean, one would intrinsically expect a larger corpus of empirically-founded linguistic investigations. Notwithstanding a considerably long-established tradition of linguistic interest, earlier works understandably hinged almost exclusively on the impressionistic data of others or literary representations of Cuban speech. And, despite the relatively recent availability of readily accessible and affordable speech analysis software, more contemporary studies have inconsistently benefitted from this instrumentation. Furthermore, long-standing political barriers between the United States and Cuba have forced many US linguists to rely on data-collection processes other than direct field work. Bearing all of this in mind, the present investigation set out to investigate gemination in Havana Cuban Spanish—specifically, to acoustically examine the qualitative and quantitative patternings of post-nuclear /l/ and /ɾ/ within the word. This study is generally intended to complement all antecedent work concerning the allophony of final liquids in Cuban Spanish and to directly address the need for empirical data-collection and analysis processes. In addition, it is believed that the present investigation will be a valuable addition to the body of extant analyses as it is uniquely based on a corpus of data derived from direct field research during two visits to Havana, Cuba, in December 2011 and the summer of 2012. It is hoped that the dialectological examination to follow affords a more descriptively precise account of the allophony of word-internal, post-nuclear /l/ and /ɾ/ so as to further specify the qualitative characteristics and quantitative patternings of a consonantal segment that is positionally subsequent to the deletion of a syllable-final liquid in western Cuban Spanish.

Compensatory Lengthening and Gemination

Compensatory lengthening (henceforth CL) subsumes a closed set of phonological phenomena in which the elimination of one segment (i.e., the trigger) is associated with a concomitant increase in the length of another (i.e., the target). Generally, the trigger and target segments are positionally adjacent within the same syllable or in neighboring syllables. Both consonants and vowels have been known to trigger as well as to be targeted by CL phenomena. Accordingly, CL can be partitioned into two principal types of compensatory processes: vowel lengthening, which is crosslinguistically more widespread, and consonant lengthening (Campos-Astorkiza 2005; Gess 2011; Morin 1992). In addition, if the target of CL phenomena is a consonant, then the compensatory mechanism entails either gemination or total assimilation (Morin 1992). While both of these compensatory outcomes have been identified in the literature as typifying characteristics of the Spanish of western Cuba (cf. Carlson 2014), it is not within the scope of the current analyses to discern whether a lengthened segment encompasses assimilation or is the outcome of gemination. All instances of /–l/ → Ø / V _.C and /–ɾ/ → Ø / V_.C in which the following consonant is lengthened will be herein understood to exemplify the phonetic process of gemination.[1]

Geminates are present in many of the world's languages and have been the topic of much discussion particularly concerning their phonological representation, the manner in which their particular behavior can be accounted for, and their phonetic implementation. Be this as it may, given the investigative focus of the present study, the long-standing debate as to their phonological behavior (cf. Hockett 1955; Swadesh 1937; Trubetzkoy 1939), the particular type of geminated sequence (i.e., lexical, assimilated, or concatenated), or the nature of their derivation (i.e., true or underlying geminates versus fake or derived geminates) will not be further discussed. Likewise, articulatory and perceptual studies and their respective results will also be excluded. Only the crosslinguistic acoustic properties of geminate consonants will be herein detailed since these are the only phonetic characteristics relevant to the data analysis portion of this investigation.

A review of the relevant literature pertaining to the phonetic differences between geminate and non-geminate consonants indicates that the only universally-consistent acoustic correlate that is crosslinguistically shared by geminates in word-internal environments is closure duration (Ridouane 2010). Although, languages that exhibit a contrast between geminates and singletons vary considerably with respect to their durational differences. Not to mention, these length contrasts appear to depend on a segment's manner of articulation, position within the word or phrase, speaking rate, and stress placement, and even these seem to be language and dialect specific (Arvaniti 1999; Aoyama and Reid 2006; Taylor 1985; Stevens 2011). All the same, average closure durations range from approximately one and a half to more than three times the length of the corresponding singleton counterpart, irrespective of the segment's manner of articulation (Aoyama and Reid 2006; Arvaniti and Tserdanelis 2000; Cohn, Ham, and Podesva 1999; Esposito and Di Benedetto 1999; Gili-Fivela et al. 2007; Hansen 2004; Ladefoged and Maddieson 1996; Lahiri and Hankamer 1988; Lehiste, Morton, and Tatham 1973; Torreira 2006). Furthermore, secondary acoustic properties that have lent, albeit inconsistently, to the perception of a geminate segment likewise appear to be language and dialect specific: voice onset time, duration of the immediately preceding and following vowels as well as burst energy and fundamental frequency values at the offset of the preceding vowel. Regardless, the sole phonetic parameter that was considered in the quantitative acoustic analyses to follow is the duration of the consonantal segment positionally subsequent to the deletion of either syllable-final liquid in word-internal position.

Review of Previous Scholarship

Among the most salient and extensively researched phonological processes of Caribbean Spanish after the categorical weakening of /–s/ is the prolific behavior of the post-nuclear liquids /l/ and /ɾ/ in both syllable- and word-final positions. Speakers of these so-called linguistically innovative dialects generally share a wide variety of allophonic variants resulting from various phonological tendencies: deletion, assimilation, gemination, lambdacism, rhotacism, hybridization, liquid gliding, and devoicing, to name the most widely attested. "Without a doubt more allophones have been attributed to the family of liquids than to any other group of sounds in the literature on Spanish dialects" (Hammond 2001, 268), which highlights not only the relative instability of the syllable coda but also that of this specific group of sonorants as compared to the rest of a limited number of consonants permissible in post-nuclear environments in Spanish.[2]

The existing literature pertaining to syllable-final /l/ and /ɾ/ in Cuban Spanish presents a spectrum of distinct phonetic manifestations. Be this as it may, the following should not be interpreted as exhaustive given that most of the articulated forms can be devoiced or weakened to varying degrees. The principal variants of /l/, as attested in the literature, are retention (/–l/ → [l]), multiple vibrantization (/–l/ → [r]), rhotacism (/–l/ → [ɾ]), hybridization (/–l/ → [$\text{l}^{\text{ɾ}}$]), liquid gliding (/–l/ → [j]), and deletion (/–l/ → Ø), while those of /–ɾ/ are retention (/–ɾ/ → [ɾ]), multiple vibrantization (/–ɾ/ → [r]), assibilation (/–ɾ/ → [ɹ̝]), lambdacism (/–ɾ/ → [l]), hybridization (/–ɾ/ → [$\text{l}^{\text{ɾ}}$]), liquid gliding (/–ɾ/ → [j]), aspiration (/–ɾ/ → [h]), nasalization (/–ɾ/ → [ɾ^{n}] or [n]), and deletion (/–ɾ/ → Ø) (Hammond 2001, 268, 289). A cursory glance at this allophonic inventory might give the erroneous impression that the lateral phoneme is the more stable of the two for its comparatively reduced number of phonetic realizations. However, if one were to consider the marked infrequency of /l/ in final environments, primarily though not exclusively due to its lack of grammatical productivity, one could then conclude then that /–l/ and /–ɾ/ are equally unstable segments.

A survey of the relatively more recent and relevant bibliographic compendia (López Morales 1994; Mota 1968; Quilis 1984; Rivas et al. 1985; Solé 1970, 1972), linguistic anthologies (Alonso and Fernández 1977), and bibliographic surveys (Alpízar Castillo 1989; Figueroa Esteva 1990; Lipski 1998; López-Íñiguez 1983; López Morales 1968; Menéndez 1999; Montes Giraldo 1989; Valdés Bernal 1978, 2007) confirms that, in spite of a considerably long-established tradition of linguistic interest dating back to the late eighteenth and early nineteenth centuries, the largest proportion of linguistic investigations concerning Cuban Spanish are lexical compilations followed by phonological or phonetic observations. And, even though the above-referenced bibliographic works span a period of approximately four decades (1968–2007), none pertain to the current decade and only one is from the previous, thereby lending possible support to the probable lack of more recent analyses in the field. In addition, a more detailed examination of this extensive bibliography reveals a number of incongruences in the analysis of Cuban Spanish dialectology overall.

Many of the earlier works on Cuban Spanish were anecdotal accounts of "aficionados entusiastas" (enthusiastic fans; López Morales 1971, 162) relying almost exclusively on the impressionistic data of others or on literary representations of Cuban speech.[3] While it is understandable that these earlier analyses perhaps did not take advantage of available audio-recording equipment and sound spectrographs given both the financial expense and the time and training necessary to use such equipment, many more-recent linguistic endeavors have yet to benefit from computer-based speech analysis software made available for free public use by Paul Boersma and David Weenink in December 1995. Furthermore, the more contemporary investigations, expressly those of US linguists, have been encumbered by Cuba's inaccessibility due to long-standing political barriers. As a result, US linguists have been unable to access investigations carried out in Cuba proper and have had to rely on investigative procedures other than direct field research. All in all, despite boasting a substantial corpus of earlier lexical studies coupled with the relatively recent growth of more scientific endeavors, the linguistic study of the language of Cuba falls a bit short of what one would expect given its cultural and historical standing in the Antilles.

It is, therefore, not unexpected that numerous scholars have noted this inherent discrepancy in the field (Almendros 1958, 171–72; Fails 1984, 305; Hammond 1976, 14; Isbăşescu 1965, 571; Lamb 1968, 11; Ruiz Hernández and Miyares Bermúdez 1984, 7, to name a few). To this respect, both Lamb (1968, 9) and López Morales (1971, 163) have commented on its underdevelopment, describing it as "relatively pristine" and "*en pañales*" (in diapers) respectively; curious observations when one considers how far back linguistic interest in Cuban Spanish dates. Others, like Alpízar Castillo (1989, vii) and Bartoš (1965, 144), recognize an inclination toward impressionistic procedures owing significantly to inharmonious development and an overwhelming absence of methodological empiricism. More recently, both Alfaraz (2000, 1) and Choy-López (1994, 442) reference significant gaps in research on Cuban Spanish since the 1970s either because of discontinuation or long-term interruption due to ongoing economic, political, and social issues.

Everything considered, the following three criteria served to narrow down the relevant scholarship to be reviewed: (1) All studies that make mention of post-nuclear liquids; (2) all studies that analyze their own data; and (3) all studies that utilize an acceptable data-collection process and a scientifically-based analysis. These constraints imposed on the literature review serve a dual purpose. First, they help to refine the number of prior investigations to only those most analogous to the current study in terms of research and analysis objectives in order to adequately compare results between these previous analyses and those of the present investigation. Second, they help to make explicit the disproportionality characteristic of the field of Cuban Spanish dialectology.

A number of scholars have investigated the allophony of post-nuclear liquids in western Cuban Spanish, either exclusively or by means of a more general analysis of such areas as vocabulary, final consonantism, consonantism, or phonology (cf. Carlson 2014, 17–20). However, only twelve of these investigations claim to have employed instrumental techniques for both the collection and analysis of their data:[4] Alfaraz (2000, 2007), Costa Sánchez (1984, 1987), Darias Concepción (2001), Fails (1984), Figueroa Esteva and Dohotaru (1994), Figueroa Esteva, Choy-López, and Dohotaru (1990), Ruiz Hernández (1978), Ruiz Hernández and Miyares Bermúdez (1984), Santana Cepero (2006), and Sosa (1974). In addition, only four of these were carried out in the past decade, and none are from the current decade, thereby calling further attention to the pressing need for more contemporary experimental endeavors. Finally, four of the previously mentioned twelve provide some acoustic evidence of their finding by means of oscillograms, sonograms, or spectrograms: Costa Sánchez (1984), Fails (1984), Ruiz Hernández and Miyares Bermúdez (1984), and Santana Cepero (2006).

Furthermore, while most of these investigations have affirmed the occurrence of gemination and universally agree that it is not the primary allophonic manifestation of the consonantal segment following deletion of /–l/ and /–ɾ/ in word-internal or word-final positions, the unanimity of the nomenclature used to designate the phenomenon as well as its corresponding phonetic description ends there: throughout the studies, it is referred to as regressive assimilation (Alfaraz 2000, 2007; Figueroa Esteva and Dohotaru 1994; Sosa 1974), regressive assimilation fundamentally realized as gemination (Darias Concepción 2001), assimilation (Fails 1984), unspecified polymorphism (Figueroa Esteva, Choy-López, and Dohotaru 1990), lengthening or partial gemination (Ruiz Hernández and Miyares Bermúdez 1984), total assimilation or gemination (Ruiz Hernández and Miyares Bermúdez 1984), deletion resulting in gemination (Ruiz Hernández 1978), complete gemination and partial gemination (Santana Cepero 2006), and gemination with varying outputs depending on the following segment (Costa Sánchez 1984, 1987). Nevertheless, what is evident from these varied descriptions is that syllable-final liquids in Cuban Spanish display an array of allophonic variants and that scientific clarity and precision as to the nature of these supposed allophones needs to be brought to light.

Finally, as previously mentioned, given strict long-standing and ongoing travel sanctions imposed between the United States and Cuba, all linguistic endeavors to date that have been carried out by US nationals (as is currently known) have had to either make recourse to secondhand recordings or direct field research of Cuban nationals recently arrived to the United States. Likewise, all data collected in the field proper have been exclusively realized by Cuban nationals (cf. Costa Sánchez

1984, 1987; Darias Concepción 2001; Figueroa Esteva and Dohotaru 1994; Figueroa Esteva, Choy-López, and Dohotaru 1990; Ruiz Hernández 1978; Ruiz Hernández and Miyares Bermúdez 1984; Santana Cepero 2006). This is an understandable yet unfortunate consequence of strained relations between the United States and Cuba post-1959. However, with the 2011 liberalization of purposeful travel to Cuba under the Obama administration, one can hope and expect to shortly see more investigations by non–Cuban nationals carried out on the island itself.

In light of the previous statements, the implications of the present investigation are many. First, it complements all previous scholarship relative to the subjects of gemination and syllable-final allophony in the Spanish of the region of Havana, Cuba, as well as more generally to the field of Cuban Spanish dialectology. Second, it is supported by an empirical investigative and analytical design. In other words, the entirety of the corpus of data was digitally captured and acoustically analyzed via current speech analysis software. Third, it is founded on a corpus of data derived from direct field research during two trips to Havana, Cuba. As is presently known, the current study is the first of its kind to have been conducted in Cuba proper by a US national. Approval to conduct the study was obtained from the Institutional Review Board of Purdue University (protocol number 1102010538).

Research Method and Design

The gemination of a consonantal segment positionally subsequent to the deletion of a syllable-final liquid has been attested in a large proportion of all prior investigations. Furthermore, gemination is said to be nearly categorical in the speech of all social status groups and most frequently, although not exclusively, affects syllable-final /l/, /ɾ/, and /s/. Nevertheless, these same descriptive analyses show a lack of systematicity with respect to the phonetic output of both underlying syllable-final liquids. As a result, the potential gamut of liquid allophony will be considered. The following research questions guided the organizational framework of the qualitative and quantitative acoustic analyses: (1) What are the specific phonetic manifestations of /–l/?; (2) What are the specific phonetic manifestations of /–ɾ/?; and (3) Which liquid segment, /–l/ or /–ɾ/, is more likely to result in gemination?

Participants were passively recruited via snowball (i.e., word-of-mouth), convenience (i.e., opportunity), and purposive (e.g., no subjects were turned away) sampling methods. Even though participants were verbally informed as to the various components and general time frame of an individual session with the investigator, the specific objectives of the study were never disclosed. Speech samples were elicited from twenty-six subjects (n=26) selected according to the following criteria: (1) Are native to the region of Havana, Cuba; (2) currently reside in the region of Havana, Cuba; (3) have not resided outside of the region of Havana, Cuba, for more than six months; and (4) are 18 years of age or older due to human-subject research protocol regulations. Those who did not fall within the required specifications were nonetheless recorded, but their respective linguistic data were excluded from the present study. In order to verify participant eligibility, each potential subject was required to show their *carné de identidad* (identification document), which unequivocally verifies place of birth (more specifically, province and municipality), among other things.

The linguistic interview was designed in both structure and content to elicit vernacular speech. More specifically, the order in which each activity within a particular session took place helped to lessen any potential unease on the part of the participant. Although the entire data elicitation process consisted of five parts (carried out in the following order: small talk, demographic questionnaire, semiformal speech elicitation task, informal speech elicitation task, and formal speech elicitation task), the present study focuses exclusively on the informal speech data. Each session would typically begin with the investigator and the participant engaging in some small talk while enjoying a cup of coffee together. Once it became evident that the conversational dynamic had become more relaxed, the investigator then proceeded to the demographic questionnaire. While both the preliminary talk and the demographic questionnaire were recorded, neither was used in data analyses since the data amassed from these two activities would not be representative of vernacular speech. Participation in the research project (more specifically, completion of all elicitation tasks) lasted on average 45 minutes to an hour, and the entirety of all informal speech elicitation tasks provided exactly 601.15 hours of recorded data. A sociolinguistic questionnaire was used to guide, as needed, the unstructured, nondirective interviews. However, not all questions were used since the participants guided the subject(s) of conversation in whichever direction they preferred. This listing of questions served more as a prompt if there happened to be a lull in the conversation or as a guide if the participant did not seem particularly interested in a chosen topic or if (s)he appeared distracted or did not proffer much response to a particular question. Following are two of the most widely employed questions for just such an occasion: (1) *Hábleme un poco de su infancia y de su juventud. ¿Cómo era la relación con sus padres o hermanos/as?* (Tell me a bit about your childhood. What was the relationship with your parents or siblings like?); and (2) *¿Qué tradiciones puede recordar creciendo con su familia? ¿Piensa mantener estas tradiciones con su propia familia?* (What family traditions can you remember growing up? Will you continue these traditions with your own family?).

All recordings were made using a Marantz solid-state handheld recorder (PMD 661) with audio input specifications set to digitize the elicited speech samples in monaural .wav format at a sampling rate of 44.1 kHz and 24-bit linear quantization by means of a unidirectional, hypercardioid condenser lavalier microphone (Countryman B25P4FF05B-HW). The acoustic data were then directly transferred from the Security Digital High Capacity (SDHC) flash media card to the investigator's notebook for initial segmentation via Sony Creative Software's audio production suite Sound Forge Pro 10.[5] Once the informal conversations were isolated, the entirety of the informal production data was manually transcribed in longhand by the investigator. All instances of underlying /l/ and /ɾ/ in syllable-final, word-internal position were highlighted so that, come time for more precise segmentation and qualitative and quantitative analyses, no occurrences would be overlooked. Mean relative intensity values for all segmented files were then normalized to 70 dB SPL via the 'scale intensity' command in Praat version 5.3.29 (Boersma and Weenink 2012) so that the average amplitude levels were constant across all files. All recordings were made in areas of convenience to the subjects. As a result, certain nonlinguistic variables, primarily ambient in nature, could neither be consistently anticipated nor prevented altogether.

Each subject contributed anywhere from 12 (subject 21) to 187 (subject 4) instances of an underlying, word-internal, post-nuclear liquid in their respective unstructured conversations. On average, however, each individual subject produced approximately 72.9 viable instances of an underlying liquid phoneme in word-internal, syllable-final position. Although it would have been ideal to have a greater number of elicited tokens per participant, in order to preserve the inherent nature of an informal, unstructured speech event, the total number of elicited tokens as per each liquid phoneme was not controlled for.

Data Analysis and Discussion

Generally, consonants can be acoustically identified by a number of characteristics evident in both their waveforms and spectra. As a result, qualitative measurements were obtained from simultaneous waveform and wideband spectrogram displays, when necessary. A further comparative examination of the Linear Predictive Coding (LPC) and the Fast Fourier Transform (FFT) spectra were utilized particularly in instances where parallel consideration of the waveform and spectrogram did not demonstrate clear enough distinctions as to the manner, place, and voicing specification of the segment under investigation. Acoustic correlates of consonant voicing, manner of articulation, and place of articulation for each of the segments under investigation were adapted from Kent and Reid (2002), Lass (1996), and Pickett (1998). Despite various, and often times discrepant, qualitative and quantitative descriptions, as far as the researcher can tell, no specific quantitative data have yet to be proffered for western Cuban Spanish. Bearing this in mind, and given that it constitutes the most comprehensive durational analysis of Spanish consonant segments, Lavoie (2001) will be referenced vis-à-vis benchmark length measurements for Spanish singleton consonants.[6] In addition, average length distinctions between singleton and geminate consonant segments from various crosslinguistic studies will serve as durational parameters for the determination of the significance of segment length in the data set. Unfortunately, none of the authors surveyed (Borzone de Manrique and Signorini 1983; Lavoie 2001; Navarro Tomás 1918;[7] Quilis 1988) quantify consonant length in syllable-final position. Still, the average durational measurements for Spanish consonants outlined in Lavoie (2001) are relatively consistent with those of Borzone de Manrique and Signorini (1983) and Quilis (1988). Additionally, none of these previously referenced quantitative examinations is founded on the analysis of Cuban Spanish (Argentinian, Mexican, Albaceteño, and various dialects respectively) or even that of a radical dialect, for that matter.

Seven allophonic variants of /–l/ and eleven for /–ɾ/ were found in the corpus of informal data. Since the deletion of /–l/ and /–ɾ/ constituted the most frequent allophonic variant of both post-nuclear liquid phonemes, four additional articulations particularly relevant to the quantitative analyses were considered for all /–l/ →

Ø and /–ɾ/ → Ø cases. In all instances where a word-internal, syllable-final liquid was elided, the length of the immediately-following consonantal segment was evaluated and classified into one of four predetermined length categories: (1) *full gemination* or those tokens displaying a 100 percent increase or more in the length of the immediately-following consonantal segment; (2) *partial gemination* or a 50 percent to 99.9 percent increase in the length of the immediately-following consonantal segment; (3) *0–49.9 percent increase* or those tokens exhibiting no durational increase to a 49.9 percent increase in the length of the immediately-following consonantal segment; and (4) *decrease in length* or all tokens displaying a decrease in the length of the immediately-following consonantal segment. The durational categories pertaining to full and partial gemination were particularly chosen since the crosslinguistic literature on geminates reveals that the length of a geminated segment can range from approximately 1.5 to 3.8 times the duration of the corresponding singleton segment (see "Compensatory Lengthening and Gemination," this chapter). Furthermore, because the current investigation considers full gemination as any segment displaying a 100.0 percent durational increase or more, it naturally followed that partial gemination would pertain to any segment that displays a 50–99.9 percent increase in length. The analyses to follow derive from a total of 1,895 tokens of word-internal, post-nuclear /l/ and /ɾ/ that were extracted from the corpus of informal data.

As table 2.1 illustrates, the larger proportion of elicited tokens were those that contained a word-internal, post-nuclear /ɾ/.

Table 2.1. Total Elicited Tokens: /Vl.C/ versus /Vɾ.C/

/Vl.C/		/Vɾ.C/	
n	%	n	%
469	24.7	1,426	75.3

More specifically, a little less than one quarter of the entirety of the informal data set (24.7 percent or 469 tokens) was composed of words with an underlying /–l/ in word-internal, post-nuclear position, as in *colcha* (bedspread), and a little more than three-quarters of the entirety of the informal data set were tokens that contained an underlying /–ɾ/ (75.3 percent or 1,426 tokens) in the same syllabic environment, as in *carta* (letter). Be this as it may, this marked difference in the frequencies of overall occurrence between /–l/ and /–ɾ/ in the present study's corpus of informal data is not surprising (cf. Alarcos Llorach 1961; Delattre 1965; Guirao and Borzone de Manrique 1972; Guirao and García Jurado 1990; Navarro Tomás 1946; Quilis and Esgueva 1980; Zipf and Rogers 1939).

Allophones of Word-Internal, Post-Nuclear /–l/

Of the 469 tokens extracted from the corpus of informal data for all twenty-six participants combined, word-internal, post-nuclear /l/ manifested a total of seven allophones: Ø, [l], [d˺], [g˺], [w], [b˺], and [m] (listed in order of frequency of occurrence in table 2.2).[8]

Table 2.2. Allophones of /Vl.C/

Allophone	n	%
Ø	254	54.2
[l]	121	25.8
[d˺]	63	13.4
[g˺]	23	4.9
[w]	4	0.9
[b˺]	3	0.6
[m]	1	0.2
Total	469	100.0

Deletion of the word-internal, post-nuclear lateral liquid (e.g., *generalmente* [he.ne.ˌɾa.ˈmen.te], 'generally') accounted for a little more than half of the entirety of the data set (54.2 percent). /–l/ maintenance (i.e., /–l/ → [l] as in *algo* [ˈal.go], 'something') accounted for 25.8 percent of the corpus of data. Two partially-assimilated allophones [d˺] (e.g., *facultad* [fa.kud˺. ˈtað], 'faculty') and [g˺] (e.g., *cualquier* [kwag˺. ˈkjeɾ], 'any') composed 13.4 percent and 4.9 percent of the entirety of the analyzed lexemes respectively. Lastly, [w] (e.g., *alguien* [ˈaw.ɣjen], 'someone') accounted for 0.9 percent of the data, a partially-assimilated [b˺] (e.g., *salve* [ˈsab˺.βe], 'save (3sg. pres.subj.)') was articulated three times (0.6 percent), and [m] (e.g., *realmente* [re.ˌam.ˈmen.te], 'really, truly') was only uttered once (0.2 percent).[9] Altogether, the three partially-assimilated allophones, [d˺], [g˺], and [b˺], accounted for 89 tokens or 19.0 percent of the corpus of informal data for word-internal, syllable-final /l/.

Spectral and temporal examination of the 254 instances of deletion of the post-nuclear lateral liquid (i.e., /–l/ → Ø / V_.C) in table 2.3 shows that the greatest number of tokens exhibiting deletion of /–l/ (n=165 or 65.0 percent) demonstrated anywhere from no increase in length to a 49.9 percent increase in the length of the immediately following consonantal segment.

Table 2.3. Length Manifestations of /–l/ à Ø / V_.C

C	n	%
Full Gemination	5	2.0
Partial Gemination	26	10.2
0%–49.9% Increase	165	65.0
Decrease in Length	58	22.8
Total	254	100.0

Fifty-eight tokens or 22.8 percent of the instances in which /–l/ was deleted showed a decrease in the length of the immediately following segment. Twenty-six tokens or 10.2 percent were classified as examples of partial gemination or tokens exhibiting a 50 percent to 99.9 percent increase in the length of the immediately subsequent consonant. Finally, 2.0 percent or 5 of 254 tokens manifested full gemination or a 100.0 percent or more increase in the length of the immediately following consonantal segment. In sum, 196 of 254 total instances of /–l/ → Ø / V_.C demonstrated anywhere from no increase in length to a 100 percent or more increase in the duration of the following segment; in other words, 77.2 percent of the entire corpus of /–l/ → Ø / V_.C tokens.

One representative spectrogram with corresponding waveform of the two most frequent length manifestations of the consonant segment immediately following the deletion of word-internal /–l/ or a 0–49.9 percent increase and a decrease in the length of the segment immediately following /–l/ → Ø is provided in figures 2.1 and 2.2 respectively. Canonical length in milliseconds (ms), actual length (in ms), and percent increase or decrease are specified for all represented tokens. The accompanying phonetic transcriptions exclusively capture the segments under investigation in the current study (i.e., word-internal, post-nuclear /l/ and the immediately following segmental environment). Other segmental environments not directly relevant to the focus of the present study (e.g., word-final position) were broadly transcribed.

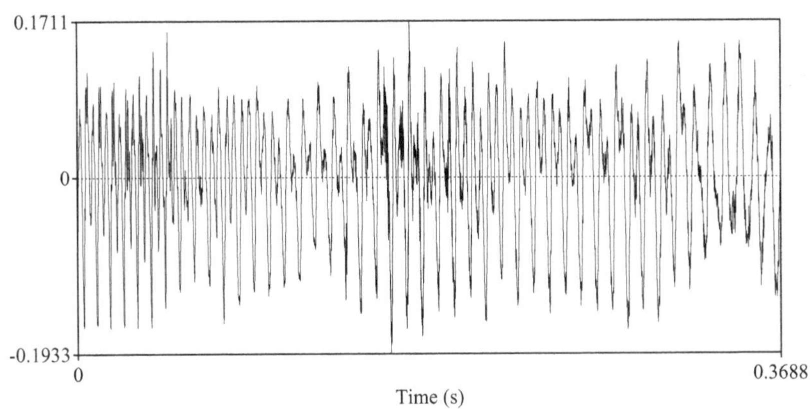

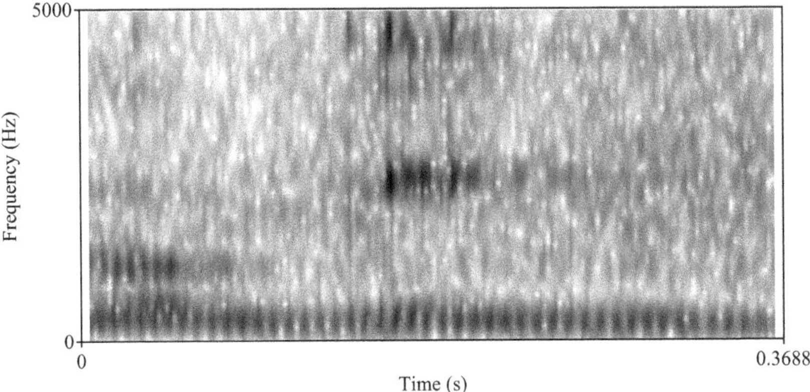

Figure 2.1. Holguin

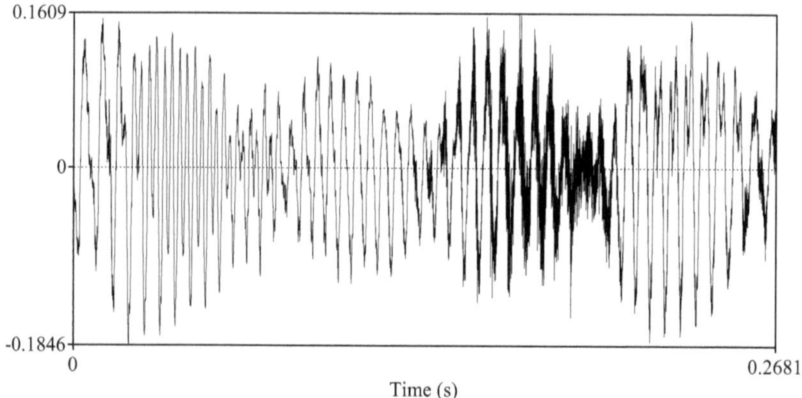

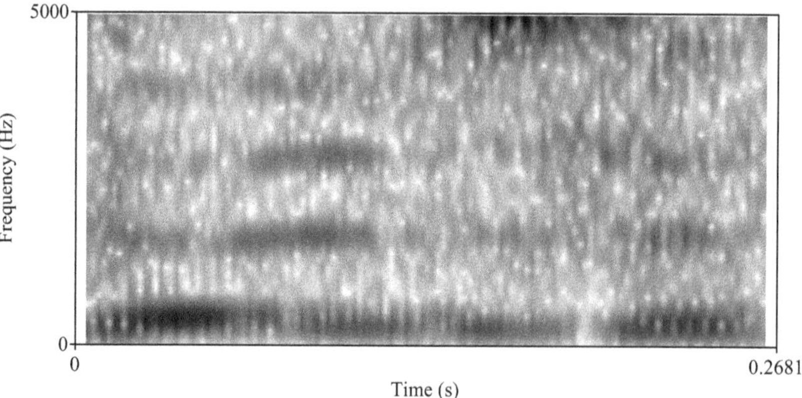

Figure 2.2. Dulce

Allophones of Word-Internal, Post-nuclear /–ɾ/

Of the 1,426 tokens extracted from the corpus of informal data for all twenty-six participants combined, word-internal, post-nuclear /ɾ/ manifested a total of eleven allophones: Ø, [g˺], [l], [d˺], [ɾ], [ɾ˺], [j], [r], [g], [b˺], and [h] (listed in order of frequency of occurrence in table 2.4).

Deletion of the word-internal, post-nuclear rhotic (e.g., *porque* [ˈpo.ke], 'because') accounted for a little more than half of the entirety of the data set (52.0 percent). When grouped together, the partially assimilated allophones [b˺], [d˺], [g˺], and [g] (n=356) (e.g., *servicio* [seb˺.ˈβi.sjo], 'service (n.)'; *importa* [im.ˈpod˺.ta], 'matters (3sg.pres.ind.)'; *porque* [ˈpog˺.ke] and [ˈpog.ke] respectively) comprised 25.0 percent of the corpus with [g˺] constituting 55.1 percent, [d˺] 44.4 percent, and [g] and [b˺] 0.3 percent each. Lambdacism (i.e., /–ɾ/ → [l] as in *suerte* [ˈswel.te], 'luck') contributed 11.9 percent of all viable tokens. /–ɾ/ maintenance (i.e., /–ɾ/ → [ɾ] or [ɾ˺] as in *recuerdos* [re.ˈkweɾ.ðos], 'souvenirs') accounted for 10.5 percent (n=150)

Table 2.4. Allophones of /Vɾ.C/

Allophone	n	%
Ø	742	51.9
[g˺]	196	13.7
[l]	169	11.9
[d˺]	158	11.1
[ɾ]	144	10.1
[ɾ˺]	6	0.5
[j]	5	0.3
[r]	3	0.2
[g]	1	0.1
[b˺]	1	0.1
[h]	1	0.1
Total	1426	100.0

of the corpus of data. /–ɾ/ → [j] (e.g., *porque* [ˈpoj.ke]) provided 0.3 percent of the data. Finally, [r] was articulated three times (0.2 percent) as in *estabilizarlo* [es.ta.βi.li.ˈsar.lo] (to stabilize it (masc.sg.)), and [h] as in *hacerlo* [a.ˈseh.lo] (to do, make it (masc.sg.)) was only uttered once (0.1 percent).

Spectral and temporal examination of the 742 instances of deletion of the word-internal post-nuclear rhotic (i.e., /–ɾ/ → Ø / V_.C) in table 2.5 shows that the greatest number of tokens exhibiting deletion of /–ɾ/ (n=361 or 48.7 percent) demonstrated anywhere from no increase in length to a 49.9 percent increase in the length of the immediately following consonant segment.

Table 2.5. Length Manifestations of /–ɾ/ → Ø / V_.C

Allophone	n	%
Full Gemination	14	1.9
Partial Gemination	130	17.5
0%–49.9% Increase	361	48.7
Decrease in Length	237	31.9
Total	742	100.0

Two hundred and thirty-seven tokens or 31.9 percent of the instances where /–ɾ/ was deleted showed a decrease in the length of the immediately-following segment. 17.5 percent (n=130) were categorized as partial gemination. Finally, 1.9 percent or 14 of 742 tokens manifested full gemination. Interestingly, frequencies of occurrence for all four manifestations of /–ɾ/ → Ø / V_.C mirror those for the post-nuclear lateral liquid; that is, the greatest proportion of tokens exhibited a slight increase in the length of the immediately-following consonantal segment (i.e., 0–49.9 percent increase) followed by a decrease in the length of the immediately-following consonantal segment. Moreover, partial gemination was favored over full gemination (compare 17.5 percent and 1.9 percent respectively).

One representative spectrogram with corresponding waveform of the two most frequent length manifestations of the consonant segment immediately following the deletion of word-internal /–ɾ/ or a 0–49.9 percent increase and a decrease in the length of the segment immediately subsequent to /–ɾ/ → Ø is provided in figures 2.3 and 2.4 respectively. Canonical length (in ms), actual length (in ms), and percent increase or decrease are specified for all represented tokens. The accompanying phonetic transcriptions exclusively capture the segments under investigation in the current study (i.e., word-internal, post-nuclear /ɾ/ and the immediately following segmental environment). Other segmental environments not directly relevant to the focus of the present study (e.g., word-final position) were broadly transcribed.

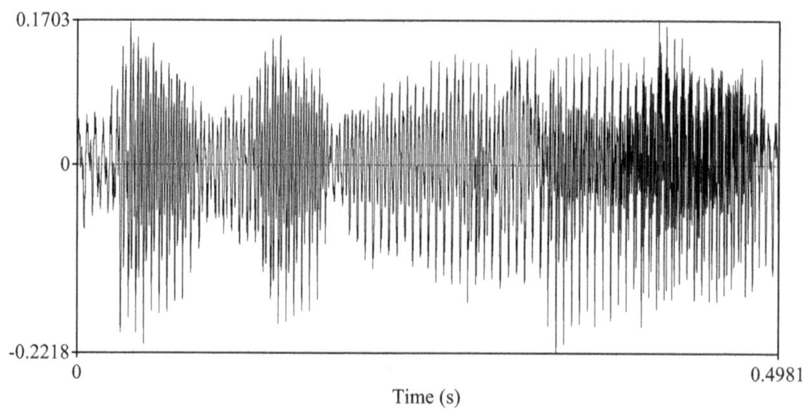

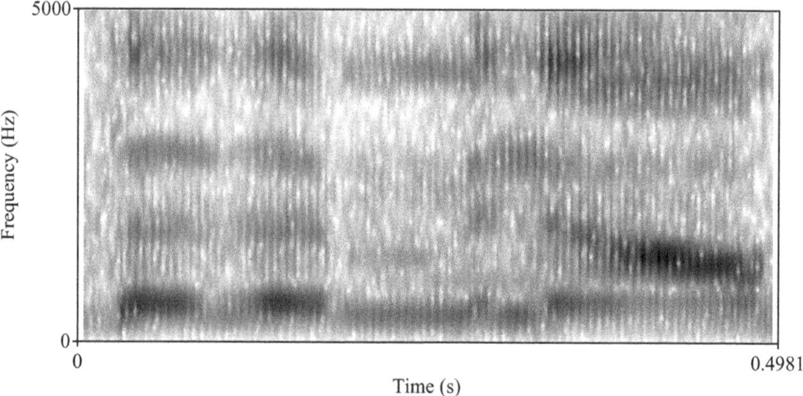

Figure 2.3. Determinados

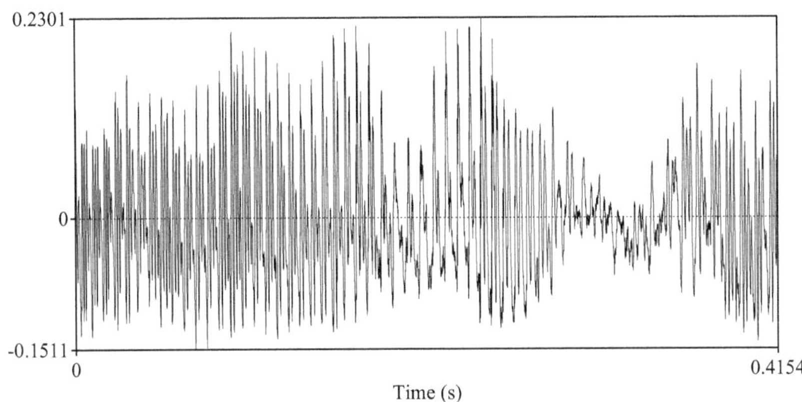

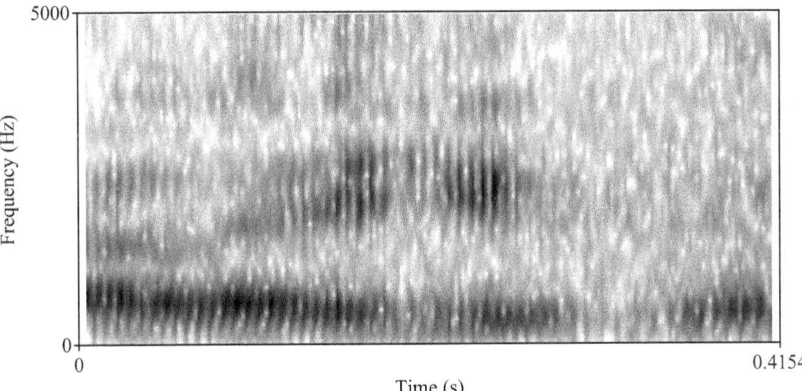

Figure 2.4. Alérgico

Conclusions

Qualitative acoustic analyses of the 1,895 tokens of word-internal, post-nuclear /l/ (n=469) and /ɾ/ (n=1,426) extracted from the corpus of informal data demonstrated seven allophones for the lateral liquid phoneme (Ø, [l], [d˺], [g˺], [w], [b˺], and [m]) and eleven for the simple vibrant phoneme (Ø, [g˺], [l], [d˺], [ɾ], [ɾ˺], [j], [r], [g], [b˺], and [h]), listed here in order of frequency of occurrence. Since deletion of both liquid segments accounted for the greatest number of allophonic cases in each respective data set (compare 54.2 percent and 51.9 percent), further quantitative acoustic analyses vis-à-vis four predetermined durational categories (i.e., full gemination, partial gemination, 0–49.9 percent increase, and a decrease in length) revealed that for both liquid phonemes a 0–49.9 percent increase in the length of the immediately-following consonantal segment was preferred overall (compare 65.0 percent and 48.7 percent respectively). Interestingly, these findings depart from previously-reviewed analyses that provided frequencies of occurrence; retention, regressive assimilation, and total assimilation were listed as the more frequent variants of either post-nuclear liquid. Thereafter, the present study's data demonstrated that both post-nuclear liquids favored a decrease in the immediately-following consonantal segment's duration (compare 22.8 percent and 31.9 percent), followed by partial gemination (compare 10.2 percent and 17.5 percent), and then full gemination (compare 2.0 percent and 1.9 percent). None of the prior-surveyed analyses mentioned a decrease in the subsequent segment's duration. In addition, both post-nuclear liquid phonemes demonstrated a large number of cases of partially-assimilated allophones. The 469 instances of /Vl.C/ manifested 89 total cases of a partially-assimilated allophone—more specifically, [d˺] (n=63), [g˺] (n=23), and [b˺] (n=3). The 1,426 occurrences of /Vɾ.C/ demonstrated 356 total instances of a partially-assimilated allophone—more specifically, [g˺] (n=196), [d˺] (n=158), [g] (n=1), and [b˺] (n=1). All surveyed investigations, with the exception of Sosa (1974), likewise attest the assimilation of a post-nuclear liquid to a following consonantal segment.

Moreover, these previous analyses have investigated the allophony of /–l/ and /–ɾ/ in varying detail. Some have focused exclusively on the potential impact of internal, linguistic variables (cf. Costa Sánchez 1984, 1987; Ruiz Hernández 1978, Santana Cepero 2006; Sosa 1974). Others have wholly concentrated on the possible influences of external, sociolinguistic factors (cf. Alfaraz 2000, 2007). Meanwhile, most have included both internal and external constraints in their respective analyses (cf. Darias Concepción 2001; Fails 1984; Figueroa Esteva and Dohotaru 1994; Ruiz Hernández and Miyares Bermúdez 1984). Nevertheless, a large proportion of these studies relied either partially or wholly on impressionistic methodological procedures, which albeit quite significant and innovative at the time of their undertaking, should be updated and reactualized as per contemporary analytical and research methodologies. Furthermore, as is currently known, all linguistic endeavors to date that have been carried out by a US national have had to either make recourse to secondhand recordings or direct field research of Cuban nationals recently arrived to the United States. With this in mind, the significance and contributions of the current investigation are multifaceted.

First, the present investigation is fully substantiated by an empirical investigative and analytical design. The entirety of the corpus of data was digitally captured and acoustically analyzed via current speech-analysis software thereby comparatively reducing the likelihood of introducing any impressionistic observations into the analyses of the data. Second, the present investigation is founded on a corpus of data derived from direct field research during two trips to Havana, Cuba. Lastly, and most importantly, the present investigation supplements all antecedent scholarship relative to gemination and syllable-final liquid allophony in the Spanish of the region of Havana, Cuba, and, more generally, Cuban Spanish dialectology. While it has demonstrated that deletion of word-internal /–l/ and /–ɾ/ is the most frequently attested articulation, this allophonic outcome is not unexpected. Cuban Spanish, in general, shares a number of common linguistic traits with the dialects of southern Spain, the Canary Islands, and the Caribbean basin. By and large, this macrodialect generally demonstrates a proclivity for the lenition of syllable- and word-final consonants. What is particularly noteworthy, however, about the 254 instances of /–l/ → Ø / V_.C and the 742 instances of /–ɾ/ → Ø / V_.C is the compensatory phonetic process of a durational increase in the length of the immediately-subsequent consonantal segment. More than three-quarters (n=196 or 77.2 percent) of the /–l/ → Ø tokens exhibited a 0–100 percent increase or more in the length of the following consonantal segment. Likewise, 68.1 percent (n=505) of the /–ɾ/ → Ø tokens manifested this same compensatory mechanism. Be this as it may, gemination has been defined in the current crosslinguistic literature as involving a durational increase of 50 percent to more than 300 percent. The current data demonstrate that the most manifested length change for both liquid segments fell within the range of no increase or decrease (0 percent) and a 49.9 percent increase (that is, below that which is universally accepted or attested as gemination); compare 65.0 percent and 48.7 percent respectively. The present study's interpretation of gemination (*partial* or a 50–99.9 percent increase and *full* or a 100 percent+ increase) only accounted for 12.2 percent and 19.4 percent of the entirety of deletion case for word-internal /–l/ and /–ɾ/ respectively; a decrease in the length of the following consonantal segment outnumbered all combined instances of full and partial gemination for both liquids (compare 22.8 percent and 31.9 percent respectively). In summary, while the body of literature pertaining to the phonetics and phonology of Cuban Spanish overwhelmingly claims gemination as a defining characteristic of said dialect area, the minimal occurrence of partial and full gemination in the data analyses of the present investigation was well below that which could be attributed to chance.

Acknowledgments

I would like to thank Alejandro Cuza and two anonymous reviewers for their helpful, constructive, and invaluable comments and feedback.

Notes

1. Hereafter, the notations "V" and "C" will be used to represent any vowel or consonant permissible in the specified syllabic environment.
2. Depending on the dialect area, fifteen phonemes are permissible in word-internal coda position, /j, w, ɾ, l, m, n, p, t̪, k, b, d̪, g, f, s, θ/, and word-final codas potentially allow nine phonemes, /j, w, r, l, n, d̪, s, h/x/χ, θ/.
3. The term *impressionistic* is defined herein as being based upon auditory observation, description, and/or assessment of acoustic events (i.e., lacking the employment of instrumental collection and measurement techniques).
4. Specific mention should be made that those analyses that neglected to indicate their methodological approach for the collection and analysis of their data were categorized as impressionistic and therefore excluded from the following classification.
5. The entirety of each participant's informal speech event (excluding the coffee talk and sociolinguistic questionnaire) was segmented into an individual long .wav file. These originating .wav files were too large for Praat to adequately upload so further segmentation was initially carried out via Sound Forge Pro 10.
6. The acoustic data from Lavoie (2001) derives from a "carefully controlled word list" (49) produced by four native speakers of northern Mexican Spanish.
7. The sole measurements found in Navarro Tomás (1918, 375) pertained exclusively to the consonant sequence of [l.d] as in *calderero* (boilermaker), *caldero* (small cauldron), and *caldo* (stock or broth).
8. The diacritic '˺' represents an unreleased articulation of the consonant segment to which it pertains.

9. Some traditional accounts of gemination (cf. Hockett 1955 and Swadesh 1937) would interpret [m.m] as a clear case of said phenomenon. Be this as it may, the present study's interpretation of gemination is that of an increase of 100 percent or more in the length of the onset segment subsequent to the deletion of either /-l/ or /-ɾ/. As a result, this one token was not included in the durational category of full gemination and, thus, was excluded from all corresponding analyses.

References

Alarcos Llorach, E. 1961. *Fonología española.* Madrid: Gredos.

Alfaraz, G. G. 2000. "Sound Change in a Regional Variety of Cuban Spanish." PhD diss., Michigan State University.

———. 2007. "Effects of Age and Gender on Liquid Assimilation in Cuban Spanish." In *Selected Proceedings of the Third Workshop on Spanish Sociolinguistics*, edited by J. Holmquist, A. Lorenzino, and L. Sayahi, 23–29. Somerville, MA: Cascadilla Proceedings Project.

Almendros, N. 1958. "Estudio fonético del español en Cuba: región occidental." *Boletín de la Academia Cubana de la Lengua* 7:138–76.

Alonso, G., and Á. L. Fernández, eds. 1977. *Antología de lingüística cubana: volúmenes 1 y 2.* Havana: Editorial de Ciencias Sociales.

Alpízar Castillo, R. 1989. *Apuntes para la historia de la lingüística en Cuba.* Havana: Editorial de Ciencias Sociales.

Aoyama, K., and L. A. Reid. 2006. "Cross-Linguistic Tendencies and Durational Contrasts in Geminate Consonants: An Examination of Guinaang Bontok Geminates." *Journal of the International Phonetic Association* 36:145–57.

Arvaniti, A. 1999. "Effects of Speaking Rate on the Timing of Single and Geminate Sonorants." In Ohala, Hasegawa, Ohala, Granville, and Bailey, *International Congress of Phonetic Sciences*, 599–602.

Arvaniti, A., and G. Tserdanelis. 2000. "On the Phonetics of Geminates: Evidence from Cypriot Greek." In *Proceedings of the 6th International Conference on Spoken Language Processing*, Volume 2, edited by B. Yuan, T. Huang, and X. Tang, 559–62. Beijing: China Military Friendship Publish.

Bartoš, L. 1965. "Notas al problema de la pronunciación del español en Cuba." *Sbornik Prací Filosoficke Fakuly Brnenske University* 14:143–49.

Boersma, Paul, and David Weenink. 2012. "Praat: Doing Phonetics by Computer." Version 5.3.29. http://www.fon.hum.uva.nl/praat/.

Borzone de Manrique, A. M., and A. Signorini. 1983. "Segmental Duration and Rhythm in Spanish." *Journal of Phonetics* 11:117–28.

Campos-Astorkiza, R. 2005. "Typological Analysis of Compensatory Consonant Lengthening." *Phonology and Phonetics in Iberia, Barcelona, 2005.* http://webs2002.uab.es/filologiacatalana/papi/files/Campos-Astorzika.pdf.

Carlson, K. M. 2014. "Compensatory Lengthening in the Spanish of Havana, Cuba: Acoustic Analyses of Word-Internal, Post-Nuclear /l/ and /ɾ/." PhD diss., Purdue University.

Choy-López, L. R. 1994. "Atlas lingüístico de Cuba (ALCu). Pasado, presente y futuro." *Anuario de Lingüística Hispánica* 10:437–42.

Cohn, A. C., W. H. Ham, and R. J. Podesva. 1999. "The Phonetic Realization of Singleton-Geminate Contrasts in Three Languages of Indonesia." In Ohala, Hasegawa, Ohala, Granville, and Bailey, *International Congress of Phonetic Sciences*, 587–90.

Costa Sánchez, M. 1984. "The Gemination of Consonants in Cuban Spanish." *Islas* 77:97–110.

———. 1987. "Características fonéticas de los fonemas consonánticos del español de la región central de Cuba (estudio de fonética experimental)." *Islas* 84:170–73.

Darias Concepción, J. L. 2001. "Variación fonética de /ɾ/ y /l/ distensivos en el español de Pinar del Río." PhD diss., Universidad de Pinar del Río.

Delattre, P. 1965. *Comparing the Phonetic Features of English, German, Spanish and French.* Heidelberg, Deu.: J. Groos.

Esposito, A., and M. G. Di Benedetto. 1999. "Acoustical and Perceptual Study of Gemination in Italian Stops." *Journal of the Acoustical Society of America* 106:2051–62.

Fails, W. C. 1984. "An Analysis of the Consonantal Phonemes of the Educated Norm of Havana." PhD diss., University of Texas at Austin.
Figueroa Esteva, M. 1990. "La lingüística en Cuba: balance y perspectivas." *Nueva Revista de Filología Hispánica* 38:1–13.
Figueroa Esteva, M., and P. Dohotaru. 1994. "Consideraciones fonéticas y fonológicas sobre el consonantismo urbano actual de Cuba (nivel universitario): fonemas tipificantes." *Gramática del Español, Revista de Filología Hispánica* 6:649–71.
Figueroa Esteva, M., L. R. Choy-López, and P. Dohotaru. 1990. "Para la caracterización fonológica del habla urbana actual de Cuba." *Revista Cubana de Ciencias Sociales* 24:20–34.
Gess, R. S. 2011. "Compensatory Lengthening." In *The Blackwell Companion to Phonology*, Volume 3, *Phonological Processes*, edited by M. van Oostendorp, C. J. Ewen, E. Hume, and K. Rice, 1513–36. Malden, MA: Wiley-Blackwell.
Gili-Fivela, B., C. Zmarich, P. Perrier, C. Savariaux, and G. Tisato. 2007. "Acoustic and Kinematic Correlates of Phonological Length Contrast in Italian Consonants." In *Proceedings of the 16th International Congress of Phonetic Sciences*, edited by J. Trouvain and W. J. Barry, 469–72. Saarbrücken, Deu.: University des Saarlandes.
Guirao, M., and A. M. Borzone de Manrique. 1972. "Fonemas, sílabas y palabras del español de Buenos Aires." *Filología* XVI:135–65.
Guirao, M., and M. A. García Jurado. 1990. "Frequency of Occurrence of Phonemes in American Spanish." *Revue Québécoise de Linguistique* 19:135–49.
Hammond, R. M. 1976. "Some Theoretical Implications from Rapid Speech Phenomena in Miami-Cuban Spanish." PhD diss., University of Florida.
———. 2001. *The Sounds of Spanish: Analysis and Application (with Special Reference to American English)*. Somerville, MA: Cascadilla Press.
Hansen, B. B. 2004. "Production of Persian Geminate Stops: Effects of Varying Speaking Rate." In *Proceedings of the 2003 Texas Linguistics Society Conference*, edited by A. Agwuele, W. Warren, and S.-H. Park, 86–95. Somerville, MA: Cascadilla Proceedings Project.
Hockett, C. F. 1955. *A Manual of Phonology*. Publications in Anthropology and Linguistics, Memoir 11. Bloomington: Indiana University
Isbăşescu, C. 1965. "Algunas peculiaridades fonéticas del español hablado en Cuba." *Revue Roumaine de Linguistique* 10:575–94.
Kent, R. D., and C. Read. 2002. *The Acoustic Analysis of Speech*. San Diego: Singular Publishing Group.
Ladefoged, P., and I. Maddieson. 1996. *The Sounds of the World's Languages*. Cambridge: Blackwell Publishers, Inc.
Lahiri, A., and J. Hankamer. 1988. "The Timing of Geminate Consonants." *Journal of Phonetics* 16:327–38.
Lamb, A. J. 1968. "A Phonological Study of the Spanish of Havana, Cuba." PhD diss., University of Kansas.
Lass, N. J. 1996. *Principles of Experimental Phonetics*. St. Louis: Mosby-Year Book, Inc.
Lavoie, L. M. 2001. *Consonant Strength: Phonological Patterns and Phonetic Manifestations*. New York: Garland Publishing.
Lehiste, I., K. Morton, and M. A. A. Tatham. 1973. "An Instrumental Study of Consonant Gemination." *Journal of Phonetics* 1:131–48.
Lipski, J. M. 1998. "Spanish Linguistics: The Past 100 Years: Retrospective and Bibliography." *Hispania* 81:248–60.
López-Íñiguez, I. 1983. "Bibliografía comentada de estudios lingüísticos publicados en Cuba (1959-1979)." *Cuban Studies/Estudios Cubanos* 13:41–68.
López Morales, H. 1968. El español de Cuba: situación bibliográfica. *Revista de Filología Española* 51:111–37.
———. 1971. *Estudios sobre el español de Cuba*. New York: Las Américas Publishing Company.
———. 1994. *Las Antillas*. Madrid: Arco Libros.
Menéndez, A. 1999. "Una rassegna degli studi dialettologici sull'isola di Cuba." *Rivista Italiana di Dialettologia* 23:371–80.

Montes Giraldo, J. J. 1989. "Breve noticia sobre la investigación lingüística en la Cuba de hoy." *Thesaurus* 44:637–44.

Morin, Y. C. 1992. "Phonological Interpretations of Historical Lengthening." In *Proceedings of the 7th International Phonology Meeting*, edited by W. U. Dressler, M. Prinzhorn, and J. Rennison, 135–55. Turin, Ita.: Rosenberg and Sellier.

Mota, F. M. 1968. *La lingüística en Cuba. Ensayo histórico y bibliográfico.* Havana: Academia de Ciencias de Cuba.

Navarro Tomás, T. 1918. "Diferencias de duración entre las consonantes españolas." *Revista de Filología Española* 5:367–93.

———. 1946. *Estudios de fonología española.* Syracuse: Syracuse University Press.

Ohala, J. J., Y. Hasegawa, M. Ohala, D. Granville, and A. C. Bailey, eds. 1999. *Proceedings of the XIVth International Congress of Phonetic Sciences.* Berkeley: University of California at Berkeley Department of Linguistics.

Pickett, J. M. 1998. *The Acoustics of Speech Communication: Fundamentals, Speech Perception Theory, and Technology.* Needham Heights, MA: Allyn & Bacon.

Quilis, A. 1984. *Bibliografía de fonética y fonología españolas.* Madrid: Consejo Superior de Investigaciones Científicas.

———. 1988. *Fonética acústica de la lengua española.* Madrid: Editorial Gredos.

Quilis, A., and M. Esgueva. 1980. "Frecuencia de fonemas en el español hablado." *Lingüística Española Actual* 2:1–25.

Ridouane, R. 2010. "Geminates at the Junction of Phonetics and Phonology." In *Papers in Laboratory Phonology 10: Variation, Phonetic Detail and Phonological Representation*, edited by C. Fougeron, B. Kühnert, M. D'imperio, and N. Vallée, 61–90. Berlin: Mouton de Gruyter.

Rivas, D., R. Ángel, G. G. Riera, H. Obregón, and I. Páez Urdaneta. 1985. *Bibliografía sobre el español del caribe hispánico.* Caracas: Instituto Universitario Pedagógico de Caracas.

Ruiz Hernández, J. V. 1978. "Las asimilaciones en contacto en Cuba- características." *Fremdsprachen* 22:269–72.

Ruiz Hernández, J. V., and E. Miyares Bermúdez. 1984. *El consonantismo en Cuba: los laboratorios de fonética.* Havana: Editorial de Ciencias Sociales.

Santana Cepero, E. 2006. "Las geminadas en el español habanero. Fonotáctica y restricciones." *Signos Lingüísticos* 4:33–64.

Solé, C. A. 1970. *Bibliografía sobre el español en América: 1920–1967.* Washington, DC: Georgetown University Press.

———. 1972. "Bibliografía sobre el español en América: 1967–1971." *Anuario de Letras* 10:253–88.

Sosa, F. 1974. "Sistema fonológico del español hablado en Cuba: su posición dentro del marco de las lenguas criollas." PhD diss., Yale University.

Stevens, M. 2011. "Consonant Length in Italian: Gemination, Pregemination and Preaspiration." In *Selected Proceedings of the 5th Conference on Laboratory Approaches to Romance Phonology*, edited by S. M. , 21–32. Somerville, MA: Cascadilla Proceedings Project.

Swadesh, M. 1937. "The Phonemic Interpretation of Long Consonants." *Language* 13:1–10.

Taylor, M. 1985. "Some Patterns of Geminate Consonants." *University of Chicago Working Papers* 1:120–29.

Torreira, F. 2006. "Coarticulation between Aspirated -S and Voiceless Stops in Spanish: An Interdialectal Comparison." In *Selected Proceedings of the 9th Hispanic Linguistics Symposium*, edited by N. Sagarra and A. J. Toribio, 113–20. Somerville, MA: Cascadilla Proceedings Project.

Trubetzkoy, N. 1969. *Grundzüge der phonologie.* Translated by C. Baltaxe. Berkeley: University of California Press.

Valdés Bernal, S. 1978. "Inquietudes lingüísticas cubanas sobre el español hablado en Cuba: siglo XVIII." *Anuario de Literatura y Lingüística* 9:121–42.

———. 2007. "Las bases lingüísticas del español de Cuba." In *La lengua en Cuba: estudios*, edited by M. A. Domínguez, 27–56. Santiago de Compostela, Esp.: Universidade de Santiago de Compostela.

Zipf, G. K., and F. M. Rogers. 1939. "Phonemes and Variphones in Four Present-Day Romance Languages and Classical Latin from the Viewpoint of Dynamic Philology." *Archives Néerlandaises de Phonétique Expérimentale* 15:111–47.

3

Code-Switching in Miami Cuban Spanish: A Preliminary Study of Suprasegmental Effects

ANN M. ALY
University of California, Los Angeles

THE WAYS IN WHICH bilinguals access and function in the languages they speak has been studied from various disciplinary angles, including linguistic, sociological, and neurological approaches. Among one of the observed phenomena from multidisciplinary research on bilinguals is that of *code-switching* (also referred to as *code-mixing*), which involves changing between two or more languages, speech styles, or dialects within a single interaction. Code-switching can be *insertional* (in which parts of Language B are inserted into a larger discourse of Language A) or *alternational* (switching between Languages A and B in larger chunks). Although code-switching was previously seen as a lack of linguistic competence or fluency (e.g., Pedraza 1978), sociolinguistic research in the 1980s (e.g., Poplack 1980) revealed the linguistic systematicity involved in code-switching and its usage by highly fluent bilinguals.

Since these initial studies, researchers have investigated various aspects of code-switching, such as the grammatical constraints of code-switching (e.g., Di Sciullo, Muysken, and Singh 1986; Poplack, Sankoff, and Miller 1988; Chan 2009), the social functions of code-switching (such as Zentella 1981, 1997; Bullock and Toribio 2009; Bhatt and Bolonyai 2011), and the neurological demands of code-switching in bilinguals of different fluency levels (such as lower processing costs in highly fluent bilinguals and higher abilities for task switching, as seen in studies like Gullifer, Kroll, and Dussias [2013] and Yim and Bialystock [2012]). Although the goals of and questions asked by these studies vary by disciplinary approach, the results of these studies all reveal code-switching as a deliberate practice that demonstrates systematic linguistic patterns and affects executive control functions.

Early work on code-switching tended to focus mostly on typologically related languages (e.g., Spanish-English in Poplack [1980]; French-English in Poplack, Sankoff, and Miller [1988]; Hindi-English and French-Italian-English in Di Sciullo, Muysken, and Singh [1986]), and these observations did not always hold for unrelated languages. Based on code-switching data from two unrelated languages (Swahili and English), Myers-Scotton (1997) proposes the *Matrix Language Framework* (MLF), in which the *matrix language* (ML), or more dominant language in the interaction, has a privileged position with respect to the *embedded language* (EL), or guest language of the interaction. More specifically, this model predicts that when there are morphosyntactic differences between languages, the ML pattern is most likely to surface.

The morphosyntactic research on code-switching has provided invaluable insights into the crosslinguistic patterns and constraints implemented by code-switching communities and has helped to reframe the previous misconceptions about code-switching as linguistically incompetent or unsystematic phenomena. However, as the understanding of code-switching continues to advance in the morphosyntactic, sociolinguistic, and psycholinguistic subfields, the phonetics and phonology of code-switching has not been studied as vigorously until recently. The following section outlines the relevant studies that investigate the phonetics of code-switching within Spanish-English bilingual communities and provide various avenues for further research, which motivate the present study.

Previous Studies

In comparison to other linguistic subfields, there are few studies on the phonetics of code-switching, most of which focus on the segmental properties of code-switches in laboratory speech. Though few, these articles have revealed various characteristics of code-switched speech and have informed researchers about the phonetics of bilingual speech during code-switching. The next section will discuss relevant previous studies on the segmental properties of Spanish-English code-switching, followed by suprasegmentals and code-switching.

Phonetics and Code-Switching

The works of Bullock and colleagues (2005, 2006), Piccinini and Arvaniti (2012, 2015), and Balukas and Koops (2014) provide important and relevant insights into the phonetics of code-switching within Spanish-speaking communities in the United States. Bullock and colleagues (2005) investigated the production of coda-position /l/ during code-switching for highly proficient Puerto Rican Spanish-English bilinguals by measuring the second formant (F2) of coda /l/ during a reading task that included Spanish and English code-switches. Their results revealed that these bilinguals maintained the difference between "clear" /l/ (typical of Spanish coda /l/ and indicated by a higher F2) and "dark" /l/ (typical of English coda /l/ and indicated by a lower F2) during code-switching.

A later study by Bullock and colleagues (2006) examined voice onset timing (VOT) in productions of /p, t, k/ during a reading task that included monolingual and code-switched contexts, which included both Spanish-dominant and English-dominant bilingual participants. Their results revealed that code-switching affected both the English-dominant and Spanish-dominant speakers' productions of English VOTs: the pre- and at-switch English VOTs were shorter than post-switch and monolingual context VOTs. The authors suggest that the asymmetrical effect on English could be due to the larger range of variation possible with long-lag VOT languages (such as English) that may facilitate compromise values more than the small range (usually 0–30 milliseconds [ms]) of short-lag VOT languages, like Spanish.

Piccinini and Arvaniti (2015) and Balukas and Koops (2014) also investigate VOT of monolingual and code-switching contexts in Spanish-English bilinguals, but use semi-spontaneous corpuses. Piccinini and Arvaniti (2012, 2015) examine the speech of early Mexican American Spanish-English bilinguals in conversational contexts with and without distraction (jigsaw puzzle). Their results revealed shorter VOTs for both English and Spanish in code-switching contexts when compared to monolingual mode. When distracted by the jigsaw tasks, VOTs in English were longer than code-switched contexts without distraction but still shorter than monolingual mode.

Balukas and Koops (2014) also measured the VOT of early New Mexican Spanish-English bilinguals from a semi-spontaneous corpus and found shorter English VOTs at and near code-switching points with no effect on Spanish VOTs when compared to monolingual modes. The authors also compared the monolingual English and Spanish of these speakers to monolingual English and Spanish populations and found that the New Mexican bilinguals' English VOTs were shorter than monolinguals and that their Spanish VOTs were on the higher range of those seen in monolingual speakers. Similar to the results and discussion in Bullock and colleagues (2006), Balukas and Koops (2014) also acknowledge the asymmetry in VOT effects between Spanish and English, suggesting that the shorter VOTs found in English could be due to the larger room for negotiation with long-lag VOT when compared to short-lag VOT (which was close to the 30 ms threshold in this population).

Suprasegmentals and Code-Switching

As mentioned in the previous section, studies on the suprasegmental properties of code-switching remain underrepresented within the subfield of phonetics and phonology. Three relevant studies on the suprasegmental properties of code-switching will be discussed in this section.

In Olson (2012), Spanish-English bilinguals of Mexican American descent read contextualized sentences in English, Spanish, and code-switched (embedded English noun) conditions. All target words were post-focal nouns in order to avoid unanticipated realizations of narrow focus. Measures of pitch (f0) maximum and duration within the stressed syllable revealed that code-switched words had a higher pitch and longer vowel duration than the monolingual English conditions. Olson (2012) posits a Hyperarticulation account for code-switching, in which the contrast in languages is inherently focused or highlighted prosodically by the speaker.

In more recent work by Olson (2015) that considers the same variables and task as Olson (2012), language mode (monolingual or bilingual) and language dominance (dominant or nondominant language) are also investigated. Olson's results reveal greater pitch range and vowel duration on code-switching in monolingual mode (i.e., insertional or embedded code-switches) when compared to bilingual (balanced) mode as well as effects on the dominant language (L1) of the participants when compared to their nondominant language (L2).

Piccinini and Garellek (2014) investigate the f0 in monolingual and code-switched utterances in one female Mexican American speaker. Stimuli consisted of monolingual sentences (Spanish and English) and code-switched contexts (both Spanish code-switches and English code-switches). Their results revealed that the f0 (in stressed syllables throughout the utterance) was the highest in English monolingual contexts, followed by code-switched contexts and Spanish monolingual contexts (lowest f0).

The studies discussed, although from a range of experimental paradigms and participants, reveal differences in code-switched and monolingual contexts for both segmental (VOT, coda /l/) and suprasegmental traits (f0, vowel duration). These differences may be affected by language dominance (as seen in Bullock et al. 2005; Olson 2012, 2015), task or cognitive load (e.g., Piccinini and Arvaniti 2015), as well as phonetic universals such as constraints on short-lag and long-lag VOT thresholds (Bullock et al. 2006; Balukas and Koops 2014).

The following section will give a brief overview on the prosodic differences between Spanish and English in order to establish the intonational categories and contrasts expected between the two languages before continuing to the current study's methodology.

Prosodic Properties of Spanish and English

The intonational phonology of Spanish and English differs in several respects. While they are both languages with head prominence, phrase-final nuclear stress, and contrastive lexical stress, they differ in their tonal inventories and distribution. Mainstream American English (MAE) has five contrastive pitch accents (as shown in table 3.1), whereas Miami Cuban (MC) Spanish has four. Additionally, the pitch accents in MAE are less positionally restricted than those in MC Spanish, as its pitch accents are typically able to occur phrase-medially (prenuclear position) and phrase-finally (nuclear position). On the other hand, MC Spanish has one default phrase-medial (prenuclear) pitch accent and three that occur in final (nuclear) position, depending on sentence type.

Table 3.1 shows the tonal inventories of both MAE, (Beckman, Hirschberg, and Shattuck-Hufnagel 2005), and MC Spanish (Aly 2014) according to their respective Autosegmental Metrical (AM; Pierrehumbert 1980; Beckman and Pierrehumbert 1986; Ladd 1996) models of intonational phonology. The pitch accents are annotated using Tone and Break Indices (ToBI) labels for each language, accompanied by a schematic phonetic description and distributional properties.[1]

In addition to tonal inventory and distribution, there are phonetic realizations of tonal events that differ between English and Spanish (and within dialects of these languages as well). As reported in Aly (2014), MC Spanish has a phonetic variant of L+H* in which the peak is realized in the posttonic syllable (delayed peak),

Table 3.1. Spanish and English tonal inventories and distribution

Pitch accent and phonetic description	Language and distribution[1]
H*: High f0 plateau in stressed syllable	**MAE**: Default pitch accent **MC Spanish**: N/A
L*: f0 trough in stressed syllable	**MAE**: Phrase medial and final position **MC Spanish**: Phrase final position only in questions
L*+H: f0 trough in stressed syllable followed by a sharp rise	**MAE**: Phrase medial position **MC Spanish**: Default pitch accent; phrase medial
L+H*: High f0 peak in stressed syllable preceded by an f0 trough	**MAE**: Phrase medial and final position **MC Spanish**: Default nuclear pitch accent; Use for phrase medial words with final stress
H+!H*: Downstepped (slightly lowered) f0 in stressed syllable from preceding high f0 target	**MAE**: Phrase medial and final position **MC Spanish**: N/A
H+L*: Low f0 trough in stressed syllable from preceding high f0 target	**MAE**: N/A **MC Spanish**: Phrase final position in declaratives

1. MAE information from Jun (2014), Dainora (2001), and Beckman, Hirschberg, and Shattuck-Hufnagel (2005); MC Spanish information from Aly (2014)

occurring more frequently in the prenuclear position of slower or read speech. MAE also contains delayed peak variants as reported in Shattuck-Hufnagel and colleagues (2004), which typically occur when the posttonic syllable is unaccented and preceded by another high tonal target. Pitch accents can also be realized with variable pitch range due to factors such as individual differences, contrastive focus, and also sentence type. For example, MAE has downstepped (lower f0) variants of high targets in sequences of high tones whereas MC Spanish shows upstepped (higher f0) variants of high tones in questions when compared to declaratives (Aly 2015).[2] Due to the continuum of phonetic and phonological realizations that exist when considering intonation, the present study will examine both categorical (pitch accent) and gradient (f0) measurements when investigating the intonation of Spanish-English code-switches, as described in the following sections.

The Present Study

The present study contributes to the work on the phonetics and phonology of code-switching by focusing on the semi-spontaneous speech of Spanish-English bilinguals from Miami, Florida. The Miami Cuban (MC) community of Spanish speakers is an understudied community in comparison to other larger communities of Spanish speakers in the United States, such as New York Puerto Ricans and Chicanos in Los Angeles. The MC community in Miami is home to the largest community of persons of Cuban descent outside of Cuba with an established, multigeneration community of MC Spanish speakers of various ethnicities, socioeconomic statuses, and linguistic affiliations (Ennis, Rios-Vargas, and Albert 2011; Carter and Lynch 2015). In addition to contributing to the existing code-switching literature on Spanish-English code-switching, the present study will consider suprasegmental properties (pitch accent type, peak alignment, and pitch range), which have not been investigated in semi-spontaneous code-switching prior to this study. The following research questions motivate the present study:

- Do MC Spanish speakers use more Spanish-like or English-like pitch accents when code-switching from Spanish to English?
- Do Spanish-English bilinguals have different f0 range and peak alignment in code-switched and monolingual contexts?
- Are there differences between early and late Spanish-English bilinguals with respect to pitch accents and f0 realization when code-switching?

Methodology and Data Analysis

This section will discuss the methods and analysis procedure for the current study, beginning with the demographic information of the speakers consulted and continuing with the experimental tasks administered. The section will conclude with details on the data analysis procedures used, including definitions and measurement criteria of variables and the inferential statistics selected for the present study's data set. After contextualizing the data collection and analysis for the present study, the results will be presented in the following section.

Speakers

The current study consults the speech of nine Cuban Spanish speakers living South Florida (Miami-Dade or Lee County). These speakers will be divided into two subgroups: those born in Cuba (Cuba-born speakers, $n = 5$) and those who were born in Miami (Miami-born speakers, $n = 4$). Cuba-born (henceforth CB) speakers moved to the United States and acquired English as adults in Miami and Miami-born (henceforth MB) speakers acquired both Spanish and English as children in Florida. Due to their respective ages of acquisition of English and Spanish, the MB group will be considered early Spanish-English bilinguals (due to exposure to both languages as children) and the CB group will be considered late Spanish-English bilinguals, having learned English in adulthood after arriving in the United States. The CB speakers were between thirty-nine and sixty-eight years old at the time of data collection (average of fifty-two years) and were between nineteen and thirty-two years old (average of twenty-five years) when they arrived in the United States and started learning English. The MB speakers were between twenty-four and thirty-six years old (average of thirty years). Apart from acquiring Spanish at home, all MB speakers reported at least one year of formal instruction in Spanish.

The reported language use by all speakers (Spanish, English, or both languages) at home, work, and with friends revealed several differences between groups. At home, all CB speakers and half of the MB speakers (1F[3], 1M) reported using Spanish, whereas the remaining MB speakers (2F, 3F) reported using English at home. At work, four CB speakers (2M, 3M, 4M, 5F) and two MB speakers (1M, 2F) reported using English and the remaining CB speaker (5F) and two MB speakers (1F, 3F) reported using both languages. Finally, with friends, all MB speakers reported using English, four CB speakers (4F, 5F, 3M, 4M) reported speaking Spanish, and the remaining CB speaker (2M) reported using both languages. Table 3.2 displays the demographic information reported by all speakers.

Experimental Tasks and Data Collection

The data from the current study comes from two experimental tasks originally designed to elicit various sentence types for prosodic analysis. The first was a discourse completion task (DCT) that was modified from Roseano and Prieto (2010) to include lexical items, expressions, and locations appropriate to Cuban Spanish and south Florida. These modifications were made by the author, a near-native speaker of Miami Cuban Spanish, and were further verified by a native Cuban Spanish speaker. The DCT consists of seventy contexts that prompt the speaker to answer freely while eliciting a specific discourse category, such as an exclamative statement, echo question, vocative, or imperative. The instructions and prompts of the DCT were provided orally to speakers by the author in Spanish. The author did not code-switch to English in the instructions or prompts during the experiment, with the exception of city names or other proper nouns mentioned during the experiment. All participants produced (unelicited) code-switches in the DCT ($n = 13$), two examples of which are shown below in example 3.1.

Example 3.1. Alternational code-switch (a) and insertional code-switch (b) from DCT

a. **Prompt:** *Estás en casa con tu compañera de casa, María, que está mirando la televisión. Dile que vas a salir un momento de compras.* (You are at home with your roommate, Maria, who is watching TV. Tell her you're about to leave to go shopping.)

   Response (3CAF): *Ok, eh, Maria voy a salir a...eh hacer algunas compras, necesitas algo?* I'll be right back. (Ok, uh, Maria, I'm going to leave...uh, to do some shopping. Do you need anything? I'll be right back.)

b. **Prompt:** *No te hacen caso y esta vez lo pides más enojada.* (They [your kids] don't listen to you [in response to a previous prompt asking them to be quiet] and you ask them again, more upset.)

   Response (7CAF): *Les he preguntado de una manera,* um, nice. *Por favor, cállense ahora.* (I asked you in a, um, nice way. Please, shut up now.)

The second task was a structured interview consisting of ten questions designed to elicit various sentence types as well as longer, semi-spontaneous utterances. Speakers were asked about topics such as their daily routines, favorite places in town, and places they would like to visit. The prompts were given by the author in Spanish and all nine speakers answered in Spanish (unelicited) code-switches to English ($n = 84$). Two examples of code-switching from the interview are shown below in example 3.2.

Table 3.2. Speaker demographics

Group	Speaker	Age	Year of arrival to US (Parents, if born in US)	Spanish in school?	Occupation	Home	Work	Friends
Miami-Born	1CAM	24	1980	1 year	Student	Spanish	English	English
	3CAF	29	1981	1 year	Student	Spanish	Both	English
	7CAF	31	1969/ 1970	2 years	Planning technician	English	English	English
	4CAF	36	1967	1 year	Office manager	English	Both	English
Cuba-Born	2CM	39	1992	N/A	Professor	Spanish	English	Both
	5CF	41	1999	N/A	Teacher	Spanish	English	Spanish
	8CM	50	1988	N/A	Mailing manager	Spanish	English	Spanish
	9CM	63	1988	N/A	Machine operator	Spanish	English	Spanish
	5F	68	1970	N/A	Retired	Spanish	Both	Spanish

Example 3.2. Alternational code-switch (a) and insertional code-switch (b) from DCT

a. **Interviewer:** *Sí, fui el otro día a la protesta con los peatones.* (Yes, I went the other day to the protest with the pedestrians).

Consultant (7CAF): Oh, that's right! Oh, yes, yes! *Yo iba a ir, pero, uh, tu sabes qué me pasó?!* (Oh, that's right! Oh, yes, yes! I was going to go, but you know what happened to me?!)

b. **Interviewer:** *¿Dónde vivía?* (Where did you live?)

Consultant: *En el* southwest *de Miami.* (In southwest Miami.)

All data was collected in Miami and Fort Myers, Florida. Speakers were recorded using an Olympus LS-11 portable voice recorder in .wav format at a 44.1 kilohertz (kHz) sampling rate and a 16-bit rate. Recordings were done in small, quiet locations for privacy and acoustic quality, such as a small, carpeted room in a home or a study room in a public library. After obtaining informed consent, the speakers filled out a demographic questionnaire and were encouraged to ask any questions before beginning. The average time elapsed per speaker for the consent process, questionnaire, and experimental tasks was approximately thirty minutes.

Data Analysis and Variables

The data collected were analyzed acoustically using Praat, version 5.4.18 (Boersma and Weenink 2015). Portions of the data that included too much background noise, interference by the interviewer, nonlinguistic noise by the participant (such as laughter or coughing), narrow focus (as elicited by the DCT), or creaky voice that disrupted the pitch track were excluded (n = 10 exclusions). Due to the imbalance of lexical categories in the sample, only nouns will be included in the present study. Table 3.3 shows the number of analyzable code-switches from each task as well as the number of code-switches by CB and MB speakers. The present study considers a word a code-switch if it is not in a monolingual Spanish dictionary, including cities, locales, and proper names in south Florida, but excluding cognates.[4] The DCT had the fewest code-switches in both groups, contributing only 13 percent of all code-switches, whereas the interview task contained 87 percent of all code-switches. MB speakers produced more code-switches (61 percent of total) than CB speakers (49 percent of total).

Categorical Measures: Pitch Accent

Utterances containing code-switches were labeled with pitch accents and boundary tones using ToBI conventions for MAE (Beckman, Hirschberg, and Shattuck-Hufnagel

Table 3.3. Pitch accents by group and task

Group	DCT	Interview	Total
Cuban-born (CB)	4	34	38
Miami-born (MB)	9	50	59
Total	13	84	97

2005) and MC Spanish (Aly 2014). The Spanish portion of the utterances were labeled with the MC Spanish ToBI and the English code-switches were labeled with both languages' tonal inventories in consideration, as the pitch accents of the code-switches could resemble either Spanish or English. These labels, along with their prosodic distribution, will help determine if the code-switches were produced with more Spanish-like intonation or English-like intonation. A total of eighty-seven code-switches from declarative utterances contained pitch accents and were labeled in Praat using the following tiers for coding different types of information (seen in figure 3.1 with (1) being the top tier and (6) being the bottom): (1) orthography, (2) stressed syllable, (3) pitch accents, (4) juncture (0–4, with 4 being the largest), (5) code-switches, and (6) peak alignment (discussed in the following section).

Continuous Measures: Peak Alignment and Pitch Range

For the continuous measures, only nuclear pitch accents (utterance final or after a pause or juncture break of four) with a high tonal target (H* or L+H*) will be included, resulting in fifty-eight tokens from the monolingual context and fifty-six from the code-switched contexts. Monolingual context tokens are from Spanish-only utterances from the reading and DCT tasks, and code-switched tokens are from the DCT and interview tasks. Both broad focus declaratives ($n = 71$) and yes-no questions ($n = 31$) were included and considered along with context (monolingual or code-switched), group (MB and CB), and self-identified gender (for pitch range only) as independent variables in the statistical analysis (explained in more detail in the following section).

Peak alignment was measured in milliseconds from the f0 max (pitch peak) in the stressed syllable to the offset of the associated syllable. To assess whether the peak occurs earlier or later in the syllable, the peak-to-syllable-offset duration was subtracted from the total syllable duration (hence, a larger number is a later peak and a smaller number is an earlier peak). Syllable and peak boundaries were placed manually in Praat and the duration was measured by a script. The peak boundary (from peak to syllable offset) was also used to measure the pitch max of the interval in order to determine pitch range. The pitch max of this interval was measured by the same script used for peak alignment, which measured f0 and duration of two interval tiers. Figure 3.1 shows an example of the interval tiers used to measure both pitch range and peak alignment for a code-switched utterance.[5] The bottom tier marks the distance from the f0 max (peak) to the end of the associated syllable, from which the peak duration (subtracted from the duration of the syllable in the second tier) and pitch max were taken.

Results

Pitch Accents Used during Code-Switches

The code-switches analyzed were primarily in phrase-final position ($n = 80$), with only seven tokens occurring in phrase-medial position. The following graph in figure 3.2 shows the frequency of pitch accent type in both groups of speakers.

MB speakers used five different pitch accents during code-switches whereas CB speakers used three different pitch accents on code-switched words. CB speakers

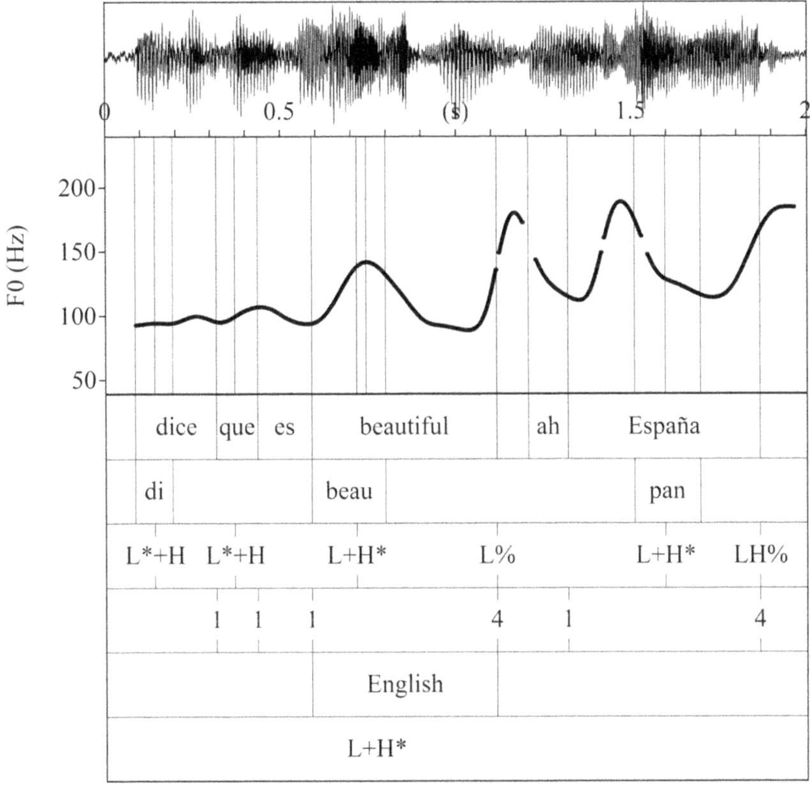

Figure 3.1. Pitch track of *Dice que es* beautiful, *ah, España* (They say it's beautiful, ah, Spain) by 9CM

preferred the L+H* pitch accent during code-switches, which exists in the tonal inventories of both MC Spanish and MAE but functions as the default nuclear pitch accent in MC Spanish. MB speakers preferred the H* pitch accent (the default pitch accent of MAE), followed by L+H* and H+!H*, the latter of which only exists in English. These group preferences suggest that the CB speakers may be code-switching with more Spanish-like intonation conventions, preferring the default nuclear pitch accent of MC Spanish, followed marginally by L* (possible in both MC Spanish and MAE) and H* (MAE only). On the other hand, MB speakers use both English-like and Spanish-like intonation when code-switching, preferring H* but also frequently using L+H*.

Peak Alignment

Peak alignment duration in milliseconds was log-transformed to reduce the amount of skew in the data for a more normal distribution. A linear mixed effects model (LMM) was administered in R (R Core Development Team 2014) using the lme4 package (Bates et al. 2015) to test for statistical significance. This model contained

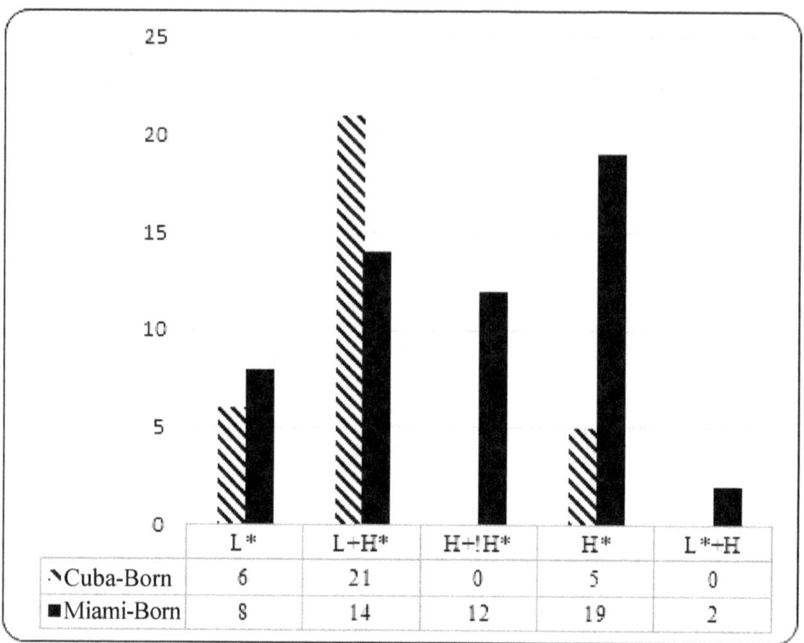

	L*	L+H*	H+!H*	H*	L*+H
Cuba-Born	6	21	0	5	0
Miami-Born	8	14	12	19	2

Figure 3.2. Pitch accents used during code-switches

log-transformed peak alignment as the dependent variable; group (MB or CB), context (monolingual or code-switched), and type (declarative or question) as fixed effects; speaker and word were random effects. Significance of fixed effects was determined using model comparison ($\alpha = 0.05$) and interactions between fixed effects were assessed with a Tukey post hoc test ($\alpha = 0.05$).

The LMM for peak alignment revealed a significant main effect for context ($\beta = 0.322$, $SE = 0.136$, $\chi^2(1) = 5.44$, $p = 0.01973$), with earlier monolingual peaks than code-switched peaks. There was also a significant interaction between group and context ($\beta = 0.642$, $SE = 0.266$, $\chi^2(1) = 5.65$, $p = 0.0175$), in which the post hoc comparisons revealed that CB speakers made a significant difference in peak alignment between monolingual and code-switched conditions ($p = 0.0035$). The plots in figure 3.3 show peak alignment by context (a) and peak alignment by group and context (b).

Pitch Range

Similar to the peak alignment variable, pitch range in hertz (Hz) was log-transformed for a more normal distribution. A LMM was administered for the dependent variable of log-transformed pitch range with group (MB or CB), context (monolingual or code-switched), type (declarative or question), and gender (male or female) as fixed effects, and speaker and word as random effects. The same significance threshold for peak alignment ($\alpha = 0.05$) is maintained for pitch range when comparing models.

The model comparison revealed significant main effects for gender ($\beta = 0.387$, $SE = 0.109$, $\chi^2(1) = 7.98$, $p = 0.0047$), in which females had a higher pitch range than males, and for type ($\beta = 0.221$, $SE = 0.048$, $\chi^2(1) = 18.81$, $p < 0.001$), in which questions had a higher pitch range than declaratives. There were no significant effects for group or context, nor any significant interactions. The plots in figure 3.4 show the difference in gender (a) and type (b).

Discussion

The three variables measured in the current study revealed several trends and patterns about the phonetics of Spanish to English code-switches in the MC Spanish community. The analysis of pitch accents revealed that while CB speakers tended to favor Spanish-like pitch accents (L+H* and L* pitch accents in nuclear position), MB speakers used both Spanish-like and English-like pitch accents, with a preference for H* (more English-like pitch accents). These results may suggest that the MB speakers, who are early bilinguals, may be able to access and utilize the intonations of both languages while code-switching, whereas the CB speakers, who are adult learners of English, may not be able to switch to English intonation during insertional code-switches as easily as the MB speakers do. However, the majority of the code-switches analyzed occurred in phrase-final position, limiting the conclusions that can be made about pitch accent preference until more data from phrase-medial position can be obtained and analyzed.

Another possibility for the frequent usage of L+H* pitch accents by both groups of speakers may be related to the findings of Olson (2012), in which code-switched items were posited to have narrow focus due to their contrast with the matrix language (as indicated by higher f0 and longer stressed vowel duration). If insertional code-switches are hyperarticulated for contrast, then the L+H* pitch accents used by both the CB and MB speakers may have also been fulfilling this purpose, as L+H* is the pitch accent used most commonly for narrow focus in both MC Spanish and MAE. However, there was no effect of context (monolingual or code-switched) in the pitch range analysis completed, which does not support the hypothesis that the MC Spanish speakers in the current data set hyperarticulated code-switched words with pitch range. The pitch range analysis instead showed significant effects for gender and (sentence) type, which is expected due to the physiological differences between male and female ranges of fundamental frequency and previous work on MC Spanish (Aly 2015) in which questions had a significantly higher pitch range than declaratives.

Although the MB speakers used a larger inventory of pitch accents when code-switching compared to CB speakers, the results of the peak alignment measures showed that only the CB speakers differentiated between monolingual and code-switched contexts with peak alignment. In monolingual context, nuclear pitch accents were significantly earlier than in code-switched contexts. This shows that CB speakers may be prosodically differentiating between monolingual and code-switched contexts phonetically with peak alignment, whereas the MB speakers may prosodically differentiate nuclear code-switched and monolingual contexts

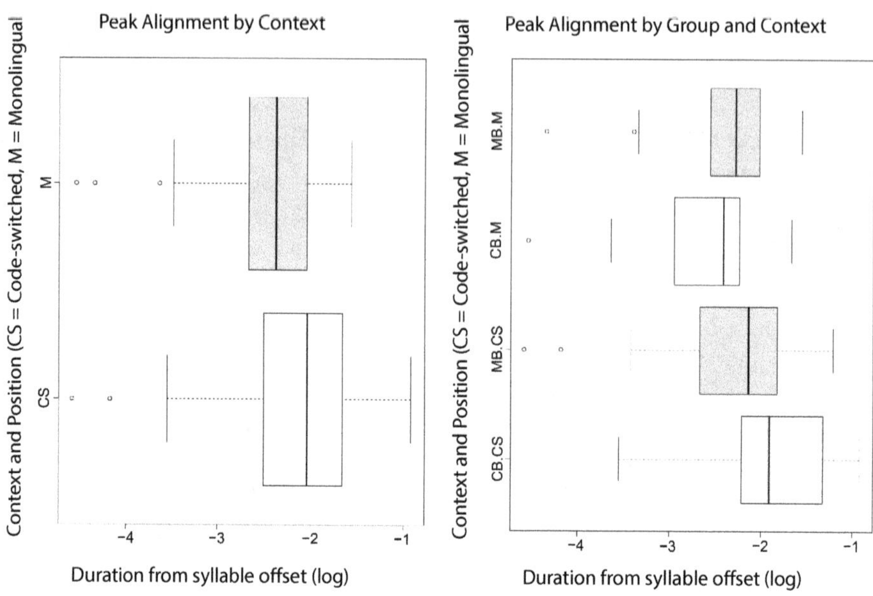

Figures 3.3a and 3.3b. Peak alignment by context and by group and context

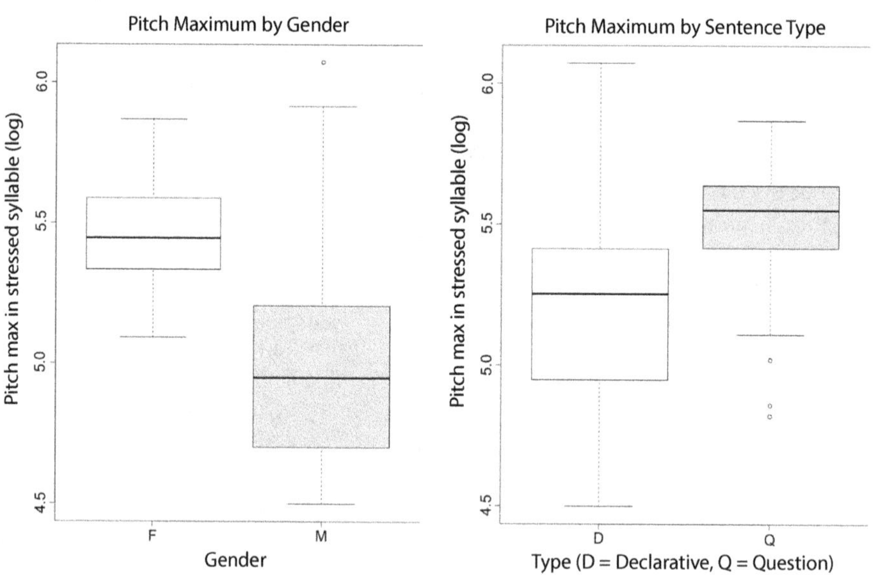

Figures 3.4a and 3.4b. Pitch maximum by gender and by sentence type

phonologically with pitch accent type. This preliminary interpretation would need to be tested on a larger corpus with more prosodic contexts, speech rate measures, and data from monolingual English contexts as well.

One limitation of the present data set is the difficulty associated with extracting an appropriate sample size of comparable tokens from a semi-spontaneous speech corpus. Although the code-switches in the present data set were not elicited by the researcher and give insights into the types of code-switches that happen in naturalistic speech, this also made it difficult to analyze and compare the properties of code-switches that varied both within and between speakers and groups. However, the tendencies and patterns found in the present dataset may serve as a preliminary starting point for further research on code-switching both within and outside of the laboratory setting, in which these variables (among others, such as discourse, social, and pragmatic factors) may be elicited more precisely and analyzed in more detail. Additionally, if larger naturalistic and controlled corpuses for various code-switching communities were formed, comparative and typological analyses may be performed that could establish universals of code-switching in bilingual speakers of different linguistic, ethnic, and fluency backgrounds.

Conclusion

The present study examined the semi-spontaneous code-switches in two groups of MC Spanish speakers: late Spanish-English bilinguals born in Cuba and early Spanish-English bilinguals born in Miami. An analysis of suprasegmental features of Spanish-to-English code-switches revealed two main findings with respect to code-switching: (1) CB speakers have a significant difference in peak alignment between code-switched and monolingual nuclear pitch accents and (2) MB speakers tend to favor English-like pitch accents (such as H*) when code-switching, compared with the CB group's preference for the default nuclear pitch accent of MC Spanish (L+H*). The descriptive and preliminary nature of this study motivates additional work on the code-switching patterns in this community as well as others in the attempt to further investigate the phonetics and phonology of code-switching.

Notes

1. The phonetic descriptions in table 3.1 are schematic and represent their typical realizations. Actual phonetic realizations of these pitch accents may differ in contexts of contrastive stress, individual pitch range, undershot tones, or other linguistic factors.
2. The phonological status of downstep in MAE is debated in studies such as Dainora (2001) and Yoon and Cole (2006).
3. To preserve their anonymity, the participants of the present study are referred to with a number (i.e. "1" or "2") and their self-identified gender ("F" or "M" for female and male, respectively). Therefore, "2M" represents the second individual who was recorded who identifies as male.
4. The author acknowledges that the dictionary criteria for code-switches does not take borrowings or recent incorporations into consideration. Due to the limited data set and preliminary nature of the study, a more detailed definition of code-switching is in progress for future work.
5. It should be noted that while this pitch track is included for demonstrating measurements, this utterance was eliminated from analysis due to the small sample of nonnoun tokens.

References

Aly, A. 2014. "Intonational Phonology of Miami Cuban Spanish: An AM Model." MA thesis, University of California, Los Angeles.

———. 2015. "The Multiple Prosodic Cues Differentiating Questions and Statements in Miami Cuban Spanish." *In Proceedings of the 18th International Congress of Phonetic Sciences*. Glasgow: University of Glasgow Press.

Balukas, C., and C. Koops. 2014. "Spanish-English Bilingual Voice Onset Time in Spontaneous Code-Switching." *International Journal of Bilingualism* 19 (4): 1–21.

Bates, D., M. Maechler, B. Bolker, S. Walker. 2015. "Fitting Linear Mixed-Effects Models Using lme4." *Journal of Statistical Software* 67 (1): 1–48. doi:10.18637/jss.v067.i01.

Beckman, M. E., and J. Pierrehumbert. 1986. "Intonational Structure in Japanese and English." *Phonology* 3 (1): 255–309.

Beckman, M., J. Hirschberg, and S. Shattuck-Hufnagel. 2005. "The Original ToBI System and the Evolution of the ToBI Framework." In *Prosodic Typology: The Phonology of Intonation and Phrasing*, edited by S.-A. Jun, 9–54. Oxford: Oxford University Press.

Bhatt, R., and A. Bolonyai. 2011. "Code-Switching and the Optimal Grammar of Bilingual Language Use." *Bilingualism: Language and Cognition* 14:522–46.

Boersma, P., and D. Weenink. 2015. "Praat: Doing Phonetics by Computer." Version 5.4.18. http://www.fon.hum.uva.nl/praat/.

Bullock, B. and A. J. Toribio. 2009. "Trying to Hit a Moving Target: On the Sociophonetics of Code-Switching." In *Multidisciplinary Approaches to Code Switching*, edited by L. Isurin, D. Winford, and K. De Bot, 189–206. Amsterdam: John Benjamins Publishing.

Bullock, B., A. J. Toribio, K. Davis, and C. Botero. 2005. "Phonetic Convergence in Puerto Rican Spanish." In *WCCFL 23: Proceedings of the 23rd West Coast Conference on Formal Linguistics*, edited by V. Chand, A. Kelleher, A. J. Rodriguez, and B. Schmeiser, 113–25. Somerville, MA: Cascadilla Proceedings Project.

Bullock, B., A. J. Toribio, V. González, and A. Dalola. 2006. "Language Dominance and Performance Outcomes in Bilingual Pronunciation." In *Proceedings of the 8th Generative Approaches to Second Language Acquisition Conference: The Banff Conference*, edited by M. Grantham O'Brien, C. Shea, and J. Archibald, 9–16. Somerville, MA: Cascadilla Proceedings Project.

Carter, P., and A. Lynch. 2015 "Multilingual Miami: Current Trends in Sociolinguistic Research." *Language & Linguistics Compass* 9:369–85.

Chan, B. H.-S. 2009. "Code-Switching between Typologically Distinct Languages." In *The Cambridge Handbook of Linguistic Code-Switching*, edited by B. Bullock and A. J. Toribio, 182–98. Cambridge Handbooks in Language and Linguistics. Cambridge: Cambridge University Press.

Dainora, A. 2001. "An Empirically Based Probalistic Model of Intonation in American English." PhD dissertation, University of Chicago.

Di Sciullo, A., P. Muysken, and R. Singh. 1986. "Government and Code-Mixing." *Journal of Linguistics* 22 (01): 1–24.

Ennis, S. R., M. Rios-Vargas, and N. G. Albert. 2011. "The Hispanic Population: 2010." 2010 Census Briefs. Washington, DC: Government Printing Office. https://www.census.gov/prod/cen2010/briefs/c2010br-04.pdf.

Gullifer, J., J. Kroll, and P. Dussias. 2013. "When Language Switching Has No Apparent Cost: Lexical Access in Sentence Context." *Frontiers in Psychology* 4:1–13.

Jun, S.-A. 2014. "Prosodic Typology: By Prominence, Word Prosody, and Macro-rhythm." In *Prosodic Typology II: The Phonology of Intonation and Phrasing*, edited by S.-A. Jun, 520–39. Oxford: Oxford University Press.

Ladd, R. 1996. *Intonational Phonology*. Cambridge: Cambridge University Press.

Myers-Scotton, C. 1997. *Duelling Languages: Grammatical Structure in Codeswitching*. Oxford: Clarendon Press.

Olson, D. 2012. "The Phonetics of Insertional Code-Switching: Suprasegmental Analysis and a Case for Hyperarticulation." *Linguistic Approaches to Bilingualism* 2 (4): 439–57.

———. 2015. "The Impact of Code-Switching, Language Context, and Language Dominance on Suprasegmental Phonetics: Evidence for the Role of Predictability." *International Journal of Bilingualism* 20 (4): 1–20.

Pedraza, P. 1978. "Ethnographic Observations of Language Use in El Barrio." Unpublished manuscript.

Pierrehumbert, J. 1980. *The Phonology and Phonetics of English Intonation*. Cambridge: Massachusetts Institute of Technology Press.

Piccinini, P., and A. Arvaniti. 2015. "Voice Onset Time in Spanish-English Spontaneous Code-Switching." *Journal of Phonetics* 52:121–37.

Piccinini, P., and M. Garellek. 2014. "Prosodic Cues to Monolingual versus Code-switching Sentences in English and Spanish." *Proceedings of the 7th Speech Prosody Conference*. Dublin: Trinity College.

Poplack, S. 1980. "Sometimes I'll Start a Sentence in English y Termino en Espanol: Toward a Typology of Codeswitching." *Linguistics* 18:581–618.

Poplack, S., D. Sankoff, and C. Miller. 1988. "The Social Correlates and Linguistic Processes of Lexical Borrowing and Assimilation." *Linguistics* 26 (1): 47–104.

Prieto, P., and P. Roseano, eds. 2010. "Transcription of Intonation of the Spanish Language." München, Deu.: Lincom Europa.

R Core Team. 2014. "R: A Language and Environment for Statistical Computing." Vienna, Aut.: R Foundation for Statistical Computing.

Shattuck-Hufnagel, S., L. Dilley, N. Veilleux, A. Brugos, and R. Speer. 2004. "F0 Peaks and Valleys Aligned with Non-prominent Syllables Can Influence Perceived Prominence in Adjacent Syllables." In *Proceedings of Speech Prosody 2004, Nara, Japan*, edited by B. Bel and I. Marlien. N.p.: SProSIG.

Yim, O., and E. Bialystock. 2012. "Degree of Conversational Code-Switching Enhances Verbal Task Switching in Cantonese-English Bilinguals." *Bilingualism: Language and Cognition* 15:873–83.

Yoon, T., and J. Cole. 2006. "Downstep in American English Is Categorical and Predictable." Presented at the 10th Conference on Laboratory Phonology, Paris, July 1.

Zentella, A. 1981. "Tá Bien, You Could Answer Me in Cualuier Idioma: Puerto Rican Code Switching in Bilingual Classrooms." In *Latino Language and Communicative Behavior*, edited by R. Durán, 109–32. Norwood, NJ: Ablex.

———. 1997. *Growing Up Bilingual: Puerto Rican Children in New York*. Malden, MA: Blackwell Publishers.

PART II

MORPHOSYNTACTIC VARIATION

4

Continuity and Change in Spanish among Cubans in New York: A Study of Subject Placement with Finite Verbs

DANIEL ERKER
Boston University

EDUARDO HO-FERNÁNDEZ
Graduate Center CUNY

RICARDO OTHEGUY
Graduate Center CUNY

NAOMI LAPIDUS SHIN
University of New Mexico

IN THE STUDY OF Spanish as it is spoken in the United States, much interest has focused on the question of cross-generational continuity and change. For the layperson and the scholar alike, it is natural to wonder whether and to what extent the language of US-born Latinos resembles that of their Latin America–born parents and grandparents. For scholars, the question is the more precise one of how exactly the Spanish of the US-born generation has remained the same as that of the Latin America–born one and in what ways it has started to differ. The authors of the present chapter have a long-standing interest in this question, studying Spanish in the US using data taken from interviews conducted in New York City, and basing the work on variable phonological, lexical, and morphosyntactic features that have been analyzed within the paradigm of variationist sociolinguistics (Erker 2012; Erker and Guy 2012; Lapidus and Otheguy 2005; Otheguy, Zentella, and Livert 2007; Otheguy and Zentella 2012; Shin 2010, 2014; Shin and Otheguy 2013). These studies join a well-established tradition of study of Spanish in the US that was pioneered by the work of renowned scholars like Richard Durán (1981), Lucía Elías-Olivares (1983), Shana Poplack (1980), and Carmen Silva-Corvalán (1994). The present chapter offers a variationist study of the position of Spanish grammatical subjects occurring with finite verbs in the speech of Cubans in New York, pinpointing precise areas of cross-generational continuity and change.

Throughout the Hispanophone world, when subjects of finite verbs are used they tend to appear before verbs (e.g., *Carlos llegó*, 'Carlos arrived'), but they are also found after verbs (*Llegó Carlos*, also 'Carlos arrived'). We are concerned with the factors that guide speakers in placing subjects in one or the other position, pre- or postverbally. We study only finite verb tokens and, naturally, only those finite verb tokens that occur with an expressed subject. That is, gerundive and infinitival verb tokens are not studied, and neither are the large numbers of finite verb tokens that appear without a subject. Examples of the types of verb tokens that are included in, and excluded from, the present analysis are in the transcribed spoken passages in examples 4.1 and 4.2. These passages and all the data for the present study are taken from the Otheguy-Zentella corpus (for details, see Otheguy and Zentella 2012). The number in brackets at the end of the passages refers to the number of the participant's interview.

Example 4.1.

> ... *entonces,* (1) *él estaba en el servicio militar y* (2) *Aba lo iba a ver siempre a Isla de Pinos, pero un buen día* (3) *Aba no fue más a verlo y* (4) *su papá le escribió y le* (5) *mandó a decir que* (6) *Aba tenía otro novio ... Entonces un día me* (7) *invitó él a Copelia, mi prima, mis dos primos, él y yo, y en Copelia* (8) *él me dijo que* (9) *estaba enamorado de mí,* (10) *yo le dije que* (11) *yo era una niña ...* (12) *Pasó el tiempo ...* [237U]
>
> '... so, he was in the military service and Aba always went to see him in Isla de Pinos, but one day Aba didn't go to see him anymore and his father wrote to him and sent word to him that Aba had another boyfriend ... So one day he invited me to Copelia, my female cousin, my two male cousins, he and I, and in Copelia he told me that he was in love with me, I told him that I was a little girl ... Time passed ...'

Verb token (4.1.1) is included in the study because it has a preverbal subject *él*. Verb tokens (4.1.2) and (4.1.3) are also included (preverbal subject *Aba*). Verbs (4.1.4) and (4.1.6) are included because they have preverbal subjects *su papá* and *Aba*, respectively. However, verb (4.1.5) is excluded because even though it is finite it occurs without a subject. Verb (4.1.7) is included (postverbal subject *él*) and so is (4.1.8) (preverbal subject *él*). However (4.1.9) is excluded because it has no expressed subject. Verbs (4.1.10) and (4.1.11) are included (preverbal subject *yo*). Verb (4.1.12) is also included because it has a postverbal subject (*el tiempo*).

Example 4.2.

> *No, no* (1) *teníamos nadie, un primo de mi papá nos* (2) *fue a ver ...* (3) *fuimos con él,* (4) *él nos llevó a conocer, a alguien de la familia de su esposa, ...* (5) *estuvimos como en un* Bar-B-Q, *una cosa así,* (6) *compartiendo una tarde ...* [376U].

> 'We didn't have anyone, a cousin of my father's came to see us ... we went with him, he took us to meet someone from his wife's family ... we were in like a Bar-B-Q, something like that, spending an afternoon together...'

Verb (4.2.1) and (4.2.3) are excluded (no expressed subject). Verbs (4.2.2) and (4.2.4) are included (preverbal subjects *un primo de mi papá* and *él*, respectively). Verb (4.2.5) is excluded (no expressed subject); verb (4.2.6) is also excluded (it is nonfinite).

The consultants whose speech we analyze are Cubans living in New York City. We study two different groups of Cubans: newcomers and New York–raised (henceforth NYR). At the time of the interview, the newcomers were seventeen years of age or older and had spent fewer than five years in New York. The NYR were born in New York or came to the city before age eight. Following convention, we often refer to our newcomers as 'first generation' and to our NYRs as 'second generation,' though it should be noted that in general usage, the term 'first generation' is often made extensive to long-time residents, whereas in the present study the first generations are all newcomers.[1] Our data consists of the transcribed interviews of the seven Cuban newcomers and the seven Cuban NYRs in the corpus (the corpus also contains transcribed interviews with Colombian, Dominican, Ecuadorian, Mexican, and Puerto Rican consultants, but they are not part of this study.) Following the approach illustrated in examples 4.1 and 4.2 above, we have drawn the first 100 eligible finite verb tokens from each of the fourteen participants' interviews. Our study is thus based on a total of 1,400 finite verb tokens, 700 from Cuban newcomers and 700 from Cuban NYRs.

The first research question posed in this study is what motivates Cuban newcomers to place subjects before or after verbs. We then ask whether these motivations persist among Cuban NYRs, or whether instead the NYRs have experienced a change in this regard. The NYRs tend to differ from the newcomers in regards to both amount of Spanish and English used and perceived proficiency in the languages, as reflected in answers to a questionnaire (for details, see Otheguy and Zentella 2012). For example, five newcomers (71 percent of them) said that their level of Spanish use was 'high' and only two (29 percent) said it was less than high. In contrast, none of the NYRs reported a high level of Spanish use; all seven of them said it was less than high. Similarly, seven newcomers said their proficiency in Spanish was 'good' or 'excellent' and none said it was just 'passable.' In contrast, none of the NYRs rated their Spanish as excellent; four said it was good and three that it was passable. Self-reports regarding English present a similar picture. None of the newcomers rated their English as excellent, whereas all but one of the NYRs did.

In addition to these different profiles of use and proficiency among the participants in our study, we note a key difference between their languages, namely that postverbal subjects in English, especially in speech, tend to be much less common than in Spanish. A natural question that arises, then, is whether these differences of frequency of use and proficiency between the generations and between the patterns of subject placement in the two languages are associated with some degree of intergenerational change in the variable placement of subjects of Spanish finite verbs.

From the extensive literature on this topic,[2] and from our own initial inspection of the data, we chose ten predictors that may be influencing the choice of subject position among the participants in our sample. As is conventional, we refer to these potential predictors of subject position as *variables*, and sometimes, as is common in the variationist literature, as *factor groups* (e.g., Tagliamonte 2012). In order to assess the predictive power of our ten chosen variables, we ran a series exploratory multivariate regressions. Of the initial set of ten, we found that five variables significantly contributed to the regression models. These five variables are listed below. For each variable, we list the values into which they are divided. We refer to these values as *factors* (and also, as they are often called in the literature, as *constraints*). Details on the factors for the first two variables follow presently. The factors that subdivide the last three variables are self-explanatory.

- *Subject type*
  Personal pronoun
  Lexical noun phrase
  Demonstrative pronoun
  Quantifier
  Clausal
- *Verb type*
  Copulative verb
  Experiencer-object or presentative verbs
  Occurrence (activity, stative, etc.)
- *Subject referent*
  Human
  Not human
- *Sentence type*
  Interrogative
  Declarative
- *Clause type*
  Main
  Subordinate

For the variable *Subject type*, the factor 'Personal pronoun' includes the forms *yo*, *tú*, *usted*, *él/ella*, *nosotros*, *ustedes*, *ellos/ellas*; the factor 'Lexical noun phrase' includes all proper and common nouns (with modifiers if any), such as *Carlos*, *los maestros*, etc.; the factor 'Demonstrative pronoun' covers the forms *este/a*, *ese/a/o*, *aquel/la*; the factor 'Quantifier' covers such forms as *alguien*, *alguno/a*, *ninguno/a*, *mucho/a/s*; and finally, the factor 'Clausal' covers items such as *que ella llegue mañana (me agrada)*. For the variable *Verb type*, the factor 'Copulative verb' consists of *ser* and *estar*; the factor 'Experiencer-object or presentative, (henceforth 'Experiencer-presentative') includes experiencer-object verbs such as *encantar* and *gustar*, as well as presentative verbs such as *ocurrir* and *suceder*. The factor 'Occurrence' includes all other verbs, including activity and stative verbs.

Deciding what variables to use and how to operationalize their factors are only two of the many decisions that need to be made in a variationist study. Additionally, because variationist analyses are based on detailed coding of naturalistic data, they should adhere to what has been called the *principle of accountability*, under which the analyst takes responsibility for every token of the type under study that is found in the chosen corpus (Labov 1966, 49; 1969, 737–38; Tagliamonte 2012, 9). The grounds on which we made the case-by-case decisions that led to the selection of the 1,400 verb tokens of our study, which were just sketched out in connection with examples 4.1 and 4.2 above, are discussed in greater detail in appendix I. The lists of individual verbs that we coded under the different factors of the different variables of the study are given in appendix II. Both appendices are available on the publisher's website (press.georgetown.edu). The details regarding the grounds on which we made our decisions on the inclusion and exclusion of the verb tokens found in our corpus, as well as the details regarding decisions on the categorization of the extracted verb types are given in an appendix only in order to facilitate the presentation, and not because we regard them as of secondary importance. These decisions are crucial to our analysis and are meant as central to the evaluation and replication efforts that we hope will be prompted by our work.

As we have mentioned, in addition to the five variables just discussed, there were another five variables that did not qualify for the study, for one of two reasons. Some variables were discarded because the regressions showed that they were not statistically significantly associated with subject placement. Other variables were discarded because the variance they cover is similar to that of other variables that turned out to have greater coverage. That is, some of the discarded variables were collinear and, in the regression analysis, were shown to subsumed under other, more strongly predictive variables.[3] The variable we called *Given / New subject* studied whether the subjects of the verb tokens under study were new in discourse or had been previously mentioned; but this variable turned out to be statistically nonsignificant in all of our exploratory analyses, and it was set aside. The variables we called *Number of words* and *Number of syllables* measured the length of the subjects of the verbs under study. But even though these variables were statistically significant, the variance captured by them was subsumed under the more strongly predictive variable *Subject type*, so they were set aside. Similarly, the variable we called *Unaccusative* studied whether verb tokens were transitive, intransitive-ergative, or intransitive-unaccusative. But the exploratory regressions showed that the variance captured by this statistically significant variable was better and more strongly accounted for by the variable *Verb class*, so *Unaccusative* was set aside.[4]

The five variables listed above together with their respective factors serve, then, to structure the research presented in this chapter. The presentation proceeds in two steps, covering two layers. First, we address the variable layer, where we investigate cross-generational similarities and differences with regard to predictor variables without yet paying attention to the factor level. Second, we go into greater detail, investigating cross-generational differences with regard to the factors of each variable.

Results: Variables

This section presents the results at the level of the variables or factor groups without mention of individual factors or direction of effects. The first part focuses on which variables significantly condition word order and the second part presents results that enable us to rank the variables.

Statistical Details on the Variables of the Study

Table 4.1 provides the basic information regarding the regression model that led us to select the variables that configure our study. Five variables are listed in alphabetical order, the left side panel showing results for newcomers and the right side panel for NYRs. Four variables were significant for newcomers, five for the NYRs (two asterisks indicate a value of $p < 0.01$ and three asterisks a value of $p < 0.001$; no asterisk indicates nonsignificance). Each of the generational models shown in table 4.1 was run twice. The first run assumed that no individual informant and no individual verb lexeme contributed uniquely to the results. The second run did not make this assumption, but rather tested it to see whether it was valid. In other words, the first regression was a fixed-effects model that included only fixed factors; the second was a mixed-effects model that included both fixed factors and two random factors, the individual participant and the individual verb lexeme. The fixed- and mixed-effects models returned identical results with respect to the (non)significance of the variables. This supports the validity of the groups of individuals and lexemes that we established at the start of our research; no individual lexeme and no individual informant is making a standout contribution to the results. The table also shows the R-square value, which specifies the amount of variance captured by each of the models for each of the generations. The Akaike Information Criterion (AIC) quotient

Table 4.1. Predictor variables of subject placement in fixed and mixed effects regressions (listed alphabetically)

Newcomers	**NYR**
AIC: 448.96	AIC: 298.26
R^2 fixed effects: 0.395	R^2 fixed effects: 0.566
R^2 mixed effects: 00.491	R^2 mixed effects: 0.585
Clause type	Clause type**
Sentence type**	Sentence type**
Subject referent**	Subject referent***
Subject type***	Subject type***
Verb type***	Verb type**

Random factors = verb lexeme and participant

given for each generational model was the lowest one of all the models we ran, indicating that these were the best-fit models for each of the two data sets.[5]

Table 4.1 shows, in the relatively high R-square coefficients, that these variables capture a minimum of 40 percent of the variance in their respective models, with the mixed-effects models capturing roughly half of the variance. With respect to the cross-generational comparison, the table tells us that four of the five variables that influence the decision to prepose or postpose subjects of finite verbs are the same for newcomers and NYRs. The only difference is that the variable *Clause type*, which distinguishes whether the verb appears in a main or subordinate clause, is significant for the NYRs but not for the newcomers.

Variable Hierarchies

Using the same regressions presented in table 4.1, we next raise the question of the relative strength of the variables in the two generations. That is, we want to know which is the strongest predictor, which is the second strongest, and so on, and we want to know whether the order for newcomers persists among the NYRs. To that end, table 4.2 compares the *variable hierarchies* of the two generations. The hierarchies are based on the Wald coefficient of each variable, quantifying a variable's strength relative to that of the others. In other words, table 4.2 lists the same variables as table 4.1, but now in order of predictive power rather than alphabetically. In table 4.2 and in subsequent tables, we dispense with the mixed-effects model and perform all analyses based on what we now know to be the valid fixed-effects models.

Table 4.2 shows that the strongest predictor of subject placement among newcomers is *Verb type*. That is, the variable that most strongly influences placement decisions regarding subjects among newcomers is whether the associated finite verb is a copulative verb, an experiencer or presentative verb, or an activity, occurrence, or stative verb. The table shows that the ranking of *Verb type* is not the same for the NYRs. In the second generation, the strongest predictor of subject placement is *Subject type*, that is, whether the subject is a personal pronoun, a demonstrative pronoun, a quantifier, a lexical noun phrase, or a clause. The table not only shows that the generations differ with regard to the top two variables, but that they differ

Table 4.2. Hierarchy of predictor variables of subject position, based on Wald, Cubans in NYC, fixed effects only

Newcomers		NYR	
R^2, fixed only: 0.39		R^2, fixed only: 0.56	
Predictor variable	**Wald**	**Predictor variable**	**Wald**
Verb type***	48.28	Subject type***	34.24
Subject type***	41.33	Verb type ***	31.67
Sentence type**	10.08	Subject referent***	21.00
Subject referent **	7.70	Sentence type**	14.64
Clause type		Clause type**	6.74

with regard to the order of the third- and fourth-place variables as well, as the ranks of *Sentence type* and *Subject referent* shift between the generations.

Summary of the Variable-Level Results

From the set of predictor variables hypothesized to be relevant to subject placement variation in Spanish, we have established which ones provide the best fit with our data. We have also established the amount of variance between preverbal and postverbal placement that is accounted for by these predictors. We have increased our confidence in the appropriateness of these variables by considering a mixed-effects model that controlled for the relevance of two random factors, namely the individual lexeme and the individual informant. By looking at the variables that motivate the choice of subject position, we have turned up two differences between the generations. First, we have found that the second generation appears to pay attention to a predictive variable that is not relevant for newcomers, namely whether the clause is main or subordinate. Second, we have discovered that the order of predictors is different between the generations. The top predictor among newcomers is the type of finite verb with which the subject occurs, whereas the top predictor among the NYR is the type of subject that is involved.

Results: Factors or Constraints

Bivariate Cross-Generational Comparisons of Individual Factors

Having established the roster of significant variables for each of the generations, and having also determined the rank order in which these variables impact subject placement for newcomers and NYRs, we are now in a position to move one layer down and investigate cross-generational differences with regard to the individual factors of each of the variables. We start by simply presenting the rates of pre- and postverbal subjects found within the factors of each significant variable. For example, for the variable *Subject referent*, we ask what is the percentage of human and nonhuman subjects that occurs preposed and the percentage that occurs postposed. Table 4.3 offers the results for newcomers; table 4.4 will compare newcomers and NYRs.

Alongside the percentages of preposed and postposed subjects for each factor of each significant variable, table 4.3 shows the total number of tokens for each constraint. The variables are presented in the order of strength of the newcomer hierarchy known from table 4.2. Inside each variable, the factors are listed in descending order of frequency of preposing. The values for *Clause type*, which as we saw above was not significant for newcomers, are not given. As mentioned, table 4.3 shows results only for newcomers; the comparison with the NYRs is in table 4.4.

Table 4.3 reflects well the clearly variable character of the phenomenon under study. Instances of preposing and postposing are found in the data for all twelve of the factors; there isn't any kind of subject that is categorically preposed or categorically postposed. Four kinds of subjects, however, approach categoricity in this regard: human subjects, personal pronouns, demonstrative pronouns, and the subjects of copulative verbs are all preposed in more than 90 percent of cases.

Table 4.3. Newcomers: Constraints and percentages

Variables	Constraints	N tokens	% preVb	% postVb
Verb type	Copulative	176	90	10
	Occurrence	482	87	13
	Expern-Presn	42	17	83
Subject type	Demonstrative	44	95	5
	Personal pro	374	94	6
	Quantifier	37	78	22
	Lexical	222	70	30
	Clausal	23	35	65
Sentence type	Declarative	677	84	16
	Interrogative	23	65	35
Subject referent	Human	523	90	10
	Not human	177	66	34
Clause type	Main			
	Subordinate			

More generally, table 4.3 shows the overall prevalence of preverbal position. Of the twelve factors on the table, ten are associated with predominantly preverbal placement. Only clausal subjects (from the variable *Subject type*), as in (4.3.2) and (4.4.1), and the subjects of experiencer-presentative verbs (from the variable *Verb type*), as in (4.4.1) and (4.4.2), are more frequently postverbal than preverbal. All other types of subjects appear mostly preverbally.

Example 4.3.

porque yo me (1) *siento cubana cien por ciento ... entonces, yo, a mí me* (2) *dolió salir de mi país.* [376U]

'because I feel 100 percent Cuban ... so, I, it hurt me to leave my country.'

Example 4.4.

a mí me (1) *parece bien haber venido. A mí me* (2) *parece bien que ... haber venido porque ya yo lo* (3) *estuve pensando* (4) *hace muchos años.* [042U]

'seems OK to me to have come over. Seems OK to me that ... having come over because I had already been thinking about it for many years.'

Taking now the variables in table 4.3 one at a time and starting with the variable *Verb type*, we see, as we have mentioned, that all types of verbs except experiencer-presentative verbs occur more frequently preverbally than postverbally, with copulative verbs approaching categorical preverbal position. For the variable *Subject type*, the table shows, as we have mentioned, that all types except clausal subjects occur in preverbal position in more than 50 percent of cases, and that two types in particular, personal and demonstrative pronouns, show a marked tendency toward preposing, approaching categorical preposing. Finally, for the variables *Subject referent* and *Sentence type*, we see that human subjects occur before verbs more frequently than nonhuman subjects and that subjects of declarative sentences occur before verbs more frequently than the subjects of interrogatives.

Table 4.4 compares factor percentages in newcomers and NYRs. The left-side panel reproduces the information in table 4.3. The right-side panel presents results for the same factors among the NYRs. The bottom row gives the totals for both generations.

Table 4.4 shows that the variable nature of subject placement persists among NYRs, but that two of the four factor values that approached categorical preverbal position among newcomers approach it even more among the NYRs. Human subjects, which were 90 percent preverbal among newcomers, are now 96 percent preverbal among the NYRs, and personal pronouns, which were 94 percent preverbal among newcomers, are now 99 percent. (The other two factors values that approach categorical preverbal position among newcomers, demonstrative pronouns and the subjects of copulative verbs, show roughly the same level of preposing among the NYRs.)

The first comparative generalization that we can make with regard to individual factors when studied in bivariate terms, then, is that there is an increased tendency toward categoricity overall among the NYRs. A chi-square (X^2) test comparing the overall distribution of pre- and postverbal subjects returns a significant difference between the two generations ($X^2 = 4.69$, $p = 0.03$). This indicates that the null hypothesis that pre- and postverbal subjects will be equivalently distributed across generations can be confidently rejected. Specifically, the number of preverbal subjects observed among the NYRs is more than expected if the null hypothesis were true.

This overall cross-generational increase, however, is not the result of an all-around increase in preposing in every factor; of the twelve factors that can be compared in table 4.4, only six factors are associated with cross-generational increases in percentages of preverbal position. Preverbal rates decrease for five factors and remain the same for one other factor. Moreover, despite the overall difference in rates between the generations, it is clear from table 4.4 that the groups are very similar in their favoring of preverbal subjects. Of the fourteen factors in table 4.4, we see for the NYRs, exactly as in newcomers, that twelve are associated with a predominance of preposing. Only two factors, namely (and again just as in newcomers), clausal subjects and experiencer-presentative verbs, are predominantly postposed. The point that newcomers and NYRs are more similar than different is well-made visually. In figure 4.1, variables are presented in the order of the newcomer constraint hierarchy, with differences in the rank order for NYR group indicated above the columns on the right. Preverbal rates observed for each factor are also presented. Despite some shifts in the ranking of variables as well as in subject position rates associated with particular factors, the picture that emerges is one of strong cross-generational continuity.

Taking the factors in the figure one variable at a time, we see for *Verb type*, preverbal position is preferred for copulative and occurrence verbs but not for verbs that are experiencer or presentative. This is true for newcomers and NYRs alike. With regard

Table 4.4. Newcomers and NYRs: Constraints and percentages

	NEWCOMERS				NYRs			
Variables	**Constraints**	**N tokens**	**% preVb**	**% postVb**	**Constraints**	**N tokens**	**% preVb**	**% postVb**
Verb type	Copulative	176	90	10	Occurrence	478	93	7
	Occurrence	482	87	13	Copulative	175	89	11
	Expern-Presn	42	17	83	Expern/Presn	42	24	76
Subject type	Demonstrative	44	95	5	Personal pro	428	99	1
	Personal pro	374	94	6	Demonstrative	30	90	10
	Quantifier	37	78	22	Quantifier	31	74	26
	Lexical	222	70	30	Lexical	189	71	29
	Clausal	23	35	65	Clausal	17	18	82
Sentence type	Interrog	23	65	35	Interrog	17	65	35
	Declarative	677	84	16	Declarative	678	88	12
Subject referent	Human	523	90	10	Human	547	96	4
	Not human	177	66	34	Not human	148	57	43
Clause type	Main				Main	447	89	11
	Subordinate				Subordinate	248	86	14
Total N		700	**84**	**16**		700	**88**	**12**

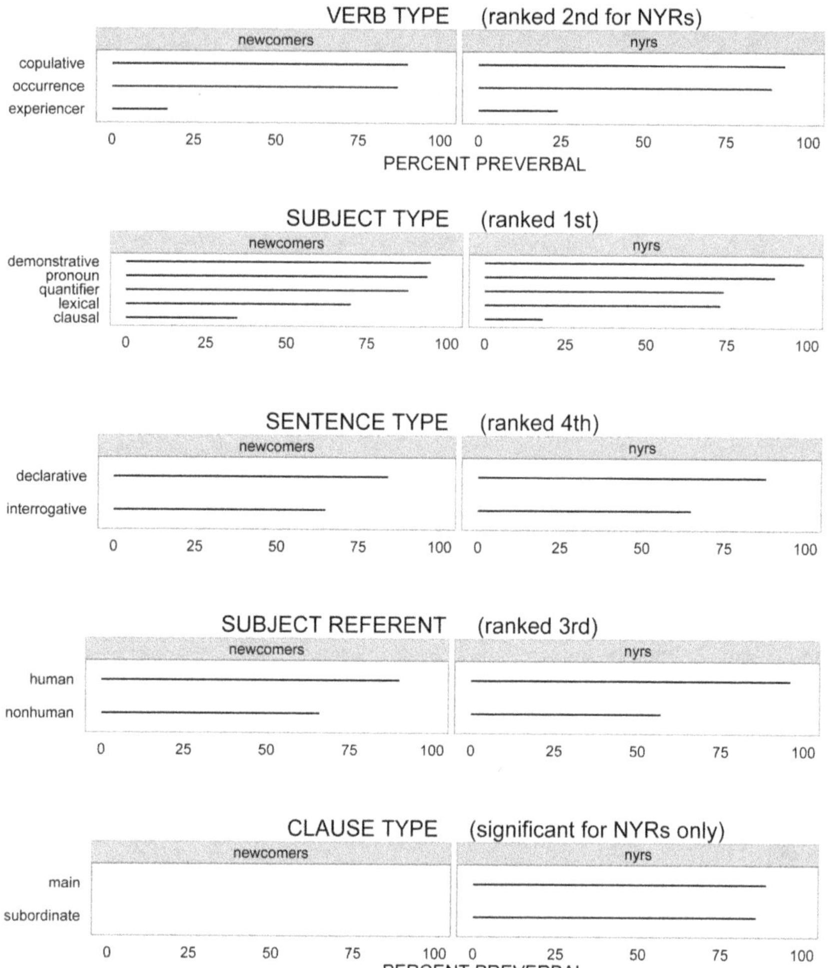

Figure 4.1. Cross-generational comparison of five constraints on subject placement

to *Subject type*, personal pronouns and demonstratives show the highest frequency of preposing, with personal pronouns, as we have mentioned, more closely approximating categorical preposing in the second generation. For *Sentence type* and *Subject referent*, we observe that in both generations the subjects of declarative sentences occur preverbally with greater frequency than the subjects of interrogatives and that human subjects occur preverbally more frequently than nonhumans (as mentioned, the preference for preposed human subjects increases in the second generation).

Multivariate Comparison of Generations at the Level of Factors

We return now to the multivariate analysis of predictors, providing more details on the regressions whose results were first outlined in tables 4.1 and 4.2. As before, in table 4.5 we list the variables in order of the newcomers' variable hierarchy. Within each variable, the factors are listed in descending order of predictive strength of preposing. The strength of each factor is expressed in terms of factor weights generated by Rbrul (Johnson 2009). The weights indicate the unique contribution that each factor makes to the preposing of the subject. The cut-off point between favoring and disfavoring preverbal position is 0.50. Weights above 0.50 indicate that the factor favors preposing when compared to overall preposing levels, that is, that subjects of the type indicated by the factor have a higher-than-chance probability of being preposed. As weights get closer to 0.50, the strength of the effects is weaker. Weights below 0.50 show that the factor disfavors preposing, that is, that the types of subject associated with the constraint have a greater than chance probability of being postposed. For each constraint, we repeat, from table 4.3, the number of tokens and the percentage of preposing.

The multivariate results in table 4.5 show some parallels with the bivariate results of table 4.3, but show as well some important differences. Consider first the variable *Subject referent*. The table shows that human subjects favor preverbal position (weight of 0.61) and nonhuman subjects disfavor it (weight of 0.39). It is important to keep in mind that the term *disfavor* is understood here in probabilistic rather than absolute terms. Both the favoring factor (human subjects) and the disfavoring one (nonhuman subjects) are, as we have seen, associated with preverbal bivariate rates greater than 50 percent (90 percent and 66 percent respectively). But the multivariate results tell us whether a given factor increases or decreases the probability of preverbal placement relative to the input probability in the data at large. Said differently,

Table 4.5. Constraint weights. Preverbal position. Regression. Rbrul

			NEWCOMERS	
Variables	**Constraints**	**N tokens**	**% preVb**	**Weight preVb**
Verb type	Copulative	176	90	**0.90**
	Occurrence	482	87	**0.87**
	Expern-presn	42	17	**0.10**
Subject type	Demonstrative	44	95	**0.91**
	Personal pro	374	94	**0.74**
	Quantifier	37	78	**0.35**
	Lexical NP	222	70	**0.31**
	Clausal	23	35	**0.13**
Sentence type	Declarative	677	84	**0.69**
	Interrogative	23	65	**0.31**
Subject referent	Human	523	90	**0.61**
	Not human	177	66	**0.39**
Clause type	Main			
	Subordinate			

the factor values indicate that the presence of a human referent increases the probability of preposing, whereas a nonhuman referent decreases that probability. For the variable *Sentence type*, we see that declaratives favor preposing while interrogatives disfavor it. For the variable *Verb type*, the table shows that only experiencer or presentative verbs disfavor preposing. But for the variable *Subject type*, a multivariate result emerges that, again, was not present in the bivariate percentages. We now see that only the demonstrative pronouns and the personal pronouns favor preposing. In contrast, quantifiers, lexical subjects, and clausal subjects all disfavor preposing.

Table 4.6 offers a comparison between the generations. The factors are presented now separate from their variables and in order of descending multivariate weights. The left-side panel repeats the information from table 4.5. Note that, unlike previous tables, table 4.6 does not show variables but rather only factors.

Table 4.6 shows evidence of both cross-generational continuity and change. The generations show their strongest similarity in that the factors that favor preverbal position (weights over 0.50) among newcomers are exactly the same ones that favor it among the NYRs. This is evidence of substantial continuity between Cuban-born and New York–raised speakers. In the speech of both generations, subjects are very likely to occur preverbally when they are pronominal, associated with either a copulative or occurrence verb, in declarative utterances, and associated with human referents. In contrast, subjects are less likely, in both generations, to occur preverbally when they are lexical or clausal in nature, when they are associated with an experiential or presentative verb, when they occur in interrogative utterances, and when they have nonhuman referents. To round off the comparison, it is worth repeating that among factors that decrease the probability of occurrence of preverbal placement, only two (clausal subjects and subjects of experiencer or presentative verbs) are associated

Table 4.6. Constraint weights. Preverbal position. Regression. Rbrul

	NEWCOMERS				NYRs		
Constraints	**N tokens**	**% preVb**	**Weight preVb**	**Constraints**	**N tokens**	**% preVb**	**Weight preVb**
Demonstrative	44	95	**0.91**	Personal pro	428	99	**0.90**
Copulative	176	90	**0.90**	Declarative	678	88	**0.82**
Occurrence	482	87	**0.87**	Copulative	175	89	**0.80**
Personal pro	374	94	**0.71**	Demonstrative	30	90	**0.73**
Declarative	677	84	**0.70**	Human	547	96	**0.72**
Human	523	90	**0.61**	Occurrence	478	93	**0.54**
Not human	177	66	**0.40**	Quantifier	31	74	**0.38**
Interrogative	23	65	**0.30**	Lexical	189	71	**0.38**
Quantifier	37	78	**0.35**	Not human	148	57	**0.28**
Lexical	222	70	**0.31**	Interrogative	17	65	**0.18**
Clausal subject	23	35	**0.18**	Expern/Presn	42	24	**0.18**
Expern-Presn	42	17	**0.10**	Clausal subject	17	18	**0.10**

with occurrence rates below 50 percent, which is to say that only these two factors are absolutely as well as probabilistically associated with postverbal placement.

Discussion

With respect to the question of intergenerational continuity and change, our results highlight the presence of the former much more so than the latter in the Spanish of Cuban New Yorkers. While it is true that a significant difference in overall rates emerges such that NYRs postpose subjects less frequently than newcomers, their behavior has not changed qualitatively. Both groups overwhelmingly prefer to use preverbal subjects. What's more, the strategies employed by both groups for making decisions about subject position are remarkably similar. This is true at both the variable and factor levels. Of the five variables that significantly constrain variation in subject position, four are shared between newcomers and NYRs. The one variable that they do not have in common, *Clause type*, which is significant only for NYRs, is the weakest of the five in that group's variable hierarchy. With respect to factors, those that increase the probability of preverbal position for the first generation also do so for the second generation. In both generations, subjects are likeliest to appear before verbs (1) when the subject is a demonstrative or personal pronoun, (2) with copulative and occurrence verbs, (3) in declarative utterances, and (4) when the referent of the subject is human. With respect to factors that disfavor preverbal position, again the generations are identical. For both groups, the probability of preverbal position decreases when the subject is (1) a quantifier, lexical, or clausal, (2) associated with an experiencer or presentative verb, (3) part of an interrogative utterance, and (4) not human.[6]

Insofar as the variable hierarchies and factor weights generated by variationist analyses reflect the probabilistic linguistic competence of language users, this study reveals broad evidence of generational continuity in the domain of subject position in Spanish. In this regard, the current investigation of variation in subject position complements and reinforces previous research on Spanish spoken in New York City. In articulating perhaps the widest generalization to emerge from their study of subject pronoun expression (e.g., *yo voy* ~ *voy*), Otheguy and Zentella (2012, 177) write that "the picture that emerges is one where newcomers have transmitted intact large portions of their grammar to the NYR." This statement is equally applicable to the variable feature under investigation here.

Alongside strong evidence of continuity, we do observe some generational differences. The most general observation is that neither the order nor the weights of the factors reported in table 4.6 above are identical between groups. That said, these facts are not, on their own, particularly surprising; they are to be expected in variationist analyses of spontaneous speech. Indeed, it is likely that a replication study using data from these same speakers collected on a different day or in a different context would reveal some minor fluctuations in factor weights and rankings within each group.

Still, some of the reshuffling in factor rank and weight is suggestive of a pattern. Specifically, some of the differences observed in the behavior of the NYRs lend support to a language contact hypothesis that would connect the greater propensity by the NYRs to prepose Spanish grammatical subjects with their relatively greater use of and exposure to English. Figure 4.2 repeats the rankings from table 4.6, highlighting three changes of interest. The arrows indicate an increase in the relative weight of the factors pronoun, declarative, and human. In addition to a shift in weight, these factors are also associated with generational increases in preverbal rates: from 94 to 99 percent with pronominal subjects, from 84 to 88 percent in declarative utterances, and from 90 to 96 percent for subjects with human referents. Together these changes suggest that for the NYRs, the variable nature of subject position is fading along these dimensions. That is, pronominal subjects with human referents as well as those occurring in declarative utterances have become more invariantly preverbal in the second generation. In this regard, such subjects more closely approximate analogous structures in English.

Another possible explanation for the generational differences that we observe appeals, beyond the matter of English influence, to the acceleration of a change in progress attested in communities of Spanish speakers in the Caribbean (e.g., Brown and Rivas 2011; Martínez-Sanz 2011; Morales 1989, 1999; Ortiz López and Dauphinais, 2016; Toribio 2000). While this is an intriguing possibility, it is not supported by the fact that the correlation between contact with English and an increased preference for preposed subjects has been noted in the speech of bilingual US Latinos of non-Caribbean origin (Raña Risso 2013; Silva-Corvalán 1994, 2014; Cuza 2012). This makes it difficult to tease apart these two potentially mutually reinforcing trends.

With regard to implications for the ongoing evolution of Spanish in the US, the changes we have documented may fit within a larger narrative of a decrease in word order flexibility with respect to finite verbs and their subjects. Indeed, the contexts in which we observe what might be called a trend toward invariance are the same contexts generally at the forefront of diachronic change toward greater propensity

Newcomers	**NYRs**
Demonstrative	**Personal pro**
Copulative	**Declarative**
Occurrence	Copulative
Personal pro	Demonstrative
Declarative	**Human**
Human	Occurrence
Not human	Quantifier
Interrogative	Lexical
Quantifier	Not human
Lexical	Interrogative
Clausal	Experiencer-Presentative
Experiencer-Presentative	Clausal

Figure 4.2. Cross-generational changes in constraint rankings

to prepose Spanish grammatical subjects. Brown and Rivas (2011, 41) propose the following series of steps as a process by which relatively freer word order might transition to a more fixed order, one in which Spanish subjects increasingly appear before their verbs:

1. Increase in subject pronoun expression →
2. Increase in preverbal placement of subject pronouns →
3. Increase in preverbal placement of subjects (all types) in declarative sentences →
4. Increase in preverbal placement of subjects (all types) in interrogatives[7]

The first step in the proposed process of change—the increase in subject pronoun expression—has been documented for Spanish in NYC in general (e.g., Otheguy and Zentella 2012) and for Cubans in NYC in particular (Shin and Otheguy 2013). In the current study we provide evidence of steps two and three. That is, we observe an increase in preverbal subject pronouns as well as an increase in preverbal placement of subjects of all types in declarative utterances. The first of these shifts has led to behavior that, for the NYRs, is almost categorical in nature (99 percent preverbal subject pronouns).

We do not, however, find evidence of the fourth step proposed above, an increase in preverbal placement of subjects in interrogatives. The preverbal rate for this factor is exactly the same for each generation (65 percent). That said, it is possible that our coding of interrogatives, which did not distinguish between types of interrogatives or whether interrogatives occurred in main or embedded clauses, may be obscuring part of the picture. Cuza (2012), for example, found that, compared to recent arrivals from Latin America, US-born bilinguals demonstrate a stronger preference for preverbal subjects, especially in embedded *wh*-questions, as in *No sé a quién Luis conoció* (I don't know who Luis met). Thus it is possible that a reoperationalization of this variable is in order, and that future analyses may in fact uncover differences between newcomers and NYRs for the subset of interrogatives that appears in embedded clauses.

A final question to consider, one that we can but mention briefly here, is why the strategies that newcomers and NYRs use to make choices about subject position are what they are. If the answers to these questions are to be found in general appeals to cognitive processing or in specific reference to principles that give structure to linguistic discourse, then one would expect the kind of results that emerged here. Similarly, if the answers are to be found in semantic properties associated with preverbal and postverbal position in Spanish, such as the preference of 'low topicality' items for postverbal position (Ocampo 2014), then one would expect results along the lines of the ones we obtained. For example, the favoring of preverbal position by pronoun subjects in general (personal and demonstrative) and the favoring of postverbal position by nominal lexical subjects may be accounted for by these factors. The referents of pronouns tend to have already made an appearance in the discourse and be of high topicality. That is, pronouns require anaphors and thus tend to be, discursively speaking, old news. To the extent that a natural ordering principle of discourse is that old information is presented first, then pronouns will tend to be preverbal, while lexical and clausal subjects, which are the means for establishing anaphors in the first place, will tend to occur postverbally. To the extent that preverbal and postverbal position in Spanish have values of high and low topicality (as in Ocampo 2014), this distribution of pronouns and nouns too is to be expected. By this logic, the right question about continuity and change is not, at its core, "Do newcomers pass along to NYRs their strategies for negotiating sites of variation in their linguistic system?" but rather, "Do they transmit structures with similar functions and semantic values?" From this perspective, the quantitative trends that we observe can be seen as the natural byproducts of speakers using linguistic systems that consist of similarly functioning elements.

Conclusion

This study examined variation in the position of grammatical subjects in the speech of fourteen Cuban New Yorkers. Analysis of 1,400 finite verbs and their subjects yielded a number of results. Our most general finding is similar to that of previous research on this topic, namely that Spanish speakers strongly favor preverbal subject position. This trend emerged for both generational groups examined here. In addition, we found, through an analysis of both variables and factors, considerable evidence of generational continuity in the behavior of speakers with regard to this feature. Indeed, newcomer and NYR variable and factor hierarchies demonstrated remarkable similarity. We also found an undercurrent of change flowing against the tide of continuity. Most notably, we observed shifts toward increased invariance in particular factors constraining the behavior of the NYRs. These trends may fit with an emerging narrative regarding a general reduction in word order flexibility in Spanish-speaking communities found in the US and abroad.

Notes

1. The conclusions that we come to regarding our newcomers may be of interest to scholars of the speech of Cubans in Cuba, as this is very likely to be closely matched by the speech of newcomers.
2. Barrera-Tobón and Raña Risso, 2016; Bentivoglio 1988; Bentivoglio and Weber 1986; Bolinger 1954; Brown and Rivas 2011; Cuza 2012; Delbecque 1988; Martínez-Sanz 2011; Mayoral Hernández 2014; Morales 1982, 1989, 1999, 2006; Ocampo 2009, 2014; Ortiz López 2010; Ortiz López and Morales-Muñoz 2015; Ortiz López and Dauphinais, 2016; Raña Risso 2013; Roggia 2011; Silva-Corvalán 1982, 2014; and Toribio 2000.
3. We arrived at these conclusions by comparing the Akaike Information Criterion (AIC) for models in which all factors were the same except one. For example, we compared a model that included *Unaccusativity* and one that included *Verb class*, and the AIC values indicated that the model with *Verb class* was a better fit.
4. Although we set *Unaccusativity* aside, it is worth noting that this variable was significant ($p < 0.001$) in a model that included *Subject type, Subject referent* (human/not human), *Sentence type* (interrogative/not interrogative), *Clause type*, and two random factors (*Participant, Verb lexeme*). In this sense our study differs from Ortiz López and Dauphinais (2016), who found that *Unaccusativity* did not constrain subject-verb word order among Cubans in Cuba (see also Ortiz López 2010). Silva-Corvalán (2014, 178–81) offers insight into why *Unaccusativity* may show up as significant in some studies, but not in others. She argues that, rather than the verb itself, it is the relative information weight of the constituents and the information structure of the sentence as a whole that matters most for subject placement.

5. AIC measures the quality of statistical models and thus provides a way to select the best model (e.g. Burnham and Anderson 2004).
6. While our results suggest that the distinction between a human and a nonhuman referent continues to guide subject placement patterns in the second generation, it may be the case that subject referent is less important for third-generation speakers. Silva-Corvalán (2014) found that as her third-generation grandsons became increasingly English-dominant, animacy of the subject referent had less of an impact on their subject placement patterns.
7. Brown and Rivas (2011) further propose that the change impacts rhetorical and quotative questions before interrogatives.

References

Barrera-Tobón, C., and R. Raña Risso. 2016. "A Corpus-Based Sociolinguistic Study of Contact-Induced Changes in Subject Placement in the Spanish of New York City Bilinguals." In *Spanish Language and Sociolinguistic Analysis*, edited by S. Sessarego and F. Tejedo, 323–42. Amsterdam: John Benjamins Publishing.

Bentivoglio, P. 1988. "La posición del sujeto en el español de Caracas: un análisis de los factores lingüísticos y extralingüísticos." In *Studies in Caribbean Spanish dialectology*, edited by R. M. Hammond and M. C. Resnick, 13–23. Washington, DC: Georgetown University Press.

Bentivoglio, P., and E. Weber. 1986. "A Functional Approach to Subject Word Order in Spoken Spanish." In *Studies in Romance Linguistics*, edited by O. Jaeggli and C. Silva-Corvalán, 23–40. Riverton, UT: Foris Publishers.

Bolinger, D. 1954. "Meaningful Word Order in Spanish." *Boletín de Filología* 8:45–56.

Brown, E., and J. Rivas. 2011. "Subject-Verb Word Order in Spanish Interrogatives: A Quantitative Analysis of Puerto Rican Spanish." *Spanish in Context* 8:23–49.

Burnham, K. P., and D. R. Anderson. 2004. "Multimodel Inference: Understanding AIC and BIC in Model Selection." *Sociological Methods & Research* 33:261–304.

Culy, C. 1997. "Logophoric Pronouns and Point of View." *Linguistics* 35:845–59.

Cuza, A. 2012. "Crosslinguistic Influence at the Syntax Proper: Interrogative Subject-Verb Inversion in Heritage Spanish." *International Journal of Bilingualism* 17:71–96.

Delbecque, N. 1988. "On Subject Position in Spanish: A Variable Rule Analysis of Constraints at the Level of the Subject NP and of the VP." *Literary and Linguistic Computing* 3:85–200.

Durán, R., ed. 1981. *Latino Language and Communicative Behavior.* Norwood, NJ: Ablex Publishing Co.

Elías-Olivares, L., ed. 1983. *Spanish in the U.S. Setting: Beyond the Southwest.* Washington, DC: National Clearinghouse for Bilingual Education.

Erker, D. 2012. "Of Categories and Continua: Relating Discrete and Gradient Properties of Sociophonetic Variation." *Penn Working Papers in Linguistics* 18:11–20.

Erker, D., and G. Guy. 2012. "The Role of Lexical Frequency in Syntactic Variability: Variable Subject Pronoun Expression in Spanish." *Language* 88:526–57.

Johnson, D. E. 2009. "Getting Off the GoldVarb Standard: Introducing Rbrul for Mixed-Effects Variable Rule Analysis." *Language and Linguistics Compass* 3:359–83.

Labov, W. 1966. *The Social Stratification of English in New York City*. Washington, DC: Center for Applied Linguistics.

———. 1969. "Contraction, Deletion, and Inherent Variability of the English Copula." *Language* 45:715–62.

———. 1972. *Sociolinguistic Patterns*. Philadelphia: University of Pennsylvania Press.

Lapidus, N., and R. Otheguy. 2005. "Overt Nonspecific *Ellos* in the Spanish of New York." *Spanish in Context* 2:157–76.

Martínez-Sanz, C. 2011. "Null and Overt Subjects in a Variable System: The Case of Dominican Spanish." PhD diss., University of Ottawa.

Mayoral Hernández, R. 2014. "Subject Position in Spanish. A Study of Factor Interactions with Prototypical Verbs." *Verba* 72:111–36.

Morales, A. 1982. "La perspectiva dinámica oracional en el español de Puerto Rico." In *El español del Caribe: Ponencias del VI Simposio de Dialectología*, edited by O. Alba, 203–19. Santiago, Dom.: Universidad Católica Madre y Maestra.

———. 1989. "Hacia un universal sintáctico del español del Caribe: el orden SVO." *Anuario de Lingüística Hispánica* 5:139–52.

——. 1999. "Anteposición de sujeto en el español del Caribe." In *El Caribe hispánico: Perspectivas lingüísticas actuales*, edited by L. Ortiz López, 77–98. Frankfurt: Vervuert.

———. 2006. "Los sujetos 'ligeros' del español y su posición en la oración." In *Haciendo lingüística. Homenaje a Paola Bentivoglio*, edited by M. Sedano, A. Bolívar, and M. Shiro, 487–501. Caracas: Universidad Central de Venezuela.

Ocampo, F. 2009. "El orden de palabras en el español hablado. La construcción Sujeto Verbo Objeto Directo." In *La lingüística como reto epistemológico y como acción social*, edited by M. Veyrat Rigat and E. Serra Alegre, 501–11. Madrid: Arco/Libros.

———. 2014. "El orden de palabras en cláusulas subordinadas relativas con un sujeto y un verbo transitivo." *Verba* 72:177–200.

Ortiz López, L. 2010. "El español del Caribe: orden de palabras a la luz de la interfaz léxico-sintaxis y sintaxis-pragmática." *Revista Internacional de Lingüística Iberoamericana* 14:75–94.

Ortiz López, L., and K. Morales-Muñoz. 2015. "Adquisición del PSN en 2L1 y L2 vs. L1: ¿Vulnerabilidad o éxito?" Paper presented at the 25th Conference on Spanish in the U.S. and 10th Conference on Spanish in Contact with Other Languages, City College of New York, March 26–29.

Ortiz López, L., and A. Dauphinais. 2016. "Microvariation in the Null Subject Parameter: Word Order in Cuban Spanish." In *Inquiries in Hispanic Linguistics: From Theory to Empirical Evidence*, edited by A. Cuza, L. Czerwionka, and D. Olson, 281–300. Amsterdam: John Benjamins.

Otheguy, R., and A. C. Zentella. 2012. *Spanish in New York: Language Contact, Dialectal Leveling, and Structural Continuity.* Oxford: Oxford University Press.

Otheguy, R., A. C. Zentella, and D. Livert. 2007. "Language and Dialect Contact in Spanish in New York: Toward the Formation of a Speech Community." *Language* 83:770–802.

Poplack, S. 1980. "Sometimes I'll Start a Sentence in English y Termino en Español: Toward a Typology of Codeswitching." *Linguistics* 18:581–616.

Raña Risso, R. 2013. "A Corpus-Based Sociolinguistic Study of Subject Pronoun Placement." PhD diss., Graduate Center of the City University of New York.

Roggia, A. 2011. "Unaccusativity and Word Order in Mexican Spanish: An Examination of Syntactic Interfaces and the Split Intransitivity Hierarchy." PhD diss., Pennsylvania State University.

Shin, N. L. 2010. "Efficiency in Lexical Borrowing in New York Spanish." *International Journal of the Sociology of Language* 203:45–60.

———. 2014. "Grammatical Complexification in Spanish in New York: 3sg Pronoun Expression and Verbal Ambiguity." *Language Variation and Change* 26:303–30.

Shin, N. L., and R. Otheguy. 2013. "Social Class and Gender Impacting Change in Bilingual Settings: Spanish Subject Pronoun Use in New York." *Language in Society* 42:429–52.

Silva-Corvalán, C. 1982. "Subject Expression and Placement in Mexican-American Spanish." In *Spanish in the United States: Sociolinguistic Aspects*, edited by J. Amastae and L. Elías-Olivares, 93–120. New York: Cambridge University Press.

———. 1994. *Language Contact and Change: Spanish in Los Angeles.* Oxford: Oxford University Press.

———. 2014. *Bilingual Language Acquisition: Spanish and English in the First Six Years.* Cambridge: Cambridge University Press.

Tagliamonte, S. 2012. *Variationist Sociolinguistics: Change, Observation, Interpretation.* Malden, MA: Wiley-Blackwell.

Toribio, A. J. 2000. "Setting Parametric Limits on Dialectal Variation in Spanish." *Lingua* 10:315–41.

5

The Variation of Subject Pronouns over Time in Cuban Spanish

GABRIELA G. ALFARAZ
Michigan State University

CARIBBEAN SPANISH HAS FIGURED prominently in research on the variation of subject pronouns and null subjects. Foundational sociolinguistic work studied the variation with data from Puerto Rican Spanish (Cameron 1992, 1993; Hochberg 1986; Morales 1986). Extensive research on the subject pronoun variable, in Caribbean and non-Caribbean varieties, has described the linguistic and social factors that condition its variation and identified similarities and differences across regions, which has been most clearly demonstrated in crosslinguistic studies on Caribbean varieties in situ as well as in the United States (Cameron 1993; Erker et al., this volume; Ortiz, Dauphinais, and Aponte Alequín, this volume; Otheguy, Zentella, and Livert 2007; Otheguy and Zentella 2012).

Two linguistic factors that have been consistently found to have a strong effect are person and number, and coreference. Person and number is often shown to be the strongest constraint (Alfaraz 2015; Bayley and Pease-Álvarez 1997; Bayley, Greer, and Holland 2013; Erker and Guy 2012; Martínez-Sanz 2011; Orozco 2015; Orozco and Guy 2008; Otheguy and Zentella 2012; Otheguy, Zentella, and Livert 2007). In varieties of the insular Caribbean, the second-person singular tends to favor overt forms more strongly than other persons (Alfaraz 2015; Ávila-Jiménez 1996; Cameron 1992; Hochberg 1986; Martínez-Sanz 2011; Otheguy, Zentella, and Livert 2007), although the first-person singular favors it more strongly in coastal Caribbean Spanish (Orozco 2015; Orozco and Guy 2008) and other varieties (Bayley, Greer, and Holland 2013; Hochberg 1986). Across dialects, singular forms have consistently been found to favor, and plural to disfavor, overt subjects (Cameron 1992; Silva-Corvalán 1994). Coreference, or switch reference, as it is often called, has been shown to have a strong, often the second strongest, effect on subject pronoun variation in both Caribbean and non-Caribbean Spanish (Alfaraz 2015; Bayley and

Pease-Álvarez 1997; Bayley, Greer, and Holland 2013; Erker and Guy 2012; Orozco 2015; Otheguy, Zentella, and Livert 2007). These findings, however, are less consistent than those for person and number; depending on how coreference is operationalized, it may rank below other linguistic factors (Martínez-Sanz 2011; Orozco and Guy 2008). Regardless of its effect size, however, the same pattern has been found in all varieties: same reference favors null subjects and switch reference favors overt subjects.

Apart from person and number and coreference, other significant linguistic factors that have been identified include verb tense, mood, and aspect (Bayley and Pease-Álvarez 1997; Bayley, Greer, and Holland 2013; Erker and Guy 2012; Martínez-Sanz 2011; Orozco 2015), syntactic verb type (Bayley and Pease-Álvarez 1997; Martínez-Sanz 2011; Orozco and Guy 2008), priming (Cameron and Flores-Ferrán 2004), and polarity (Travis and Torres Cacoullos 2012). Frequency effects have been demonstrated (Erker and Guy 2012) and contested (Bayley, Greer, and Holland 2013). Social factors, such as age, are significant in some studies on Caribbean varieties (Ávila-Jimenez 1996; Morales 1986; Orozco 2015; Orozco and Guy 2008) but not in others (Alfaraz 2015; Martínez-Sanz 2011; Otheguy and Zentella 2012).

Given the vigorous research on the variable, working descriptions and explanations of the variation have been reported for many varieties. Although subject pronoun variation has been discussed for Cuban Spanish in contact with English (Lipski 1996; Flores-Ferrán 2007) and studies of newcomers to New York City (Otheguy, Zentella, and Livert 2007) have examined the influence of internal constraints, the social and linguistic constraints that influence the variable in monolingual Cuban Spanish are understudied. Some descriptive information about the rates of pronominal and null subjects has been reported, but the rates vary considerably. Ávila-Shah (2000) reports 40.4 percent (n = 390/965) overt pronouns for a control group of twelve Cuban monolinguals with which bilingual Puerto Ricans were compared (the rate for adult Puerto Ricans was 41.4 percent [n = 316/764]). In contrast, the rates in Otheguy, Zentella, and Livert (2007) show that Cuban newcomers were more conservative in their use of overt pronouns (33 percent) than new arrivals from the Dominican Republic (41 percent), and slightly more so than newcomers from Puerto Rico (35 percent). Beyond the overall rate of subject expression, however, the linguistic and social constraints that influence subject variation in the Cuban variety have not been described. The present study contributes to previous research by taking into account the time dimension in a comparative analysis of logistic regressions of three time periods.

The research discussed here studied subject variation in Cuban Spanish, with data from Cubans born on the island who were either interviewed while living there, while traveling outside the island, or after arriving in the US. The goal of this research was to understand the linguistic and social factors that conditioned the variation of null subjects and overt subject pronouns. The full sample of 8,305 tokens was examined using a logistic regression analysis in order to examine the factors that influenced the variation and to establish a basis for comparison with other studies. More importantly, to examine subject variation over time in Cuban Spanish, separate logistic regression analyses were conducted on the data sets for three groups, established according to year of birth—1885–1911, 1929–36, and 1959–70. The findings from these analyses were compared in order to identify similarities and differences in the significance and influence of predictors and the patterning of constraint hierarchies over time.

Methodology

The data used in the study are from three different sources. The first data set, collected by the author in the late 1990s in Miami, Florida, has seventeen participants born in Cuba between 1959 and 1970 and six participants born in Cuba between 1929 and 1936. The second data set, from the *Norma Culta* project (*Proyecto de Estudio Coordinado de la Norma Lingüística de las Principales Ciudades de Iberoamérica y de la Península Ibérica*), was collected in the late 1960s in Miami, Florida, and has twenty participants born in Cuba between 1929 and 1936. The third data set, from interviews in the Díaz-Ayala Collection (Florida International University) made in the early 1970s and 1980s in various locations, including Miami, Florida, and Havana, Cuba, has fourteen individuals born in Cuba between 1885 and 1911. The three data sets are from interviews with one or more participants. The discourse contains adjacency pairs (questions and answers) and personal narratives. Genre was run in a preliminary logistic regression analysis, but significant differences were not found, so it was not included in the final analysis. All fifty-seven individuals included in the sample were born in Cuba. The interviewers were speakers of Cuban Spanish in the author's corpus, in the Díaz Ayala collection, and in some of the *Norma Culta* interviews; in others, the interviewer was a native speaker of Spanish who was not a speaker of Cuban Spanish, but because other Cuban participants were often in the interviews, and there does not appear to be evidence of accommodation or leveling of either marked or unmarked regional variants.

The social factors (also referred to as predictors) included in the study were year of birth, gender, and social status. Although year of birth was also analyzed as a continuous factor, the analysis with the year-of-birth groups provided information on the factor weights; thus, the results will present the findings for year-of-birth groups as a fixed factor. As a social predictor, gender was taken as a binomial factor based on the individual's sex. A total of thirty women and twenty-seven men were included in the study. The third social predictor, social status, was calculated based on the occupation of participants and coded as high, medium, and low. The sample, based on the available data, consisted primarily of high- and middle-status individuals—the low-status group had only five individuals because the majority fell into the high and middle groups, which had twenty-seven and twenty-five individuals respectively.

Tokens of inflected verbs were coded for the linguistic predictors: subject type, person and number, verb tense, mood, and aspect (TMA), verb type, polarity, coreference, and specificity. Exclusions included impersonal constructions with *haber*, *hacer*, *ser*, *se*, verbs in relative clauses with a subject head, and discourse markers with obligatory pronouns. Subject type was either null or overt. Overt forms included subject, indefinite, and definite pronouns, although only subject pronouns were later analyzed. Person and number included first, second, and third, singular and plural, and were coded based on verb inflection. Verb TMA was coded as present, preterite, imperfect, future, conditional, indicative, and subjunctive. Compound forms were coded according to the tense of the inflected verb—*ha hablado* was present and *había hablado* was imperfect. Type of verb was classified as copula, transitive, or intransitive, which was further coded as either unergative or unaccusative. Polarity (Travis and Torres Cacoullos 2012) was coded as either positive or negative. Coreference was coded according to whether the referent of the verb was the same or different from the referent of the immediately preceding inflected verb. Although same reference was mostly observed with the same person and number, it also occurred with different verb inflection. Similarly, a switch in reference commonly occurred with a change in verb morphology, but a different referent could appear with the same verb inflection. Referents occurring after the plural forms *nosotros*, *ustedes*, and *ellos* were coded as same reference if they were part of the set referred to with the plural pronoun (Cameron 1992). The specificity of second-person singular and third-person plural forms was coded as specific and nonspecific.

The logistic regression analysis and descriptive statistics were carried out with Rbrul. The analyses reported below were run with only subject pronouns, excluding definite and indefinite pronouns, which tended to occur more frequently in the later data sets than the earliest one. The second-person plural subject pronoun, *ustedes*, was excluded from the analyses because it had a low number of tokens. Similarly, future and conditional verb forms were excluded because they occurred at low rates. Another adjustment was the combination of the two intransitive types, unergatives and unaccusatives, because they were not significantly different. Furthermore, specificity was excluded from the final logistic regression analyses reported below after it was confirmed that specific and nonspecific forms were not significantly different. A logistic regression analysis that included year of birth as a fixed effect was run on 8,305 tokens from the combined data sets. Separate logistic regression analyses with the linguistic and social (gender and status) factors described above were also carried out on each of the three year-of-birth groups for the comparative analysis.

Results: Full Sample

The overall proportion of null and overt subjects indicated that null subjects were considerably more frequent than overt subject pronouns (table 5.1). Null subjects accounted for 64.6 percent (n = 5,363) and overt subject pronouns for 35.4 percent

Table 5.1. Rates of null subjects and overt subject pronouns by year of birth

	Null		Overt		Total
	%	N	%	N	N
1885–1911	62.6	1657	37.4	991	2648
1929–36	66.0	2239	34.0	1155	3394
1959–70	64.8	1467	35.2	796	2263
Total	64.6	5363	35.4	2942	8305

(n = 2,942) of the total 8,305 tokens included in the study. The rates for the year-of-birth groups indicated that null subjects ranged between 62.6 percent and 66 percent, and overt subjects between 34 percent and 37.4 percent. The rate trend for the year-of-birth groups was not incremental, however, because the 1885–1911 group had a higher rate of overt subjects (37.4 percent) than the 1929–36 (34 percent) and the 1959–70 (35.2 percent) groups.

The results of the logistic regression analysis, in table 5.2, organized according to the significance of predictors, showed that the linguistic predictors were all highly significant. Of the social predictors, gender and social status were not significant, but year of birth was significant at the 0.05 level. The most significant constraint was the person and number of the verb, followed by coreference, TMA, verb type, polarity, and, finally, year-of-birth group. To understand the results, the centered weight can be used as a guide to interpret the strength of each item within predictors: a factor weight (FW) of 0.50 is neutral, factor weights closer to 1.0 favor the occurrence of overt subject pronouns, whereas weights closer to 0.0 disfavor overt forms.

In the results for person and number, the strongest predictor, second-person singular strongly favored (FW = 0.77) overt pronouns; this included both *tú* and *usted*, which was frequent in the data of individuals born before 1936. First-person singular also favored (FW = 0.65) overt forms, and third-person singular slightly favored (FW = 0.54) them. First-person plural (FW = 0.36) and third-person plural (FW = 0.20) disfavored overt forms. The results for coreference, the second strongest predictor, confirmed that switch reference favored overt subjects (FW = 0.62), and same reference disfavored them (FW = 0.38). Verb TMA favored overt subjects in the case of the imperfect indicative (FW = 0.58). There was a very small favorable influence for the present subjunctive (FW = 0.53), and the imperfect subjunctive was

Table 5.2. Logistic regression for the overall sample

Predictor	Factor	N	Weight	Factor	N	Weight
Person-number[a]	2 sg.	824	0.77	1 pl.	816	0.36
	1 sg.	3681	0.65	3 pl.	1170	0.20
	3 sg.	1814	0.54			
Coreference[a]	Switch	4584	0.62	Same	3721	0.38
TMA[a]	Imperf. ind.	1670	0.58	Pres. ind.	4196	0.46
	Pres. subj.	166	0.53	Pret.	2141	0.42
	Imperf. subj.	132	0.51			
Verb type[a]	Cop.	771	0.59	Intr.	2264	0.44
	Trans.	5270	0.47			
Polarity[a]	Pos.	7309	0.54	Neg.	996	0.46
Year of birth[b]	1885–1911	2648	0.52	1959–70	3394	0.49
	1929–36	2263	0.49			

a. $p < 0.0001$, b. $p < 0.05$, Grand mean 0.354; Input 0.297

essentially neutral (FW = 0.51). The present indicative (FW = 0.46) and preterite (FW = 0.42) somewhat disfavored overt pronouns. The results for verb type indicated that copulas (FW = 0.59) favored overt forms, but transitive (FW = 0.47) and intransitive verbs (FW = 0.44) disfavored them. Lastly, positive polarity slightly favored (FW = 0.54), and negative polarity slightly disfavored (FW = 0.46) overt pronouns. The results for year of birth indicated a small, nearly neutral (FW = 0.52) preference for the overt variant for the years 1885–1911. A separate analysis was carried out with the data from the year-of-birth groups in order to examine the ordering of significant predictors and strength of factors for each group. The results of the comparative analysis are described after the discussion of the logistic regression analysis of the entire sample.

Discussion: Full Sample

The frequency of overt pronouns for the entire sample was 35 percent, which is similar to the rates reported in Otheguy and Zentella's studies in New York City: 33 percent for Cuban newcomers (Otheguy, Zentella, and Livert 2007) and 38 percent for Cubans with varying lengths of residence (Otheguy and Zentella 2012). The frequency of overt pronouns according to year of birth—37 percent in the group born between 1885 and 1911, 34 percent in the one born between 1929 and 1936, and 35 percent for the group born between 1959 and 1970—are remarkably similar across groups and to the frequencies reported for Cuban speakers in New York City. The similarity of rates in different corpora, different time, and different regions provides strong evidence that the variation of null subjects and overt pronouns is stable in Cuban Spanish. These rates do not show the entire story, however; a comparison of constraint ordering and strength of factors is necessary to explore internal changes.

The constraint ranking from the regression analysis (table 5.3) confirmed similarities with the findings of studies on Caribbean and non-Caribbean Spanish. Person and number, which tends to be the strongest predictor (Alfaraz 2015; Bayley, Greer, and Holland 2013; Bayley and Pease-Álvarez 1997; Erker and Guy 2012; Martínez-Sanz 2011; Orozco 2015; Orozco and Guy 2008; Otheguy and Zentella 2012), was ranked first here, and it was also first for Caribbean newcomers in Otheguy, Zentella, and Livert (2007). Coreference ranked second here, as in other studies (Bayley, Greer, and Holland 2013; Bayley and Pease-Álvarez 1997; Erker

Table 5.3. Constraint ranking overall

Predictor	Significance
Person-number	$p < 0.0001$
Coreference	$p < 0.0001$
TMA	$p < 0.0001$
Verb type	$p < 0.0001$
Polarity	$p < 0.0001$
Year of birth	$p < 0.05$

and Guy 2012; Otheguy and Zentella 2012), and it was the second constraint for Caribbean newcomers in Otheguy, Zentella, and Livert (2007). The parallel with Otheguy, Zentella, and Livert (2007) extends to verb TMA, which was also ranked third for Caribbean newcomers. In all, the ranking of predictors found for the overall sample is in line with the findings of earlier studies.

The results for person and number, which had the strongest influence on the variation of subject pronouns, showed that the second-person singular favored overt forms most strongly, a tendency commonly found in Caribbean varieties (Alfaraz 2015; Ávila-Jiménez 1996; Cameron 1992; Flores-Ferrán 2004; Hochberg 1986; Holmquist 2012; Martínez-Sanz 2011; Otheguy and Zentella 2012; Otheguy, Zentella, and Livert 2007). The first-person singular also favored overt forms, as found for Puerto Rican and Dominican varieties (Alfaraz 2015; Ávila-Jiménez 1996; Cameron 1992; Holmquist 2012; Martínez-Sanz 2011). The strength of the first singular and third singular forms were reversed here compared to the Caribbean newcomer group in Otheguy, Zentella, and Livert (2007), for whom a small favorable influence was found for both the first- and third-person singular. The tendency for plurals to strongly disfavor overt pronouns was evident here for the first- and third-person plural forms (Ávila-Jiménez 1996; Bayley and Pease-Álvarez 1997; Cameron 1992; Enríquez 1984; Erker and Guy 2012; Martínez-Sanz 2011; Orozco and Guy 2008; Otheguy, Zentella, and Livert 2007; Silva-Corvalán 1994).

The results for coreference reflected the tendency for overt forms to be preferred when there is a switch in reference, but not when the reference is the same. This strong trend has been demonstrated for Cuban Spanish (Ávila-Shah 2000; Domínguez 2013), Caribbean varieties (Alfaraz 2015; Ávila-Jiménez 1996; Cameron 1992, 1995; Flores-Ferrán 2004; Hochberg 1986; Holmquist 2012; Martínez-Sanz 2011; Orozco 2015; Otheguy and Zentella 2012; Otheguy, Zentella, and Livert 2007), and non-Caribbean varieties (Bayley and 1997; Bayley, Greer, and Holland 2013; Cameron 1992; Enríquez 1984; Otheguy, Zentella, and Livert 2007; Prada Pérez 2009; Silva-Corvalán 1982, 1994). Thus, the strength of coreference and the direction of influence confirmed the anticipated pattern.

The predictors related to properties of the verb also reflected patterns observed in Caribbean Spanish. Although different approaches to coding TMA make direct comparisons across studies difficult, some conclusions can be drawn from a comparison with Dominican Spanish, for which Martínez-Sanz (2011) also reports that the imperfect favored (FW = 0.57) and the preterite disfavored (FW = 0.42) subject pronouns. More verb types were examined in Martínez-Sanz than the three studied here; nonetheless, another parallel can be drawn for the favoring effect of statives, including *ser*, on overt pronouns. Transitives and intransitives, both unergatives and transitives, had the opposite effect, disfavoring rather than favoring subject pronouns; although those results were influenced by other verb types that disfavored overt forms.

Social factors, including age, do not tend to surface as significant in studies on subject pronoun variation. Otheguy and Zentella (2012), for instance, did not find gender, age, or social status significant for varieties of Caribbean Spanish (Dominican, Puerto Rican, Cuban), although they were significant for the mainland varieties studied.

Considered as an indication of change in progress in apparent-time studies, age was not significant in Dominican Spanish (Martínez-Sanz 2011). However, studies on Puerto Rican Spanish found a significant difference when age groups were compared (Ávila-Jiménez 1996; Morales 1986), although the age distribution in Ávila-Jiménez (1996) indicates an age-graded pattern in which twenty- to forty-nine-year-olds used more overt pronouns (43 percent) than ten- to nineteen-year-olds (33 percent) and persons fifty and over (37 percent). Orozco and Guy (2008) similarly report a preference for overt forms among the oldest group (FW = 0.60) compared to twenty- to fifty-year-olds (FW = 0.49) and adolescents (FW = 0.40), which was attributed to the prestige of the mainland standard in the coastal Colombian region. The findings for year-of-birth groups showed a small significant influence on the variation, and a small preference for overt pronouns was evident in the group born at the earliest time. A comparison of the constraints in the three year-of-birth groups was conducted to examine the variation beyond the similar frequency rates.

Comparative Analysis: Year of Birth

Separate logistic regression analyses were carried out on the three year-of-birth groups to compare similarities and differences in the variation across time. Following methods in comparative sociolinguistics, three types of evidence are presented in tables 5.4 through 5.8: statistical significance, strength of the predictors, and constraint hierarchies (Poplack and Tagliamonte 2001; Tagliamonte 2011, 2013). For each predictor, the tables present the centered factor weights, the significance level, the overall rank, and the range, represented by the difference between the highest and lowest weights within the predictor, which indicates the strength of its influence on the variation. Because the social predictors—gender and social status—were not significant in the analyses carried out for each group, they are not discussed here. Thus, the tables below present the findings for the linguistic factors—person and number, coreference, TMA, verb type, and polarity.

The results for person and number (table 5.4) showed that it had the strongest influence on the variation of overt and null subjects, ranking first across groups. The pattern reported above for the overall analysis was replicated for each group. The difference in the range score was only two points in the three groups. The results for factors within the predictor indicated that second-person singular, corresponding to *tú* and *usted*, had a strong favoring influence on overt forms, and first-person singular also favored overt forms, but somewhat more strongly in the 1885–1911 (FW = 0.69) group than the other two groups, particularly the group born between 1929–36 (FW = 0.63). The third-person singular somewhat favored the overt variant equally in the 1885–1911 (FW = 0.56) and 1929–36 (FW = 0.56) groups, but its influence was neutral in the 1959–70 group (FW = 0.50). The first-person plural disfavored overt forms, but the effect was stronger in the 1885–1911 group (FW = 0.31) than in the groups born in 1929–36 (FW = 0.37) and 1959–70 (FW = 0.39). The third-person plural disfavored the overt variant equally in all three groups (FW = 0.20).

Coreference was the second strongest predictor of the variation for each year-of-birth group (table 5.5). In all three, switch reference favored and same reference

Table 5.4. Person and number by year of birth

	1885–1911	1929–36	1959–70
2nd sg	0.76	0.76	0.78
1st sg	0.69	0.63	0.65
3rd sg	0.56	0.56	0.50
1st pl	0.31	0.37	0.39
3rd pl	0.20	0.20	0.20
Sig.	$p < 0.0001$	$p < 0.0001$	$p < 0.0001$
Rank	1	1	1
Range	56	56	58

Table 5.5. Coreference by year of birth

	1885–1911	1929–36	1959–70
Switch	0.63	0.62	0.61
Same	0.37	0.38	0.39
Sig.	$p < 0.0001$	$p < 0.0001$	$p < 0.0001$
Rank	2	2	2
Range	26	24	22

disfavored overt pronouns. Although the factor weights were generally similar across the groups, the range scores indicated that the influence of coreference was slightly weaker in the 1959–70 group (Range 22) than the 1885–1911 group (Range 26). An analysis of the frequency rates of null subjects and subject pronouns with same and switch references (figure 5.1) indicated that in same-reference contexts the rate of overt subjects was higher for the 1885–1911 group (27.3 percent) than the 1929–36 (22.5 percent) and 1959–70 (25.8 percent) groups, and in switch-reference contexts there were more overt forms in the 1885–1911 group (49 percent) than the 1929–36 (42 percent) group and the 1959–70 group (41.6 percent). Thus, although the frequencies point to fewer overt forms in same-reference contexts, the strength of the predictor's influence on the variable appears to be declining.

The results for the TMA of the verb, coded for presence or absence of an overt subject pronoun and run in separate analyses for each year-of-birth group (table 5.6), revealed differences in the statistical significance, the rank, and the range of the predictor, as well as differences in the ordering of individual factors. The significance of TMA was greater in the first two groups ($p < 0.0001$), but it decreased considerably in the 1959–70 group ($p < 0.05$). The predictor's ranking dropped from third in the 1885–1911 group to fourth in the 1929–36 group and fifth in the 1959–70 one, which is reflected in the successively lower range score from 21 in the first group to 13 in the last. Compared to the factor weights of the earliest group, there was a difference in the 1929–36 group in the ordering of present subjunctive and imperfect subjunctive, and ordering differences in the 1959–70 group involved these as well as the

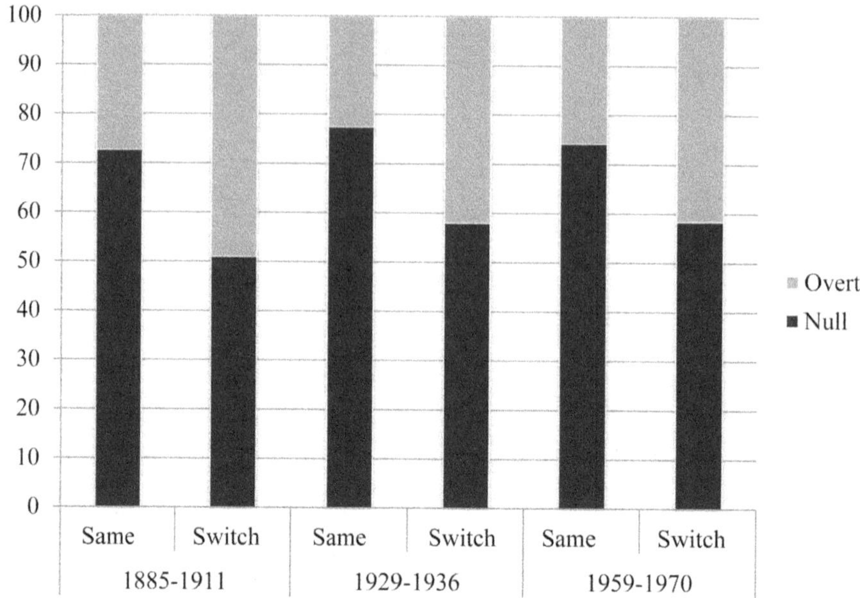

Figure 5.1. Rates of overt and null subjects in same and switch reference contexts

imperfect indicative and the present indicative. Across groups, the imperfect indicative favored the overt variant, although more strongly in the early group (FW = 0.61) than the later group (FW = 0.56). The present subjunctive favored overt forms more strongly in the later group (FW = 0.57) than the others, and the imperfect subjunctive favored overt forms in the middle group (FW = 0.57) but disfavored them in the later one (FW = 0.44). In all three groups, present indicative and preterite disfavored overt subject pronouns.

The verb type predictor proved to be different in the three groups when significance, ranking, and range were compared (table 5.7). Verb type was more significant in the analysis of the 1929–36 group ($p < 0.0001$) than the other two groups

Table 5.6. TMA by year of birth

	1885–1911	1929–36	1959–70
Imperfect indicative	0.61	0.58	0.56
Present subjunctive	0.53	0.51	0.57
Imperfect subjunctive	0.50	0.57	0.44
Present indicative	0.47	0.44	0.47
Preterite	0.40	0.42	0.45
Sig.	$p < 0.0001$	$p < 0.0001$	$p < 0.05$
Rank	3	4	5
Range	21	16	13

Table 5.7. Verb type by year of birth

	1885–1911	1929–36	1959–70
Copula	0.57	0.64	0.57
Intransitive	0.47	0.40	0.49
Transitive	0.46	0.46	0.44
Sig.	p < 0.01	p < 0.0001	p < 0.01
Rank	4	3	3
Range	11	18	13

(p < 0.01). In the 1885–1911 group, verb type ranked fourth among the predictors, but in the later groups it ranked third. The influence of verb type, as indicated by the range score, was stronger in the 1929–36 group (18) than the earlier (11) and later (13) ones. In all three groups, the copula favored overt subjects, with the same favoring weight in the 1885–1911 (FW = 0.57) and 1959–70 (FW = 0.57) groups, and a stronger weight in the 1929–36 (FW = 0.64) group. Transitives were slightly disfavored across the three groups, with the same weight in the first two groups (FW = 0.46), and a small difference in the last (FW = 0.44). In the first and last groups, intransitives had similar weights indicating a slightly disfavoring effect for the 1885–1911 group (FW = 0.47) and a generally neutral one for the 1959–70 group (FW = 0.49). In the middle group, however, intransitives were more strongly disfavored (FW = 0.40). The order of factors was flipped in the 1929–36 group, and this predictor was more significant and had a stronger influence. These differences, however, did not persist in the group born between 1959 and 1970.

The findings for polarity in the three year-of-birth groups (table 5.8) showed similarities in the factor weights. Positive polarity favored the overt variant somewhat and negative polarity disfavored it. The predictor was more significant in the later two groups (p < 0.01) than the early one (p < 0.05). Its rank increased to fourth in the 1959–70 group from fifth in the other groups. Overall, the influence of polarity, though significant, was small. Polarity was found to have different effects on the variation of first-person singular *yo* with cognitive and noncognitive verbs in Colombian Spanish (Travis and Torres Cacoullos 2012); the direction of influence was the opposite of these findings, because negative polarity favored the overt pronoun *yo*. These results indicate that positive polarity favored overt subject pronouns in each of the three groups of Cubans studied.

Table 5.8. Polarity by year of birth

	1885–1911	1929–36	1959–70
Positive	0.54	0.54	0.55
Negative	0.46	0.46	0.45
Sig.	p < 0.05	p < 0.01	p < 0.01
Rank	5	5	4
Range	8	8	10

The comparison of significant predictors according to year of birth revealed some differences in the significance, strength, and ordering of predictors. The constraint rankings for each group, with level of significance indicated, are shown in table 5.9. Person and number ranked first and coreference ranked second across groups. Differences appeared in the last three predictors: verb TMA, verb type, and polarity. Verb TMA was stronger in the 1885–1911 group but it lost strength as year of birth increased, so that it dropped from third to last in the ranking. Verb type increased to third position in the 1929–36 group and remained in that position in the 1959–70 group. Finally, polarity rose from last position in the ranking in the first two groups to fifth position, before TMA, in the last group. Apart from person and number and coreference, which were strong in all three groups, the predictors were not as strong for the group born between 1959 and 1970 as they were for the other groups. The differences found in the comparative analysis of year-of-birth groups suggest changes in the constraints over time.

Table 5.9. Constraint ranking by year of birth

1885–1911	1929–36	1959–70
Person-number[a]	Person-number[a]	Person-number[a]
Coreference[a]	Coreference[a]	Coreference[a]
TMA[a]	Verb type[a]	Verb type[b]
Verb typeв	TMA[a]	Polarity[b]
Polarity[c]	Polarity[b]	TMA[c]

a. $p < 0.0001$, b. $p < 0.01$, c. $p < 0.05$

Discussion: Year of Birth

The comparative analysis of the variation in year-of-birth groups showed that the person and number predictor, commonly found to exert a stronger influence than other linguistic predictors on the variation of overt pronouns and null subjects, was ranked first in the constraint rankings for each group and had similar levels of significance and range scores across groups. The factor weights were generally similar too, although small differences were found in the third-person singular, which favored overt forms in the first two groups but was neutral in the last, and in the first-person plural, which had a stronger disfavoring effect in the 1885–1911 group. In general, however, the comparison of person and number at the time dimensions represented by the year-of-birth groups indicated that it was stable and was the primary constraint on the variation of overt subject pronouns and null subjects.

The comparison of coreference by year of birth confirmed that it had the same level of significance and constraint ranking in all three groups. Mirroring the results commonly found in studies of the variable, a preference was found for overt subjects in switch-reference contexts and null subjects in same-reference contexts. The range scores suggested a slightly smaller influence in the 1959–70 group compared to the two earlier groups, although a comparison of the rate distribution by context showed that overt pronouns were more frequent in same-reference contexts in the 1885–1911 group than the 1929–36 and 1959–70 groups. Nonetheless, a smaller effect for coreference was observed in the middle and later groups, suggesting possible, although perhaps minor, adjustments in the influence of the coreference constraint over time. Coreference has been found in some studies to have less influence on the expression of pronouns and null subjects among bilingual second- and third-generation speakers of Spanish (Flores-Ferrán 2004; Silva-Corvalán 1994), but other studies found no significant effect (Ávila-Shah 2000). For example, a comparison of Cuban monolinguals in Cuba and late bilinguals in Miami found no significant differences in the use of overt pronouns with and without topic shifts (Domínguez 2013).

When verb TMA was compared in the year-of-birth groups, differences were found in the predictor's significance, rank, and range, as well as the ordering of factors in the middle and later time groups. In the later time group, TMA was less significant and its rank fell from third to fifth. The range score dropped from 21 in the earliest time group to 13 in the later. These differences, along with some changes in the strength of individual factors, indicate a weakening of the influence of TMA and changes in the reorganization of constraints on the variation of overt and null subjects over time.

The comparative analysis of verb type showed differences in its significance, ranking, and range. Its significance was greater in the 1929–36 group when compared to the 1885–1911 group, and its strength on the variation increased, as indicated by a larger range score and an increase from fourth to third position in the hierarchy. Furthermore, intransitives were more strongly disfavored in the 1929–36 group compared to the 1885–1911 group. Differences in the level of significance and the influence of intransitives did not carry over into the later group (1959–70), although verb type continued to be ranked third. The increase in the strength of the predictor was nonetheless linked to the weakening influence of TMA on the variation.

The findings from the comparative analysis pointed out the similarities and some of the main differences in the ranking of constraints in the three year-of-birth groups. The two constraints at the top of the hierarchy, person and number and coreference, exerted a similarly strong influence throughout the time periods represented. As described above, no evidence of change was found for person and number, which showed, across the groups, a consistent pattern commonly found in variation studies (Alfaraz 2015; Bayley and Pease-Álvarez 1997; Bayley, Greer, and Holland 2013; Erker and Guy 2012; Martínez-Sanz 2011; Orozco and Guy 2008; Otheguy and Zentella 2012; Otheguy, Zentella, and Livert 2007). Coreference appeared to be undergoing slight weakening, but its overall effect on the variation continued to be strong, consistent with studies on Caribbean and non-Caribbean varieties (Alfaraz 2015; Ávila-Jiménez 1996; Ávila-Shah 2000; Cameron 1992, 1995; Flores-Ferrán 2004; Hochberg 1986; Holmquist 2012; Martínez-Sanz 2011; Otheguy and Zentella 2012; Otheguy, Zentella, and Livert 2007; Prada Pérez 2009; Silva-Corvalán 1994). The last three predictors in the hierarchy—TMA, verb type, and polarity—shifted in the ranking from the earliest to the latest time. TMA experienced weakening, to the extent that in the 1959–70 group it was the last predictor in the hierarchy and had a considerably lower significance level. In contrast, verb type strengthened in the middle and last groups; its significance level, however, was lower in the last group compared to the middle and early groups, suggesting that the influence of the constraint is decreasing over time.

In sum, the comparison of three time periods represented by year of birth shows the constant strength of the predictors at the top of the hierarchy and highlights changes and weakening of the other predictors in the group born between 1959 and 1970. Change was not evident in the proportion of overt subject pronouns over time, because the frequency rates were generally stable for Cubans born between 1885 and 1970 and in line with the rates reported for Cuban Spanish in Otheguy, Zentella, and Livert (2007). Nonetheless, differences observed in the constraint hierarchies indicate changes over time in the variable grammar (Poplack and Tagliamonte 2001; Tagliamonte 2011, 2013). It will be necessary to examine further the predictors that appear to be changing—TMA and verb type—to determine whether their effect on the variation continues to change. The study of subject variation over time in Cuban Spanish highlighted the fact that despite differences and changes in the variable hierarchy the predictors that constrain the variation tend to be similar across varieties of Spanish.

Conclusion

This research studied subject pronoun variation in Cuban Spanish with 8,305 tokens extracted from the speech of fifty-seven Cubans born in Cuba in the years between 1885 and 1970. A logistic regression analysis showed that person and number, coreference, verb TMA, syntactic verb type, and polarity were significant predictors. The results for linguistic predictors were in line with the findings of other studies: person and number had the strongest effect on the variation, followed by coreference, TMA, verb type, and polarity. Of the social predictors studied, gender and social status were not significant, but year of birth, included as a fixed predictor, had a small, significant effect. The findings showed that subject pronouns were favored by the earliest years of birth, between 1885 and 1911. A comparison of results from separate logistic regression analyses on three groups, defined by year of birth, showed similarities in the predictors person and number and coreference, but differences in TMA, polarity, and verb type, suggesting changes over time in the conditioning of the variation. These constraints should be investigated in future studies on Cuban Spanish.

References

Alfaraz, G. G. 2015. "Variation of Overt and Null Subject Pronouns in the Spanish of Santo Domingo." In *Subject Pronoun Expression in Spanish: A Cross-Dialectal Perspective*, edited by A. M. Carvalho, R. Orozco, and N. L. Shin, 3–16. Washington, DC: Georgetown University Press.

Ávila-Jiménez, B. I. 1996. "Subject Pronoun Expression in Puerto Rican Spanish: A Sociolinguistic, Morphological, and Discourse Analysis." PhD diss., Cornell University.

Ávila-Shah, B. I. 2000. "Discourse Connectedness in Caribbean Spanish." In *Research on Spanish in the United States: Linguistic Issues and Challenges*, edited by A. Roca, 238–51. Somerville, MA: Cascadilla Press.

Bayley, R., K. Greer, and C. Holland. 2013. "Lexical Frequency and Syntactic Variation: A Test of a Linguistic Hypothesis." *University of Pennsylvania Working Papers in Linguistics* 19 (2): 21–30.

Bayley, R., and L. Pease-Álvarez. 1997. "Null Pronoun Variation in Mexican-Descent Children's Narrative Discourse." *Language Variation and Change* 9 (3): 349–71.

Cameron, R. 1992. "Pronominal and Null Subject Variation in Spanish: Constraints, Dialects, and Functional Compensation." PhD diss., University of Pennsylvania.

———. 1993. "Ambiguous Agreement, Functional Compensation, and Nonspecific *Tú* in the Spanish of San Juan, Puerto Rico, and Madrid, Spain." *Language Variation and Change* 5 (3): 305–34.

———. 1995. "The Scope and Limits of Switch Reference as a Constraint on Pronominal Subject Expression." *Hispanic Linguistics* 6:1–28.

Cameron, R., and N. Flores-Ferrán. 2004. "Perseveration of Subject Expression across Regional Dialects of Spanish." *Spanish in Context* 1 (1): 41–65.

Domínguez, L. 2013. *Understanding Interfaces: Second Language Acquisition and First Language Attrition of Spanish Subject Realization and Word Order Variation*. Amsterdam: John Benjamins Publishing.

Enríquez, E. V. 1984. *El Pronombre Personal Sujeto En La Lengua Española Hablada En Madrid*. Madrid: Consejo Superior de Investigaciones Científicas.

Erker, D., and G. R. Guy. 2012. "The Role of Lexical Frequency in Syntactic Variability: Variable Subject Personal Pronoun Expression in Spanish." *Language* 88 (3): 526–57.

Flores-Ferrán, N. 2004. "Spanish Subject Personal Pronoun Use in New York City Puerto Ricans: Can We Rest the Case of English Contact?" *Language Variation and Change* 16 (1): 49–73.

———. 2007. "A Bend in the Road: Subject Personal Pronoun Expression in Spanish after 30 Years of Sociolinguistic Research." *Language and Linguistics Compass* 1 (6): 624–52.

Hochberg, J. G. 1986. "Functional Compensation for /s/ Deletion in Puerto Rican Spanish." *Language* 62 (3): 609–21.

Holmquist, J. 2012. "Frequency Rates and Constraints on Subject Personal Pronoun Expression: Findings From the Puerto Rican Highlands." *Language Variation and Change* 24 (2): 203–20.

Lipski, J. 1996. "Patterns of Pronominal Evolution in Cuban-American Bilinguals." In *Spanish in Contact: Issues in Bilingualism*, edited by A. Roca, and J. B. Jensen, 159–86. Somerville, MA: Cascadilla Press.

Martínez-Sanz, C. 2011. "Null and Overt Subjects in a Variable System: The Case of Dominican Spanish." PhD diss., University of Ottawa.

Morales, A. 1986. "La Expresión Del Sujeto Pronominal En El Español De Puerto Rico." In *Gramáticas En Contacto: Análisis Sintácticos Sobre El Español De Puerto Rico*, edited by A. Morales, 89–100. San Juan: Editorial Playor.

Orozco, R. 2015. "Pronominal Variation in Colombian Costeño Spanish." In *Subject Pronoun Expression in Spanish: A Cross-Dialectal Perspective*, edited by A. M. Carvalho, R. Orozco, and N. Lapidus Shin, 17–38. Washington, DC: Georgetown University Press.

Orozco, R., and G. Guy. 2008. "El Uso Variable De Los Pronombres Sujetos: ¿Qué Pasa en la Costa Caribe Colombiana?" *Selected Proceedings of the 4th Workshop on Spanish Sociolinguistics*, edited by M. Westmoreland and J. A. Thomas, 70–80. Somerville, MA: Cascadilla Proceedings Project.

Otheguy, R., and A. C. Zentella. 2012. *Spanish in New York: Language Contact, Dialectal Leveling, and Structural Continuity*. Oxford: Oxford University Press.

Otheguy, R., A. C. Zentella, and D. Livert. 2007. "Language and Dialect Contact in Spanish in New York: Toward the Formation of a Speech Community." *Language* 83 (4): 770–802.

Poplack, S., and S. A. Tagliamonte. 2001. *African American English in the Diaspora: Tense and Aspect*. Malden, MA: Blackwell.

Prada Pérez, A. de. 2009. "Subject Expression in Minorcan Spanish: Consequences of Contact with Catalan." PhD diss., Pennsylvania State University.

Silva-Corvalán, C. 1982. "Subject Expression and Placement in Mexican-American Spanish." In *Spanish in the United States: Sociolinguistic Aspects*, edited by J. Amastae and L. Elías-Olivares, 93–120. Cambridge: Cambridge University Press.

———. 1994. *Language Contact and Change: Spanish in Los Angeles*. Oxford: Oxford University Press.

Tagliamonte, S. A. 2013. "Comparative Sociolinguistics." In *The Handbook of Language Variation and Change*, edited by J. K. Chambers, and N. Schilling-Estes, 128–56. Malden, MA: John Wiley and Sons.

———. 2011. *Variationist Sociolinguistics: Change, Observation, Interpretation*. Hoboken: Wiley-Blackwell.

Travis, C. E., and R. Torres Cacoullos. 2012. "What Do Subject Pronouns Do in Discourse? Cognitive, Mechanical and Constructional Factors in Variation." *Cognitive Linguistics* 23 (4): 711–48.

6

Cuban Spanish: Is It a Null Subject Parameter Dialect?

LUIS A. ORTIZ LÓPEZ
University of Puerto Rico

ASHLEE DAUPHINAIS
Ohio State University

HÉCTOR APONTE ALEQUÍN
University of Puerto Rico

CARIBBEAN SPANISH HAS TRADITIONALLY been understood as the varieties of Spanish spoken in Cuba, Puerto Rico, and the Dominican Republic (e.g., Lipski 1994; López Morales 1992; Zamora and Guitart 1982). However, from a linguistic standpoint, Caribbean Spanish also extends to coastal Colombia, Venezuela, Panama, and Mexico (Claes and Ortiz 2011; Lipski 1994; Rodríguez Cadena 2009). Independent of its diatopic extension, the majority of studies have been based on data from Puerto Rico, the Dominican Republic, Miami, Venezuela, and Barranquilla, Colombia. This has been more so in regards to natural data examining syntactic and morphosyntactic issues, with only a handful of recent studies (Cuza and Frank 2011; Dorta, Díaz Cabrera, and Hernández 2015; Dauphinais and Ortiz López 2016; Fúster 2012; Pascual y Cabo 2013). In the past decades, the overwhelming majority of research on Cuban Spanish (CS) has been limited to the Cuban American community in Miami, with little data originating from the island of Cuba itself, and is focused on phonology and intonation, leaving a dearth of information about this dialect in all other aspects of linguistics. Furthermore, the data from previous studies are principally based on acceptability judgment tasks (AJTs) and thus lack empirical evidence, especially from Cubans on the island. In other words, studies on the syntax of CS are limited. The studies available mainly deal with overt or null pronouns and with data from Cubans in New York (Otheguy and Zentella 2012). Recently, researchers have conducted work on word order and pro/PRO (null or explicit pronoun + infinitive verb; Aponte Alequín and Ortiz López 2015; Erker et al., this volume).

In this chapter, we investigate the syntax of CS, with special attention to three properties of the null subject pronoun (NSP)—overt or null pronominal subjects (PSs), syntactic order (subject verb versus verb subject [SV/VS]), and pro versus PRO in infinitival clauses (C2)—using naturally occurring data from the island. Our ultimate goal is identifying the linguistic restrictions that govern each one of these properties, as part of the dialectal microvariation in Caribbean Spanish. The main research questions in this study are the following:

1. What is the distribution of these three properties of the NSP in CS?
2. What linguistic factors restrict these three properties of the NSP in CS?
3. What hierarchical role does the syntactic-semantic-pragmatic interface play in these properties of NSP in CS?

This chapter is structured as follows: First we'll present a review of previous literature and arguments regarding these properties in Spanish and, in particular, Caribbean Spanish, and the debate surrounding the syntactic-semantic and syntactic-pragmatic interfaces. Then we'll discuss the methodology of the study and presents the results. And finally we'll present the study's discussion and conclusions.

The NSP and Caribbean Spanish

According to the minimalist model, the NSP is restricted by the Extended Projection Principle (EPP; e.g., Chomsky 1995; D'Introno 2001). The EPP proposes that each sentence in the exteriorized language (E) must have a subject, and that the variation between languages rests on whether or not the subject pronoun is phonetically produced. Verbal agreement [+ strong] legitimizes a phonetically null pronoun as it occurs in Spanish, Italian, Portuguese, and other languages.[1] Other languages require a phonetically explicit pronoun, such as English, French, Haitian Creole, and others. In pro-drop languages, it is also possible to have flexible subject placements, the absence of null pleonastic pronouns, the absence of effects of COMP + trace, and the extraction of subjects over long distances (Dowty 1991; Jaeggli 1982; Rizzi 1982). The NSP, therefore, separates languages into distinct categories according to the syntactic patterns of their sentences. It has been used as a starting point for generativist, variationist, and acquisitionist proposals.

Spanish has been traditionally classified by grammatical descriptions as a pro-drop language, with free variation in terms of subject-verb order (SV/VS), PRO with [– fin verb], and no expletive pronouns. Caribbean Spanish, however, has been documented to challenge certain properties of the NSP (Camacho 2013; Carvalho, Orozco, and Shin 2015; Claes 2011; Lipski 1997 Martínez-Sanz 2011; Pöll 2015), especially those related to the overt and null PSs (Morales 1997, 1999; Otheguy and Zentella 2012), the SV/VS order (Ortiz López 2010), present expletives (Martínez-Sanz 2011; Toribio 1994), and preverbal subject pronouns with infinitives [{pro/SD}V -fin] (Aponte Alequín and Ortiz López 2015; Suñer 1983, 2001, 2003). According to these studies, Caribbean Spanish has demonstrated a tendency toward a greater presence of overt pronouns, a more fixed SV order, and pro with [– FLEX verb].

The overt or null pronouns property, however, has been the focus of many studies on Caribbean Spanish (e.g., Aponte Alequín and Ortiz López 2015; Camacho 2013; Claes and Ortiz López 2011; Martínez-Sanz 2011; Orozco 2015; Otheguy and Zentella 2012; Pöll 2015). These previous works have shown that PS is optional, and that optionality is associated with different linguistic factors. These factors respond to syntactic-semantic-pragmatic interfaces. The statistical analysis from these studies shows a ranking of the effects of these factors: syntactic (grammatical persons > the first person singular and second person singular, singular pronoun forms, clause type); semantic (nonspecific pronouns, such as */uno/* [one] and */tú/* [you], verb semantics); and pragmatic (nonfocal, noncontrastive and nonambiguous contexts). These factors present the highest rates of appearance. Regarding CS from the island, we do not have evidence about these factors, but our predictions suggest the same restrictions (see hypothesis 1).

On the other hand, word order and pro/PRO properties have scarcely been studied in these dialects. Word order is linked to the lexical-semantic class of the verb (Cardinaletti 1997; Roggia 2011) and pragmatic focus (Sorace 2003, 2005, 2011). In Spanish, a subject-verb-object (SVO) language, verb type has been said to reflect on the position of the subject: unergative verbs, or 'pure intransitives,' which have a deep subject or agent properties—such as *sonreír* (smile), *patinar* (skate), *trabajar* (work), *llorar* (cry)—favor SV, whereas unaccusative verbs, which have theme or patient properties (i.e., object-like)—such as *llegar* (arrive), *florecer* (bloom), *quedar* (remain), *faltar* (lack)—tend to be VS. These lexical-semantic differences present structural consequences that are manifested in many languages through different linguistic resources, such as lexicon, morphology, and syntax. Opposing the unaccusative hypothesis, Sorace (2011) proposes that SV/VS variation is conditioned by pragmatic focus. Also, she proposes the Split Intransitivity Hierarchy, defined by aspectual notions, in which different types of verbs are gradiently classified as more unaccusative or more unergative according to the degree of agentivity of the verb. According to this proposal, the differences between unaccusative and unergative verbs can be reduced to telicity and agentivity, which would alter the syntax of the Split Intransitivity Hierarchy. This sensibility to contextual or compositional factors is also related to the distance between the verb and its head: stative and nonagentive verbs would be the most affected, and, therefore, most susceptible to syntactic changes, such as word order (Sorace 2011).

It is said that Spanish word order allows for certain free variation, contrary to other languages (e.g., English, French, Creole), in particular in the SV position (Bosque and Gutiérrez-Rexach 2009), as in example 6.1.

Example 6.1.

a. ***María** se fue a la fiesta.*
María refl. went. 3sg to the party
María went to the party.

b. *Se fue* ***María*** *a la fiesta.*
refl. went. 3sg María to the party
María went to the party.

The variation found in Spanish has been associated with semantic factors related to the verb and pragmatic uses of focus (Bosque and Gutiérrez-Rexach 2009; Silva-Corvalán 1982). Nevertheless, recent research on this topic has documented Caribbean Spanish (and Brazilian Portuguese) as distancing themselves from previous descriptions of other dialects, given that they present a greater tendency toward SV order without producing substantial semantic or pragmatic changes (Bentivoglio and Weber 1986; Camacho 2012; Cameron 1993; Morales 1999; Ortiz López 2011; Pöll 2015). This tendency toward a more fixed SV order has been documented in questions (example 6.2), subordinate clauses (example 6.3), infinitives with expressed subjects (example 6.4), and imperatives (example 6.5).

Example 6.2. Fixed SV order in questions

a. *¿Qué quiero* ***Ø****?*
b. *¿Qué quiero* ***yo****?*
c. *¿Qué* ***yo*** *quiero?*
d. ***Yo****, ¿qué quiero?*
'What do **I** want?'

Example 6.3. Fixed SV order in subordinate clauses

a. *Mis padres saben que viene* ***mi hermano*** *mañana.*
b. *Mis padres saben que* ***mi hermano*** *viene mañana.*
My parents know that **my brother** is coming tomorrow.

Example 6.4. Fixed SV order in infinitives with expressed subjects

a. *Al salir* ***Ø*** *de casa, empezó a llover.*
b. *Al salir* ***nosotros*** *de casa, empezó a llover.*
c. *Al* ***nosotros*** *salir de casa, empezó a llover.*
Upon **Ø** leaving home, it started to rain.

Example 6.5. Fixed SV order with imperatives

a. *¡Llámame* ***Ø****,* por favor*!*
b. *¡Llámame* ***tú****, por favor!*
c. *¡****Tú****, llámame, por favor!*
'**Ø** Call me, please!'

Also, this categorization is manifested in different ways in some dialects, such as those found in Caribbean Spanish, which have shown greater rigidity in SV order. Both the flexibility found in other non-Caribbean varieties of Spanish and the decreased frequency of variation in Caribbean Spanish have received little attention. Eliciting discursive contexts, such as those in examples 6.2–6.5, present methodological difficulties due to a scarcity of quantitative data from spontaneous speech in these different contexts. In the last few years, however, research has been renewed in studies that examine grammaticality judgment tasks (Ortiz López 2010) that look at interrogative (Comínguez 2013) and infinitive clauses with preverbal subjects (Aponte Alequín and Ortiz López 2015). The results from these studies show a high acceptability rate of these fixed SV structures, as in example 6.2c and example 6.4c, independent from the semantic class of the verb (unergative or unaccusative). The results also demonstrate a loss of semantic and pragmatic restrictions to organizing word order in Spanish into a hierarchy. Furthermore, they show that despite SV word order being more frequent (see hypothesis 2), there are contexts in which sentences without inversion are not acceptable, such as in example 6.6a.

Example 6.6.

a. *¿Qué **los padres de la familia que vive al lado** quieren?
b. ¿Qué quieren **los padres de la familia que vive al lado**?
What do **the parents of the family who lives next-door** want?

Regarding the third property, as in example 6.4, the panorama is also complicated according to the EPP model. Spanish is subjected to a microparameter (which predicts the secondary derivations whenever the subject position is filled): the features of time, person, and number in T (tense) must be checked, with phonetic materialization in the verb that generates them (Bosque and Gutiérrez-Rexach 2009; D'Introno 2001; Poole 2011). If this principle is not fulfilled, there would not be a clear interpretation of the speech in question. There are, however, semantic restrictions that allow for the occurrence of this type of structure in very controlled environments, such as the situation of verbs with generic interpretation (Van der Wurff 2007), as in example 6.7.

Example 6.7.

$[$*Trotar*$]_{C1}$ $[$*es bueno para la salud*$]_{C2}$.
Running is good to be healthy.

A sentence without inflection would result in a structure without a clear interpretation, since it would contain unchecked categorical features in violation of the Principle of Syntactic Reconstruction (Bosque and Gutiérrez-Rexach 2009), as in example 6.8.

Example 6.8.

a. **Ella saber mucho.*
She to know much.
b. **Yo tener hambre.*
I to have hungry.

In Spanish, there are environments that allow for the lack of verbal inflection in one of the two clauses with a generic interpretation. Grammars have traditionally classified this type of clause, where C2 appears with a {pro/SD} + V [– fin], as *ungrammatical* (Bosque and Gutiérrez-Rexach 2009). These structures are produced in Caribbean

Spanish, as in examples 6.9 and 6.10, and have been described as "strange" since the early research done by Henríquez Ureña (1940) and Navarro Tomás (1948), among others. Despite this, they coexist alongside verbal forms with inflection, described traditionally as part of the language and in variation with the indicative (example 6.9b) and the subjunctive (example 6.10b).

Example 6.9.

a. **Esa misma que tú ves ahí... la dueña del taxi... yo le ofrezco* ***yo ayudarla*** *y ella no quiere.* (M, Cuba, 29)
That person you see there... the taxi owner... I offer **(I)** her **help**, and she doesn't want.
b. *Esa misma que tú ves ahí... la dueña del taxi... yo le ofrezco* ***ayuda*** *y ella no quiere.* (M, Cuba, 29)
That person you see there... the taxi owner... I offer her **help**, and she doesn't want.

Example 6.10.

a. **Todo lo que tú pagaste* ***por tú llegar*** *aquí... eso mismo es lo que sucede.* (F, Cuba, 57)
All that you paid for you to **get** here... that's exactly what happens
b. *Todo lo que tú pagaste para que* ***llegaras*** *aquí... eso mismo es lo que sucede.* (F, Cuba, 57)
All that you paid to **get** here... that's exactly what happens.

The presence of the pronominal (and lexical) subject has scarcely been studied as a factor that could impact infinitive-indicative-subjunctive variation (Aponte Alequín 2008, 2014; De Mello 1995; Kempchinsky 2009; Morales 1999; Serrano 2005). Recently, Aponte Alequín and Ortiz López (2015) have considered the modality scope of this type of variation (infinitive-indicative), regarding, as independent factors, the subject (PRO versus explicit pro, person, coreferentiality, and discourse-actant marking), the semantic class of the verb of the matrix clause, and the preposition. The results demonstrate that Caribbean dialects, including CS, accept and use infinitive verbal forms with overt subjects with greater frequency than other varieties of Spanish (e.g., Peru and Mexico). These acceptations and uses are motivated by semantic and pragmatic restrictions (see hypothesis 3).

As mentioned earlier, previous work on SV/VS order (examples 6.1–6.3) and [PRO/pro +/– fin] (examples 6.4, 6.9, and 6.10) is limited and shows little natural empirical evidence from Spanish and its dialectal varieties, particularly Cuban Spanish. It is therefore necessary to investigate the nature of these three properties in this dialect and the factors that govern their variation. From this overview, we assume that these three properties are related to overt subject pronouns before finite [+ fin] or nonfinite [– fin] verbs. Given these proposals, we present the following hypotheses:

Hypothesis 1: The subject pronoun in CS has been extended beyond contrastive and ambiguous contexts by semantic and pragmatic influences from subject pronouns.

Hypothesis 2: The SV order in CS is imposed as a consequence of the weakening of the semantic and pragmatic functions of the subject.
Hypothesis 3: CS favors pro before V [– fin] in CS by semantic and pragmatic restrictions.

The Study

This study is based on data collected in situ in Cuba between 2013 and 2014. The data collection took place primarily in the province of Havana and consisted of a sample of forty-three Cuban participants, residents of Havana. The data were obtained following the snowball sampling technique. Factors such as age, gender, level of formal instruction, province of origin, and time of residence in Havana, were taken into account; however, such factors will not form part of this first approach to analyzing the data. We followed the model of the sociolinguistic interview, based on open topics, such as daily life in Cuba, weather, sports, food and diet, and so on. The interviews had an average duration of thirty minutes (Labov 1966; Tagliamonte 2006, 2011) and were later transcribed and coded. Given the complexity of working with the [pro/PRO +/– fin] property, we employed grammaticality judgment tasks. Table 6.1 summarizes the participants of the study according to each property.

The envelope of variation was determined by extracting all the expressed subjects in the corpus and then examined and coded for (1) overt and null pronouns, (2) SV/VS word order, and (3) [pro/PRO +/– fin]. All of the extracted tokens were coded for the following linguistic factors: type of subject pronoun and lexical subject, clause type, semantic class of the verb, semantic features of the subject, and type of subordinate proposition subjects +/– actant (in the results section, the dependent and independent variables will be presented). We excluded idiomatic expressions,

Table 6.1. Participants and instruments, according to NSP properties

NSP Properties	Methods/ instruments	Participants	Social Factors
(1) *Overt/Null pronouns*	semi-spontaneous interviews	12	8F 4M 28–65 years university level
(2) *Word order SV/VS*	semi-spontaneous interviews	43	26F 17M 28–65 years 5 pre-university 38 university level
(3) *pro/PRO ± fin*	semi-spontaneous interviews	12	8F 4M 28–65 years university level
	grammaticality judgments questionnaire	24	6F 6M (21–30 years) 6F 6M (50 years or more) university level

such as *¡Ya tú sabes!* (You know it!), *¿Qué sé yo?* ('What do I know?' or 'How would I know?'), *¡Yo qué sé!* (What do I know?); structures with impersonal verbs, such as *Hace frío* (It's cold); constructions with impersonal *se*, such as *No se podía hacer* (It couldn't be done); reported speech from other persons; and psych verbs, since they present a different type of structure that deserves its own analysis. For the pro/PRO property, the interviews offered few tokens; therefore, it was necessary to turn to a questionnaire, as in example 6.11. The Likert scale from –2 to 2 measures the judged acceptability of the structure (–2 and –1 are unacceptability values and 1 and 2 are acceptability values).

Example 6.11.

A Bryan se le va el día en un dos por tres. Se levanta al mediodía y siente que, a las 3:00 de la tarde, ya no puede hacer ninguna diligencia. Si se despertara más temprano, tendría más tiempo para hacer sus cosas [– *actante*].
Bryan's days fly by he gets up at noon and feels like, by 3 o'clock in the afternoon, he can't run any more errands. If he were to wake up earlier, he would have more time to do his things. [– actant].

a. *Todo se le atrasa por* [*preposición*] *él* [*sujeto patente, 3s*] *no madrugar* [*infinitivo*].
Everything is delayed by [preposition] he [overt subject 3rd person] not getting up early [infinitive].
–2 –1 0 1 2

b. *Todo se le atrasa porque* [*preposición*] *él* [*sujeto patente, 3s*] *no madruga* [*indicativo*].
Everything is delayed him because [preposition] he [overt subject 3rd person] doesn't get up early [indicative].
–2 –1 0 1 2

On the premise that each item from the questionnaire delimits the discursive sequence without scratching on hypercontextualization (Brown and Yule 1993; Cornips and Corrigan 2005; Terkourafi 2011), the subject was identified as +/– actant in the discursive tense and was integrated in the present continuum T. These semantic features are reflected in the first option with a C2 [– fin] and in the second one with a C2 [+ fin], with V2 in the present indicative. Both C1s contain declarative isosemy ([+ declaration] C1- C2).

The data, both naturally occurring and from the questionnaire, were then subjected to a multivariate analysis using GoldVarb X (Sankoff, Tagliamonte, and Smith 2005) to calculate the simultaneous conditioning of the independent factors on the variable phenomenon (Tagliamonte 2011). For each independent factor (overt or null, SV/VS, and pro/PRO), it calculates the probability or factor weight represented by coefficients ranging from 0.0 to 1.0. A factor weight greater than 0.5 implies that the independent variable favors the dependent variable (table 6.2), while a value less than 0.5 implies disfavor. We expect the order of values within each factor group to reveal a hierarchy from which the impact of individual factors within a factor group can be determined. By examining the range found within the factor groups, each group's relative impact on the variation can be measured as well.

Results

In this section, we analyze the results of the three properties, according to the participants and the instruments described above.

Null and Overt Pronouns

For this first property, there were twelve participants and 1,000 tokens (instances of declarative sentences with an expressed subject), for an average of 83 tokens per participant. Table 6.2 presents the rate of the null and overt pronouns. A total of 697 tokens (69 percent) were null pronouns, as in example 6.12, and 303 (30 percent) were overt pronouns, as in example 6.13.

Table 6.2. Null and overt pronouns, according to independent factors

Default: Overt Pronoun		**Weight**	**%**	**N**
Pronoun Type	*tú/usted/ustedes* (you, sing. and plural)	**0.554**	31%	79
	yo (I)	**0.562**	24%	120
	él (he) / *ella* (she)	0.362	42%	42
	ellos/ellas (they)	0.481	25%	25
	nosotros (we)	0.432	35%	14
	uno (one)	0.143	**71%**	23
Range = 419				
Context	contrast	**0.059**	**85%**	28
	ambiguity	0.023	89%	93
	focus	0.014	96%	121
	redundant	**0.788**	8%	65
Range = 729				
Specificity	+ spec	**0.514**	28%	277
	– spec	0.220	**60%**	26
Range = 294				
Number	singular	**0.500**	30%	270
	plural	**0.547**	26%	33
Range = 54				

Corrected mean	0.746
Log likelihood	Log = 265, 747
Total N	1,000

Example 6.12.

> *...pero cuando tú llegas a Rusia, ya Ø no lo vas a ver.* (M, Cuba, 52)
> ...but when you get to Russia, **you** won't see it anymore.

Example 6.13.

> *Y cuando **tú** ibas por Europa, lo que era Italia, Francia, **tú** veías la gente de noche bailando, y **nosotros** locos por brincar pa'llá.* (M, Cuba, 52)
> And when **you** would go through Europe, what was Italy, France, **you** would see the people dancing at night, and **we** [were] crazy to jump over there.

When compared with all other languages, the pronominal rate in CS is one of the highest (Carvalho, Orozco, and Shin 2015; Ortiz López 2011; Otheguy and Zentella 2012). However, CS has one of the lowest pronominal rates found in Caribbean Spanish varieties, compared to 49 percent in Dominican Republic Spanish (Ortiz López 2011), 42.3 percent in Santo Domingo Spanish (Alfaraz 2015), 44.8 percent in San Juan Spanish (Cameron 1993), 34.2 percent in Barranquilla, Colombia, Spanish (Orozco 2015), and 33 percent in NYC Cuban Spanish (Otheguy and Zentella 2012). The pronominal rate in CS is higher than the mainland varieties (Ecuatorians, Colombians, and Mexicans of New York City; Spaniards; and Mexicans of Mexico City), with an average overt pronoun production rate of 23 percent, or rather, a clear preference for null pronouns (Lastra and Butragueño 2015; Otheguy and Zentella 2012). Regarding the type of null pronouns that are preferred, table 6.2 suggests that pronoun expression is not consistent in discourse. The most overt pronouns in discourse are the singular forms *tú* and *yo*. More-specific forms are distinguished, although the less-specific form *uno* has a high percentage. The pronominal form *yo* appears due to the influence of the semantic verb class; it fundamentally occurs with verbs of knowledge and desire and stative verbs. The null pronouns are fundamentally plural, although there is not a marked difference between singular and plural. The pragmatic functions of contrast and ambiguity forced the overt pronouns, while the null pronouns responded mostly to redundant contexts, with a weight of 0.788. These findings have been amplified and studied in detail with samples of speech from forty-three participants, whose results are summarized in table 6.3.

Word Order: SV/VS

When SV/VS order is analyzed exclusively, the pronouns occupy SV position with a weight of 0.065 compared to lexical subjects (0.026). In an AJT, pronominal subjects in preverbal position (as in examples 6.12 and 6.13) reached 97 percent, compared to nominal subjects in preverbal position with 81 percent, data that coincide with Ortiz López (2010). Despite the fact that the majority of the pronouns are found preverbally, not all pronouns presented the same probabilistic weight. Second person pronouns, both singular and plural, evidence a pre-position of the pronoun, with significant weights. The few cases of these types of pronouns in postverbal position appear to respond to certain pragmatic and discursive functions, particularly

Table 6.3. Factor groups for word order (SV/VS)

App: SV		Weight	%	N
Subject type	Pronominal	**0.65**	97%	1806
	Nominal	0.26	81%	893
Range=39				
Pronoun type	*tú/usted/ustedes* (you, sing. and plural)	**0.70**	99%	556
	Yo (I)	0.39	97%	703
	Él (he) / *ella* (she) / *ellos/ellas* (they)	0.38	97%	277
	uno (one)	0.27	94%	86
	nosotros (we)	0.25	93%	97
	other pronouns	0.19	92%	88
Range = 51				
Subject Complexity	simple NP	**0.53**	83%	792
	P + Comp	0.31	66%	101
Range = 22				
Clause type	independent	**0.53**	92%	2214
	subordinate	0.44	90%	409
	relative	0.16	78%	76
Range = 37				
Unaccusativity	unergative	0.61	92%	218
	unaccusative	0.47	85%	748
Range = 14				

Corrected mean	0.91
Log likelihood	–743.171
Total N	2,968

when it comes to affirming, rejecting, or doubting something previously said, as in example 6.14. However, further evidence and more data are needed to come to any conclusions about this behavior, which appears to occur principally with verbs such as *pensar* (think), *decir* (say), and *creer* (believe).

Example 6.14.

a. *Estoy, como digo* ***yo****, en un periodo de estancamiento.* (F, Cuba, 65)
I'm, as **I** say, in a period of stagnation.

b. *Que pienso* ***yo*** *que no es el mismo de antes.* (F, Cuba, 31)
Which **I** think is not the same as before.

The levels of syntactic complexity (proper nouns, common nouns, including Determiner (Det) + Noun Phrase (NP), and structures composed of a more syntactically 'complex' NP) are more frequent with pronouns than NPs. Sixty six percent of the complex NPs were in a preverbal position, compared to eighty-three percent of the simple NPs. These data suggest that CS has a clear preference for preverbal subjects and that pronouns have become all but fixed in the preverbal position, with rare exceptions, as in example 6.15.

Example 6.15.

a. *Es que no pasaba* ***la guagua****.* (F, Cuba, 30)
   It's just that **the bus** never came.
b. *Ya te está hablando* ***una oncóloga****, ¿ves?* (M, Cuba, 50)
   And now **an oncologist** is talking to you, you see.

As seen in figure 6.1 below, there are interesting trends that differ between different types of subjects, with an increase in postverbal subjects depending on the pronoun and syntactic complexity of nominal subjects.

According to the statistical analysis, unaccusativity was not a significant factor group. These results overwhelmingly weaken the lexical hypothesis or unaccusative hypothesis as it relates to word order. Both the unaccusative and the unergative verbs presented fairly similar behavior in terms of percentages (92 percent versus 85 percent). However, unergativity has a greater statistical weight (0.61). This finding demonstrates that the semantic class of the verb still presents some restriction in CS, but with less strength than in other varieties of Spanish. The weakening of the semantic class of the verb is greater among pronominal subjects, as seen in figure 6.1. The

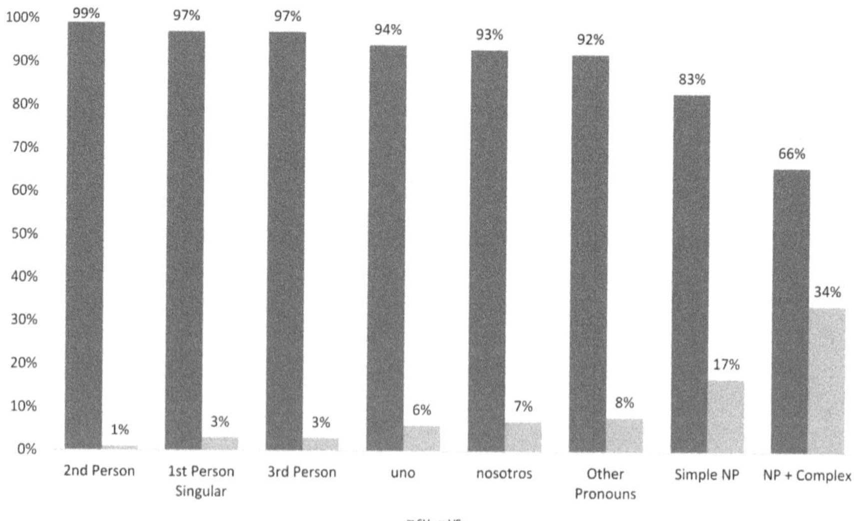

Figure 6.1. Word order (SV/VS) according to pronoun

tendency in CS is clearly toward an SV word order independently of the semantic class of the verb (example 6.16).

Example 6.16.

a. *Ese día que* ***ellos*** *vinieron a la exposición.* (F, Cuba, 35)
That day that **they** came to the exposition.
b. ***Este muchacho de Calle 13*** *grita de aquí allá.* (M, Cuba, 53)
This boy from Calle 13 screams from here, there.

Clause type has also been cited as an important factor in determining word order in Spanish (Martínez-Sanz 2011; Morales 1997; Orozco and Guy 2008; Otheguy and Zentella 2007, 2012). Postverbal subjects tend to be produced with greater frequency in relative clauses, compared to independent and subordinate clauses. Results from this study confirm this, with independent and subordinate clauses presenting similar rates of preverbal subject expression (92 percent and 90 percent, respectively), while in relative clauses a more variable pattern was found (78 percent), in favor of SV order (table 6.3). These results indicate that there are significant syntactic factors (clause type, subject type) that are affecting word order, while the semantic variable of unaccusativity no longer appears to be a significant factor affecting subject position.

pro/PRO + V [– fin]

The SV/VS order presents variation in subordinate clauses with infinitives [– fin] in comparison with verbs [+ fin] in CS.[2] Explicit pronouns in PRO position favor the option C2 [pro, – fin, V infinitive], while subjects tied to pro favor the preservation of option C2 [+ fin, V indicative] or C2 [PRO, – fin, V indicative]. Eighty percent favor the infinitive with the distribution of Ø filled in C2—that is, in a position reserved for PRO—with a factor weight of 0.712 (table 6.4).

Subject type is a determinate factor in favor of the nonfinite clause (0.712) in CS. The semantic factor specificity plays an important role as well. The nonspecificity of the subjects of C2 significantly influences the selection of clauses [– fin], with a weight of 0.873, as *tú* in example 6.17.

Example 6.17.

[*Es bien fácil*]$_{C1}$ [***tú llegar*** *aquí hablando pestes del régimen*]$_{C2}$ (H, Cuba, 29)
[Is very easy]$_{C1}$ [**you arrive-INF** here talking stenches of-the régime]$_{C2}$
It is very easy for you to blame the régime just when **you arrive** in here.

It is shown that the greater the specificity presented by subject pronouns, the greater the impact of the mood [+ fin] (terminative aspect) and vice versa: the less specific the subject pronoun, the lesser the specificity of the mood [– fin] (nonterminative aspect). Pronominal forms, such as */tú/* and */uno/*, would be, precisely, the materialized version of PRO in CS (and Caribbean Spanish in general, contrary to what occurs in Peruvian and Mexican; Aponte Alequín 2014; Aponte Alequín and Ortiz López

Table 6.4. Factor groups for clause type (pro/PRO + V +/– fin)

Default: C2 [– fin]		**Weight**	**%**	**N**
Subject type	PRO / pro (null)	0.240	11%	80
	pro (explicit) / lexical subject	**0.712**	80%	576
Range = 22				
Specificity	– specific	**0.873**	87%	626
	+ specific	0.127	12%	36
Range = 24				
Actant	+ actant	**0.855**	86%	619
	– actant	0.145	15%	108
Range = 88				

Corrected mean	0.73
Log likelihood	–189.349
Total N	720

2015), as in examples 6.17–6.20. There is consistency in that the explicit pronoun occurs in + specific environments, but the nonspecific /*tú*/ and /*uno*/ gain territory in this variety, as demonstrated in the previous quantitative data. The explicit pronouns, +/– specific, act as actants (0.855), both in subordinate environments [+/– fin] and in [+ fin], as in examples 6.17–6.20. This pragmatic variable refers to those situations in which the subject is identified with the source of intentionality and the capacity to generate change in the possible world that surrounds the conversation (Brown and Yule 1993, 112), of the type C2 [– fin, Vinf], and in examples 6.18–6.20, of the type C2 {Prep}[– fin, Vinf].

Example 6.18.

[*Y de repente te dan el premio*]$_{C1}$ [***por tú hacer*** *las mejores ventas*]$_{C2}$ (M, Cuba, 70)
[And of sudden you-OBJ give-3S the reward]$_{C1}$ [**for you make-INF** the best sells]$_{C2}$
And all of a sudden you receive the reward **because you did** so great at sales.

Example 6.19.

[*Pues... miran a uno mal*]$_{C1}$ [***por uno llegar*** “fresh off the boat”]$_{C2}$ (H, Cuba, 29)
[Then… see-3PL to one bad]$_{C1}$ [**for one arrive-INF** “fresh off the boat”]$_{C2}$
Well, they look at you disrespectfully **because you are** just “fresh off the boat.”

In example 6.20, the pronoun *él* is specific, but because it is an actant in the discourse, it appears to favor the adoption of [nom] by the subject of the subordinate clause [nom] and, therefore, its materialization.

Example 6.20.

[*Lo que* ***él*** *tiene es*]$_{C1}$ [*que* ***él intentar*** *dejar la bebida*]$_{C2}$ (M, Cuba, 28)
[OBJ3MS what **he** has is]$_{C1}$ [that **he try-INF** leave-INF the drink]$_{C2}$
What **he** has to do is to stop drinking.

The speaker positions themself as the protagonist of the action and wishes to convince the listeners of an idea that they have about themself or another topic, within a framework of cooperation (Grice 1975). The description of the state of things in the world that the indicative mood characterizes (Haverkate 2002; Martínez-Sanz 2011; Mensching 2000; Pires 2001) appears to go through a second plane in relation to the intention of explaining this persuasion and directing the conversation to a few particular intentions (Terkourafi 2011). The verb can appear consequently in its naked form, [– fin], with the subordinate clause without inflection, but the appearance of the syntactic subject must be completed. The quantitative analysis supports this claim, since the [+ actant] variable appears with a weight of 0.855 in favor of the subordinate nonfinite clause with an infinitive.

Discussion

Caribbean Spanish presents a considerable increase of NSP in preverbal position, as a result of three factors: an adjustment in the verbal inflexion, a decrease in the functional or semantic specialization, and a possible sentence restructuring (Camacho 2012). CS data coincide with Camacho's proposal (2012) and support hypothesis 1 of this study, as we will discuss in this section. Thus, the morphosyntactic factors that intervene between the subject and verb appear to influence the pronominal behavior (Camacho 2012; Poplack 1979). The singular and plural first person pronominal forms present differences in pronoun expression—the pronoun *nosotros* barely appears in the discourse, and the generic pronominal nonspecific form *uno* appears to be taking on territory of the first person singular, *yo*, and of the first person plural, *nosotros*. These differences, for example, between *uno*, *nosotros*, and other pronouns (including demonstratives and indefinites) appear to imply that this semantic distinction is extending to patterns of syntactic order. Despite the fact that its morphology corresponds to the third person, it does not share the same pattern of word order as other third person pronouns. With respect to the second person, *tú*, Brown and Rivas (2011) have proposed, with the support of the lexical representation and the frequency of use (Bybee 2001), that this pronoun positions itself before the verb to form one single lexical unit. This would explain why the frequent use of a structure such as *tú vives* (you live) makes it possible to store it as a unit or lexical set. Lipski (1997) refers to this unit as a cliticization process, in which preverbal pronominal subjects function as clitics and in which *pronoun + verb* has converted into a nexus combination. Pronominal subjects appear more fixed to the left than lexical subjects. The necessary question here is: What is it that motivates this subparameter of a noun or pronoun in place of a null pronoun in the preverbal position in CS and Caribbean Spanish in general? The generic pronouns, *uno* and *tú*, best represent the materialization of the null subjects, but the specific forms of *yo* and *tú* maintain high pronominal frequencies. As the data from this study indicate, the process of preverbal placement of pronominal subjects has dragged along other pronominal subjects and also some lexical subjects, although complex or heavy lexical subjects present greater syntactic restrictions on SV/VS order compared to pronouns. At the same time, proper nouns and common nouns have fewer restrictions on movement to the left than those subjects with greater syntactic complexity. This appears to support, in theory, the proposal that long and complex phrases and growing or heavier elements tend to materialize at the end of their clauses (Arnold et al. 2000). The relative clauses that represent greater variation in terms of subject position need to establish coreference with the antecedent in the matrix clause. In terms of the unaccusative and unergative distinction (Bullock and Toribio 2008; Roggia 2011; Sorace 2011), it has been demonstrated that CS does not establish significant differences between the two, and both the agent and the theme occupy the preverbal position without radical semantic or pragmatic distinctions. This CS data refutes the idea that in Spanish unergative verbs are generated in preverbal position and unaccusative verbs in postverbal, as defended by formal syntactic descriptions of Spanish word order (Bosque and Gutiérrez-Rexach 2009). According to this data, CS distances itself from general patterns of Spanish in that it does not respond to the lexical restrictions of the verb, as is predicted by hypothesis 2, although some of these restrictions will extend to more conservative dialects (Lastra and Martín Butragueño 2015) but not in all syntactic structures.

These findings are consistent with other recent works on different sentence structures, which evidence that Caribbean Spanish tends to have preverbal subject placement, particularly in pronouns, independent of the type of verb, including in interrogative sentence and with personal infinitives (Aponte Alequín 2014; Comínguez 2013; Martínez-Sanz 2011). The CS data support that variation among pro/PRO is restricted by syntactic, semantic, and pragmatic factors. Therefore, there is a hierarchy among syntactic (explicit pronoun > pronominal person), pragmatic (+ actant feature), and semantic (+/– specificity) factors that restrict the three properties under study, as anticipated by hypothesis 3. The interfactic sequence of the procedural meaning flows into the acceptability of the subordinate nonfinite clauses as an apparent subparameter for Cuban speakers. In CS, the subject, with greater pronominal frequency and independent of the type of clause ([+ fin], as in examples 6.13– 6.15, or [– fin], as in examples 6.17–6. 20, relative or interrogative), acquires a nominative case, and therefore is materialized principally by means of a pronoun: *Eso te pasa por tú ir demasiado rápido* (That's what you get for you go. INF too fast), *Yo dije que ella era de La Habana* (I told you that she was from La Habana), and *¿Dónde tú vives?* (Where do you live?). In these environments, pronouns acquire a nominative case which materializes pronominally, such as a part of a hierarchical process between syntactic (expressed pronoun), pragmatic (+ actant feature), semantic (+/– specificity), and dialectal factors. The actant function accounts for why the first person and the nonspecific form *uno* have positioned themselves before the verb in CS. The actant function is defined as the series of situations in which the subject is identified with the source of intentionality and the capacity to generate change in the possible world that surrounds the conversation (Brown and Yule 1993). According to

Grice (1975), the speaker assumes protagonism in the action to convince the interlocutor about an idea or proposal, within a frame of cooperation. It is not surprising that in finite sentences, declarative or interrogative, these pronouns, specific and nonspecific, exert a significant effect in CS. This study supports the proposal that in CS there is a subparameter in which a hierarchy intervenes between the syntactic factors (explicit pronouns > pronouns > proper > common nouns), pragmatic factors (the feature + actant), and semantic features (specificity) of the pronoun. This finding is concurrent with the results for the rest of the insular and continental Caribbean, in opposition to Mexican Spanish (Dauphinais and Ortiz López 2013; Ortiz López 2010; Aponte Alequín and Ortiz López 2015). This CS subparameter (and Caribbean Spanish subparameter in general) confirms—even optionally—a feature of [case: nominative] in the PRO position (and other clauses, as shown with words). In the case of [– fin] clauses, this feature is in the head or specifier position. It is important to point out, however, that because this is a continuum from the other two semantic, syntactic, and pragmatic features present in an environment, a very specific group that is very difficult to isolate, it is important to investigate other factors, such as the effect of the preposition on the selection of C_2 nonfinite or finite, the figure of +/– declaration in C_2, and the verbal semantics of C_2.

Conclusions

This chapter aimed to answer three research questions: (1) What is the distribution of these three properties of the NSP in CS? (2) What linguistic factors restrict these three properties of the NSP in CS? and (3) What hierarchical role does the syntactic-semantic-pragmatic interface play in these properties of NSP in CS? In terms of the first question, the results from the study show that CS presents 30 percent overt pronouns and 70 percent null pronouns. Explicit pronouns (*yo, tú, uno* [– Spec] and *uno* [+ Spec]) appear almost categorically in preverbal position, independent of the type of clause [+/– fin]. These data agree with previous studies on CS in New York (Otheguy and Zentella 2012) and Miami (Ortiz López 2010). Questions 2 and 3 were intended to find answers on the factors that condition the properties under study and the restrictions at the level of the interfaces. In this respect, we can affirm that the three properties present a complex hierarchy of syntactic, semantic, and pragmatic factors and restrictions. There are some pronouns that have become fixed to the left of the verb; the first-person and second-person singular are situated in preverbal position almost categorically. To date, previous studies about personal pronouns have identified the Dominican dialect as the most innovative or advanced Spanish variety in terms of pronominal expression (Alfaraz 2015; Toribio 2000; Ortiz López 2010, 2011; Otheguy and Zentella 2012). This study supports the idea that this is possibly a Caribbean phenomenon (Aponte Alequín and Ortiz López 2015; Dauphinais and Ortiz López, in press; Ortiz López 2011), but CS exhibits less NSP than Dominican Spanish (Alfaraz 2015; Ortiz López 2010, 2011). CS is in a process of transition in terms of the NSP. It is situated between dialects with greater pronominal expression in preverbal position and in pro [+/– fin] clauses, close to the 33 percent that NY Cubans presented (Otheguy and Zentella 2012).

These findings are relevant for Spanish syntax in general and for the NSP debate in particular. At first glance, these data appear to challenge the typology of Spanish, traditional grammatical descriptions, and the supposed free variation this language presents. It is necessary, however, to refine these general findings in order to investigate the restrictions that allow SV/VS order and pro/PRO and also to examine some syntactic and semantic variables that regulate word order in Spanish in general and in CS specifically. It is also important to explore other semantic questions regarding the verb, since this study has raised evidence of some frequency effect occurring within this phenomenon (Brown and Rivas 2011). It would, therefore, be opportune to study this behavior in terms of frequency, and to examine other linguistic variables such as adverbial presence, previous information, and focus, as well as social factors. This would allow us to account for the diachronic and synchronic extent of these properties, which, due to lack of space, has been outside the scope of the analysis presented in this chapter.

Notes

1. There are examples of languages that contradict this generalization. Some languages, such as Chinese, do not have verbal morphemes to mark person, but do allow sentences with tacit subjects. It has been proposed that these languages are "oriented towards discourse," while Romance and Germanic languages, among others, are "oriented towards the sentence" (Huang 1982, 122).
2. In the oral interviews, there were few structures with [– fin] verbs. This prevented us from carrying out statistical analysis on this property with natural oral data. For this reason, we applied a questionnaire of acceptability judgments, as in example 6.11.

References

Alfaraz, G. 2015. "Variation of Overt and Null Subject Pronouns in the Spanish of Santo Domingo." In Carvalho, Shin, and Orozco, *Subject Pronoun Expression in Spanish*, 19–40.

Arnold, J., A. Losongco, T. Wasow, and R. Ginstrom. 2000. "Heaviness vs. Newness: The Effects of Structural Complexity and Discourse Status on Constituent Ordering." *Language* 76 (1): 28–55.

Aponte Alequín, H. 2008. "Infinitivos frente a subjuntivos: ¿procesos lingüísticos internos/universales o variación dialectal?" In *Actas del XV Congreso de la Asociación de Lingüística y Filología de América Latina*, edited by M. Luján and R. Ávila, 120–35. Montevideo, Ury.: Pontificia Universidad Católica del Perú.

———. 2014. "Desafíos del español caribeño: el debate sobre el modo y la microvariación modal." PhD diss., University of Puerto Rico.

Aponte Alequín, H., and L. A. Ortiz López. 2015. "Variación dialectal e interfaz sintáctica/ semántica/ pragmática: la anteposición de sujetos en cláusulas subordinadas en infinitivo." *Spanish in Context* 2 (3): 396–418.

Bentivoglio, P., and E. Weber. 1986. "A Functional Approach to Subject Word Order in Spoken Spanish." In *Studies in Romance Linguistics*, edited by O. Jaeggli and C. Silva-Corvalán, 23–40. Dordrecht, Nld.: Foris.

Bosque, I., and J. Gutiérrez-Rexach. 2009. *Fundamentos de sintaxis formal*. Madrid: Akal.

Bullock, B., and A. J. Toribio. 2008. "Kreyol Incursions into Dominican Spanish: The Perception of Haitianized Speech." *Bilingualism and Identity: Spanish at the Crossroads with other Languages* 37:175–98.

Brown, G., and G. Yule. 1993. *Análisis del discurso*. Madrid: Visor.

Brown, E., and J. Rivas. 2011. "Subject-Verb Word Order in Spanish Interrogatives: A Quantitative Analysis of Puerto Rican Spanish." *Spanish in Context* 8 (1): 23–49.
Bybee, J. 2001. *Phonology and Language Use*. Cambridge Studies in Linguistics 94. Cambridge: University Press.
Camacho, J. 2012. "The Null Subject Parameter Revisited: The Evolution from Null Subject Spanish and Portuguese to Dominican Spanish and Brazilian Portuguese." Unpublished manuscript in review by Rutgers University.
———. 2013. *Null Subjects*. Cambridge: Cambridge University Press.
Cameron, R. 1993. "Ambiguous Agreement, Functional Compensation, and Non-specific *tú* in the Spanish of San Juan, Puerto Rico, and Madrid, Spain." *Language Variation and Change* 5: 305–34.
Cardinaletti, A. 1997. "Agreement and Control in Expletive Constructions." *Linguistic Inquiry* 28 (3): 521–33.
Carvalho A., R. Orozco, and N. Shin. 2015. *Subject Pronoun Expression in Spanish: A Cross-Dialectal Perspective*. Washington, DC: Georgetown University Press.
Chomsky, N. 1995. *The Minimalist Program*. Cambridge, MA: MIT Press.
Claes, J. 2011. "¿Constituyen las Antillas y el Caribe continental una sola zona dialectal? Datos de la variable expresión del sujeto pronominal en San Juan de Puerto Rico y Barranquilla, Colombia." *Spanish in Context* 8 (2): 191–212.
Claes, J., and L. A. Ortiz López. 2011. "Restricciones pragmáticas y sociales en la expresión de futuridad en el español de Puerto Rico." *Spanish in Context* 8 (1): 50–72.
Comínguez, J. 2013. "Microvariation in Caribbean Spanish Interrogative wh- Movement." Research presented at the International Workshop: The Syntactic Variation of Catalan and Spanish Dialects, Barcelona, España, Universidad Autónoma de Barcelona, June 26–28.
Cornips, L., and K. Corrigan. 2005. "Toward an Integrated Approach to Syntactic Variation: A Retrospective and Prospective Synopsis." In *Syntax and Variation: Reconciling the Biological and the Social*, edited by L. Cornips and K. Corrigan, 1–30. Amsterdam: John Benjamins.
Cuza, A., and J. Frank. 2011. "Transfer Effects at the Syntax-Semantics Interface: The Case of Double-*Que* Questions in Heritage Spanish." *Heritage Language Journal* 8 (2): 66–89.
Dauphinais, A., and L. A. Ortiz López. 2016. "Microvariation in the Null Subject Parameter: Word Order in Cuban Spanish." In *Inquiries in Hispanic Linguistics: From Theory to Empirical Evidence*, edited by A. Cuza, L. Czerwionka, and D. Olson, 281–300. Amsterdam: John Benjamins.
De Mello, G. 1995. "Preposición + Sujeto + Infinitivo: 'Para yo hacerlo.'" *Hispania* 78 (4): 825–36.
D'Introno, F. 2001. *Sintaxis generativa del español: evolución y análisis*. Madrid: Cátedra.
Dorta, J., C. Díaz Cabrera, and B. Hernández. 2015. "La entonación cubana en zonas rurales: La Habana y Santa Clara." In *Perspectivas actuales en el análisis fónico del habla: tradición y avances en la fonética experimental*, edited by A. Cabedo Nebot, 44–55. Valencia: Universitat de València.
Dowty, D. 1991. "Thematic Proto-roles and Argument Selection." *Language* 67:547–619.
Fúster, N. 2012. "Percepciones y actitudes lingüísticas de habaneros y santiagueros en Cuba." MA diss., Universidad de Puerto Rico.
Grice, P. 1975. "Logic and Conversation." In *Syntax and Semantics*, vol. 3, *Speech Acts*, edited by P. Cole and J. Morgan, 41–58. New York: Academic Press.
Haverkate, H. 2002. *The Syntax, Semantics and Pragmatics of Spanish Mood*. Amsterdam: John Benjamins.
Henríquez Ureña, P. 1940. *El español de Santo Domingo*. Buenos Aires: Biblioteca de Dialectología Hispanoamericana.
Huang, J. 1982. "Logical Relations in Chinese and the Theory of Grammar." PhD diss., MIT.
Jaeggli, O. 1982. *Topics in Romance Syntax*. Dordrecht, Nld.: Foris.
Kempchinsky, P. 2009. "What Can the Subjunctive Disjoint Reference Effect Tell Us about the Subjunctive?" *Lingua* 119:1788–810.
Labov, W. 1966. *The Social Stratification of English in New York City*. Washington, DC: Center for Applied Linguistics.
Lastra, Y., and P. M. Butragueño. 2015. "Subject Pronoun Expression in Mexican Spanish." In *Subject Pronoun Expression: A Cross-Dialectal Perspective*, edited by A. Carvalho, R. Orozco, and N. Shin. Washington, DC: Georgetown University Press.

Lipski, J. 1994. *El español de América*. Madrid: Cátedra.
———. 1997. "Preposed Subjects in Questions." *Hispania* 60:61–7.
López Morales, H. 1992. *El español del Caribe*. Madrid: Mapfre.
Martínez-Sanz, C. 2011. "Null and Overt Subjects in a Variable System: The Case of Dominican Spanish." PhD diss., University of Ottawa.
Mensching, G. 2000. *Infinitive Constructions with Specified Subjects: A Syntactic Analysis of the Romance Languages*. Oxford: Oxford University Press.
Morales, A. 1997. "La hipótesis funcional y la aparición de sujeto no nominal: el español de Puerto Rico." *Hispania* 80 (1): 153–65.
———. 1999. "Anteposición de sujeto en el español del Caribe." In *El Caribe hispánico: perspectivas lingüísticas actuales*, edited by L. Ortiz López, 77–98. Frankfurt: Vervuert.
Tomás Navarro, T. 1948. *El español de Puerto Rico*. Río Piedras, Pri.: Editorial Universitaria.
Orozco, Rafael. 2015. "Pronominal Variation in Colombian Costeño Spanish." In Carvalho, Shin, and Orozco, *Subject Pronoun Expression in Spanish*, 19–40.
Ortiz López, L. A., 2010. "El español del Caribe: orden de palabras a la luz de la interfaz léxicosintaxis-y sintáxis-pragmática." *Revista Internacional de Lingüística Iberoamericana* 14:75–94.
———. 2011. "Spanish in Contact with the Haitian Creole." In *Handbook of Hispanic Sociolinguistics*, edited by M. Díaz-Campos, 418–45. New York: Blackwell.
Otheguy, R., and A. Zentella. 2012. *Spanish in New York. Language Contact, Dialectal Leveling, and Structural Continuity*. Oxford: Oxford University Press.
Otheguy, R., A. C. Zentella, and D. Livert. 2007. "Language and Dialect Contact in Spanish in New York: Toward the Formation of a Speech Community." *Language* 83 (4): 770–802.
Pascual y Cabo, D. 2013. "Knowledge of *Gustar*-Like Verbs in Spanish Heritage Speakers." In *Proceedings of the 12th Generative Approaches to Second Language Acquisition Conference* (GASLA), edited by J. Cabrelli Amaro, T. Judy, and D. Pascual y Cabo, 162–69. Somerville, MA: Cascadilla Proceedings Project.
Pires, A. 2001. "The Syntax of Gerunds and Infinitives: Subjects, Case and Control." PhD diss., University of Maryland.
Pöll, B. 2015. "Caribbean Spanish = Brazilian Portuguese? Some Comparative Thoughts on the Loss of Pro-Drop." *Studies in Hispanic and Lusophone Linguistics* 8 (2): 317–54.
Poole, G. 2011. *Syntactic Theory*. Basingstoke, Eng.: Palgrave Macmillan.
Poplack, S. 1979. "Function and Process in a Variable Phonology." PhD diss., University of Pennsylvania.
Rizzi, L. 1982: *Issues in Italian Syntax*. Dordrecht, Nld.: Foris.
Roggia, A. 2011. "Unaccusativity and Word Order in Mexican Spanish: An Examination of Syntactic Interfaces and the Split Intransitivity Hierarchy." PhD diss., Pennsylvania State University.
Rodríguez Cadena, Y. 2009. "Variación y cambio fonético en el Caribe Colombiano: Estudio Sociolinguístico sobre la ciudad de Barranquilla." PhD diss., Colegio de México.
Sankoff, D., S. Tagliamonte., and E. Smith. 2005. "Goldvarb X: A Variable Rule Application for Macintosh and Windows." Software. Department of Linguistics, University of Toronto.
Serrano, M. 2005. "Entre la gramática y el discurso: las completivas con 'para' + infinitivo/subjuntivo en un contexto socio-comunicativo." Special issue: *Bilingualism and Emotions* 5 (1): 130–50.
Silva-Corvalán, C. 1990. "Subject Expression and Placement in Mexican-American Spanish." In *Spanish in the United States: Sociolinguistic Aspects*, edited by J. Amastae, and L. Elías-Olivares, 93–120. Washington, DC: Georgetown University Press.
Sorace, A. 2003. "Near-Nativeness." In *Handbook of Second Language Acquisition*, edited by M. Long and C. Daughty, 130–52. Oxford: Blackwell.
———. 2005. "Syntactic Optionality at Interfaces." In *Syntax and Variation: Reconciling the Biological and the Social*, edited by L. Cornips and K. Corrigan, 26–111. Amsterdam: John Benjamins.
———. 2011. "Gradience in Split Intransitivity: the End of the Unaccusative Hypothesis?" *Archivio glottologic oitaliano* 96 (1): 67–86.
Suñer, M. 1983. *Subjects of Infinitives in Standard and Caribbean Spanish*. Ithaca: Cornell University Press.

———. 2001. "The Puzzle of Restrictive Relative Clauses with Conjoined DP Antecedents." In *Features and Interfaces in Spanish and French: Essays in Honor of Heles Contreras*, edited by J. Herschenson, E. Mallén, and K. Zagona, 212–28. Amsterdam: John Benjamins.

———. 2003. "The Lexical Preverbal Subjects in a Romance Null Subject Language. Where Are Thou?" In *A Romance Perspective on Language Knowledge and Use*, edited by E. R. Núñez-Cedeño, L. López, and R. Cameron, 341–57. Amsterdam: John Benjamins.

Tagliamonte, S. 2006: *Analyzing Sociolinguistic Variation*. Cambridge: Cambridge University Press.

———. 2011. *Variationist Sociolinguistics: Change, Observation, Interpretation*. Malden, MA: Wiley-Blackwell.

Terkourafi, M. 2011. "The Pragmatic Variable: Toward a Procedural Interpretation." *Language in Society* 40:343–72.

———. 1994. "Dialectal Variation in the Licensing of Null Referential and Expletive Subjects." In *Aspects of Romance Linguistics: Selected Papers from the Linguistics Symposium on Romance Languages XXIV*, edited by C. Parodi, C. Quicoli, M. Saltarelli., and M. L. Zubizarreta, 409–32. Washington, DC: Georgetown University Press.

———. 2000. "Setting Parametric Limits on Dialectal Variation in Spanish." *Lingua* 110 (5): 315–41.

Van der Wurff, W., ed. 2007. *Imperative Clauses in Generative: Studies in Honour of Frits Beukema*. Linguistik Aktuell 113. Amsterdam: John Benjamins.

Zamora, J., and J. Guitart. 1982. *Dialectología hispanoamericana: Teoría, descripción, historia*. Salamanca, Esp.: Ediciones Almar.

7

Recomplementation as an Unexplored Locus of Dialectal Variation: The Status of Reduplicative *Que* in Cuban Spanish

JOSHUA FRANK
University of Texas at Austin

ALMEIDA JACQUELINE TORIBIO
University of Texas at Austin

THE PRESENT CHAPTER SCRUTINIZES complementizer reduplication in Cuban Spanish, a phenomenon characterized by dislocated arguments and circumstantial adjuncts sandwiched between a primary and a secondary complementizer, as illustrated in example 7.1. Although prescriptively restricted, the use of the doubled complementizer, or recomplementation, to introduce a syntactically dependent clause is reported to be widespread in dialects of Spanish, especially in unguarded spoken language.[1]

Example 7.1. Recomplementation in Spanish

a. *La señora de las ONG, que nunca ha trabajado, que no sabe qué es trabajar, le dice* ***que*** *al presidente* ***que*** *trabaje.*
   The woman from the NGOs, who has not worked, who doesn't know what it means to work, says to the president **that** he should work.
   ("Daniel Urresti ofrecería a PPK el Ministerio de Economía si gana elecciones." Video, *Perú21: Noticias del Perú y del Mundo*, August 3, 2015.)
b. *La reelección es un tema* ***que*** *francamente* ***que*** *si se plantea hay que saber cómo y cuándo se va a plantear.*
   Reelection is a theme **that** frankly **that** if raised, that one must know how and when it will be raised.
   ("Reelección le quitaría concentración y tranquilidad al Presidente Hernández." *La Tribuna Honduras*, August 23, 2014.)

Although commonly attested in conversational registers, the status of the secondary *que* remains unsettled. Scholars working within syntactic-theoretical frameworks (e.g., Cerrudo Aguilar and Gallego 2014; Demonte and Fernández-Soriano 2009, 2013; Frank 2016; López 2009; Rodríguez-Ramalle 2003; Villa-García 2012, 2015) have sought to explain how the secondary *que* is licensed and why it is lexicalized. Villa-García (2012) suggests that in Peninsular Spanish the reduplicative *que* is always present, but may undergo optional deletion at phonological form (PF), parallel to *that* deletion in English. However, it is not known whether such a representational-based account holds true of Spanish in general. In addition, it remains to be examined why speakers elide or express the reduplicative complementizer.

Taking note of the 'extra' complementizer in English oral vernacular, as in example 7.2, Casasanto and Sag (2008) undertake a psycholinguistic study of the phenomenon—the lone such study known to the present authors—and conclude that the supplementary complementizer functions to lower processing costs.

Example 7.2. Recomplementation in English

a. My hope is **that** by the time we meet **that** we'll have made some progress. (President Obama, press conference, BBC Radio 5, cited in Radford 2013, 19)
b. They were so cold **that** if they were sitting on the launch pad in this aluminum tank **that** they would form sheets of ice on the outside. (NPR Morning Edition, July 12, 2005, cited in Casasanto and Sag 2008, 602)

Adopting this theory of performance, according to which the forms of spoken sentences are determined by processing mechanisms, we can make predictions about the variable presence versus absence of reduplicative *que* in Spanish: The longer the distance between the redundant complementizer and the complement clause, the more likely the occurrence of recomplementation with secondary *que*. In fact, Frank (2016) argues in support of this prediction in a study on Colombian Spanish. The empirical study set forth herein tests this prediction by reference to oral production in Cuban Spanish; in so doing, we lend evidence to syntactic-theoretical constructs and contribute to theories of language processing with new data from an understudied variety.

Comparing the results from this study to existing research on non-Caribbean dialects also sheds light on recomplementation as an unexplored locus for dialectal variation. Caribbean varieties in general deserve special interest, as they share many morphosyntactic properties that distinguish them from other Spanish dialects.[2] In the present volume several chapters consider this very theme. As noted in Cuza and Camacho's chapter on pronominal subject expression with inanimate referents, third person subject pronouns in Spanish typically have animate antecedents. However, these pronouns in Cuban and other Caribbean dialects can also take animate referents. In a study on subject-verb word ordering, Erker explains that Cubans, along with Spanish speakers of other Caribbean dialects, demonstrate a higher rate of preposing of the subject when compared to the rest of the Spanish-speaking world. Furthermore, while it is commonly accepted that Cubans, Dominicans, and Puerto Ricans use overt subject pronouns at higher rates when compared to other non-Caribbean Spanish speakers, Ortíz López, Dauphinais, and Aponte Alequín's chapter paints a more complex picture of the phenomenon via analysis of three interrelated properties of the null subject parameter. In summary, the present study builds upon the themes of this volume, and complements several chapters therein, by investigating an understudied linguistic phenomenon that may add to the list of uniquely Caribbean morphosyntactic properties.

The remainder of the chapter is organized as follows. First we review the pertinent literature on the articulation of the left periphery as well as selected analyses from the psycholinguistic literature that are germane to the processing of complex constructions such as the ones at issue here. Then we delineate the research questions and the elicitation stimuli and methods employed in pursuing them. The following section rehearses the results of the controlled studies and submits these to statistical analyses. Finally, we conclude the chapter with discussion of the insights from the present findings for grammar- versus processing-based accounts of recomplementation and for an unexplored locus of dialectal variation.

Background Literature

The complex structure of the left periphery has inspired a rich body of research, much of it devoted to the cartography of the complementizer phrase (CP) layer of matrix clauses.[3] More recently, scholars have focused on the structure above the canonical position of the embedded subject. Villa-García (2012, 2015) offers a thoroughgoing review of extant literature on recomplementation configurations and an analysis that has broad implications for the articulation of the embedded CP-layer in Spanish specifically. In particular, the author attends to the relationship between the secondary complementizer and the intervening fronted material, arguing for an analysis in which the *que* lexicalizes Top°, whose specifier hosts the dislocated phrase. Garrett (2013) extends the work of Villa-García to take account of supplemental data from cliticization and polarity data from Asturian, Galician, and Portuguese (see González i Planas 2010, 2014; Gupton 2010), and he reinforces the status of the intervening XPs and the supplemental *que* as topic-related entities, as in example 7.3.

Example 7.3.

$[_{ForceP}$... *que* $[_{TopP*}$... *XP** *que* $[_{FinP}$...

While the aforementioned investigations of the CP architecture are consistent in identifying the supplemental *que* as a topic phrase element, researchers like Garrett encourage additional study of the phenomenon. Complementing efforts based on introspective grammaticality judgments on constructed examples, Radford (2013) examines the occurrence of multiple lexicalized *that* in a large corpus of unscripted broadcasts from popular British radio and television programming. He reports on a diversity of utterances that provide evidence for a cartographic template in which each occurrence of *that* may be merged in situ in the head position of various projections of the left periphery in subordinate finite clauses. On this view, *that* can lexicalize any peripheral head in the template in example 7.3, but the heads can also be null, under conditions yet to be determined.

A potential explanation for the occurrence of multiple complementizers is found in language processing. Indeed, processing explanations are proving increasingly promising as researchers reevaluate syntactic phenomena that were formerly understood in grammatical terms, by reference to parsing (see O'Grady 2010). Specific to multiple complementizers, Casasanto and Sag (2008) investigated the processing of English recomplementation structures by manipulating variables of length of intervening material and secondary *that* in sentences such as those in example 7.4.

Example 7.4. Stimuli from Casasanto and Sag (2008)

a. John reminded Mary that soon (**that**) his brother would be ready to leave.
b. John reminded Mary that after he was finished with his meeting (**that**) his brother would be ready to leave.

Their first experiment tested whether the presence of a secondary complementizer reduced the acceptability of a sentence, and, if so, whether the cost in acceptability rating was modulated by the distance between the two complementizers. Results show that the presence of reduplicative *that* reduces acceptability and local violations carry greater acceptability costs. In the second experiment, the authors examined the function of the secondary complementizer by testing whether it incurs a penalty in reading time and whether the outcome is dependent on locality. Results of this latter study reveal that reading times were improved on the subject of the complement clause when the intervening material is long. Taken together, these findings suggest that although the extra *that* is not licensed by the formal grammar, it facilitates processing by minimizing the integration cost of the subordinated clause.

Casasanto and Sag adopt a distance-based theory of linguistic complexity, where the integration cost associated with two syntactically dependent elements is equal to the distance between them (Gibson 2000). Distance can be measured in terms of letters, syllables, words, or constituents. The authors elect to measure distance at the level of words.[4] As a result, the integration cost of the complement in example 7.4a is equal to one, and in example 7.4b, equal to seven. In summary, the benefit of the reduplicated complementizer is derived from the fact that it reiterates the information provided by the first; it signals the beginning of an ensuing complement. It merits noting that the results reported by Casasanto and Sag on the presence of multiple complementizers are consonant with those of Jaeger (2006, 2010) for single complementizers. Single complementizers are more likely to be lexicalized in English when the complement clause is less predictable, such as when there is a material intervening between the complement-taking verb and the subordinate clause. Thus, there is a processing benefit that is accrued by lexicalizing the complementizer in English, whether in single or multiple complementizer sentences.

When compared to English, the distribution of complementizer-drop in Spanish is much more limited. However, in a study on Spanish-English bilinguals from Los Angeles, Silva-Corvalán (1993) finds that the complementizer is often omitted in argument clauses. Given that the participants resided in California, the author suggests that the tendency in English to drop the 'that' may influence the bilinguals' behavior in Spanish. More recently, in a Twitter corpus study, Riccelli (forthcoming) found more instances of *que*-drop in tweets from Mexico City than from LA. This finding is important because it suggests that higher-than-expected *que*-drop tendencies need not be driven by direct contact with English. Furthermore, in personal communication with Riccelli, he explains that while instances of *que*-drop are abundant in Mexico City tweets, they are almost nonexistent in Peninsular Spanish tweets.

In Spanish, lexicalization of the primary subordinating complementizer is prescribed. Interestingly, for indirect questions specifically, formal research argues that the primary *que* is optional after *ask* or *wonder* verbs of saying (e.g., *preguntar*, 'to ask') but obligatory after non-ask or non-wonder verbs (e.g., *decir*, 'to say or tell'). This analysis has also been extended to the reduplicative *que* in equivalent but more complex constructions, those with left-dislocated elements (Brovetto 2002; Frank 2016; Villa-García 2015). The claim is that the *wh*-complement will be interpreted as a statement in the case that the complementizer is not spelled out, as in example 7.5a, but as an indirect question when it is lexicalized, as in example 7.5b (e.g., Plann 1982; Suñer 1993).

Example 7.5. Prescribed interpretation

a. Statement
   Me dijo cuándo iban a salir.
   S/he told me when they were going to leave.
b. Indirect question
   Me dijo que cuándo iban a salir.
   S/he asked me when they were going to leave.

Cuza and Frank (2015) investigated bilingual speakers' production of primary *que* in these prescribed obligatory contexts. Interestingly, many participants from the Cuban-speaker control baseline produced the null *que* variety. The authors speculate that prosody and extra-sentential information might serve to disambiguate the otherwise semantically ambiguous *wh*-complement. Importantly, they leave open the option that an increased tendency to drop *que* may be a locus for dialectal variation. In summary, research on the Spanish complementizer suggests that *que*-drop is a linguistic phenomenon that varies across the Spanish-speaking world. Furthermore, instances of *que*-drop are not limited to contact varieties.

In this chapter, we investigate the secondary complementizer *que* in both indirect question and statement constructions, which like English *that* is optionally realized. Fontana (1993) argues that multiple complementizer constructions are restricted to "nonstandard" dialects of Spanish, and even among these dialects, the range of the material that can intervene between the two complementizers is more restricted in modern Spanish than in older varieties of the language. The status and exponence of the secondary complementizer and the length and type of intervening material is discussed by Frank (2016) in a study of embedded questions (example 7.6a) and statements (example 7.6b) in Colombian Spanish.

Example 7.6. Stimuli from Frank (2016)

a. *Me dijo que esa camisa fea, (**que**) cuándo iba a devolverla.*
S/He asked me when I was going to return that ugly shirt.
b. *Me dijo que esa camisa fea, (**que**) iba a devolverla.*
S/He told me that s/he was going to return that ugly shirt.

Ratings of aural stimuli in a speeded acceptability judgment task point to participants' preference for the simple, single complementizer condition over the more complex, recomplementization condition, a result that is robust across both statement and question items. Frank notes, however, that while participants may prefer the less complex form, the ratings associated with the doubled *que* are nevertheless within the acceptable range of the Likert scale. Furthermore, he contends that a decrement in acceptability judgment does not equate to a rejection of the structure; in point of fact, participants' responses show ample variation, with some respondents judging both the null and expressed *que* options equally acceptable and a few preferring the overt variety. Curiously, this finding can still be reconciled with a strictly processing-based account of the phenomenon if one is to consider the increased processing demands associated with the speeded nature of the task. Frank concludes that the reduplicated *que* is not optional per se in Colombian Spanish, but conditioned by processing demands. The acceptance and variable expression of recomplementation are further examined here by reference to production in Cuban Spanish.

The Present Study

In the present study, we pursue a controlled investigation of complementizer use in Spanish-language production, toward the aim of illuminating the variable appearance of the duplicated complementizer in the processing of complex structures. More specifically, we examine whether multiple complementizers are formally licensed in elicited spoken sentences and whether the lexicalization of secondary *que* is facilitative of integration of sentential complements that are separated from the selecting predicate by topicalized arguments or adverbial phrases. Our focus on Cuban Spanish is motivated by the first author's observation of variable *que* in the Cuban baseline in Cuza and Frank (2015), which is contrary to prescribed Spanish norms. Thus, we consider recomplementation as a possible locus for syntactic variation and an understudied psycholinguistic phenomenon whose study has the potential to augment our base of knowledge on the Caribbean Spanish lect.

The following research questions guide the study:

1. Is reduplicative *que* acceptable in Cuban Spanish?
2. If so, is the presence of reduplicative *que* sensitive to dependency distance between the matrix verb and the complement clause?

In accordance with the findings reported for English recomplementation, we predict that complex constructions with extra material will be more difficult to process and, as a result, speakers will produce resumptive *que* with long intervening dislocated phrases (example 7.7a), but not with short interveners (example 7.7b).

Example 7.7. Recomplementation with long versus short interveners

a. *Me dice que ese postre para la fiesta de cumpleaños, (**que**) lo va a dejar en la cocina.*
S/he tells me that that dessert for the birthday party (**that**) s/he will leave it in the kitchen.

b. *Me dice que ese postre, (**que**) lo va a dejar en la cocina para la fiesta de cumpleaños.*
S/he tells me that that dessert (**that**) s/he will leave it in the kitchen for the birthday party.

In testing this prediction, we enlisted (n − 25) native Spanish speakers in Havana, Cuba to participate in two production tasks that elicit secondary *que* and test the effect of the length of the dislocated element on its usage. Selected metadata collected via a demographic and language history questionnaire are summarized in table 7.1.

Table 7.1. Participant profiles

Demographic questionnaire	Elicited information
Place of birth	Cuba
Current residence	Havana
Gender	11 male 14 female
Age	18–78 (mean: 34)
Highest level of education	18 university 4 technical school[a] 3 high school

a. Technical school equates to a two-year community college degree.

The participants' respective occupations included student, teacher, engineer, accountant, journalist, physical therapist, army employee, and retiree, among others. Spanish was not only the first language of all participants, but it was the language of education for all participants across primary, high school, and postsecondary levels of education. Furthermore, Spanish was also the first language of their parents, as reported in all cases. Finally, twenty-two out of twenty-five participants reported that they used 'only' or 'mainly' Spanish both at work and in social contexts, while the remaining three used 'slightly more' Spanish.

In order to preclude the effects of prescriptivist restrictions of written stimuli, we elicited recomplementation by recorded prompts, in two tasks. In the first task, participants were presented with an aural prompt that they were asked to repeat orally (e.g., Hamayan 1978; Pérez-Leroux, Cuza, and Thomas 2011). The underlying assumption is that constructions that are consistent with the speakers' grammars will be faithfully reproduced whereas those that are not will be altered (e.g., with suppression of the doubled complementizer in example 7.8). We additionally examine the alternative possibility that a secondary complementizer will be employed as a strategy for integrating complement clauses when required by a long intervener (i.e., that example 7.8b will be reproduced with the lexicalized secondary complement, while example 7.8a will not). In the second task, participants listened to a contextualizing preamble followed by a prompt that included a short or long intervener (example 7.9), the latter intended to elicit reduplicative *que*; again, the length of the material in the CP field preceding the embedded subject was manipulated (e.g., *si gano* versus *si gano la competencia de arte anual*). Participants were instructed to first repeat the incomplete sentence prompt and then complete it in accordance with the preamble.

Example 7.8. Task one: Elicited imitation

a. *Me dice que sin duda (**que**) va a haber mucho daño al techo después de la tormenta severa.*
   S/he tells me that without doubt (**that**) there will be significant damage to the roof after the severe storm.
b. *Me dice que sin duda después de la tormenta severa (**que**) va a haber mucho daño al techo.*
   S/he tells me that without doubt after the severe storm (**that**) there will be significant damage to the roof.

Example 7.9. Task two: Oral sentence completion

Preamble

Si ganas (la competencia de arte anual), ¿cómo vas a gastar el premio monetario?
If you win (the annual art competition), how will you spend the monetary prize?

Prompt

Me pregunta que si gano (la competencia de arte anual)...
S/he asks me that if I win (the annual art competition)...

Forty items were created for testing: twenty-four for the elicited imitation task and sixteen for the oral sentence completion task.[5] Intervening \ elements included direct and indirect objects, as well as *si*-clauses and adverbials, and sentence types included both indirect questions and statements. Across both tasks, the length of the dislocated element was operationalized as short (two words) versus long (seven words). Overall sentence length for task one was controlled at seventeen words (not including optional reduplicative *que*). Pilot results determined that this length is sufficient to challenge the participant, but not so difficult that it interferes with successful completion of the task. The aforementioned target items were scrambled with thirty-four and sixteen distractors respectively, so as to ensure no two identical conditions appeared consecutively. Distractors were of comparable length and targeted unrelated linguistic phenomena: subject-verb inversion and pronoun realization.

All stimuli were read by a native speaker of Spanish and recorded and edited on the latest version of Audacity recording software. For task two specifically, editing consisted of removing the complement from the original recording in order to create a prompt with authentic prosody and continuation rise (Cuza and Frank 2015). In order to avoid the effects associated with presentation order, two versions of each test were created, with the items presented in reverse orders. One half of the participants took version A, while the other half took version B. In all cases, the oral sentence completion task was administered first in order to avoid any potential priming effects associated with having heard the reduplicative *que* in the elicited imitation task.

Participants were recruited in Havana by a research assistant as well as via snowball sampling. During testing, stimuli were presented using Windows Media Player and individual responses were recorded on Audacity with unidirectional head-mounted microphone. Each participant was exposed to a battery of tasks that make up a larger project, which spanned a total of 1 hour and 30 minutes over one testing session. All sessions were conducted either in a quiet room in the residence of the investigator's host family or in an equivalent setting in the participants' home. For their efforts, participants were fairly compensated.

Results

In order to shed light on the guiding research questions, data collected from task one and task two are submitted to statistical analyses. The results of these efforts are presented in this section.

Task One

The elicited imitation data was coded in the following manner: Accurate imitation of the null and overt secondary *que* across the four conditions received a score of 1; conversely, inaccurate imitation (*que* insertion or omission in the null and overt conditions, respectively) received a score of 0. Excepting the critical reduplicative *que*, only sentences that were imitated with a maximum of two word omissions, alterations, or insertions were included in the final analysis. This coding was arbitrarily adopted as a metric for attention to task. If the participant had not been paying attention, then s/he might not have listened to the critical *que* region, which would have rendered the item unusable. As a result, a total of forty-nine sentences from the six-hundred-item corpus were discarded. A sample response is reproduced in example 7.10.

Example 7.10. Elicited imitation: sample prompt and non-target response

Prompt

Me dice que esta pintura clásica colgada en la sala, ***que*** *la va a vender la próxima semana.*

S/he tells me that the classic picture hanging in the living room, **that** s/he is going to sell it next week.

Non-target Response

Me dice que esta pintura clásica colgada en la sala, la va a vender la próxima semana.

S/he tells me that the classic picture hanging in the living room, s/he is going to sell it next week.

Following the above coding scheme, the elicited repetitions were labeled target or nontarget. Importantly, this terminology does not refer to grammatical accuracy but rather to successful word-for-word repetition of the prompt. A breakdown of the responses in the corpus is provided in table 7.2.

Table 7.2. Descriptive statistics by condition for elicited imitation task

Condition	Target Imitation	Nontarget Imitation	Proportion Target	*SD*
Short/Null	131	3	0.98	0.06
Long/Null	136	7	0.95	0.10
Short/Overt	32	104	0.23	0.32
Long/Overt	38	100	0.27	0.26

As demonstrated, independent of the distance between the matrix verb and the complement clause (two words versus seven words), the test group performs at ceiling across both null complementizer conditions, producing an accurate imitation 96 percent of the time (267/277 items). In other words, participants insert a reduplicative *que* into a null complementizer prompt in only 4 percent of the items. However, across both overt complementizer conditions, accurate imitation with secondary *que* falls to 26 percent (70/274 items), or, in other words, reduplicative *que* omission is displayed in 74 percent of the test items.

A binary logistic regression was performed to elucidate these descriptive statistics. Specifically, a two-predictor model was fitted to the data to investigate the effects of reduplicative *que* and distance of intervening material on the accuracy of the imitated sentence. The analysis was conducted in SPSS (SPSS 22 IBM, New York, USA). As alluded to above, the reduplicative *que* was found to be a significant predictor of the model ($B = -5.347$, $p < 0.001$). Neither distance nor the interaction between the two factors reached significance ($B = -0.163$, $p = 0.243$ and $B = 0.202$, $p = 0.181$, respectively). Stated differently, regardless of the length of the intervening material, the null reduplicative *que* conditions were imitated with greater accuracy than the overt ones.[6]

Task Two

In order to triangulate the experimental design and to control for a potential task effect, participants also completed an oral sentence completion task. Responses with and without reduplicative *que* were coded with the numerical value of 1 and 0 respectively. Furthermore, data was carefully scanned for items where the preamble was not repeated; this repetition is essential because it allows the investigator to distinguish between direct versus indirect speech. Six of the four hundred test items were without preamble and thus were discarded. Finally, another nine items were removed because the response did not match the information elicited by the prompt. A sample sentence completion item appears in example 7.11.

Example 7.11. Oral sentence completion: sample prompt and response

Prompt

Al viejo, ¿cuándo le vas a ofrecer un trabajo?
To the old man, when will you offer him a job?

Response

Me pregunta que al viejo... cuándo le voy a ofrecer un trabajo.
S/he asks me that to the old man... when I will offer him a job.

Coding the oral responses by insertion or absence of *que*, the data reflects the breakdown provided in table 7.3.

Table 7.3. Descriptive statistics by condition for oral sentence completion task

Condition	*Que* Insertion	No *que* Insertion	Proportion *Que*	*SD*
Short	1	192	0.005	0.024
Long	3	189	0.015	0.054

As demonstrated in table 7.3, participants do not reduplicate the *que* in the oral sentence completion task, where only 1 percent of the test items (4/385 items) display *que* insertion. Furthermore, the distance between the primary complementizer and the complement does not appear to be a significant factor. A binary logistic regression was performed in order to further consider the effects of the distance variable on the insertion of reduplicative *que*. This model was adopted to maintain a consistent statistical design across tasks. In support of the descriptive analysis, as well as the results from task one, distance was not found to be a significant predictor of the model (B = 0.223, $p = 0.336$). In summary, regardless of the length of the material that intervenes between the primary *que* and its complement, reduplicative *que* was not an adopted strategy in the oral sentence completion task.

Discussion and Conclusion

The findings from the elicited imitation task and the sentence completion task together suggest that Cuban Spanish is a variety in which recomplementation is not licensed by the grammar. Furthermore, we find no evidence that it serves a facilitative function in production. These findings do not tally with those of previous studies on other dialects of the Spanish-speaking world. Recall that Villa-García (2012, 2015) argues that the reduplicative *que* is optional in Peninsular Spanish and offers a grammar-based account of the phenomenon. Nor are our findings commensurate with explications in which a secondary complementizer is inserted as a processing strategy, for example, Casasanto and Sag's (2008) psycholinguistic study. While the present study does not find support for this trade-off between grammaticality and processing complexity, it is important to note that the design of the present study diverges from that of Casasanto and Sag in crucial ways: The latter study adopted an online measurement (reading times) and was not oral in nature (self-paced reading paradigm). Thus, while it appears likely that Cuban Spanish does not license recomplementation, it is premature to conclude that it does not present this grammaticality versus processing compromise.

The findings from the study are also dissimilar from those presented in Frank's (2016) unified grammar-and-processing accounts of recomplementation in Colombian Spanish. He argues that both null and overt reduplicated *que* constructions are shown to be licensed by the grammar, though the less complex forms are preferred when integration costs are low. Instead, our results offer yet another interpretation of this linguistic phenomenon. The two tasks adopted in this study demonstrate that the presence of a doubled *que* is not only minimally sensitive to dependency distance between the matrix verb and the complement clause, but that it is also not properly internalized in the grammar. More specifically, the lack of secondary *que* insertion in the null condition of task one, as well as across task two, suggests that doubled *que* provides little processing benefit to the complexity associated with the given tasks.

What is more, the omission of the secondary *que* in the overt condition in the elicited repetitions of task one supports the claim that recomplementation is a violation of Cuban Spanish grammar. Recall that the working assumption in an elicited imitation task is that constructions that are consistent with the speakers' grammars will be faithfully reproduced, while those that are not will be distorted or manipulated during production (e.g., Hamayan 1978; Pérez-Leroux et al. 2011; Radloff 1991). In this task, an unlicensed secondary complementizer is suppressed during elicited repetition in 74 percent of the test items, despite the participants having explicitly been instructed to repeat the sentence word for word. Our interpretation of the data is drawn from a robust set of test items, which include indirect questions and statements, as well as left-dislocated elements that comprised direct objects, indirect objects, *si*-clauses, and adverbials, both short and long.

Given that there is little evidence that the reduplicated *que* is licensed in Cuban Spanish, we argue that this dialect distinguishes itself from Peninsular and Colombian varieties (see Villa-García 2012; Frank, 2016). Interestingly, Cuban Spanish resembles US English in regard to this property. Recall that Casasanto and Sag (2008) demonstrate that recomplementation is ungrammatical in English. They motivate its use by strictly appealing to processing costs. In their view, the secondary complementizer reduces complement integration costs, which are determined by the strain on working memory, operationalized as the distance between the matrix verb and the ensuing complement. In much the same way, we believe that a processing-based account will shed light on the productive nature of this phenomenon in Cuban Spanish. Online data has been collected in order to further consider this claim.

As pointed out by an anonymous reviewer, in a future study it will be important to consider the contrastive behaviors associated with different left-dislocated elements. We are aware that the grammatical status of the doubled complementizer may not be uniform across the many sentences in which it can be found (see Frank, 2016). This is in fact why we included so many sentence types: We did not want our results to be biased in either the grammatical or ungrammatical direction. Still, our test was not designed to have the statistical power to consider any variable other than length of intervener; this is material for a future study. In a similar vein, it would be interesting to investigate different types of complementizer-complement dependencies. For example, the jussive/optative *que*, which is for the most part considered obligatory in the Spanish norm (Villa-García 2012), remains unexplored. We do predict that it will be less obligatory in Cuban as opposed to Peninsular Spanish. In summary, it will be important to investigate as many sentence types as possible with the support of statistical analysis. This is particularly true given the hypothesis that our findings could be related to a more general *que*-drop property.

In conclusion, one of the central goals of the greater volume is to consider the linguistic properties that are unique to Cuban Spanish and Caribbean varieties more generally. The present study points to recomplementation as an unexplored locus for dialectal variation across the Spanish-speaking world. In so doing, it provides an initial study of an understudied morphosyntactic property in Cuban Spanish. Future studies should be devoted to replicating these experiments with other populations; it would be interesting to see if other Caribbean varieties pattern what is found here. Then it would be of value to replicate the study on non-Caribbean varieties. This would shed light on whether the linguistic phenomenon might not only contribute to our knowledge of the Cuban variety, but also to our knowledge of the morphosyntactic properties that separate Caribbean from non-Caribbean varieties.

Notes

1. The term recomplementation was coined by Higgins (1988). Here we also use the terms multiple/double complementizers for signaling the co-occurrence of a primary and a secondary, reduplicative complementizer.
2. For research on Dominican Spanish, for example, see Bullock and Toribio (2009); Camacho (2006a, 2006b, 2013); Ordóñez and Olarrea (2001, 2006); and Toribio (2000a, 2000b, 1992, 1993a, 1993b).
3. Consult the seminal work of Rizzi (1997) and the large number of works inspired therefrom.
4. As an anonymous reviewer points out, measuring distance at the word level is a less precise measure. In spite of this fact, we have adopted a similar distance measure in order to remain consistent with Casasanto and Sag's study.
5. The oral sentence completion task is modeled on the production task used in Cuza and Frank (2011, 2015), which successfully elicited primary *que* in indirect questions without left dislocation.
6. Five participants did imitate at least 50 percent of the overt complementizer items accurately. However, even among this subgroup, accuracy was higher in the null as compared to the overt conditions, 92 percent versus 68 percent respectively.

References

Bullock, B. E., and A. J. Toribio. 2009. "Reconsidering Dominican Spanish: Data from the Rural Cibao." *Revista Internacional de Lingüística Iberoamericana* 7 (2): 49–73.

Brovetto, C. 2002. "Spanish Clauses without Complementizers." In *Current Issues in Romance Languages: Selected Proceedings from the 29th Linguistic Symposium on Romance Languages*, edited by T. Satterfield, C. Tortora, and D. Cresti, 33–46. Amsterdam: John Benjamins.

Camacho, J. 2006a. "Do Subjects Have a Place in Spanish?" In *New Perspectives on Romance Linguistics*, vol. 1, *Morphology, Syntax, Semantics, and Pragmatics*, edited by C. Nishida and J.-P. Y. Montreuil, 51–66. Amsterdam Studies in the Theory and History of Linguistic Science series 4, Current Issues in Linguistic Theory 275. Amsterdam: John Benjamins.

———. 2006b. "In Situ Focus in Caribbean Spanish: Towards a Unified Account of Focus." In *Selected Proceedings of the 9th Hispanic Linguistics Symposium*, edited by N. Sagarra and A. J. Toribio, 13–23. Somerville, MA: Cascadilla Proceedings Project.

———. 2013. *Null Subjects*. Cambridge Studies in Linguistics 137. Cambridge: Cambridge University Press.

Casasanto, L. S., and I. A. Sag. 2008. "The Advantage of the Ungrammatical." *Proceedings of the Annual Conference of the Cognitive Science Society* 30:601–6.

Cerrudo Aguilar, A., and Á. J. Gallego. 2014. "Contextos de (des) aparición de 'que.'" BA thesis, Universitat Autònoma de Barcelona, Departament de Filologia Espanyola.

Cuza, A., and J. Frank. 2011. "Transfer Effects at the Syntax-Semantics Interface: The Case of Double-*Que* Questions in Heritage Spanish." *Heritage Language Journal* 8 (2): 66–89.

———. 2015. "On the Role of Experience and Age-Related Effects: Evidence from the Spanish CP." *Second Language Research* 31 (1): 3–28.

Demonte, V., and O. Fernández-Soriano. 2009. "Force and Finiteness in the Spanish Complementizer System." *Probus* 21:23–49.

———. 2013. "Evidentials *Dizque* and *Que* in Spanish. Grammaticalization, Parameters and the (Fine) Structure of Comp." *Revista de Estudos Linguísticos da Univerdade do Porto* 211: 234.

Fontana, J. M. 1993. "Phrase Structure and the Syntax of Clitics in the History of Spanish." PhD diss., University of Pennsylvania.

Frank, J. 2016. "On the Grammaticality of Recomplementation in Spanish." In *Inquiries in Hispanic Linguistics: From Theory to Empirical Evidence* 12:39–52.

Garrett, J. 2013. "Which *Que* Is Which?: A Squib on Reduplicative *Que* Complementizers in Iberian Spanish Embedded Clauses." *Indiana University Linguistics Club Working Papers* 13:1–9. https://www.indiana.edu/~iulcwp/wp/article/view/13-05/26.

Gibson, Edward. 2000. "The Dependency Locality Theory: A Distance-Based Theory of Linguistic Complexity." In *Image, Language, Brain: Papers from the First Mind Articulation Project Symposium*, edited by A. Marantz, Y. Miyashita, and W. O'Neil, 95–126. Cambridge, MA: MIT Press.

González i Planas, F. 2010. "Cartografia de la Recomplementació en les Llengües Romàniques." MA thesis, University of Girona.

———. 2014. "On Quotative Recomplementation: Between Pragmatics and Morphosyntax." *Lingua* 146:39–74.

Gupton, T. M. 2010. "The Syntax-Information Structure Interface: Subjects and Clausal Word Order in Galician." PhD diss., University of Iowa.

Hamayan, E. 1978. "Differences in Performance in Elicited Imitation between French Monolingual and English-Speaking Bilingual Children." *International Review of Applied Linguistics in Language Teaching* 16 (4): 330–39.

Higgins, R. 1988. "Where the Old English Sentence Begins." MA thesis, University of Massachusetts, Amherst.

Jaeger, T. F. 2006. "Redundancy and Syntactic Reduction in Spontaneous Speech." PhD diss., Stanford University.

———. 2010. "Redundancy and Reduction: Speakers Manage Syntactic Information Density." *Cognitive Psychology* 61 (1): 23–62.

López, L. 2009. *A Derivational Syntax for Information Structure*. Oxford Studies in Theoretical Linguistics 23. Oxford: Oxford University Press.

O'Grady, W. 2010 . "An Emergentist Approach to Syntax." In *The Oxford Handbook of Linguistic Analysis*, edited by H. Narrog and B. Heine, 257–84. Oxford: Oxford University Press.

Ordóñez, F., and A. Olarrea. 2001. "Weak Subject Pronouns in Caribbean Spanish and XP Pied-Piping." In *Features and Interfaces in Romance: Essays in Honor of Heles Contreras*, edited by J. Herschensohn, E. Mallén, and K. Zagona, 223–38. Amsterdam Studies in the Theory and History of Linguistic Science series 4, Current Issues in Linguistics 222. Amsterdam: John Benjamins.

———. 2006. "Microvariation in Caribbean/Non-Caribbean Spanish Interrogatives." *Probus* 18 (1): 59–96.

Pérez-Leroux, A. T., A. Cuza, and D. Thomas. 2011. "Clitic Placement in Spanish–English Bilingual Children." *Bilingualism: Language and Cognition* 14 (2): 221–32.
Plann, S. 1982. "Indirect Questions in Spanish." *Linguistic Inquiry* 13:297–312.
Radford, A. 2013. "The Complementizer System in Spoken English. Evidence from Broadcast Media." In *Information Structure and Agreement*, edited by V. Camacho-Taboada, Á. L. Jiménez-Fernández, J. Martín-González, and M. Reyes-Tejedor, 11–54. Amsterdam: John Benjamins.
Radloff, C. 1991. *Sentence Repetition Testing for Studies of Community Bilingualism.* Arlington: Summer Institute of Linguistics and University of Texas at Arlington.
Riccelli, A. Forthcoming. "Complementizer Drop in Two Varieties of Spanish." In *Language Variation and Contact-Induced Change: The Spanish Language across Space and Time*, edited by J. King and S. Sessarego. Amsterdam: John Benjamins.
Rizzi, L. 1997. "The Fine Structure of the Left Periphery." In *Elements of Grammar*, edited by L. Haegeman, 281–337. Dordrecht, Nld.: Kluwer Academic Publishers.
Rodríguez-Ramalle, T. M. 2003. *La Gramática de los Adverbios en -mente o cómo Expresar Maneras, Opiniones y Actitudes a Través de la Lengua.* Madrid: Ediciones de la Universidad Autónoma de Madrid.
Silva-Corvalán C. 1993. "On the permeability of grammars: Evidence from Spanish and English contact." In *Linguistic Perspectives on Romance Languages*, edited by W. Ashby, M. Mithun, and G. Perissinotto, 19-43. Amsterdam: John Benjamins.
Suñer, M. 1993. "About Indirect Questions and Semi-Questions." *Linguistics and Philosophy* 16 (1): 45–77.
Toribio, A. J. 1992. "Proper Government in Spanish Subject Relativization." *Probus* 4 (3): 291–304.
———. 1993a. "Lexical Subjects in Finite and Non-finite Clauses." *Cornell Working Papers in Linguistics* 11:149–78.
———. 1993b. "Parametric Variation in the Licensing of Nominal." PhD diss., Cornell University.
———. 2000a. "Minimalist Ideas on Parametric Variation." In *Proceedings of the North East Linguistic Society 30*, edited by M. Hirotani, A. Coetzee, N. Hall, and J.-Y. Kim, 627–38. Amherst: University of Massachusetts, Graduate Linguistic Student Association.
———. 2000b. "Setting Parametric Limits on Dialectal Variation in Spanish." *Lingua* 110 (5): 315–41.
Villa-García, J. 2012. "Recomplementation and Locality of Movement in Spanish." *Probus* 24 (2): 257–314.
———. 2015. *The Syntax of Multiple* -que *Sentences in Spanish: Along the Left Periphery.* Issues in Hispanic and Lusophone Linguistics 2. Amsterdam: John Benjamins.

8

The Sociolinguistic Profile of *Ser* and *Estar* in Cuban Spanish: An Analysis of Oral Speech

MANUEL DÍAZ-CAMPOS
Indiana University

IRAIDA GALARZA
Indiana University

GIBRAN DELGADO-DÍAZ
Indiana University

THE ANALYSIS OF COPULA choice in adjectival constructions has been the center of many investigations in Spanish, and they have focused on theoretical accounts (Clements 1988, 2006), sociolinguistic perspectives (e.g., Alfaraz 2012; Brown and Cortés-Torres 2012), first-language (e.g., Requena, Román-Hernández, and Miller, 2015), and second-language acquisitional contexts (e.g., Geeslin 2003), and language-contact situations in the US (Silva-Corvalán 1986) and Spanish in contact with other languages (Geeslin and Guijarro-Fuentes 2008). This work has contributed to our understanding of the factors involved in predicting copula choice as well as in describing the patterns of variation and change across varieties of Spanish.

The present investigation focuses on the extra-linguistic factors influencing copula choice in Cuban Spanish, a dialect of Spanish where recent research on this subject is scarce. This study also compares Cuban Spanish with other dialects such as Puerto Rican, Mexican, and Venezuelan Spanish in order to gain a broader understanding of the grammatical change involving [*ser*/*estar* + adjective] under a grammaticalization perspective. This chapter is organized as follows: First, a review of the previous literature is presented. In this section, a brief historical development of variation between *ser* and *estar* is discussed as well as analyses on the extra-linguistic factors that condition their use. The second section describes the present study and the methodology used. In the results section, a statistical analysis of the factors conditioning the use of *ser* and *estar* in Cuban Spanish is offered and a comparative analysis across Latin American dialects is examined. The implications of these findings are discussed to gain a better understanding of the path of language change affecting [*ser*/*estar* + adjective] in contemporary Spanish. Finally, we offer some conclusions and future research directions.

Previous Literature

Traditional accounts have explained copular distribution in the construction [copula + adjective] in semantic terms, attributing different functions to each of the copulas, and thus attributing it a meaningful alternation. For instance, it has been argued that while *ser* expresses the permanent properties of a referent, *estar* expresses transitory, contingent, or circumstantial states (Gili Gaya 1961). For example, in 8.1 *ser* presents the quality attributed to the subject as permanent and in 8.2 *estar* presents the quality as contingent.

Example 8.1.

Pedro ***es saludable***.
Peter **is healthy**.

Example 8.2.

Pedro ***está enfermo***.
Peter **is sick**.

However, Gili Gaya (1961), based on the work of Hanssen (1913), explains that the distinction of *ser* and *estar* goes beyond the simplicity of the treatment it has received in the most traditional descriptive studies. Gili Gaya argues that in studying the distinction between *ser* and *estar*, the aspectual notion of imperfective and perfective as used by Hanssen may be useful. *Ser* would represent an imperfective predicate and *estar* would be used to indicate a perfective predicate. For instance, in example 8.3 *ser* is used to express a quality that is presented in its duration, while in example 8.4 the quality is seen as the result of an action, transformation, or change (both examples are from Gili Gaya 1961, 62).

Example 8.3.

Este jarro ***es blanco***.
This vase **is white**.

Example 8.4.

Este jarro ***está roto***.
This vase **is broken**.

Gili Gaya further explains that in an example like 8.1 the quality is seen without taking into account its origin, while in an example like 8.2, the quality is seen as the result of a change that could be either real or assumed by the speaker. How do we know that a change has taken place according to this distinction? Gili Gaya argues that the experience of the speaker with the referent is a key factor. For example, in the case in 8.5 the use of *ser* + *fría* corresponds to a general description that is independent of the speaker's immediate experience. In contrast, example 8.6 represents an assessment of a description that depends on the immediate experience. (Both examples come from Gili Gaya 1961, 62.)

Example 8.5.

> *La nieve* ***es fría***.
> Snow **is cold**.

Example 8.6.

> *Aquella nieve* ***está fría***.
> That snow **feels cold**.

This subtle difference in the use of *ser* and *estar* in Spanish tends to be difficult for non-native speakers to capture. Gili Gaya explains that for English native speakers it is useful to consider if, in the sentence with a copula, one can use verbs such as to feel or to look (e.g., 'the coffee **feels hot**'/*el café* ***está caliente***). In this case, not only is the perfective aspect present, the immediate experience with the referent is also seen. In the following section, a brief but concise review of the most important diachronic and synchronic patterns of change in copula choice is presented in order to provide the necessary context to understand current studies on this subject.

Diachronic and Synchronic Variation of ser and estar

Several scholars have argued that copular verbs in Spanish are in a process of diachronic change, in which *estar* is expanding to functions originally fulfilled by *ser* (e.g., Batllori and Roca 2011), as well as grammaticalizing new functions (cf. Torres Cacoullos 2011). *Ser* and *estar* have their roots in Latin *esse* and *stare*, respectively.[1] Latin *stare* had different meanings related to the posture and location of the referent, which can be translated as 'to stand,' 'to be situated,' and 'to stay' (Díaz-Campos and Geeslin 2011; Pountain 1982). As Batllori, Castillo, and Roca-Urgell (2009, 461) state, *stare* was used with a full lexical meaning in locative constructions in Latin, both in intransitive constructions (e.g., *Pugna stetit*, 'The battle continued') and constructions with locative expressions (e.g., *Stabat ad ianuam*, '[It] was at/in front of the door'). Pountain (1982) observes that *stare* was not nearly as frequent in either Classical or Vulgar Latin as it is now in contemporary Spanish. Thus, the locative function fulfilled by *stare* was also expressed by other Latin verbs (*adesse*, 'to be present,' 'to be here/there'; *sedere*, 'to sit'; and *esse*, 'to be,' among others). Moreover, Batllori, Castillo, and Roca-Urgell (2009) indicate that some copulative uses of *stare* were already present in Latin when the predicate was to be interpreted as "remaining or being in some place"; in other words, when the adjectival construction had a strong locative meaning. As a result, Batllori, Castillo, and Roca-Urgell consider this construction with *stare* in Latin as the precursor of the copulative uses of *estar* in Spanish (see Batllori, Castillo, and Roca-Urgell 2009 and Batllori and Roca 2011 for further discussion). Consequently, the historic development of Spanish copulas, *ser* and *estar*, can be described as a process whereby *estar* has expanded its functional contexts of occurrence, overlapping with contexts in which *ser* was previously exclusively used (Batllori and Roca 2011; Marco and Marín 2015). Thus, the use of *estar* has developed from a locative construction in Latin, with a full postural meaning, to its current use in locative, attributive, and progressive constructions in contemporary Spanish (Batllori and Roca 2011).

It has been argued that the semantic distinctions between *ser* and *estar* in the attributive construction may have their origins in the copulas' diachronic lexical sources (Marco and Marín 2015). Consequently, the original locative meaning of *estar* has been extended to express temporally bounded states, such as temporally delimited adjectives (Marco and Marín 2015). This evolutionary path is consistent with semantic change of locative expressions. Bybee, Perkins, and Pagliuca (1994, 25) show that, crosslinguistically, many locative expressions develop temporal and aspectual meanings over time due to grammaticalization processes. Grammaticalization refers to a set of phonological, morphosyntactic, semantic, and pragmatic processes by which grammatical constructions are created out of discursive patterns of use (Bybee, Perkins, and Pagliuca 1994; Torres Cacoullos 2011, 149). These processes operate gradually in concrete instances of language use; thus, in this view, language use in context creates and shapes grammatical material (Bybee, Perkins, and Pagliuca 1994). For instance, the original locative meaning of *estar* developed different aspectual meanings both in [*estar* + gerund] constructions (which have a grammaticalized progressive meaning), and in [*estar* + adjective] constructions in Spanish. Bybee, Perkins, and Pagliuca (1994) argue that the temporal and aspectual senses that develop out of locative expressions have to do with the fact that both spatial and temporal meanings are present in locative expressions, even though spatial meaning is the principal sense of the form. Thus, the development of aspectual and temporal meaning consists of the loss of the spatial meaning and the strengthening of the temporal sense already present in the locative construction. In grammaticalization theory, the process whereby a form loses specific features of meaning is known as generalization of meaning, and is one of the many mechanisms involved in semantic change (Bybee 2010; Bybee, Perkins, and Pagliuca 1994). This type of semantic change has implications for the distribution of the grammaticalizing form since by having a more generalized or abstract meaning the form can occur in a greater number of contexts, thus extending its contexts of occurrence. This may result in instances in which two or more forms compete over a semantic domain, creating overlapping usage. Another possibility is that two forms develop contrasting meanings (e.g., was doing/did; Bybee, Perkins, and Pagliuca 1994). Regarding the grammaticalization path of copulative expressions, Devitt (1990) argues that there seems to be a crosslinguistic affinity between locatives and the expression of temporary states since many locative expressions across languages develop copulative functions with temporary states before gaining more general copulative functions. These findings reveal a pattern of grammaticalization according to which *estar* has acquired new functions based on a process of semantic generalization, allowing it to occur in more copulative contexts.

Copula Choice in Cuban Spanish

Regarding previous research specifically focused on copula choice in Cuban Spanish, the only recent variationist investigation is presented by Alfaraz (2012). This scholar analyzed two sets of recorded interviews from Cubans. The first set belongs to *el Estudio Coordinado de la Norma Lingüística Culta de las Principales Ciudades de Iberoamérica y de la Península Ibérica* (Coordinated Study of the Educated Linguistic Norm of the Main Iberian-American Cities and Iberian Peninsula), which includes material recorded in the 1960s. The second set of recordings comprises sociolinguistic interviews of speakers who had recently arrived to the US from Cuba at the moment of the study (Cubans in Miami). This last set is from the 1990s. With respect to the variable context, Alfaraz did not include in the analysis contexts in which referents are compared to themselves in two different points in time. Therefore, this study did not examine the copular distribution taking into account the factor frame of reference, which was found to be significant in other studies (Brown and Cortés-Torres 2012; Díaz-Campos and Geeslin 2011; Gutiérrez 1994; Silva-Corvalán 1986). The analysis is limited as it only includes one linguistic factor, adjective type, disregarding crucial linguistic factors found to be significant in previous studies of copula choice (e.g., resultant state, frame of reference, susceptibility to change, and experience with the referent). The analysis also includes two sociolinguistic factors: generation and gender. The author reports 116 instances (19.3 percent) of "innovative" use of *estar*. 'Innovative' in this context is a categorization based on criteria established using reference grammars of Spanish, which do not necessarily reflect the actual corpus analyzed. Recall that recent research on other varieties of Spanish has revealed that *ser* is still the predominant form and that the contexts in which *estar* has expanded are somewhat more limited than what has been proposed in previous work. Regarding the effect of linguistic variable adjective type, Alfaraz (2012) shows that categories such as physical properties (e.g., *suave*, 'soft,' *sólido*, 'solid') favor the use of *estar* with a weight of 0.59 and evaluative adjectives (e.g., *bueno*, 'good,' *bello*, 'beautiful') also favor the use of *estar* with a weight of 0.56. However, while the use of *ser* and *estar* may be variable with these adjectives, it is not clear that complete neutralization of meaning distinctions has occurred with some of the adjectives included in these two categories. The analysis of social factors indicates that only the factor generation was selected as significant and included in the statistical model. These results show an increased use of *estar* by the younger generation of the 1990s, which, according to Alfaraz, may suggest a change in progress. However, the analysis of other relevant sociolinguistic factors may be needed to corroborate that interpretation. In summary, one of the limitations of this study is that it only takes into account a single linguistic factor, namely adjective class, to explain all copular alternation in Cuban Spanish, despite the evidence that copula choice is influenced by a composite of linguistic and social factors. Moreover, this study left out of the analysis contexts in which *ser* and *estar* can alternate, such as the contexts in which the speakers compared referents to themselves. The next section is dedicated to describing the factors used in the present study.

Linguistic and Social Factors on Copula Variation

Several empirical studies have included a variety of linguistic and social factors in order to determine the nature of the variability of [*ser*/*estar* + adjective]. A crucial aspect in the design of these investigations has to do with the definition of the envelope of variation and the criteria used to classify *ser* and *estar* in attributive contexts. Related to the idea of the development of new contextual uses of *estar*, previous research has made the assumption that the synchronic variation in the [copula + adjective] construction observed in Spanish is due to the extension of *estar* into contexts previously occupied by *ser*. Several studies have focused on the description of the so-called innovative uses of *estar* (Alfaraz 2012; Silva-Corvalán 1986). Implicit in these studies is the definition of the dependent variable based on the categorization of cases according to "normative" uses of *ser* and *estar* as described in prescriptive Spanish grammars. In contrast, studies such as Brown and Cortés-Torres (2012) and Díaz-Campos and Geeslin (2011) have based their classification of the dependent variable in the actual cases found in the corpora by differentiating tokens with only *ser*, only *estar*, and both copulas, reflecting the distribution of them in the corpus. This methodology permits identifying the actual envelope of variation for copula choice according to speaker's patterns of use. Table 8.1 summarizes all the linguistic factors that have been found to condition copula choice and the direction of the effects documented in these studies.

The Role of Social Factors

Processes of language variation and change can be mediated by social factors (e.g., Labov 1972). Social stratification of the use of *ser* and *estar* has been examined in several varieties of Spanish, including Venezuelan, Cuban, Puerto Rican, Costa Rican, and Mexican, among other dialects. However, in contrast to the effect of the linguistic variables discussed above, the results of the social variables are less consistent, revealing different patterns of variation according to the specific speech community under study. Table 8.2 summarizes all the social factors that have been found to condition copula choice and the direction of the effects documented in these studies.

These previous investigations and the independent variables discussed above are central pieces in the design of the present investigation. As will be described and explained in the methodology section, several factors included in the literature review are also used in the empirical analysis of Cuban Spanish in this study.

The Present Study

The present study provides an empirical, quantitative analysis of copula choice in contemporary Cuban Spanish using the tools of variationist sociolinguistics. The specific purpose is to examine the linguistic and extralinguistic factors predicting

Table 8.1. Summary of linguistic factors previously studied according to the direction of the effect and investigations providing support

Factor	Direction of effect	Investigation providing support
Predicate type	Individual level → *ser* Stage level → *estar*	Aguilar-Sánchez 2009; Batllori, Castillo, and -Urgell 2009; Batllori and Roca 2011; Camacho 2012; Clements 1988, 2006; Díaz-Campos and Geeslin 2011, 2011; Geeslin 2003; Juárez-Cummings 2014; Leonetti 1994; Marco and Marín 2015
Resultant state	[– resultant] → *ser* [+ resultant] → *estar*	Aguilar-Sánchez 2009; Brown and Cortés-Torres 2012; Díaz-Campos and Geeslin 2011a; Geeslin 2003; Juárez-Cummings 2014
Semantic class of the adjective	Status → *ser* Observable traits → *ser* Mental and physical states → *estar*	Brown and Cortés-Torres 2012; Cortés-Torres 2004; Díaz-Campos and Geeslin 2011a; Gutiérrez 1992, 1994; Juárez-Cummings 2014; Ortiz López 2000; Silva-Corvalán 1986
Frame of reference	[– comparison] → *ser* [+ comparison] → *estar*	Brown and Cortés-Torres 2012; Díaz-Campos and Geeslin 2011a; Gutiérrez, 1994; Silva-Corvalán 1986
Susceptibility to change	Not changeable → *ser* Changeable → *estar*	Díaz-Campos and Geeslin 2011a; Juárez-Cummings 2014; Silva-Corvalán 1986
Experience with the referent	Indirect → *ser* Ongoing → *ser* Immediate → *estar*	Brown and Cortés-Torres 2012; Díaz-Campos and Geeslin 2011a; Guijarro-Fuentes and Geeslin 2006; Geeslin and Guijarro-Fuentes 2007 2008

the use of *ser* and *estar* in oral corpus from Havana, Cuba, since there are not recent studies that analyze the speech of Cubans on the island. This investigation also has the broad objective of describing this phenomenon in Cuban Spanish and comparing the results with other varieties, including Puerto Rican, Mexican, and Venezuelan Spanish, with the purpose of assessing synchronically an ongoing process of language variation and change. Following grammaticalization theory, a discussion of the findings is presented. With these objectives in mind the following research questions are proposed:

1. What are the linguistic and sociolinguistic factors that significantly predict copula choice in the [copula + adjective] construction in Cuban Spanish?
2. How does Cuban Spanish compare to other Spanish dialects (San Juan, Puerto Rico, Caracas, Venezuela, and Mexico City, Mexico) with respect to the linguistic and sociolinguistic constraints?
3. How can the results of the comparative analysis be accounted for within grammaticalization theory?

Table 8.2. Summary of social factors previously studied according to the direction of the effect and investigations providing support

Social Factor	Dialect and direction of the effect	Investigation providing support
Socioeconomic status	Venezuela Lower class → estar Mexico Lower and middle class → estar	Díaz-Campos and Geeslin 2011; Juárez-Cummings 2014
Age	Puerto Rico 20–29 y/o → estar Mexico 35–44 y/o → estar Venezuela 46+ → estar	Brown and Cortés-Torres 2012; Díaz-Campos and Geeslin 2011a; Juárez-Cummings 2014
Level of education	Cuernavaca, México lower educational level → estar Costa Rica lower educational level → estar	Aguilar-Sánchez 2009; Cortés-Torres 2004
Gender	Costa Rica Women → estar Puerto Rico Men → estar	Aguilar-Sánchez 2009; Ortiz López 2000
Language contact	Bilinguals → estar Monolinguals → estar No uniform effect Basque and Galician bilinguals → estar Catalan and Valencian bilinguals → ser No effect	Brown and Cortés-Torres 2012; Geeslin and Guijarro-Fuentes 2008; Gutiérrez 1994; Ortiz López 2000; Silva-Corvalán 1986

Methodology

Participants

The corpus used for this analysis comes from a sample of native Spanish speakers from Havana, Cuba. The corpus is part of the Project for the Sociolinguistic Study of Spanish from Spain and America (Proyecto para el Estudio Sociolingüístico del Español de España y de América or PREESEA). The sample is composed of eighteen native Spanish speakers from Havana, Cuba. These recordings were recently completed and electronically published in 2014. The data contained in this sample are composed of sociolinguistic interviews lasting around 45 minutes for each speaker. The conversations included the following topics: greetings, weather, place where the subject lives, family and friends, traditions, danger of death situations, etc. The data is evenly distributed according to level of education (i.e., illiterate or primary education, high school, and college education), age (i.e., 20–34, 35–54, and 55 or more) and gender (i.e., male or female).

Envelope of Variation and Coding Scheme

The variable context was circumscribed following the notion of functional equivalence (Lavandera 1978), which delimits the envelope of variation in terms of a given grammatical or discursive function. Thus, it is not based on the traditional definition of sociolinguistic variables as "alternate ways of saying 'the same' thing" (Labov

1972, 188). As has been extensively discussed (Lavandera 1978; Schwenter 2011; Terkourafi 2011), the idea of equivalence in meaning is problematic in the case of linguistic variables that go beyond the phonological level, since the choice between two morphosyntactic structures can have an effect on the referential meaning expressed (Lavandera 1978).

In the present study, all cases of *ser* and *estar* that co-occurred with adjectives in the corpus were extracted. These [copula + adjective] constructions have a general attributive function in which a quality or characteristic is related to a referent (Díaz-Campos and Geeslin 2011; Geeslin and Gudmestad 2010). However, with this definition of the envelope of variation we are aware that not all of the cases examined have the same semantic or pragmatic interpretation, and in many cases the copulas are not necessarily interchangeable. Since the main goal of this study is to examine the variation between *ser* and *estar*, we left out other verbs that may also fulfill an attributive function, such as *sentir* (to feel) and *parecer* (to seem), but see Geeslin and Gudmestad (2010) for such an analysis. After extracting all of the relevant cases from the corpus, we coded each of them for five linguistic factors (*resultant state*, *frame of reference*, *dependence on experience*, *adjective class*, and *susceptibility to change*) and three sociolinguistic factors pertaining to the speaker (*age*, *education level*, and *gender*). The selection of factors was based on the previous literature and particularly following the methodology used in Díaz-Campos and Geeslin (2011). A description of the dependent variable and the independent variables are below.

Dependent variable: The dependent variable of this investigation is the copulative construction composed of [*ser*/*estar* + adjective]. As seems obvious from this description, the dependent variable has two variants:

- 8.6 *Ser*
  ...más simples eeh tienen otro pensamiento ya cuando ***son adultos*** *eeh su pensamiento va cambiando.*
  ...more simple ehh they have other ideas when they **are adults** eeh their ideas are changing. (LHAB_H13_073)

- 8.7 *Estar*
  ...o la esperanza de que ***esté*** *más* ***pintadita*** */ de que* ***esté*** *más* ***arreglada.***
  ...or the hope that it **would be painted** / that it **would be in better shape**. (LHAB_M13_079)

Independent variables: Based on the review of the previous literature, this investigation tests the predictive power of five linguistic variables and three extralinguistic variables.[2] A description of these factors and examples of each one of them follow.

Resultant state: This variable used in previous studies (e.g., Aguilar-Sánchez 2009; Díaz-Campos and Geeslin 2011; Brown and Cortés-Torres 2012) distinguishes adjectives that derive from a dynamic situation (i.e., processes or activities and events or achievements and accomplishments; see a conceptual description in the work of Clements 2006). It is generally the case that these adjectives are derived from a verb form.

- 8.8 [+ Resultant]
  Son los lugares / que a esa hora ***están abiertos*** */ que por lo menos a mí no me llaman mucho.*
  They are places / that **are open** at that time / that at least they don't call me often. (LHAB_H23_085)
- 8.9 [– Resultant]
  (23) *Mi apartamento* ***es muy amplio****.*
  My apartment **is very big**. (LHAB_M13_079)

Semantic class of the adjective: As pointed out in Díaz-Campos and Geeslin (2011, 77) adjective class has received the widest attention in the previous literature. Some of the limitations of examining this variable are related to the fact that in naturally occurring data, some categories occur with greater frequency than others. For this reason, we have created broader categories to facilitate the quantitative analysis. The three categories created are mental states, observable traits (e.g., appearance, size, color), and adjectives of social class and status.

- 8.10 Mental states
  Personas de... de su generación / ***están conscientes*** *de las necesidades de...*
  People from… his generation / **are aware** of the needs of… (LHAB_M23_091)
- 8.11 Observable traits
  Ya hablábamos de las características de él / él ***es delgado*** *por naturaleza.*
  We were talking about his characteristics / he **is thin** by nature. (LHAB_M23_091)
- 8.12 Status
  …porque entonces ya el papá del niño y yo ya ***estábamos separados****.*
  …because by then the father of my son and I **were separated**. (LHAB_M22_055)

Frame of reference: As explained above while reviewing the previous literature, this independent variable distinguishes between individual and class frames of reference in comparison contexts. An individual frame compares an entity to itself at different points in time. In contrast, a class frame compares a referent with a group of similar entities. It is expected that individual frame of reference will favor the use of *estar* based on empirical findings from previous research (e.g., Díaz-Campos and Geeslin 2011; Brown and Cortés-Torres 2012; Silva-Corvalán 1986).

- 8.13 [+ Comparison] Individual frame of reference
  No es un hombre feo // es trigueño bueno ahora ***está canoso*** *porque ya* ***está viejo*** *// pero bueno.*
  He is not ugly // he is tanned well now **he has grey hair** because **he is old** // but hey. (LHAB_M32_067)

- 8.14 [– Comparison] Class frame of reference
  *...porque mi mamá y mi tía **son asmáticas** y **son alérgicas** / fulminante al pelo de del gato.*
  ...because my mother and aunt **are asthmatics** and **are allergic** / immediately to cat's hair. (LHAB_M11_007)

Susceptibility to change: This independent variable is designed to capture properties of the adjective and referent that can be considered changeable from those that cannot change (e.g., Díaz-Campos and Geeslin 2011; Juárez-Cummings 2014, Silva-Corvalán 1986).

- 8.15 Susceptible
  *Piden muchas hamburguesas / parece que / **están muy buenas**.*
  They order lots of hamburgers / it seems that / **they are good**. (LHAB_H21_013)

- 8.16 Not susceptible
  *Pero mi sangre **es gallega** // es la realidad / y no lo puedo negar.*
  My blood **is Galician** // it is the reality / and I cannot deny it. (LHAB_H33_097)

Experience with the referent: Originally proposed by Guitart (2002), this independent variable is design for the analysis of contexts where speakers indicate having firsthand experience with the referent. Three variants are distinguished for this variable: immediate experience, ongoing, and indirect experience.

- 8.17 Immediate
  *Me gusta pero como está hoy que hace sol sí **está aceptable**.*
  I like it but how it is today that it is sunny it **is acceptable**. (LHAB_H12_037)

- 8.18 Ongoing
  *No fue una carrera muy fácil fue... **fue** bastante **difícil** / tuve que estudiar bastante.*
  It was not an easy degree ... **it was** very **difficult** / I had to study hard. (LHAB_H13_073)

- 8.19 Indirect
  *...cosas diferentes / los amigos cuando / cuando uno **es adulto** por lo general se hace amigo de personas...*
  ...different things / friends when / when one **is an adult** in general one becomes friends with people... (LHAB_M13_079)

The coding scheme also includes social independent variables for the *age*, *gender*, and *socioeconomic class* of the speaker. The next section provides some details concerning the statistical analysis used in the present investigation.

Analysis

The data were analyzed using Rbrul, a computer program designed for modeling sociolinguistic variation (Johnson 2009). The implementation of Rbrul is based on R statistical software. We performed a mixed-effects logistic regression statistical test. This type of analysis allowed us to examine the effects of the linguistic and social factors on copula choice in the [copula + adjective] construction, while accounting for the effect of the individual. In other words, the independent variables described above are treated as fixed effects, while the individual is treated as a random effect.

In the Rbrul analysis, the probability coefficients are expressed in log-odd units, which can be a positive or negative number: a positive log-odd value is interpreted as a favoring effect (i.e., an effect that favors the application value, such as *estar* in the present analysis), a negative value indicates a disfavoring effect, and 0 corresponds to a neutral effect (Johnson 2009). This is the natural logarithm of the odds of success, with the same concept as an odds ratio. Rbrul also expresses the probability coefficients in the traditional factor weight units, ranging from 0 to 1, so that the results obtained with the Rbrul analysis can be easily compared to studies that have reported their results using probabilistic weights (Johnson 2009). In the present analysis, we treated *susceptibility to change*, *frame of reference*, *dependence on experience*, *resultant state*, *adjective class*, *age*, *education level*, and *gender* as fixed factors, whereas *speaker* was treated as a random effect. The results of such analysis will be discussed in the following section.

Results

A total of 873 [copula + adjective] constructions were obtained from the corpus. *Estar* was used in 208 cases (23.8 percent), while *ser* had a higher usage rate in the [copula + adjective] construction, with 665 cases (76.2 percent). This copular distribution is consistent with other studies (e.g., Brown and Cortés-Torres 2012; Díaz-Campos and Geeslin 2011; Juárez-Cummings 2014), in which *ser* is the most frequently used copula or the default copula (Clements 2006, 182) in the adjectival construction. Clements (2006) attributes this distribution to the semantic underspecification of *ser*, which allows this copula to occur with a larger number of adjectives. To discuss the results of the regression, we follow the three courses of action commonly used in variationist sociolinguistics: (1) identify the significant factors that condition the variation; (2) examine the relative strength or significant contribution of each factor group (i.e., the magnitude of effect); and (3) identify the direction of the effect within a factor group (i.e., constraint hierarchy) (Poplack and Tagliamonte 2001, 92–94). These aspects of the results are considered in variationist research to represent the underlying variable grammar of a particular set of speakers.

Results from the mixed-effects logistic regression show that the best model for the prediction of [copula + adjective] in Cuban Spanish included the *speaker* as random effect, and *resultant state*, *frame of reference*, *dependence on experience*, and *adjective class* as fixed effects. The factors that did not significantly contribute to the use of *estar* were *susceptibility to change*, *age*, *education level*, and *gender*. Consequently, only semantic and pragmatic linguistic factors explained copula choice in Cuban Spanish in the attributive function. These results are summarized in table 8.3.

Resultant state is by far the most significant predictor of *estar* in the Cuban data. An adjective classified as [+ resultant] favored the use of *estar*, with a weight of 0.862, whereas a [– resultant] adjective disfavored the use of *estar* with a weight of 0.138.[3] The use of *estar* with [+ resultant] adjectives reflects the observation that there is an aspectual difference between *ser* and *estar* (Clements 2006; Fernández Leborans 1995; Luján 1981). In this case, this difference is manifested through the preference of *estar* with adjectives that have an underlying dynamic situation as source (Clements 2006). In other words, the adjectives that express the end point of a process or event tend to favor the use of *estar*. Thus, this result is consistent with the predictions made by Clements (2006) with respect to the different classes of adjectives across time stability categories, and their distribution with the copular verbs. This factor has also proven to be relevant in other dialectal areas such as Caracas, Venezuela, Mexico City, Mexico, and Puerto Rico (see comparative analysis below).

The second factor selected as significant by the model is a discourse-pragmatic one (Clements 2006; Geeslin 2003): frame of reference. Specifically, in contexts in which a referent was compared to itself [+ comparison], the use of *estar* was favored, with a weight of 0.844. In contrast, the cases in which the referent was classified as a member of a class disfavored the use of *estar* with a weight of 0.156. This is consistent with the results of other studies (Brown and Cortés-Torres 2012; Cortés-Torres 2004; Díaz-Campos and Geeslin 2011; Gutiérrez 1992, 1994; Juárez-Cummings 2014; Silva-Corvalán 1986). Moreover, the significant result of this factor provides empirical support to the semantic-pragmatic feature [+ nexus] proposed by Clements (1988), in which *estar* but not *ser* connects the referent to other (assumed or expected) situations or states. Consequently, these results show that *estar* tends to be favored in the discursive contexts when there is a comparison of the referent with itself.

The following significant factor included in the model was the discourse-pragmatic factor dependence on experience. An *immediate* experience with the referent favored the use of *estar* in the data, with a weight of 0.90, while both an *indirect* and an *ongoing* experience with the referent disfavored the use of *estar*. The preference for *estar* in contexts in which the speaker has a firsthand experience with the referent concurs with the results of other studies (Brown and Cortés-Torres 2012; Díaz-Campos and Geeslin 2011; Geeslin and Guijarro-Fuentes 2007, 2008; Juárez-Cummings 2014). The significant effect of this variable relates to the evidential (Roby 2009) and subjective uses of *estar* to express a reaction or surprise with respect to the subject referent (Guitart 2002).

Finally, adjective class also had an effect on the use of *estar* in the data. Particularly, mental adjectives favor the use of *estar*, with a weight of 0.786, whereas *status* and *observable traits* adjectives do not contribute to the use of *estar*. This result agrees with previous empirical studies (e.g., Brown and Cortés-Torres 2012; Díaz-Campos and Geeslin 2011; Juárez-Cummings 2014) and with theoretical accounts of the copular verbs in adjectival contexts (Clements 2006), since mental adjectives often represent transitory states.

Table 8.3. Results of the mixed-effect model analysis with Rbrul indicating the linguistic factors that significantly favor [*estar* + adjective] in Cuban Spanish

Factors	Log-odds	Cases/ total	Percentage %	p-value	Centered Factor Weight
Resultant State				7.92e–41[1]	
+ Resultant	1.834	96/131	73.3		0.862
– Resultant	–1.834	112/742	15.1		0.138
Range	72				
Frame of Reference				4.3e–42	
+ Comparison	1.691	99/149	66.4		0.844
– Comparison	–1.691	109/724	15.1		0.156
Range	69				
Dependence on Experience				8.46e–25	
Immediate	2.258	60/69	87		0.905
Indirect	–0.989	8/42	19		0.271
Ongoing	–1.269	140/762	18.4		0.219
Range	68				
Adjective Class				1.71e–07	
Mental	1.299	63/99	63.9		0.786
Status	–0.629	23/65	35.4		0.348
Observable traits	–0.670	122/709	17.2		0.339
Range	44				

Speaker standard dev
0.338

Deviance	Df	Intercept	Mean	Input probability
451.278	8	1.847	0.238	0.864

1. P values are presented in scientific E notation. Therefore, p = 7.92e–41 equals 0.0000000000000000 0000000000000000000000792.

The model for copula choice in Cuban Spanish shows a rich patterning of both semantic (resultant state, adjective class) and discourse-pragmatic factors (frame of reference, dependence on experience). However, it is worth noticing that the predictor model did not include any social factors (i.e., age, level of education, gender). The lack of social stratification is consistent with other sociolinguistic studies that analyze morphosyntactic variation, in which the social factors do not necessarily have an effect in the observed patterns of variation. In fact, Díaz-Campos and Geeslin 2011 point out the following in their study of copula choice in Caracas Spanish: "While frequent and productive phonological change can be associated with certain social groups, syntactic change tends to be less frequent and its social value more elusive. In fact, the history of copula choice in Spanish suggests a pattern of development with long periods of stability and the strong conditioning of linguistic factors" (2011, 91).

To further explore copula choice in Cuban Spanish, we analyzed the distribution of adjectives with each copular verb. Table 8.4 shows that *ser* occurs with a larger number of adjectives (241 different adjectives or 67.70 percent of the total adjective count), whereas *estar* occurs with a smaller number of adjectives (26.40 percent). It is worth noting that the adjectives that were used only with *estar* were mostly participial adjectives (59.57 percent of the total adjectives occurring with only *estar*), such as *restaurado* (restored), *sentado* (sat), and *vestido* (dressed), among others. When *ser* occurs with past participles it can express another function, that of passive voice (e.g., *Hasta de muerte **fue** herido*, 'He **was** fatally wounded' [LHABH21]). However, some participial adjectives are found with only *ser* in attributive contexts, such as *enamorado* (in love), *agradecido* (thankful), and *callado* (quiet), among others. These participial adjectives were used to describe personality traits of the referent (e.g., *Pero tenía un defecto, que **era** demasiado enamorado*, 'But he had a defect, **he was** a womanizer' [LHABH33]).

The adjectives that were used in the corpus with both *ser* and *estar* accounted for only 5.90 percent of the total adjectives. This number of variable adjectives was smaller than in the Caracas study (8 percent; Díaz-Campos and Geeslin 2011) and the Puerto Rico study (16 percent; Brown and Cortés-Torres 2012). Furthermore, similar to the results found by Díaz-Campos and Geeslin (2011), even though there were fewer variable adjectives, these were the most frequently used adjectives in the corpus, with an average rate of use of 11.33 times each. Table 8.4 illustrates the distribution of the nine most frequent variable adjectives in the corpus.

Regarding the variable adjectives, those shown in table 8.5 account for 70.59 percent of the total variable adjective cases. Furthermore, the majority of these adjectives belong to three adjective classes: evaluative class (57.90 percent of the total variable cases), such as *bueno* (good; e.g., *El cine europeo es muy bueno*, 'European films are very good' [LHABM33]; *El programa de television está bueno*, 'The tv show is good' [LHABH31]); age class (20 percent) such as *joven* (young) and *viejo* (old) (e.g., *cuando muchacho iba mucho... cuando era joven*, 'when I was a teenager I used to go a lot... when I was young' [LHABH23]; *me sentía bien, estaba joven*, 'I felt good, I was young' [LHABH32]); and physical appearance class (10 percent), such as *gordo* (fat; e.g., *físicamente me siento bien así porque estaba bien gorda*, 'physically I feel well like this because I was very fat' [LHABM21]; *me gustaba ser aeromoza pero era muy gorda*, 'I liked being a flight attendant but I was very fat' [LHABM2]). Taken together, these three adjectival classes account for 87.92 percent of the variable adjectives. Thus, variation is limited to certain adjective classes and the specific lexical items within them.

Tracking Synchronic Variation and Grammaticalization across Dialects

In this section, we compare the patterning of linguistic and sociolinguistic factors for copula choice in Cuban (Havana), Puerto Rican (Brown and Cortés-Torres 2012),

Table 8.4. Distribution of ser and estar according to adjectives

	Number of adjectives	Pecentage of adjectives	Number of cases	Percentage of cases	Average rate of use[1]
Only *ser*	241	67.70%	477	54.64%	1.98
Only *estar*	94	26.40%	158	18.10%	1.68
Variable: *ser* and *estar*	21	5.90%	238	27.26%	11.33
Total	356	100%	873	100%	

1. Following Díaz-Campos and Geeslin (2011b) and Geeslin (2013), we calculated the average rate of use of adjectives, the number of cases in each category was divided by the total number of adjectives in each category.

Venezuelan (Caracas; Díaz-Campos and Geeslin 2011), and Mexican (Mexico City; Juárez-Cummings 2014) Spanish in order to assess the synchronic grammaticalization stages of *ser* and *estar* in copulative constructions across these Spanish dialects. Recent investigations have proposed that grammaticalization processes can be observed synchronically in dialectal variation (Bybee 2010; Torres Cacoullos 2011; Silva-Corvalán 2001).

In order to carry out the comparisons across dialects, we follow the variationist comparative method (Poplack and Tagliamonte 2001). This method consists of comparing the independent regression models obtained for the different dialects, following the three lines of evidence mentioned above (i.e., significant factors, their relative strength, and the direction of their effects; Poplack and Tagliamonte 2001). Consequently, if the dialects under study share the same factor configuration along these three lines of evidence, and if the grammaticalizing forms show comparable frequency of use, it is taken as evidence that the dialects are in the same grammaticalization stage (Torres Cacoullos 2011). In contrast, dialectal differences may represent diverse grammaticalization stages or even dissimilar clines (Torres Cacoullos 2011). Therefore, comparing and contrasting the configuration of the linguistic factors that constrain the use of the copular verbs in different dialects may help determine the grammaticalization stage of the [copula + adjective] construction in Spanish.

In the present study, the cross-dialectal comparisons are possible because the studies chosen for the analysis used similar dependent and independent variables, and employed similar coding schemes. However, there are some differences across studies. For instance, Brown and Cortés-Torres (2012) did not include predicate type in their analysis, and split the adjective class factor into five categories (mental traits, physical traits, evaluation and description, age, and size), instead of the three categories used in the Cuban, Venezuelan, and Mexican studies (mental and physical traits, status traits, observable traits). Similarly, predicate type was not included in the Cuban analysis.

Another difference in the partition of the data has to do with the social factor age, since all of these studies classified their participants into different age groups. For instance, while the Mexican, Cuban, and Puerto Rican studies have similar age groupings (Mexican and Cuban age groups: 20–34, 35–54, 55+; Puerto Rican age groups: 20–29, 30–59 and 60+), in the Caracas study there were only two large

Table 8.5. Distribution of *ser* and *estar* with the most frequent variable adjective in the Cuban corpus

Adjective	*Estar*	*Ser*	Total
Bueno (good)	7 (14.3%)	42 (85.7%)	49 (100%)
Joven (young)	4 (16.7%)	20 (83.3%)	24 (100%)
Grande (big)	4 (20%)	16 (80%)	20 (100%)
Difícil (difficult)	1 (6.3%)	15 (93.8%)	16 (100%)
Igual (same)	1 (7.7%)	12 (92.3%)	13 (100%)
Viejo (old)	9 (69.2%)	4 (30.8%)	13 (100%)
Bonito (pretty)	1 (9.1%)	10 (90.9%)	11 (100%)
Chiquito (small)	1 (9.1%)	10 (90.9%)	11 (100%)
Fuerte (strong)	2 (18.2%)	9 (81.8%)	11 (100%)

age groups that included much younger participants than the other studies (Caracas age groups: 14–45, 46+). Moreover, studies differed with respect to other extralinguistic factors: While the Mexican and Venezuelan studies included socioeconomic level as a factor (upper, middle, lower), the Cuban study analyzed the level of education of the speakers (illiterate, primary education, high school, or college education), and the Puerto Rican study coded for the degree of bilingualism of the participants (monolingual, bilingual) instead. Nonetheless, cross-dialectal comparisons can still be made since there are more similarities than differences in the coding schemes, especially with respect to the linguistic factors. The results of the four independent multivariate analyses are shown in table 8.6.[4]

Regarding the use of *ser* and *estar* in attributive constructions, table 8.6 shows that cross-dialectally *ser* is the predominant copula used in the majority of adjectival contexts (between 61 percent and 76.2 percent of the time, depending on the dialect). This result further corroborates the observation that *ser* is the default copula in Spanish (Clements 2006). Moreover, this distributional pattern suggests that *ser* has a more generalized meaning, which allows it to occur with a larger number of adjectives. For this reason, it is argued that the older Spanish copula, *ser*, has more copulative contexts of use due to its more grammaticalized (i.e., less specific) meaning. Similarly, the diachronic evidence put forward in the diachronic and synchronic section suggests that *estar* has also gone through loss of its specific locative meaning in the attributive construction, which has allowed it to expand its contexts of use within the copulative construction. However, the lower frequency of *estar* across dialects (between 23.8 percent and 39 percent depending on the dialect) in contrast to *ser* suggests that there are features of its meaning that restrict it to certain copulative contexts and adjectives. This idea will be explored next by taking into account the configuration of semantic and pragmatic factors across dialects.

The linguistic factors predicting the use of copulas in the dialects under study include the following independent variables in all varieties: resultant state, experience with the referent, and adjective class. All dialects studied (i.e., Cuban, Puerto Rican, Mexican, and Venezuelan) are conditioned in the selection of copula choice by these linguistic factors. While the impact of these independent variables may be

Table 8.6. Linguistic and social factors that significantly favor the use of [*estar* + adjective] across Latin American dialects

Havana, Cuba (Present study)	Puerto Rico (Brown and Cortés-Torres 2012)	Mexico City (Juárez-Cummings 2014)	Caracas, Venezuela (Díaz-Campos and Geeslin 2011)
ser (76.2%)	*ser* (61%)	*ser* (62.43%)	*ser* (74.2%)
estar (23.8%)	*estar* (39%)	*estar* (37.57%)	*estar* (25.8%)
Resultant state	**Frame of reference**	**Adjective class**	**Resultant state**
+ Resultant 0.862	Individual-level 0.893	Mental/physical states 0.99	+ Resultant 0.92
– Resultant 0.132	Class 0.107	Observable traits 0.23	– Resultant 0.34
		Status 0.12	
Frame of reference	**Experience with the referent**	**Experience with the referent**	**Adjective class**
+ Comparison 0.844	Immediate 0.848	Immediate 0.95	Mental/physical states 0.88
– Comparison 0.156	Ongoing 0.321	Ongoing 0.47	Status 0.69
	Indirect 0.274	Indirect 0.09	Observable traits 0.42
Experience with the referent	**Resultant state**	**Socioeconomic class**	**Predicate type**
Immediate 0.905	+ Resultant 0.735	Lower class 0.74	Stage-level 0.79
Indirect 0.271	– Resultant 0.265	Middle class 0.67	Individual 0.37
Ongoing 0.219		Upper 0.06	
Adjective class	**Adjective class**	**Resultant state**	**Experience with the referent**
Mental states 0.786	Mental states 0.837	+ Resultant 0.88	Immediate 0.89
Status 0.348	Physical state 0.75	– Resultant 0.28	Indirect 0.58
Observable traits 0.339	Evaluation/description 0.392		Ongoing 0.48
	Age 0.313		
	Size 0.182		
	Age	**Susceptibility to change**	**Susceptibility to change**
	20–29 y/o 0.582	Changeable 0.87	Changeable 0.56
	30–59 y/o 0.505	Not changeable 0.31	Not changeable 0.33
	60+ 0.414		
		Age	**Socioeconomic level**
		35–44 y/o 0.64	Lower class 0.57
		20–34 y/o 0.51	Upper class 0.50
		55+ 0.39	Middle class 0.42
			Age
			46+ y/ o 0.57
			14–45 0.44
			Frame of reference
			[+ comparison] 0.59
			[– comparison] 0.48

different, the direction of the effect is the same across varieties. This is indicative that *estar* fulfills the same semantic and pragmatic functions across dialects: expressing resultant states comparing the referent with itself, describing immediate experiences with the referent, and, with predicates, describing mental states (changeable states and stage-level predicates). Frame of reference was selected as a significant linguistic predictor in three of the four dialects compared in the present study (i.e., Cuban, Puerto Rican, and Venezuelan). Susceptibility to change was found to be a significant linguistic predictor in dialects from Mexico and Venezuela. Finally, predicate type is only significant for Venezuelan Spanish. Recall that the direction of the effect in all cases shows the expected tendencies as acknowledged in table 8.1. The implication of these findings is that the dialects under study (Cuban, Puerto Rican, Mexican, and Venezuelan) seem to be in the same grammaticalization stage with respect to [copula + adjective] construction. Therefore, *estar* fulfills specific semantic and pragmatic functions within the copulative construction that are synchronically similar across Spanish dialects.

It is fair to say that social factors are at the periphery in the statistical models obtained in the different studies. This means that they can be considered the least significant factors, with some exceptions in the Mexican data. The factor age was selected as a significant predictor in Puerto Rican, Mexican, and Venezuela Spanish. Once again, while the magnitude of effect of this social variable is different according to the dialect, the direction of the effect in dialects from Puerto Rico and Mexico shows similarities with younger speakers favoring the use of *estar*. This does not necessarily suggest a change in progress as the present linguistic analysis indicates similar uses of *estar* across varieties. The fact that younger speakers used *estar* more often in some studies is not indicative of change in progress as there are some adjectives that are used only with *estar* and others, only with *ser*, while others occur with both copular verbs in a similar fashion. In addition, *estar* is used more by older speakers in Venezuela Spanish (see Díaz-Campos and Geeslin 2011 for a complete discussion of the social factors in this particular group of speakers). Furthermore, the fact that this variable was significant in Puerto Rico, Mexico, and Venezuela may be due to the nature of the interview, the adjectives used by the participants, or other outliers. Future research should take into account this issue in order to disentangle this possible effect. In the present study the social stratification of the copula choice is not evident as the statistical analysis suggests. Gender was not selected as significant in any of the studies, but socioeconomic class was selected as significant in the cases of Mexico and Venezuela, with lower socioeconomic groups favoring the use of *estar*. Therefore, in order to argue that there is a change in progress, future investigations have to account for the effect of the specific lexical items (i.e., individual adjectives) speakers use to better assess the influence of the sociolinguistic factors. This implies limiting the envelope of variation and the contexts in which neutralization has happened (see table 8.7).

Discussion

This investigation sought to analyze the linguistic and extralinguistic factors that constrain the use of *ser* and *estar* in copulative constructions in Cuban Spanish as well as

Table 8.7. Summary of comparative analysis across dialects of Spanish

Factors	Cuba	Puerto Rico	Mexico	Venezuela
Linguistic Factors				
Resultant State	+	+	+	+
Frame of reference	+	+	–	+
Experience with the referent	+	+	+	+
Adjective class	+	+	+	+
Susceptibility to change	–	–	+	+
Predicate Type	n/a	n/a	–	+
Social Factors				
Age	–	+	+	+
Gender	–	–	–	–
Socioeconomic class	–	–	+	+

carry out a comparative analysis with other Spanish dialects. It was found that the use of *estar* in Cuban Spanish was restricted by semantic (resultant state, adjective class) and pragmatic (frame of reference, experience with the referent) factors. This finding concurs with recent investigations of these copular constructions because they share the same linguistic constraints and direction of the effect (see table 8.6). However, it was found that age, gender, and socioeconomic class were not significant. This result contrasts with some of the previous studies because Díaz-Campos and Geeslin (2011) and Juárez-Cummings (2014) found that socioeconomic class influenced the use of *estar*. Additionally, Brown and Cortés-Torres (2012), Díaz-Campos and Geeslin (2011), and Juárez-Cummings (2014) found that age significantly influenced the use of *estar*. Nonetheless, the findings of these previous investigations may be due to the nature of the interviews, the topics discussed, and the specific discursive contexts triggered by the interviews. Therefore, we recommend using an experimental task in order to control for these variables.

The second research question inquired about the dialectal comparison. This analysis revealed that *estar* is conditioned by the same linguistic factors. This allows us to determine, following Brown and Cortés-Torres (2012, 67), a cross-dialectal prototypical meaning of *estar* in attributive contexts: [temporally bounded, immediate, + comparative]. These results further dispute the claim made in several studies that there is a generational change in progress favoring *estar* (i.e., Alfaraz 2012; Silva-Corvalán 1986). On the contrary, we argue that the consistency of the linguistic constraints across dialects suggests a stable phenomenon in Spanish (Díaz-Campos and Geeslin 2011). However, this does not deny that the copulative structure in Spanish is slowly changing since grammaticalization processes operate gradually and are best observed in the diachronic dimension (Bybee, Perkins, and Pagliuca 1994; Torres Cacoullos 2011). According to Bybee (2010), the more we understand the diachronic development of structures the more we can explain their synchronic patterns of use.

Similarly, the results of this investigation suggest that the dialects under study (i.e., Cuban, Puerto Rican, Mexican, and Venezuelan) are in the same grammaticalization stage with respect to copulative uses. This hypothesis is based on the fact that the uses of *ser* and *estar* in attributive function have the same linguistic configurations (i.e., the same underlying variable grammar) across Spanish varieties. Even though there were differences in terms of the relative magnitudes of the effects of the significant factors, the direction of the effect (i.e., the constraint hierarchy) was constant across dialects.

This study also points out the importance of individual lexical items and their frequency of use on copula choice in Spanish. Regarding the results for Cuban Spanish, we found that a larger number of adjectives occurred with only *ser* in the corpus and that adjectives occurring with only *estar* were less numerous, while variable adjectives (i.e., those occurring with both *ser* and *estar*) were even scarcer in the data. However, variable adjectives had a higher rate of use in the corpus. Additionally, with respect to the adjective class, the multivariate analysis only selected mental adjectives as a significant predictor of *estar*, since the majority of mental adjectives (63 percent) were used with this copular form. However, our analysis shows that evaluative, age, and physical aspect adjective classes are also important to copula choice in Cuban Spanish, as they tended to show the most copular variability (i.e., they accounted for the 87.2 percent of the variable cases). Thus, it is argued that variation is mediated by certain adjective classes, the specific lexical items within these categories, and by their frequency of use.

Furthermore, grammaticalization theory can explain the patterns of use of *ser* and *estar* in copulative function in contemporary Spanish. According to Bybee, Perkins, and Pagliuca (1994), grammaticalizing forms interact with each other in the same functional domain by competing for the same uses or by covering different areas of meaning. For instance, there were cases in which the meaning of the constructions was subtle, as in examples 8.20 and 8.21. In these examples, the uses of *ser* and *estar* do not create a contrast in the interpretation, since both express a comparison of the referent with itself. On the other hand, there are contexts in which a contrast in meaning is maintained with the uses of *ser* and *estar,* such as in examples 8.22 and 8.23. In these examples, the adjective *buenas* in the construction with *estar* and a referent related to food (example 8.22) carry the interpretation of flavor and taste, whereas the same adjective in the construction with *ser* and a referent denotes behavior (example 8.23). Consequently, it is important to take into account the construction as a whole in the analysis, since, after all, grammaticalization processes operate within specific constructions and the particular elements within them have an impact on the resultant meaning (Bybee 2010; Torres Cacoullos 2011).

Example 8.20.

Ahora es bella también pero en aquel momento ***era*** *más* ***bella***.
Now she is pretty too but in the past she **was** even **prettier**. (LHABH22)

Example 8.21.

*¡Qué **bella está**!*
'How **beautiful you are**!' (LHABH33)

Example 8.22.

*Me piden muchas hamburguesas parece que **están** muy **buenas**.*
'They order many hamburgers it seems that **they taste** really **good**.' (LHABH21)

Example 8.23.

*Mi niño **es bueno**, mi familia es unida.*
'My child **is good**, my family is **close**.' (LHABM23)

Conclusions

The main goals of this investigation were to determine the linguistic and extralinguistic factors that constrain the use of copula choice in Cuban Spanish, and to contrast its linguistic and extralinguistic configuration with Mexican, Puerto Rican, and Venezuelan Spanish with reference to the grammaticalization theory. The results of this investigation indicate that these dialects have similar linguistic constraints: resultant state, experience with the referent, and adjective class. However, it was found that these dialects differed in terms of the social factors that predict the use of *estar*. The present study did not find any social factor to be significant in Cuban Spanish. However, age was significant in Puerto Rican, Mexican, and Venezuelan Spanish and socioeconomic class was significant in Mexican and Venezuelan Spanish. We argue that these differences may be due to the specific discursive contexts of the interview. Therefore, it is suggested that these copular constructions are stable, contrary to what has been stated in previous investigations (Alfaraz 2012; Silva-Corvalán 1986). In fact, it is proposed that these constructions are at the same grammaticalization stage. Nonetheless, this does not reject the notion that the copulative forms in Spanish are slowly changing because grammaticalization processes operate gradually and are best observed in the diachronic dimension (Bybee, Perkins, and Pagliuca 1994; Torres Cacoullos 2011). Consequently, future studies should incorporate contact varieties of Spanish in order to complete a picture of the phenomenon within bilingual communities in comparison to monolingual varieties. Finally, there were instances where the distinctions between *ser* and *estar* were subtle, but there were also contexts where copulas maintained a clear contrast. These findings support the grammaticalization theory because grammaticalizing forms interact with each other in the same functional domain by competing for the same uses or by covering different areas of meaning (Bybee, Perkins, and Pagliuca 1994). On the other hand, this theory predicts that there are contexts in which a contrast in meaning is maintained. Therefore, it is argued that it is important to take into account the constructions and the surrounding elements in the analysis because grammaticalization processes operate within specific constructions and each particular elements have an impact on the meaning (Bybee 2010; Torres Cacoullos 2011).

Notes

The authors would like to thank Juan Escalona, the two anonymous reviewers, and the editor of this volume. Any mistakes remain our own.

1. Ford (1899) and Poutain (1982) mention that the precursor of Spanish *ser* was Vulgar Latin *essere* instead of Classical Latin *esse*. Moreover, Spanish *ser* obtained many of its forms from Latin *sedere* (to sit, to be seated), such as the infinitive form, the present participle, the future indicative, the conditional, the imperative, and the present subjunctive (Batllori and Roca 2011; Ford 1899).
2. Predicate type (individual-level and stage-level distinction) was not taken into account in the analysis of Cuban Spanish since it highly correlated with frame of reference factor ([+ comparison] and [– comparison] frames), resulting in the nonorthogonality (i.e., nonindependence) of the two linguistic factors. This correlation issue may apply to all Spanish varieties.
3. Since the dependent variable is binary in the present study, a favoring effect is interpreted as favoring the application value, *estar*, whereas a disfavoring effect can be interpreted as favoring *ser* (Tagliamonte 2012, 127).
4. The Cuban and Puerto Rican studies (Brown and Cortés-Torres 2012) performed a mixed-effects logistic regression through Rbrul, while the Mexican (Juárez-Cummings 2014) and Venezuelan studies (Díaz-Campos and Geeslin 2011) performed a binary logistic regression through Goldvarb X.

References

Aguilar-Sánchez, J. 2009. "Syntactic Variation: The Case of Copula Choice in the Spanish of Limón, Costa Rica." PhD diss., Indiana University.

Alfaraz, G. 2012. "The Status of the Extension of *estar* in Cuban Spanish." *Studies in Hispanic and Lusophone Linguistics* 5 (1): 3–27

Batllori, M., E. Castillo, and F. Roca-Urgell. 2009. "Relation between Changes: The Location and Possessive Grammaticalization Path in Spanish." In *Diachronic Linguistics*, edited by J. Rafel, 443–93. Girona, Esp.: Universitat de Girona publication services.

Batllori, M., and F. Roca. 2011. "Grammaticalization of *ser* and *estar* in Romance." In *Grammatical Change: Origins, Nature, Outcomes*, edited by D. Jonas, J. Whitman, and A. Garrett, 73–92. New York: Oxford University Press.

Brown, E., and M. Cortés-Torres. 2012. "Syntactic and Pragmatic Usage of the [estar + Adjective] Construction in Puerto Rican Spanish: *¡Está brutal!*" In *Selected Proceedings of the 14th Hispanic Linguistics Symposium*, edited by K. Geeslin and M. Díaz-Campos 61–74. Somerville, MA: Cascadilla Proceedings.

Bybee, J. 2010. *Language, Use and Cognition*. Cambridge: Cambridge University Press.

Bybee, J., R. Perkins, and W. Pagliuca. 1994. *The Evolution of Grammar: Tense, Aspect, and Modality in the Languages of the World*. Chicago: University of Chicago Press.

Camacho, J. 2012. 22 "Ser and Estar: The Individual/Stage-Level Distinction and Aspectual Predication." *Handbook of Hispanic Linguistics* 69:453–74.

Clements, J. C. 1988. "The Semantics and Pragmatics of the Spanish <COPULA + ADJECTIVE> Construction." *Linguistics* 26:779–822.

———. 2006. "*Ser-estar* in the Predicate Adjective Construction." In *Functional Approaches to Spanish Syntax: Lexical Semantics, Discourse, and Transitivity*, edited by J. C. Clements and J. Yoon, 161–202. London: Palgrave MacMillan.

Cortés-Torres, M. 2004. "¿Ser o estar? La variación lingüística y social de estar más adjetivo en el español de Cuernavaca, Mexico." *Hispania* 87:788–95.

Devitt, D. 1990. "The Diachronic Development of Semantics in Copulas." *Proceedings of the Sixteenth Annual Meeting of the Berkeley Linguistics Society* 16:103–15.

Díaz-Campos, M., ed. 2011. *The Handbook of Hispanic Sociolinguistics*. Malden, MA: Wiley-Blackwell.

Díaz-Campos, M., and K. Geeslin. 2011. "Copula Use in the Spanish of Venezuela: Is the Pattern Indicative of Stable Variation or an Ongoing Change?" *Spanish in Context* 8 (1): 73–94.

Fernández Leborans, M. J. 1999. "La predicación: Las oraciones copulativas." *Gramática descriptiva de la lengua española*, edited by I. Bosque and V. Demonte, 2354–460. Madrid: Espasa.

Ford, J. D. M. 1899. "Sedere, Essere and Stare in the Poema del Cid." *Modern Language Notes* 14:4–10.

Geeslin, Kimberly. 2003. "A Comparison of Copula Choice in Advanced and Native Spanish." *Language Learning* 53 (4): 703–64.

———. 2013. "Future Directions in the Acquisition of Variable Structures: The Role of Individual Lexical Items in Second Language Spanish." In *Selected Proceedings of the 15th Hispanic Linguistics Symposium*, edited by C. Howe, M. Lubbers, and S. Blackwell, 187–204. Somerville, MA: Cascadilla Press.

Geeslin, K., and A. Gudmestad. 2010. "An Exploration of the Range and Frequency of Occurrence of Forms in Potentially-Variable Structures in Second Language Spanish." *Studies in Second Language Acquisition* 32 (3): 433–63.

Geeslin, K., and P. Guijarro-Fuentes. 2007. "Linguistic and Social Predictors of Copula Use in Galician Spanish." In *Spanish in Contact: Policy, Social and Linguistic Inquiries*, edited by K. Potowski and R. Cameron, 253–73. Amsterdam: John Benjamins.

Geeslin, K. L., and Guijarro-Fuentes, P. 2006. "Second Language Acquisition of Variable Structures in Spanish by Portuguese Speakers." *Language Learning* 56 (1): 53–107.

———. 2008. "Variation in Contemporary Spanish: Linguistic Predictors of *Estar* in Four Cases of Language Contact." *Bilingualism: Language and Cognition* 11 (3): 365–80.

Gili Gaya, S. 1961. *Curso superior de sintaxis española*. Barcelona: Biblograf.

Guitart, J. 2002. "Spanish ser and estar in cognitive/pragmatic perspective." Paper presented at the Kentucky Foreign Language Conference, Lexington, Kentucky, April 19–21.

Gutiérrez, M. 1992. "The Extension of estar: A Linguistic Change in Progress in the Spanish of Morelia, Mexico." *Hispanic Linguistics* 5:109–41.

———. 1994. "Simplification, Transfer, and Convergence in Chicano Spanish." *Bilingual Review* 19 (2): 111–21.

Hanssen, F. 1913. *Gramática histórica de la lengua castellana*. Buenos Aires: Halle.

Johnson, D. E. 2009. "Getting Off the GoldVarb Standard: Introducing Rbrul for Mixed Effects Variable Rule Analysis." *Language and Linguistics Compass* 3 (1): 359–83.

Juárez-Cummings, E. 2014. "Tendencias de uso de Ser y Estar en la Ciudad de México." *IULC Working Papers*, 14 (2): 120–37.

Labov, W. 1972. *Sociolinguistic Patterns*. Philadelphia: University of Pennsylvania Press.

Lavandera, B. 1978. "Where Does the Sociolinguistic Variable Stop?" *Language in Society* 7:171–82.

Leonetti Jungl, M. 1994. "Ser y estar: estado de la cuestión." *Pliegos de la ínsula Barataria* 1:182–205.

Luján, M. 1981. "The Spanish Copulas as Aspectual Indicators." *Lingua* 54:165–210.

Marco, C., and R. Marín. 2015. "Origins and Development of Adjectival Passives in Spanish: A Corpus Study." In *New Perspective in the Study of ser and estar*, edited by I. Pérez-Jiménez, M. Leonetti, and S. Gumiel Molina, 239–66. Amsterdam: John Benjamins.

Ortíz López, L. A. 2000. "Extensión de estar en contextos de ser en el español de Puerto Rico: ¿evolución interna o contacto de lenguas?" *Boletín de la Academia Puertorriqueña de la Lengua Española*, 98–118.

Poplack, S., and S. Tagliamonte. 2001. *African American English in the Diaspora: Tense and Aspect*. Malden, MA: Blackwell Publishers.

Pountain, C. 1982. "Essere/Stare as a Romance Phenomenon." *Studies in the Romance Verb: Essays Offered to Joe Cremona on the Occasion of His 60th Birthday*, edited by N. Vincent and M. Harris, 139–60. London: Croom Helm.

Requena, P., A. Román-Hernández, and K. Miller. 2015. "Children's Knowledge of the Spanish Copulas *Ser* and *Estar* with Novel Adjectives." *Language Acquisition* 22 (2): 193–207.

Roby, D. B. 2009. *Aspect and the Categorization of States: The Case of Ser and Estar in Spanish*. Philadelphia: John Benjamins.

Schwenter, S. 2011. "Variationist Approaches to Spanish Morpho-Syntax: Internal and External Factors." In Díaz-Campos, *Handbook of Hispanic Sociolinguistics*, 123–47. Malden, MA: Wiley-Blackwell.

Silva-Corvalán, C. 1986. "Bilingualism and Language Change: The Extension of Estar in Los Angeles Spanish." *Language* 62:587–608

Terkourafi, M. 2011. "The Pragmatic Variable: Toward a Procedural Interpretation." *Language in Society* 40:343–72.

Torres Cacoullos, R. 2011. "Variation and Grammaticalization." In Díaz-Campos, *Handbook of Hispanic Sociolinguistics*, 148–67. Malden, MA: Wiley-Blackwell.

PART III

LEXICAL VARIATION

9

The Social Diffusion of English-Based Lexical Innovations in Miami Cuban Spanish

ANDREW LYNCH
University of Miami

DURING THE LATTER HALF of the twentieth century, the continuous en masse arrival of Cubans in South Florida produced a social, cultural, and linguistic transformation—concomitant with the population growth and economic development of Miami—that made the city popularly synonymous with *cubanidad* by the new millennium (Portés and Stepick 1993; Boswell 1994; Lynch 2000; Otheguy, García, and Roca 2000; De La Torre 2003; Laguna 2010). Miami's intimate links to Cuba predate Castro's 1959 revolution, however. As Pérez (1999) highlights, commerce and tourism in Miami during the 1940s and 1950s were already characterized by ample Spanish language use. The author of a *New York Times* article wrote of Miami in 1948 that: "almost as much Spanish as English is heard on the streets and in business establishments. '*Se habla español aquí*' appears in the show window of almost every store, and it is not uncommon to find most of the customers inside speaking Spanish" (Phillips 1948, X11). Celebrated Cuban journalist Eladio Secades affirmed in 1957 that: "All we Cubans have gone to Miami by now.... Spanish is spoken everywhere in Miami: in restaurants, in the shops, in the hotels, on the streets. There are moments in which the foreigner could think that what is not spoken in Miami is English" (cited by Pérez 1999, 439). During the 1960s and 1970s, the highly entrepreneurial and politically active exiles of Cuba's upper and upper-middle socioeconomic strata arriving in Miami would thus successfully establish a legitimacy for Spanish use in a relatively small urban area where the language was already so prevalent in economic life and intertwined in its short history. As Carter and Lynch (2015) note, Miami is now surely the most bilingual major metropolitan area of the US, and perhaps arguably of the Americas.

Nonetheless, with Spanish clearly remaining secondary to English in institutional and official terms, and Anglophone popular culture pervading the mass media and processes of socialization among Miami youth, English dominance among second- and third-generation Cubans unquestionably emerges. This pattern of cross-generational shift has led some scholars to doubt the potential duration of Spanish in South Florida (e.g., Porcel 2006) as well as the purported evolution of a variety—or varieties—of the language that might be properly called 'US Spanish' (e.g., Lynch 2013). The great social, cultural, and economic vitality of Spanish in the face of societal and political inequalities among immigrant groups (see Aranda, Hughes, and Sabogal 2014), and sociolinguistic discontinuity among the Miami-born, creates an immensely complex scenario for scholars interested in processes of variation and change in Spanish, as well as notions of what constitutes a 'speech community' (cf. Otheguy and Zentella 2012).

Since the 1990s, Miami's Spanish-speaking population has become highly diverse; Cuban-origin speakers comprised only about half of that population in the 2010 US Census. There are now large contingents of Colombians, Nicaraguans, Hondurans, Puerto Ricans, Dominicans, Venezuelans, Peruvians, and Argentines in Miami (Aranda, Hughes, and Sabogal 2014, 24), and important sociolinguistic divisions have become apparent among the city's longstanding Cuban population (Alfaraz 2014; Lynch 2009a, 2009b). In these regards, the opportunity that Miami provides for studies of Spanish dialect contact and the influence of English on the varieties of Spanish spoken in the US is unparalleled. Among the more compelling areas of inquiry is the lexicon, as this is arguably the most malleable structural aspect of languages in contact and, as such, lexical innovations are readily apparent in the speech of first-generation adult immigrants who have spent relatively little time in the US setting (Klee and Lynch 2009; Silva-Corvalán 2001; Varra 2013).

With the aim of offering further insight into the continuous transculturation of Cuban Spanish within a highly dynamic migratory context (cf. Otheguy, García and Roca 2000), this chapter analyzes the diffusion of English-based lexical innovations among Cuban-origin speakers in Miami, relying upon theoretical principles of sociolinguistic variation (Silva-Corvalán 2001). The empirical study that provides the basis of the chapter is a loose replication of an investigation carried out by Otheguy and García among Cubans in Miami in 1983 and subsequently published in 1988. The present study aims to confront Otheguy and García's findings regarding diffusion of lexical innovations among Cubans in Miami three decades later. In what follows, I describe their original study and then turn to the methods of the present research and discussion of its findings, drawing relevant comparisons. My hope is that readers will perhaps gain a better perspective on the nature of language contact at the lexical level, the role that sociolinguistic factors play in the diffusion of lexical innovations of various types, and the impact that English language ability has on the variety of Spanish spoken among Miami's diverse Cuban-origin population. In all likelihood, the principles and processes that characterize lexical crosslinguistic influence within Miami's Cuban communities are also readily observable among other Spanish-speaking groups across the US. Although a considerable amount of theory and empirical research on lexical innovation among US Latinos has been published since the time of Otheguy and García's study (cf. Klee and Lynch 2009; Otheguy 2011), I adhere rather strictly to the theoretical framework and methodology followed by these authors three decades ago in order to facilitate comparison of the two studies.

Diffusion of Lexical Innovations in the Spanish of Cuban Americans: Otheguy and García's (1988) Study

The stated motivations for Otheguy and García's study three decades ago were to provide quantitative insights into the diffusion of lexical innovations in the situation of Spanish-English contact in the US, and to understand better the effect that lexical structure itself has on the diffusion of innovations of various types (1988, 203). To this end, they drew a typology of four distinct types of innovations, defined below in their terms, with some examples from their written survey.

1. *Loanwords*, by which a linguistic sign "is imported whole from a source language [English], with greater or lesser phonological adaptation to the recipient language [Spanish]" (Otheguy and García 1988, 212–13), as in the following items: *Necesito hacer un* **part-time** *para ganar dinero*; *¿Tienes un* **quarter** *que me prestes?*
2. *Phonologically merged word calques*, wherein a single-word element in Spanish calques the usage of a phonologically similar single-word element in English "based on an equation established between [the two forms] that rests on similarities in the meaning and also on similarities in the signal" (Otheguy and García 1988, 213–14), as in the following items: *En la fiesta te voy a* ***introducir*** *a una señora muy agradable* (calqued on English 'introduce'); *El martes me* ***registré*** *en la universidad* (English 'register').
3. *Phonologically independent word calques*, which reflect the same calquing process as phonologically merged word calques (above) but without the similarity of phonological form, or, in other words, "the connection between [the two forms] is being established only on semantic grounds," independent of phonological parallelism (Otheguy and García 1988, 214–15), as in the following items: ***Corrió*** *para gobernador en las últimas elecciones, pero no ganó* (calqued on English 'run for political office'); *El maestro les* ***dio un examen*** *muy difícil* (English 'give an exam'); *Quiero que* ***camines al niño*** *hasta la escuela* (English 'walk the child to school').
4. *Phrasal calques*, which resemble word calques "in that elements that belong to the borrowing language [Spanish] in their own right are being used in the manner of the lending language [English]," but without any readily detectable modification of the Spanish forms or their traditional or normative meanings (Otheguy and García 1988, 215). These sorts of calques convey an American English–speaking sort of message without altering Spanish language form or meaning at all; in other words, this sort of calquing "leaves the linguistic system untouched" (216). Some examples are: *Pregúntale si* ***sabe cómo***

> ***hacerlo*** (calqued on English 'know how to…' versus Spanish *saber hacerlo*); *Su presencia* ***hará la diferencia*** (English 'make the difference' versus Spanish *ser importante*); *Con todos los problemas que tengo,* ***lo último que necesito*** *es un dolor de garganta* (English 'the last thing I need' versus Spanish *lo que me faltaba*).

To arrive at a composite concept of *diffusion*, defined as "the degree to which the innovation is a somewhat permanent feature of the language" (Otheguy and García 1988, 208), the authors asked study participants to respond 'yes' or 'no' to each of the following three questions regarding forty items that reflected these different types of lexical phenomena (including the examples given above): 'Have you heard it?' (variable of awareness); 'Do you use it when speaking?' (variable of adoption); and 'Do you consider its use correct in speech?'(variable of acceptability). A diffusion index was calculated for each of the four types of lexical innovations, based upon the percentage of responses on each of these three variables (awareness, adoption, acceptability).

A total of seventy-four Cuban-origin Spanish speakers responded to Otheguy and García's written survey in 1983, which included basic social background questions regarding sex, age, birthplace, years in the US, level of formal education, and proficiency in both Spanish and English. All of the participants were managers and employees of a large Cuban-owned lumberyard where Spanish was the predominant language of everyday use. Of their sample, 88 percent were Cuban-born (Otheguy and García 1988, 207). Young adults (under thirty years old) constituted 54 percent; the remaining 46 percent were over the age of thirty. Although 77 percent reported that they "spoke English well," almost everyone (99 percent) reported that they spoke Spanish "always or almost always" at home, and the great majority (77 percent) reported the same at work (207–8). Because those identified as 'bilinguals' in Otheguy and García's sample reported rarely using English at home and relatively rarely at work, they most likely had high levels of oral proficiency in both languages. One could thus assume that their heightened sensitivity to English-based structural modifications in Spanish was probably attributable to a rather highly nuanced lexical and discursive ability in both languages. In the present results, we will see similar cross-generational effects in the data, in which everyday language use is clearly implicated.

The principal finding of Otheguy and García's study was that among those respondents whom they identified as 'monolingual' Cubans, there was a greater willingness to adopt and accept English-based lexical variants than among more bilingual Cubans (i.e., those who knew and used English to a greater extent). The authors attributed this finding possibly to a greater tendency among monolinguals to consider such innovations as mere characteristics of the Spanish of Miami, while bilinguals likely perceived them differentially, as elements of English. In terms of types of innovations, the authors observed greater awareness and adoption of loanwords than calques in general. Within the category of calques, phonology appeared to exert a determining influence: merged calques were more readily perceived and adopted than independent calques. Phrasal calques were deemed most acceptable and loanwords least acceptable, despite being the most widespread type of innovation in terms of use.

Structural differences had a much greater determining effect on the degree of diffusion of lexical innovations among bilingual speakers than among those with more limited knowledge of English. The authors argued that "the willingness of [Spanish] monolinguals to regard English signals independently of their meanings appears to explain why their Spanish—contrary to what happens with the Spanish of bilinguals—shows essentially the same level of diffusion for all types of lexical innovations" (Otheguy and García 1988, 206). In sum, Otheguy and García found that, overall, phrasal calques manifested the highest indices of diffusion in Cuban Miami; phonologically independent word calques were the least diffused and were met with slightly lower rates of acceptability than merged word calques among bilinguals, but not monolinguals, in their sample. They reasoned that, among the latter, "the mechanism of blending of two signals that defines the phonologically merged word calque is not operative among monolinguals" (225). As we will see in the findings of the present study, phonologically independent word calques reflect a different degree of diffusion among English-dominant third-generation Cuban bilinguals than they did among Otheguy and García's more Spanish-dominant second-generation bilinguals three decades earlier, when Spanish-speaking Miami was still beginning to coalesce socially.

The Present Study

Survey

The written survey used in the present inquiry replicated the one used by Otheguy and García in Miami in 1983, with a few modifications. The first section on the respondents' social background included questions regarding age, gender, birthplace and/or age of immigration to the US, parents' birthplace and/or age of immigration (in order to determine generation in the US), years of residence in Miami, occupation, level of formal education attained by respondents as well as by their parents, ability to speak and understand Spanish and English, and extent of use of both languages with family members, friends, people on the street, and in television, movie, and music choices. It also included a question regarding the importance of being able to speak Spanish in the US context, to which almost everyone responded very positively.

On Otheguy and García's original questionnaire, respondents were provided the binary option of 'always or almost always' or 'almost never or never' for responding to questions regarding the use of Spanish and English at home, at work, in social activities, and in mass media. On the present questionnaire, however, participants responded to language use questions via a Likert scale that ranged from 1 ('Spanish almost always') at one extreme to 5 ('English almost always') at the other. The same was true for items concerning self-reported proficiency in Spanish and English. Otheguy and García's data were based on the binary options 'very good or good' or 'not good or none' in response to questions regarding ability in both languages; for the present study, a 1-to-5 scale was provided, ranging from 'little ability' to 'excellent ability.' I reasoned that this methodological issue might possibly be important, as an account of more intermediate degrees of self-reported ability and use of the two languages could potentially lend itself to a rather more nuanced interpretation of the relationship between English language influence and the diffusion of lexical innovations in Spanish. This is especially true for the now quite numerous third-generation adult population of Miami Cubans, who are all English-dominant and have variable degrees of bilingual ability in Spanish.

Replicating the second section of Otheguy and García's original questionnaire with a few modifications (described below), participants were presented a series of forty-three sentences written in Spanish. As in the 1983 survey, each sentence contained a bolded and underlined word or phrase to which participants must respond 'yes' or 'no' for each of the following three questions aimed at interpreting the level of diffusion in local speech: (1) *¿Ha oído Ud. la frase o palabra subrayada?* [Have you heard the underlined phrase or word?]; (2) *¿Usa Ud. esta frase o palabra al hablar?* [Do you use this phrase or word when speaking?]; (3) *¿Considera correcto su uso al hablar?* [Do you consider its use correct when speaking?]. Of the forty test items composing this section of Otheguy and García's survey, thirty-two were retained in their original form. Eleven new items were added to reflect the contemporary usage of Anglicisms in relation to technology (*Mi* **laptop** *fue más caro que el de mi hermano*; *Los jóvenes pasan muchas horas* **chateando** *en Internet*, etc.), and to investigate the diffusion of several commonly heard loanwords (*La tienda se encuentra en el* **mall** *más grande de Miami*), word calques (*Puedes llevar ropa* **casual** *para la fiesta el sábado*; *Esta máquina no está* **trabajando** *en este momento*, etc.), and phrasal calques (*Si le dejas un mensaje, seguro que te* ***llama para atrás***; ***¿Cómo te gustó la película*** *que vimos anoche?*, etc.). The selection of retained items and new items was made with the goal of maintaining Otheguy and García's original distinction between loanwords, phonologically merged word calques (which I will henceforth refer to as *phonological calques*), phonologically independent word calques (which I will simply call *semantic calques*), and phrasal calques for purposes of analysis and subsequent comparison of the two studies.

All of the quantitative written survey data for the social and linguistic variables were entered into SPSS for statistical analysis. For the binary questions on the dependent variables (awareness, adoption, acceptability) for each lexical item, 'yes' was assigned a value of 1 and 'no' was assigned a value of 2. From a qualitative perspective, more than thirty participants responded to the written survey in my presence, commenting on particular items aloud without my questioning any of their responses. Several others allowed me the opportunity to ask them specific questions regarding their responses after they had completed the survey. Their comments and observations provided helpful insights into why particular items garnered certain sorts of reactions and responses. Some of these are mentioned in the discussion below.

Sample

A total of 130 Spanish speakers of Cuban origin residing in the Miami metropolitan area completed the written survey between fall 2014 and fall 2015. A snowball sampling method was used in order to reach participants residing all across the metropolitan area, which is geographically and socioeconomically marked by a north-south divide (with the Atlantic Ocean to the east and the Everglades to the west). Roughly speaking, areas to the north and northwest of Miami center can be characterized as lower to lower-middle socioeconomic class, and more firmly middle and upper-middle class areas are found to the south and southwest. While Spanish is unequivocally prevalent in all areas of the city, its use in home and public life is more pervasive in the northwesterly areas of the metropolitan area (labeled 'NW' for our purposes), for example, Hialeah (where Spanish was spoken in 94 percent of homes in 2010 census data), Doral (89 percent Spanish-speaking homes), and Miami Lakes (82 percent Spanish-speaking homes). It must be pointed out, however, that both Doral and Miami Lakes are firmly middle socioeconomic class neighborhoods, with median household incomes of $69,300 and $66,369, respectively, in 2010 census data, versus $31,648 in Hialeah. In northwesterly areas, Cuban-origin speakers constitute a majority. Of the present sample, 38 percent resided in NW.

Areas of the city labeled 'South' for the present analysis included South Miami, Kendall, and Dadeland, which all contain firmly middle-class neighborhoods. Also included in the South category was the city of Coral Gables, one of Miami's most affluent areas, where the median household income was $84,027 in 2010 census data and home Spanish use exceeded 50 percent. It is important that the reader bear in mind that, unlike in other major urban areas of the US (e.g., Los Angeles, Chicago, Houston), home Spanish use is no less prevalent in middle- and upper-income neighborhoods than in lower-income areas (Carter and Lynch 2015). Indeed, in Miami's most exclusive address, Key Biscayne (median household income of $104,554 in 2010 census data), a non-English language was used in 80 percent of homes; in the great majority of those homes that language was Spanish. Of the present sample, 44 percent resided in South (with 12 percent of the total sample residing in Coral Gables).

Areas around downtown Miami, including the historic bastion of Cuban exile popularly referred to as Calle Ocho, as well as other neighborhoods located roughly within Miami's broad north-south divide (e.g., West Miami, Flagler, the MIA airport area), were categorized as 'Center' for the present purposes. Homes found in these zip codes are largely Spanish-speaking, and mostly lower to lower-middle in terms of socioeconomic status. The city of Miami proper, a geographically small area that includes only downtown and its immediate vicinity, was 70 percent Hispanic/Latino in 2010 census data, and the median household income was $29,621. A non-English language was reportedly spoken in more than 77 percent of homes, with Spanish constituting the overwhelming majority of those. One must bear in mind that the city of Miami proper is greatly mixed in terms of socioeconomic status, with highly educated and extremely wealthy transients living in high-rise luxury apartment buildings that are only blocks away from some of the city's most impoverished and destitute neighborhoods. In and of itself, downtown is largely a banking and commercial district with relatively few permanent residents. Calle Ocho, immediately to the southwest of downtown, is a lower-income neighborhood; it no longer contains a Cuban majority. Of the present sample, 18 percent resided in Center.

Since English language ability proved to be a crucial factor in Otheguy and García's (1988) findings, and because lexical features could perhaps be differentially distributed in geographic space, a careful attempt was made to include respondents who had differential degrees of ability in English from all areas of the city. Table 9.1 reflects the distribution of the present study participants according to these two independent variables. It is worth noting that the majority of respondents (65 percent) reported having high levels of aural ability in English (>3.9 on the given Likert scale). This percentage is probably representative of Miami's Cuban population in overall terms, if one includes Cuban Americans of the 1.5, second, and third generations. Even among most first-generation Cuban immigrants who have been in Miami for several years, aural abilities in English are quite high (perhaps contrary to popular belief); this is especially true of young adult immigrants.

Table 9.1. Distribution of respondents according to area of residence and English ability

Area of residence in Miami	Low English ability	Mid English ability	High English ability
NW	12	8	27
Center	6	1	16
South	10	6	41
Total	28 (22%)	15 (12%)	84 (66%)

Note: Three respondents did not answer the questions regarding English language ability.

Generational groups in the US were defined according to the following criteria: Group 1 were those who immigrated to Miami from Cuba at age seventeen or later; Group 2 were those who immigrated sometime between the ages of eleven and sixteen; Group 3 were those who arrived in Miami before age ten or who were born in the US to Group 1 or Group 2 parents; and Group 4 included those Miami-born respondents whose parents corresponded to the definition of Group 3. The generational distribution of the present respondents according to gender is displayed in table 9.2. The reader should take note that the sample was slightly skewed in terms of gender: 68 percent of respondents were female. This is a limitation of the present data. Perhaps most importantly, however, among Group 1 participants, for whom English language ability and awareness of crosslinguistic influence would likely be crucial variables, there was a statistically strong balance of female and male respondents (53 percent versus 47 percent, respectively).

Table 9.2. Distribution of respondents according to immigrant generation and gender

Immigrant generation in Miami	Females	Males
Group 1	24	21
Group 2	19	5
Group 3	30	9
Group 4	15	7
Total	88 (68%)	42 (32%)

Because initial statistics clearly showed that the responses of Group 3 and Group 4 participants patterned very similarly, it was decided that they would be merged into a single category for purposes of statistical testing. For this reason, in the results section below, the findings are reported in terms of three generational groups labeled as follows: Group 1 respondents = G1; Group 2 respondents = G1.5 (because they are popularly referred to as the '1.5 generation'); Group 3 and Group 4 respondents = G2.

Both formal education level and extent of use of Spanish and English were tested as independent social variables in the present study. Education levels were classified as follows: primary schooling (value of 1 on the given Likert scale), secondary or high school education (2), some postsecondary or college studies (3), college degree or *licenciatura* (4), and graduate or professional studies (5). As already mentioned, language use items were based on a Likert scale that ranged from 'Spanish almost always' (value of 1), 'Mostly Spanish' (2), 'Both languages equally' (3), 'Mostly English' (4), to 'English almost always' (5). Table 9.3 shows the distribution of respondents according to these two independent variables.

As Table 9.3 reflects, the majority of respondents who indicated using both languages equally or principally English on an everyday basis had completed at least some postsecondary studies.

Table 9.3. Distribution of respondents according to formal education level and language use

Formal education level	Principally Spanish	Both languages	Principally English
Low (≤2)	15	6	5
Mid (3)	9	32	14
High (≥4)	9	26	11
Total	33 (26%)	64 (50%)	30 (24%)

Note: Three respondents did not answer all of the items regarding language use.

A wide range of occupations was represented: unskilled workers comprised 18 percent of the sample (e.g., cleaning and maintenance workers, manual construction laborers, store cashiers, parking attendants, restaurant servers); skilled workers or semiprofessionals were 29 percent (e.g. trained office staff workers, low-level managers and skilled employees of Miami's vital service and tourist industries, professional salespeople, medical assistants, and laboratory technicians); professionals constituted 20 percent (e.g., physicians, lawyers, upper-level managers, financial advisers, certified schoolteachers); and another 30 percent were retired. Five participants did not report their occupation. No one included in the present study was involved in any sort of language-related profession (e.g., journalists, writers, advertising professionals, language teachers, interpreters or translators).

Finally, the distribution of age ranges was as follows: eighteen to twenty-five years old = 36 percent of the sample; twenty-six to thirty-nine years old = 20 percent; forty to fifty-nine years old = 26 percent; sixty years old or more = 18 percent (the youngest participants were eighteen and the oldest was ninety-two). With respect to birthplace, 68 percent were born in Cuba (versus 88 percent in Otheguy and García's

1983 sample). Some 45 percent of respondents had immigrated from Cuba to Miami during the 1960s and 1970s or were the children or grandchildren of early exiles; about 20 percent corresponded to migrations of the 1980s and 1990s; and another 35 percent of respondents had arrived since the year 2000 (cf. Lynch 2009a).

Results and Discussion

General Findings

Following Otheguy and García (1988, Table 1, 218), table 9.4 displays the quantitative findings for each of the dependent variables (awareness, adoption, acceptability) according to the four types of lexical innovation under scrutiny (loanwords, phonological calques, semantic calques, phrasal calques), as well as a series of distractor or 'dummy' items taken as a sort of baseline. In each cell, the mean of responses from all 130 participants is given, calculated from the 'yes' (1) / 'no' (2) binary (i.e., values closer to 1 reflect a greater majority of affirmative responses and those closer to 2 indicate a preponderance of negative responses). Otheguy and García reported their results in terms of percentages of those who "answered yes" on each of the dependent variables. In the present study, because not all respondents answered yes to all of the particular lexical items that composed each analytical category (loanwords, phonological calques, semantic calques, and phrasal calques), I chose to calculate the mean responses, reasoning that this figure would afford the reader better insight into the range of variability in the data. The final column of table 9.4 displays a composite diffusion variable, calculated by taking the mean of all of the responses for the dependent variables (awareness, adoption, acceptability). While Otheguy and García derived their diffusion index from the average of percentages of yes answers on the dependent variables (Otheguy and García 1988, 218), the present diffusion index was based upon the mean of responses on all three dependent variables, calculated using the 'compute variable' function in SPSS. In mathematical terms, the same principle was followed in both studies; the diffusion index reflects an 'average of percentages' (Otheguy and García 1988) or a 'mean of means' (the present inquiry).

Comparing the present results (table 9.4) with those of Otheguy and García (1988, Table 1, 218), one can appreciate striking similarities. For the awareness

Table 9.4. Mean responses to items regarding awareness, adoption, and acceptability: YES [1]---------------------[2] NO

Innovation Type	**Awareness** *Hear it?*	**Adoption** *Use it?*	**Acceptability** *Is it correct?*	**Diffusion Index**
Loanwords	1.07	1.31	1.76	1.38
Phonological Calques	1.09	1.39	1.53	1.34
Semantic Calques	1.20	1.49	1.58	1.42
Phrasal Calques	1.16	1.39	1.48	1.34
Distractors	1.09	1.24	1.29	1.20

variable, loanwords were most the salient type of lexical item, even slightly more so than the distractor items (1.07 versus 1.09, respectively), and phonological calques were as commonly heard as the distractor items (both 1.09). This is precisely the same pattern reported by Otheguy and García three decades ago. The fact that in both studies there was greater awareness of loanwords than of any other type of item—including the distractors—lends further support to those authors' assertion that "high visibility produces high awareness" (219)—in other words, loanwords stand out in terms of form, easily recognized as having an English-language origin. Semantic calques were the least salient (mean of 1.20), with phrasal calques being a bit more common (1.16). Again, this is the same pattern of awareness observed by Otheguy and García. It is noteworthy, though perhaps expected, that females were significantly more likely to be aware of all four types of innovations than male respondents ($p > .05$) in one-way ANOVA tests; however, gender did not yield significant differences in terms of adoption or acceptability.

In terms of use (the adoption variable), the same pattern observed by Otheguy and García again emerged in Miami three decades later: semantic calques were least used (mean of 1.49), followed by phrasal calques and phonological calques (both 1.39). Of the English-origin innovations, loanwords were the most commonly used (1.31) and, as expected, distractor items reflected the highest indices of use (1.24).

The acceptability variable yielded interesting findings with respect to loanwords, in that despite their being the most perceptually salient and commonly used type of lexical innovation, they received the lowest acceptability ratings by far. Indeed, the majority of respondents deemed them incorrect (mean of 1.76), despite reporting that they used them. Semantic calques received the next lowest acceptability rating (1.58), followed by phonological calques (1.53) and phrasal calques (1.48). Once again, this overall pattern was the same as that observed by Otheguy and García (1988).

For the composite diffusion variable, the results reflected a similar trend as in Otheguy and García's 1983 sample, with semantic calques being the least diffused of all types of innovations. Because loanwords were the most highly stigmatized feature, they reflected a diffusion index that was perhaps lower than deserved in light of their highly widespread use. As Otheguy and García explain, "loans do not violate the integrity of any signs. And they are, in fact, the only way to be completely true to the English message while speaking in Spanish. Speakers appear to be aware of these qualities of loans and are willing to adopt them even when they recognize them as not Spanish" (1988, 222). One potentially interesting—albeit minor—difference between the two studies was related to the diffusion of phonological calques. In García and Otheguy's 1983 data, phrasal calques were more widely diffused than phonological calques, yet in the present study both appear equally diffused (value of 1.34). While this difference could merely be attributed to sampling, one might speculate that phonological calques have become somewhat more integrated in the variety of Spanish spoken among Cubans in Miami (in diachronic fashion), and in the US more generally.

Because both phonological and phrasal calques reflected the same degree of diffusion in the present data, one could speculate that first-generation speakers go about incorporating these two phenomena in their speech in similar ways (cf. table 9.6 below) since both conform easily to the structure of normative Spanish. Indeed, one young interviewee from Hialeah who had been in the US for only two years and had limited abilities in English remarked that the words *introducir*, *registrarse*, and *aplicación* reflected a "more formal Spanish" than that spoken in Cuba; she commented the same regarding the phrasal calque *está supuesta a llegar*. This leads us to the significance of English language ability as a variable conditioning the use of such innovations.

The Influence of English Language Ability and Everyday Language Use Patterns

Perhaps Otheguy and García's most unexpected and thought-provoking finding was that "there is greater diffusion of lexical innovations among those members of the community that do not know the language of origin of the innovations than among those that do" (1988, 205). In other words, those speakers in their sample who knew the least amount of English were in fact the ones who used and accepted English-based lexical innovations the most. Statistical analysis of the present data set revealed a rather more nuanced portrait of the sociolinguistic phenomenon underscored by Otheguy and García. Testing the singular effect of English language ability on each of the three different dependent variables (awareness, adoption, acceptability), one-way ANOVAs yielded significance, specifically on the following (table 9.5): the acceptability of loanwords, the awareness of phonological calques and semantic calques, and the acceptability of phrasal calques.

Table 9.5. Mean responses to items regarding awareness, adoption, and acceptability according to English language ability (low vs. mid to high): YES [1]---------------------[2] NO

Innovation Type	**Awareness** *Hear it?*		**Adoption** *Use it?*		**Acceptability** *Is it correct?*	
English ability	**low**	**mid / high**	**low**	**mid / high**	**low**	**mid / high**
Loanwords	1.08	1.07	1.25	1.32	1.53	1.82*
Phonological Calques	1.14	1.07*	1.41	1.38	1.45	1.55
Semantic Calques	1.27	1.17*	1.57	1.46	1.54	1.59
Phrasal Calques	1.19	1.14	1.38	1.40	1.39	1.50*

$*p < 0.05$

As table 9.5 reflects, among the present participants, stronger abilities in English condition lower acceptance of all four types of lexical innovations, just as Otheguy and García observed in their 1983 sample (cf. 1988, Table 3, 226). One-way ANOVAs of the present data revealed that the differences of acceptability were significant only for loanwords and phrasal calques, however. As for adoption, all four types of lexical innovations appeared to be used by both groups (i.e., those with low-level abilities in English and those with mid- to high-level abilities). It is noteworthy that although stronger abilities in English seemed to condition greater use of semantic calques in Spanish (not significantly, though), such abilities did not have the same effect on other types of lexical innovations. In terms of awareness, English language abilities made participants significantly more cognizant of phonological calques and semantic calques; this was also true for phrasal calques, although the difference between groups was not statistically significant. Rather expectedly, both groups were equally aware of loanwords (1.08 and 1.07), as their salience is very high. In sum, this evidence suggests that English language abilities lead Spanish speakers to be: (1) more aware of calques of all types; (2) somewhat less likely to use loanwords, yet more likely to use semantic calques; and (3) more likely to consider all types of English-origin innovations incorrect. This finding lends support to Varra's (2013) conclusion regarding lexical borrowing among bilinguals in New York City: "Where Spanish is maintained, the likelihood and extent of permanent change to its lexicon may decrease as the individual and the community becomes more aware of and gains in knowledge of English" (214).

Because high levels of English language ability are a given among all Cuban Spanish speakers in Miami except first-generation immigrants and, even among the latter, daily exposure to and use of English can still be very frequent, the extent of use of Spanish and English was tested separately. For this purpose, a composite variable was created from the five different questions regarding use of both languages with family, friends, people on the street, in movies and television programs, and in music choices. By testing everyday language use as a composite variable, the question of English ability is addressed from a different angle. Moreover, the potential impact of differences between, on one hand, those bilingual participants who used more English beyond the home and in mass media and music consumption, and, on the other hand, those who used more Spanish in those same domains, could be better taken into account.

The result for language use was quite revealing with respect to loanwords, in that those who used English the most in everyday life were significantly less likely to be aware of them yet, at the same time, significantly more likely to deem them unacceptable on the questionnaire. For calques, a similar effect was not observed. This finding is particularly interesting since English language ability did not appear to exert any effect on the awareness of loanwords (table 9.5, above), but on the measure of actual use of English, higher frequency of use was significantly correlated with lower awareness. A closer look at specific items suggests a possible cause of this phenomenon, to wit: words for which low-frequency users of Spanish (i.e., Group 3 and Group 4 bilinguals) might be less likely to find an equivalent in Spanish are the ones that are significantly more likely to be reported as not having been heard (vacuum cleaner, quarter, mall, laptop, *chatear* [online], ATM [bank]). In light of this finding, one might conclude that the predominant use of English has a seemingly paradoxical effect on the overall diffusion of loanwords, desensitizing bilingual speakers to their presence (thus potentially allowing for their proliferation) while, at the same time, conditioning more negative appraisals of their acceptability when explicitly underscored, especially in written form or metalinguistic commentary (cf. Varra 2013). As we will see below, rather predictably, higher levels of formal education accentuate this phenomenon, in conjunction with cross-generational language use trends related to English dominance.

Immigrant Generation and the Impact of Formal Education

As table 9.6 shows, G1 speakers were significantly more likely than G1.5 and G2 bilinguals to use loanwords and deem them as acceptable. This finding is fully in line with Otheguy and García's results and their argument that first-generation Spanish-dominant or near-monolingual Cubans in Miami "are more willing to adopt [lexical innovations] and to accept them as correct because...they simply see the innovations as the Spanish of Dade County, as the way, that is, that this language is spoken in the new—and to them Spanish monolingual—community that, as all new communities, can be expected to have its linguistic quirks" (1988, 226).

Table 9.6. Mean responses to items regarding awareness, adoption, and acceptability according to generation (G1, G1.5, G2): YES [1]---------------------[2] NO

Innovation Type	Awareness *Hear it?*			Adoption *Use it?*			Acceptability *Is it correct?*		
Generation	**G1**	**G1.5**	**G2**	**G1**	**G1.5**	**G2**	**G1**	**G1.5**	**G2**
Loanwords	1.08	1.01	1.09	1.28*	1.34	1.31	1.60*	1.87	1.82
Phonological Calques	1.14	1.03*	1.08	1.48	1.44	1.31*	1.54	1.66*	1.47
Semantic Calques	1.29	1.10*	1.17	1.64	1.52	1.37*	1.64	1.62	1.53*
Phrasal Calques	1.19	1.11	1.15	1.45	1.47	1.32*	1.49	1.62*	1.41

*$p < 0.05$

For phonological calques, G1.5 speakers appeared most sensitive, as they were significantly more likely to be aware of them and to consider them incorrect; G2 speakers were significantly more likely to use them. Given that bilingual abilities tend to be stronger among G1.5 speakers than in the other two groups, this finding is not surprising. It is also not surprising that G2 speakers, who are all English-dominant bilinguals in Miami, would be the most likely group to accept and use them (significantly so). For phrasal calques, the same pattern applies: G1.5 speakers were most aware of them and significantly more likely to consider them incorrect; G2 speakers were significantly more likely to use them and, in comparison with G1.5 speakers, to deem them acceptable.

It is noteworthy that, in terms of the acceptability of both phonological and phrasal calques, G2 speakers patterned more closely with G1 speakers than with

G1.5 speakers (table 9.6, last column). One might suppose that G1 speakers find both these types of calques more acceptable than G1.5 speakers for the reason proposed by Otheguy and García (i.e., they consider these innovations merely as part and parcel of the variety of Spanish spoken in Miami). On the other hand, I suppose that G2 speakers find these calques more acceptable because of their less frequent use of Spanish and lower levels of overall ability in the language. The English dominance of G2 speakers might also serve to explain why G2 speakers were significantly more likely to use and accept semantic calques than the other two groups (G1 and G1.5 speakers), a type of innovation that met with the lowest rates of use and approval among those identified as bilinguals in Otheguy and García's 1983 sample. One could hypothesize that as bilingualism now extends into the third generation of adult Cubans in Miami (the present G2 participants), beyond the more Spanish-dominant bilingualism of the 1983 sample just twenty years after the Revolution, calques of all types have reached higher indices of diffusion across the city.

It is indeed remarkable that, as table 9.6 reflects, the present G2 participants—farther away in time from the Cuban Spanish bilingualism of Otheguy and García's sample—demonstrate the greatest use and acceptance of all three types of calques, and significantly more so in the case of semantic calques. Rather lacking the intimate sort of knowledge of Spanish syntax and lexicon required to recognize semantic calques (which bear no semblance of English language structure, unlike phonological or phrasal calques), third-generation speakers use and accept them almost as readily as the other two types of calques. G1.5 speakers, in the meantime, continue to align with G1 speakers regarding their incorrectness (1.64 and 1.62, respectively). In sum, these data provide compelling evidence that as more English-dominant bilingual varieties of Spanish in South Florida coalesce, calques of all sorts may become more syntactically integrated into the social fabric of Miami's Cuban speech communities. This hypothesis depends, of course, on the vitality of Spanish language use among the fourth generation of Cubans, who are still small children in their great majority. For them, much likely rides upon access to formal education in Spanish and recontact with the language through interpersonal relationships with first-generation immigrants (cf. Silva-Corvalán 2014; Lynch 2000).

Because they did not take education level into account in their quantitative analysis, Otheguy and García questioned whether lower levels of formal education among their Spanish monolingual sample—rather than lack of English language ability per se—could have possibly driven the result of greater use and acceptance of lexical innovations among that group (1988, 227). For that reason, the present analysis took formal education level into statistical account. Because all or nearly all of the formal education of those who arrived in Miami as children or were born there (G2 participants) would have been in English, the statistical inquiry presented in table 9.7 was limited only to those who immigrated to the US from Cuba as teens or adults (i.e., G1 and G1.5 participants). As table 9.7 shows, the findings suggest that formal education only conditions the degree of acceptability of all types of innovations; it does not significantly impact the awareness or adoption of any of them.

As Otheguy and García suspected yet did not test (1988, 227), those G1 and G1.5 speakers with lower levels of formal education (primary or secondary schooling)

Table 9.7. Mean responses to items regarding awareness, adoption, and acceptability according to education level (G1 and G1.5 speakers only): YES [1]--------------------[2] NO

Innovation Type	**Awareness** *Hear it?*			**Adoption** *Use it?*			**Acceptability** *Is it correct?*		
Education level	**low**	**mid**	**high**	**low**	**mid**	**high**	**low**	**mid**	**high**
Loanwords	1.08	1.03	1.06	1.33	1.29	1.29	1.56	1.73	1.76
Phonological Calques	1.13	1.05	1.13	1.43	1.43	1.52	1.39*	1.60	1.73
Semantic Calques	1.25	1.15	1.28	1.51	1.64	1.61	1.44*	1.67	1.72
Phrasal Calques	1.18	1.13	1.18	1.43	1.53	1.42	1.39*	1.61	1.55

*$p < 0.05$

were significantly more likely than their more educated counterparts (those with at least some postsecondary studies or a college degree) to deem all types of calques acceptable. For loanwords, the same pattern occurred, although the difference did not reach statistical significance. It thus seems that while English language ability has the potential to impact both the awareness and acceptability of different types of innovations, the effect of formal education is rather more restricted to the realm of perceived acceptability; it does not appear to play a significant role in determining whether Cuban Spanish speakers in Miami will be more aware of or make greater use of lexical innovations in general. In sum, a perusal of tables 9.4–9.7 clearly suggests that phrasal calques were deemed the most acceptable type of lexical innovation by the present sample and, alongside phonological calques, were the most widely diffused. Unlike phonological calques, however, the structural trace of English that phrasal calques carry is linguistically subtle. As Otheguy and García remark, phrasal calques are perhaps "the most distinctive characteristic of US Spanish" in that they convey a "sense of strangeness" by virtue of being entirely Spanish in form yet English in their message (1988, 223). At the same time, according to Otheguy and García, this type of innovation "resembles traditional usage the most" (223). Given this rather special quality, in what follows I explore the diffusion of phrasal calques by profiling three specific items that appear to reflect differential degrees of sociolinguistic integration in Miami Cuban Spanish, based on the present data.

A Sociolinguistic Profile of Three Phrasal Calques in Miami Cuban Spanish

This subsection is intended to provide the reader with a mere illustration of the myriad ways in which phrasal calques may become socially integrated in particular speech communities. For this purpose, three syntactically different sorts of phrasal calques were chosen, all of which reflected very high rates of awareness among the present sample (i.e., they are all widely heard throughout Miami) yet appeared to carry different degrees of social value: (1) *déjame saber* (let me know); (2) *está supuesta/o a…* (s/he is supposed to); and (3) *llamar para atrás* (to call back). None of these phrasal calques, now widely diffused in Miami, were included in Otheguy and García's original 1983 survey.

Déjame saber

Perhaps the most interesting aspect of the profile of the phrasal calque *déjame saber* is that it appears not to have taken on any sort of social differentiation within the context of Cuban Miami (i.e., it does not constitute a sociolinguistic variant). As table 9.8 reflects, its diffusion is in no way socially stratified according to area of the city. It is used just slightly more among those with low levels of English language ability and formal education and among those who speak principally Spanish in daily life (differences that were insignificant). Its use meets with slightly higher indices of disapproval among those with greater English ability and higher levels of formal education, and among those who speak both languages in fairly equal amounts in everyday life. Furthermore, both males and females claim to hear, use, and accept it equally.

Table 9.8. Mean responses to items regarding awareness, adoption, and acceptability of ***Déjame saber*** *si puedes ayudarme mañana:* YES [1]----------------------[2] NO

Factor	Awareness *Hear it?*			Adoption *Use it?*			Acceptability *Is it correct?*		
English ability	low	mid / high		low	mid / high		low	mid / high	
	1.00	1.04		1.21	1.15		1.18	1.25	
Sex	females	males		females	males		females	males	
	1.02	1.05		1.16	1.18		1.22	1.26	
Language use	+Spa	Both	+Eng	+Spa	Both	+Eng	+Spa	Both	+Eng
	1.00	1.02	1.10	1.24	1.14	1.13	1.18	1.29	1.20
Generation	G1	G1.5	G2	G1	G1.5	G2	G1	G1.5	G2
	1.00	1.00	1.07	1.20	1.13	1.15	1.23	1.33	1.20
Education level	low	mid	high	low	mid	high	low	mid	high
	1.05	1.02	1.04	1.23	1.15	1.15	1.14	1.25	1.26
Area of Miami	NW	Centr	South	NW	Centr	South	NW	Centr	South
	1.02	1.04	1.04	1.15	1.13	1.19	1.21	1.26	1.23

*p < 0.05

Similar to the case of *llamar para atrás* (table 9.10 below), those who use principally Spanish or principally English in everyday life deem it correct in similar numbers (1.18 and 1.20, respectively), perhaps suggesting that the heightened disapproval of this variant among G1.5 speakers who use both languages frequently in daily life (i.e., more 'socially balanced' bilinguals) is attenuated by English-dominant bilinguals of the Miami-born second and third generations (labeled G2 speakers for the present purposes).

It is important to note that, unlike the other two phrasal calques considered below, *déjame saber* is heard on the island of Cuba, albeit with relatively low frequency; forms such as *avísame*, *dime*, or *mantenme al tanto* are more commonly used there. The fact that there is some incidence—albeit quite low—of this variant among monolinguals in Cuba might serve to explain, at least in part, why it garners no sort of social attention in Cuban Miami. At the same time, its structural parallelism with the English form 'let me know' assures that its use and diffusion are sociolinguistically accelerated within the context of bilingualism in South Florida, at the expense of other variants more frequently used among monolinguals in Cuba (cf. Silva-Corvalán 1994).

Está supuesta/o a...

Different than *déjame saber*, the phrasal calque *está supuesta/o a...* is not part of Cuban monolingual repertoires and, because of its probable "sense of strangeness" to ears unaccustomed to bilingual varieties of Spanish in the US, it attracts some attention on the part of recently arrived Cuban immigrants and Spanish monolingual visitors in Miami. Comparing tables 9.8 and 9.9, one realizes that this form is much more firmly entrenched than *déjame saber* in the repertoires of those who have low levels of English ability and formal education and who use principally Spanish in everyday life. As table 9.9 shows, the differences for these social variables in terms of acceptability of this form proved statistically significant in the present sample.

Table 9.9. Mean responses to items regarding awareness, adoption, and acceptability of *Ella* ***está supuesta a llegar*** *hoy a las 5:00:* YES [1]----------------------[2] NO

Factor	Awareness *Hear it?*			Adoption *Use it?*			Acceptability *Is it correct?*		
English ability	low	mid / high		low	mid / high		low	mid / high	
	1.04	1.10		1.33	1.34		1.26*	1.53	
Sex	females	males		females	males		females	males	
	1.03*	1.21		1.29*	1.47		1.45	1.53	
Language use	+Spa	Both	+Eng	+Spa	Both	+Eng	+Spa	Both	+Eng
	1.03	1.09	1.13	1.34	1.38	1.24	1.25*	1.53	1.57
Generation	G1	G1.5	G2	G1	G1.5	G2	G1	G1.5	G2
	1.02	1.00	1.16*	1.40	1.42	1.28	1.38	1.61	1.49
Education level	low	mid	high	low	mid	high	low	mid	high
	1.10	1.05	1.13	1.29	1.32	1.40	1.24*	1.48	1.58
Area of Miami	NW	Centr	South	NW	Centr	South	NW	Centr	South
	1.04	1.13	1.11	1.33	1.45	1.32	1.43	1.52	1.51

*$p < 0.05$

The fact that high-frequency users of Spanish accept this particular phrasal calque significantly more than the other two groups (language use variable), taken together with the near absolute salience of this variant among G1 and G1.5

speakers—significantly greater than among G2 Cubans—leads one to conjecture that it is a more characteristically Spanish-speaking variant in Cuban Miami than an English-dominant bilingual variant.

The fact that G2 speakers indicate using *está supuesta/o a...* somewhat more than G1 and G1.5 speakers and find it rather more acceptable than their G1.5 counterparts might at first blush seem negligible for purposes of sociolinguistic speculation, yet, when confronted with three other social facts reflected in table 9.9, these differences seem to lend support to the hypothesis that this variant has begun to acquire social value in Cuban Miami. The other relevant facts are the following: (1) There are significantly greater rates of acceptability and substantially higher rates of adoption of this variant among those with low versus high levels of formal education in the overall sample (cf. Sullivan 2008); (2) this variant is somewhat more socially diffused (though not significantly so) in northwesterly areas of the city, which are generally lower socioeconomic class (including Hialeah); and (3) females are significantly more aware of the form and significantly more likely to use it than males; they also consider it slightly more correct than males. In light of all this evidence taken together, one could well speculate that this form has begun to acquire the profile of a sociolinguistic variant. If that is the case, in time, the phrase *está supuesta/o a...* could reach the sociolinguistic status already attained by the now rather iconic form *llamar para atrás*, described below.

Llamar para atrás

This phrasal calque is surely one of the most frequently cited examples of so-called Spanglish and widely noted particularities of the Spanish of US Latino bilinguals in both popular and scholarly commentaries (cf. Otheguy 1993). It is perhaps a paragon example of what Otheguy (2011) characterizes as conceptual convergence involving grammatical meaning but not linguistic form. Otheguy affirms in this particular case that: "The form of English ['to call back'] has been ignored by the bilinguals, who have copied the conceptual content instead.... There is little room for thinking that what we have here is anything other than imitation at the conceptual rather than the formal level" (2011, 517). In this regard, this variant is structurally different than the other two phrasal calques profiled above, in that the syntactic form of the other two mirrors English form; this is not the case of *llamar para atrás*. Perhaps this is but one of the reasons why *llamar para atrás* ultimately attracts such great social scrutiny.

The present evidence suggests, rather unequivocally, that *llamar para atrás* has acquired social value in Cuban Miami and can be characterized as a sociolinguistic variant. As table 9.10 reflects, Cubans with lower levels of English language ability and formal education are significantly more likely to use it, as are those who use principally Spanish in daily life. As in the case of *déjame saber*, the heightened disapproval of this variant that manifests among G1.5 speakers who use both languages frequently in daily life (i.e., more socially balanced bilinguals) is attenuated by English-dominant bilinguals of the Miami-born second and third generations, labeled G2 speakers. In the case of this phrasal calque, however, the differences within these social variables (i.e., language use and immigrant generation) are statistically significant, while they are not in the case of *déjame saber*. It is remarkable that high-frequency and low-frequency users of Spanish disapprove of *llamar para atrás* to similar degrees (mean responses of 1.64 and 1.60, respectively), while those who use both languages equally in daily life are significantly more likely than the other two groups to consider it unacceptable (1.89). Similarly, G1 and G2 respondents disapprove of this form to an equal extent (1.73 and 1.72, respectively), and G1.5 respondents are nearly categorical in their disdain (1.92), significantly surpassing the other two generational groups. This is perhaps suggestive of a pattern of social normalization in cross-generational terms. This hypothesis may be supported by the fact that there are no differences of awareness, adoption, or acceptability of this form between females and males.

Table 9.10. Mean responses to items regarding awareness, adoption, and acceptability of *Si le dejas un mensaje, seguro que te* ***llama para atrás***: YES [1]----------------------[2] NO

Factor	Awareness *Hear it?*			Adoption *Use it?*			Acceptability *Is it correct?*		
English ability	low		mid / high	low		mid / high	low		mid / high
	1.04		1.05	1.18*		1.51	1.64		1.79
Sex	females		males	females		males	females		males
	1.03		1.08	1.43		1.44	1.77		1.74
Language use	+Spa	Both	+Eng	+Spa	Both	+Eng	+Spa	Both	+Eng
	1.03	1.03	1.10	1.27*	1.53	1.43	1.64	1.89*	1.60
Generation	G1	G1.5	G2	G1	G1.5	G2	G1	G1.5	G2
	1.02	1.04	1.07	1.39	1.46	1.46	1.73	1.92*	1.72
Education level	low	mid	high	low	mid	high	low	mid	high
	1.05	1.03	1.06	1.18*	1.45	1.53	1.14	1.25	1.26
Area of Miami	NW	Centr	South	NW	Centr	South	NW	Centr	South
	1.02	1.04	1.07	1.40	1.35	1.51	1.67	1.70	1.86*

*p < 0.05

More remarkably still, *llamar para atrás* is the only phrasal calque included in the present survey that reflected significant differences of acceptability according to area of the city, suggesting that it has become a marker of socioeconomic status in Cuban Miami. Residents of South areas (which include the affluent city of Coral Gables and the firmly middle-class neighborhoods of Dadeland, South Miami, and Kendall) are significantly more likely to consider this form unacceptable than their lower and lower-middle class counterparts in Miami center, Hialeah, and other north-westerly neighborhoods. The former are also less likely to use this form (although the difference does not reach statistical significance in the present data set).

In reflective interviews, most participants commented explicitly on the use and acceptability of *llamar para atrás* without being asked to do so, providing further evidence that this variant has become a sociolinguistic marker in Cuban Miami. Several laughed when commenting on its use, stressing its quality of "español malhablado" and affirming that it "sounds uneducated." Interestingly, as participants made these comments, many pronounced the phrase with a rather affected intonation, emphasizing the truncation of the prepositions *para atrás* and exaggerating the aspiration or deletion of the final /s/, as in [pa-tráh] or [pa-tráø]. Others also exaggerated the tendency to geminate the final /r/ in *llamar* before the following stop consonant, as in [ya-máp-pa-trá ø]. The gemination of liquids before following consonants (particularly stops) is a distinguishing dialect feature of Cuban Spanish (Lipski 1994), which prior to the Revolution reflected socioeconomic stratification on the island; it possibly continues to do so in Cuban Miami. The aspiration and deletion of final /s/ has already been documented as a sociolinguistic marker in Cuban Miami, particularly to differentiate the speech of the second- and third-generation Miami-born children and grandchildren of the early exiles of the 1960s, who represented Cuba's middle and upper socioeconomic strata, from that of Marielitos and more recent arrivals (Lynch 2009b).

Conclusion

A comparison of the results of Otheguy and García's (1988) study (based on data gathered in 1983) with those of the present inquiry (based on data gathered from late 2014 to late 2015) reveals remarkable similarities. By loosely replicating those authors' methodology, the present study serves to confirm their contention that, contrary to what might be expected, ability in English generally conditions lower degrees of adoption and acceptability of English-influenced lexical innovations. Stronger abilities in English led samples of Cuban Spanish speakers in both studies—more than three decades apart—to be more aware of all types of calques and somewhat less likely to use loanwords. The bilinguals of Otheguy and García's inquiry in 1983 appeared less willing to use semantic calques than their more monolingual counterparts; but in the present data, which included more English-dominant second- and third-generation bilinguals, semantic calques reflected higher rates of use for the latter than among first-generation Cubans with low-level abilities in English.

Higher-level abilities in English also made G1.5 speakers more likely to consider all types of English-origin lexical innovations incorrect. While such abilities appeared to condition both the awareness and acceptability of different types of innovations, formal education exerted an influence only in terms of acceptability, and did not make the present sample of Miami Cuban Spanish speakers more aware of lexical innovations nor condition greater use of them. Phrasal calques were deemed the most acceptable type of lexical innovation by the present sample and, alongside phonological calques, were the most widely diffused. The acceptability ratings for both phonological and phrasal calques among G1 speakers patterned more closely with those of G2 speakers than those of G1.5 speakers. This finding can likely be attributed to a tendency of the former to perceive these types of calques as integral characteristics of the variety of Spanish spoken in Miami; the same is true of loanwords. Toward the other end of the bilingual spectrum, G2 speakers probably find all types of calques—including semantic calques—more acceptable because of their less frequent use of Spanish and lower levels of ability in the language.

A plausible hypothesis is that, diachronically, all types of calques will reach higher indices of diffusion in Miami (comparing the findings of the 1983 study and the present inquiry) due to the growing influence of the speech patterns of third- and fourth-generation bilinguals. The profiles of three different sorts of phrasal calques now widely diffused in Miami but not included in Otheguy and García's original survey (*déjame saber*, *está supuesta/o a…*, and *llamar para atrás*) cursorily illustrate how this might happen from a sociolinguistic theoretical perspective. This diachronic hypothesis, of course, depends upon sustained Spanish language use among future generations of Miami-born Cubans in the years ahead. Patterns of sociolinguistic discontinuity presently observable in the adult third and child fourth generations of Miami Cubans make this a rather dubious scenario, however (Carter and Lynch 2015; Gutiérrez-Rivas 2007; Porcel 2006).

The sociolinguistic concept of diffusion within a context of transitional societal bilingualism perhaps loses some of its explanatory power, since generational discontinuity precipitates structural discontinuity, not just at the lexical level but at the phonological, morphosyntactic, pragmatic, and discursive levels as well (cf. Gutiérrez-Rivas 2007). Across the three (apparent time) generations surveyed for the present study, what is ostensibly an incipient stage of societal diffusion of calques in what one could abstractly label 'Miami Cuban Spanish' could ultimately be falsified by ensuing English-language dominance and more highly restricted social use of Spanish, concomitant with limited awareness of lexical normativity in Spanish as well as the discourse-pragmatic patterns of use beyond the US context (cf. Lynch 2013). This pattern is likely to be all the more prevalent in other Spanish-speaking immigrant communities across the US, beyond the confines of the socioeconomic prestige and cultural dynamism that the unique urban setting of Miami provides for Spanish-English bilingualism.

References

Alfaraz, G. 2014. "Dialect Perceptions in Real Time: A Restudy of Miami Cuban Perceptions." *Journal of Linguistic Geography* 2:74–86.

Aranda, E., S. Hughes, and E. Sabogal. 2014. *Making a Life in Multiethnic Miami: Immigration and the Rise of a Global City*. Boulder: Lynne Rienner Publishers.

Boswell, T. 1994. *The Cubanization and Hispanicization of Metropolitan Miami*. Miami: Cuban American National Council.

Carter, P. M., and A. Lynch. 2015. "Multilingual Miami: Current Trends in Sociolinguistic Research." *Language and Linguistics Compass* 9:369–85.

De La Torre, M. 2003. *La Lucha for Cuba. Religion and Politics on the Streets of Miami*. Berkeley: University of California Press.

Gutiérrez-Rivas, C. 2007. "Variación pragmática del español de los cubanos y cubanoamericanos en Miami. El efecto de género y generación en el uso de estructuras discursivas." PhD diss., University of Florida.

Klee, C., and A. Lynch. 2009. *El español en contacto con otras lenguas*. Washington, DC: Georgetown University Press.

Laguna, A. S. 2010. "'Aquí está Álvarez Guedes': Cuban choteo and the Politics of Play. *Latino Studies* 8:509–31.

Lipski, J. 1994. *Latin American Spanish*. London: Longman.

Lynch, A. 2000. "Spanish-Speaking Miami in Sociolinguistic Perspective: Bilingualism, Recontact, and Language Maintenance among the Cuban-Origin Population." In *Research on Spanish in the United States: Linguistic Issues and Challenges*, edited by A. Roca, 271–83. Somerville, MA: Cascadilla Press.

———. 2009a. "Expression of Cultural Standing in Miami: Cuban Spanish Discourse about Fidel Castro and Cuba." *Revista Internacional de Lingüística Iberoamericana* 14:21–48.

———. 2009b. "A Sociolinguistic Analysis of Final /s/ in Miami Cuban Spanish." *Language Sciences* 31:767–90.

———. 2013. "Observaciones sobre comunidad y (dis)continuidad en el estudio sociolingüístico del español en Estados Unidos." In *El español en los Estados Unidos: E pluribus unum? Enfoques multidisciplinarios*, edited by D. Dumitrescu and G. Piña-Rosales, 67–83. New York: Academia Norteamericana de la Lengua Española.

Otheguy, R. 1993. "A Reconsideration of the Notion of Loan Translation in the Analysis of U.S. Spanish." *In Spanish in the United States: Linguistic Contact and Diversity*, edited by A. Roca and J. M. Lipski, 21–41. Berlin: Mouton de Gruyter.

———. 2011. "Functional Adaptation and Conceptual Convergence in the Analysis of Language Contact in the Spanish of Bilingual Communities in New York." In *Handbook of Hispanic Sociolinguistics*, edited by M. A. Díaz-Campos, 504–29. Malden, MA: Blackwell Publishers.

Otheguy, R., and O. García. 1988. "Diffusion of Lexical Innovations in the Spanish of Cuban Americans." In *Research Issues and Problems in United States Spanish: Latin American and Southwestern Varieties*, edited by J. Ornstein-Galicia, G. Green, and D. Bixler-Márquez, 203–43. Brownsville, TX: Pan American University.

Otheguy, R., O. García, and A. Roca. 2000. "Speaking in Cuban: The Language of Cuban Americans." In *New Immigrants in the United States*, edited by S. McKay and S. Wong, 165–88. Cambridge: Cambridge University Press.

Otheguy, R., and A. C. Zentella. 2012. *Spanish in New York: Language Contact, Dialect Leveling, and Structural Continuity*. Oxford: Oxford University Press.

Pérez, L. 1999. *On Becoming Cuban: Identity, Nationality & Culture*. Chapel Hill, NC: University of North Carolina Press.

Phillips, R. H. 1948. "Cubans Enliven Miami Season." *New York Times*, September 5, X11.

Porcel, J. 2006. "The Paradox of Spanish among Miami Cubans." *Journal of Sociolinguistics* 10:93–110.

Portés, A., and A. Stepick. 1993. *City on the Edge: The Transformation of Miami*. Berkeley: University of California Press.

Silva-Corvalán, C. 1994. *Language Contact and Change: Spanish in Los Angeles*. Oxford: Clarendon Press.

———. 2001. *Sociolingüística y pragmática del español*. Washington, DC: Georgetown University Press.

———. 2014. *Bilingual Language Acquisition: Spanish and English in the First Six Years*. Cambridge: Cambridge University Press.

Sullivan, C. M. 2008. "A Mechanism of Lexical Borrowing." *Journal of Language Contact* (*VARIA*) 1:17–28.

Varra, R. 2013. "The Social Correlates of Lexical Borrowing in Spanish in New York City." PhD diss., City University of New York.

10

Cuban Spanish versus Peninsular Spanish: A Quantitative Lexical Approach

PASCUAL CANTOS-GÓMEZ
Universidad de Murcia

THE SIMILARITIES OR DIFFERENCES people perceive while comparing two or more language varieties are always relative. However, the analysis of these linguistic contrasts can be formalized either from different angles and linguistic levels (phonetic or phonological, morphological, syntactic, semantic, pragmatic, diachronic, etc.) or from different research methodologies (inductive, deductive, descriptive, etc.).

For any native Peninsular Spanish speaker, the encounter with any variant of Latin American Spanish is always an interesting experience, sometimes peculiar, sometimes even disconcerting, but never boring. On the one hand, one is excited and impressed by the ability to travel from Mexico to Chile using a single language; on the other hand, one is constantly discovering differences in pronunciation, morphology, syntax, and vocabulary (including idioms, collocations, etc.) between the Peninsular Spanish and its Latin American counterparts.

However, the differences are not only to be found between the general peninsular variety and the Latin American varieties, but also among different variants of Peninsular Spanish and Latin American Spanish. There is no such thing as a single 'Latin American Spanish' in a more or less homogeneous sense, but rather many variants of Latin American Spanish with different degrees of divergence from their originator: Peninsular or Castilian Spanish. The Spanish varieties spoken in America have been thoroughly studied (Lipski 1994; Silva-Corvalán 1997; Davis 1999; Arias and Meléndez 2002; Penny 2002; Roca and Colombi 2003). Nevertheless, researchers have rarely coincided in their synchronic or diachronic descriptions of the language varieties in the New World (Firsova 2007; Rojas-Arregocés 2008; López-Morales 2013). Despite the ample literature and a recent bibliographical repertoire of dictionaries on Latin-American Spanish (see Haensch and Omeñaca 2004), research and findings on these variants of Spanish still remain incomplete and fragmentary.

For a given Latin American area you might find, for example, a study on phonetics but nothing on lexis or morphosyntax, and vice versa. The current situation is even worse in terms of dictionaries, vocabularies, or glossaries devoted to Latin American Spanish (Haensch 1991; Asociación de Academias de la Lengua Española [ASALE] 2010). Another related issue is the unresolved problem of dialect-speaking regions in America, such as, for instance, the Caribbean Spanish base (Valdés Bernal 1989; López-Morales 1999; Lipski 1994, 2004a, 2004b).

As for Cuba, there is an extensive bibliography (e.g., Isbăşescu 1968; López-Morales 1971, 1992, 2003; Varela and Armistead 1992; Bernal 1993); however, most studies focus on analyzing the lexicon of Cuban Spanish, highlighting the potpourri of elements borrowed from the different cultures that have passed through the country (e.g., Oliver 1965; Bernal 1993; Castellanos and Castellanos 1988; Fabelo 1998; Cárdenas, Tristá, and Werner 2000; Cabrera and Castellanos 2001).

The purpose of this comparative study between Cuban Spanish and Peninsular Spanish is not to find and identify different lexical items that make Cuban Spanish different from Peninsular Spanish and vice versa; it is to define the underlying lexical structure. We will process, analyze, and extract meaningful linguistic information from large amounts of linguistic data (approximately 120 million words), and offer, for the first time, objective and reliable quantitative data on the "visibility" of both language varieties and on the structure and structuring of the lexical inventory in both language varieties (lexical variability, lexical growth, types, lexical and functional types and lemmas, most common types and lemmas, etc.). This study also approaches the different underlying mathematical properties of Cuban Spanish (CS) and Peninsular Spanish (PS).

The Spectrum of the Spanish-Speaking Community

According to the 2015 Annual Report of the Instituto Cervantes,[1] there are 470 million native speakers of Spanish[2] and 559 million Spanish learners;[3] Spanish is the second most spoken language. It is expected that by 2030, the number of native speakers could reach 533 million, that is, 7.5 percent of the world population. The figures do not necessarily match across all sources. For example, according to Ethnologue,[4] Spanish is spoken in thirty countries, totaling nearly 400 million speakers. These divergences could be due to the different source years used by Ethnologue, ranging from 2005 to 2014 depending on the country.

We can also check the status of language vitality and endangerment of Spanish using the Expanded Graded Intergenerational Disruption Scale (EGIDS; Fishman 1991). This scale focuses on different aspects of vitality at ten different levels: 0 (International) is a category reserved for those few languages that are used as the means of communication in many countries for political purposes and international commerce, whereas 10 is given to weakest levels of vitality (Extinct). Figure 10.1 shows how Spanish is represented by a large top-left purple dot, meaning that it is extremely vital (x-axis; 0-level) and is not considered endangered (y-axis indicates the large number of L1 speakers).

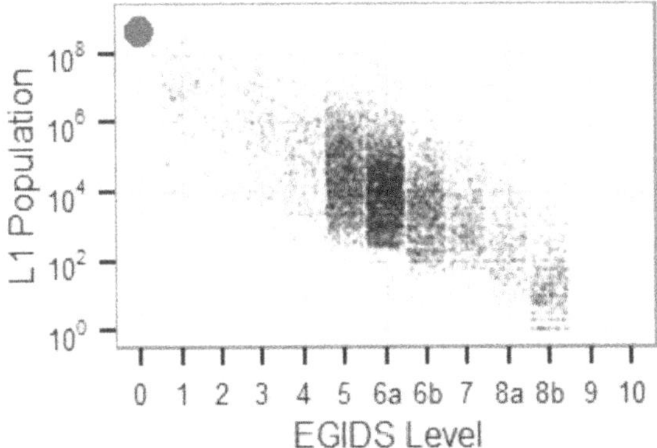

Figure 10.1. EGIDS level for Spanish (source: http://www.ethnologue.com/cloud/spa)

Visibility of PS versus CS

CS is the form of Castilian Spanish spoken in Cuba, and is, in general, not greatly different from its Castilian origin. However, due to diverse influences, CS inevitably has unique vocabulary items, grammatical structures, and pronunciation features that make it different from any other Spanish variety. The Cuban variety is predominantly influenced by (1) the Spanish spoken in the Canary Islands, due to the significant waves of emigration from these islands to Cuba, (2) the indigenous tribes who lived there before the Spanish colonization, and (3) the Caribbean culture (see, for example, Oliver 1965; Bernal 1993; Castellanos and Castellanos 1988; Fabelo 1998; Cabrera and Castellanos 2001). Apart from these influences, English has also played a role in the development of Spanish in Cuba, due to both the period when Cuba was under US control and its proximity to the US (Lipski 1990, 1994, 2004c).

The number of Peninsular Spanish natives compared to Cuban Spanish ones is roughly three times more, although it is true that the statistics do not fully coincide across the sources consulted; the collection criteria seem to differ in some parameters. The data on speakers of the two varieties are summarized in table 10.1.

Table 10.1. Peninsular vs. Cuban Spanish natives

	Native Speaking Population	%
Peninsular Spanish	46,771,341	0.646%
Cuban Spanish	11,176,434	0.154%
World population	7,238,184,000	100.000%

However, the isolated figures of native Peninsular Spaniards and Cubans might not be reliable enough to evaluate the visibility of each language variety. A more realistic view would be to add a further potential variable for language visibility, such as the amount of publically available resources written or published (books, journals, websites, etc.) in both varieties. Of course, the issue of language visibility is a research area of its own and it is not our purpose to explore it here; for purely practical reasons, we shall solely focus our attention on websites (.es versus .cu)[5] as a potential valid language visibility indicator.

There are 128,643,420 websites with an .es domain (the top-level country code domain for Spain),[6] and 1,337,196 for .cu, which, compared to the total number of websites (968,882,453), gives 1.327 percent for PS and 0.138 percent for CS (table 10.2). Comparatively, this places both varieties in extreme positions. So, for PS there is a ratio of 2.75 websites per native speaker, compared to 0.119 websites for each Cuban; that is, the interratio website visibility is 23.109 times greater for PS. This means that PS is potentially 23 times more visible on the Internet than the CS variety, though the population of the former is only 4 times more. Of course, this descriptive comparison constitutes a tentative approach for evidencing the visibility of both language varieties and should be taken cautiously as it is by no means conclusive and focuses just on web domains with .es and .cu. We have deliberately disregarded any other potential factors involved (i.e., economy, GNP, Internet users, Internet restrictions, websites with other code level domains, etc.).[7]

Table 10.2. Websites with *.es* and *.cu* domain

	Websites	**%**
Peninsular Spanish	128,643,420	1.327%
Cuban Spanish	1,337,196	0.138%
Total	968,882,453	100.000%

Lexicon Size

The issue of the inventory of the words that make up a language has always been a heated one. It is quite common to hear people say that this language is lexically more diverse than that language, and it is by no means an easy or trivial matter to decide. In general, the words of a language reflect the conceptualizations native speakers make about the reality they perceive. Therefore, a language with a huge word repertoire, or lexicon, could be also understood as a more conceptualized language with an extensive communicative potential. A richer lexicon implies that the native speakers of that language deal with or are able to deal with more concepts. For instance, “shopping” implies a subjacent reality only present in developed and industrialized countries where malls and shopping centers exist; “shopping” also implies the coexistence of other conceptualizations and realities, such as products, sales, competitiveness, money, credit cards, loans, etc. This context would be unthinkable in primitive societies. If this reality did not exist, its conceptualization among the community would not exist either. Concepts, objects, and realities are the origins of words, and we need these words to refer back to those concepts, objects, or realities. Consequently, it is impossible to define or account exactly for the number of words in a language, as this would imply the possibility of defining all the concepts these native speakers have at their disposal. Having said this, it becomes clear that we cannot just state that English is lexically richer or lexically more prolific than German or Spanish, or even that CS has a greater lexicon than PS or vice versa. In addition, because of the constant change of a language, we would never be in a position to elaborate a precise and extensive lexical repertory of any language.

Dictionaries (in paper or electronic format) have so far been the standard tools to refer to the lexicon of a language, and no other reliable substitutes for dictionaries, as we know and perceive them at present, have been found. Regarding Spanish reference dictionaries, the edition of the Royal Academy of the Spanish Language (*Real Academia Española*) contains approximately 93,000 entries,[8] whereas the first corpus-based dictionary,[9] *Gran Diccionario de Uso de la Lengua Española*, accounts for 70,000 headwords. Could we say that the lexicon for standard Spanish totals around 70,000–90,000 different entries? Might this rule of thumb work? Hanks (2009) suggests that there is somewhere around 250,000 types (different word forms) in regular use in English at any one time. By analogy, if lemmas in English account for about 45–50 percent of the total types (Sánchez and Cantos 1997b),[10] then we might state that 250,000 types are likely to be equivalent to 112,500–125,000 lemmas. Unfortunately, we do not know of any similar studies for Spanish.

Corpora, Words (Tokens), and Word Forms (Types)

Early corpus linguistics had little impact on lexicography (Hanks 2009). The reasons were essentially the poor computational resources available (slow processing time and little, as well as very expensive, memory capacity) and the small size of the corpora, which were not large enough to account for most facts and evidences of most words and patterns. The situation started to change in the late '80s, with the compilation of the *Cobuild Dictionary* in 1987 as computers became cheaper and corpora increased significantly in size. In *Cobuild*, for the first time, the corpus became the central reference component for lexicographers: it was used extensively (1) to structure the meanings of a word (placing the most common meanings first), (2) to reformulate the meaning definitions of words (trying to resemble the way native speakers use and perceive these words), and (3) as the source for real examples. There is no doubt that size became essential (Hofland and Johansson 1982) as larger corpora can shed new light on the utilization of words in different varieties of a language and can additionally constitute a starting point for other studies.

As for our study, we tried to find representative and comparable corpora for PS and CS, but this was not an easy task. We could not obtain any two comparable representative corpora.[11] We finally decided to use the *esTenTen11 (European, Freeling, v4)* corpus for PS and the *esTenTen11 (American, Freeling, v4)* for CS. The *TenTen* family of corpora is a project for building very large web corpora (Sharoff 2006; Baroni et al. 2009). The process for creating a *TenTen* corpus is: (1) crawl the web with Spiderling (Pomikalek and Suchomel 2012); (2) remove nontextual material (Pomikalek 2011; the algorithm used is linguistically informed, rejecting material that does not have a high proportion of tokens that are the grammar words of the language); and (3) tokenize the corpus into words, lemmatize, and part-of-speech tag.

The *esTenTen11 (European, Freeling, v4)* is entirely devoted to PS (with a total size of 2,021,756,831 tokens), whereas the *esTenTen11 (American, Freeling, v4)* totals 7,475,645,291 tokens (originally designed to have 8.38 billion words) broken down between nineteen different national varieties (as identified by URL): Argentina, Bolivia, Chile, Colombia, Costa Rica, Cuba, Dominican Republic, Ecuador, El Salvador, Guatemala, Honduras, Mexico, Nicaragua, Panama, Paraguay, Peru, Uruguay, and Venezuela. The total token size for the Cuban variety accounts for 121,166,000 tokens. As Sharoff and Baroni and colleagues have shown (Sharoff 2006; Baroni et al. 2009), web corpora give a useful and interesting picture of 'general language' and, where we can compare the picture of the language given by the web corpus with that given by some other reference corpus, the picture from the web corpus is, for many purposes, as good as or better than that given by the reference corpus (see also Kilgarriff 2012).[12] According to Kilgarriff and Renau (2013), since all the national subcorpora have been created using exactly the same method, it is plausible that they all contain the same mix of different types of texts: blog, newspaper, academic journal, sports report, club page, company report, personal home pages, etc.

In order to carry out a reliable comparison between both language varieties, for PS we randomly extracted 121,166,000 tokens from the *esTenTen11 (European, Freeling, v4)*, the same size as the CS part in the *esTenTen11 (American, Freeling, v4)*. An initial description of the two corpora is given in table 10.3. Succinctly, both corpora are equivalent in size, though the Cuban variety evidences a greater number of types (33,766 types more).

A first approach to the data reveals that CS seems to be lexically richer in types (word forms).[13] The simple type-token ratio (TTR) formula is below:

$$TTR = \frac{Types}{Tokens}$$

This formula applied to PS and CS indicates that for PS we get, on average, forty-five new types (word forms) for every ten thousand words of running text, compared to forty-eight new types for CS, which confirms the greater lexical variability of CS.[14]

$$TTR_{PS} = \frac{546,478}{121,166,000} = 0.0045$$

$$TTR_{CS} = \frac{580,244}{121,166,000} = 0.0048$$

Table 10.3. Peninsular and Cuban Spanish corpora used

	Corpus	Tokens	Types
Peninsular Spanish	*esTenTen11* (European, Freeling, v4)	121,166,000	546,478
Cuban Spanish	*esTenTen11* (American, Freeling, v4)	121,166,000	580,244

Analogously, we can also explore the mean repetition of types (MRT) in both varieties:

$$MRT_{PS} = \frac{121,166,000}{546,478} = 221.7216$$

$$MRT_{CS} = \frac{121,166,000}{580,244} = 208.819$$

In concordance with what we just stated above, CS has a minor mean repetition rate of types; it repeats, on average, each type approximately 209 times, compared to 222 repetitions in PS; that is, PS is more repetitive as it repeats each type 6.18 percent more than CS.

Distribution of Tokens, Types, and Lemmas

A further step is to analyze the relationship between tokens and types in both Spanish varieties in more depth. This might shed new light and bring forth further differences on how the lexicon is structured in both language varieties.

In order to avoid the size-dependent problem of the TTR, we applied an alternative measure. The quantitative technique used instead is:

$$Types = K\sqrt{Tokens}$$

This formula (Sánchez and Cantos 1997) is size independent and therefore a stable indicator for determining the relationship between types and tokens.[15] Its application is straightforward: instantiate the initial data on types and tokens and get the *K* (constant value) for each language variety (CS and PS). Once the *K*s are calculated, the greater of the two values indicates greater increased rhythm in types within that language variety. That is, the language variety with a greater *K*-value is the one that allows the incorporation of more items to its lexicon and is, consequently, lexically more prolific. Additionally, the formula can be used for predicting the type size of any potential corpora without the need to compile them, with a tolerable reliability (Sánchez and Cantos 1997, 1997b).

Notice that the *K*-value determines the increase rhythm of the types of each language variety. It is a unique indicator, size-independent, that differs for any language, language variety, text type, genre, author, and so on, and might be understood as a kind of textual DNA.[16] To calculate the individual *K*-value, we just need to rewrite the original formula:

$$K = \frac{Types}{\sqrt{Tokens}} = \frac{Types}{Token}\sqrt{Token}$$

The resulting Ks for CS and PS are as follows:[17]

$$K_{CS} = \frac{580,244}{121,166,000}\sqrt{121,166,000} = 52.7133$$

$$K_{PS} = \frac{546,478}{121,166,000}\sqrt{121,166,000} = 49.6457$$

A preliminary analysis of the K-values for both varieties indicates a greater pace increase for new types in CS, compared to PS. In addition, we can now also project both language varieties and compare their lexical-type growth for hypothetical text sizes, greater than the one analyzed here (121,166,000 tokens) and even for smaller ones. Table 10.4 shows the comparison between both Spanish language varieties regarding the relation between size (tokens) and lexical increase (types).[18]

Table 10.4. Type growth in Peninsular and Cuban Spanish

	Types			
Tokens (in million)	Cuban Spanish	Peninsular Spanish	Diff. CB-PS	Diff. CB-PS Increase
50	372,739	351,048	21,691	21,691
100	527,133	496,457	30,676	8,985
150	645,603	608,033	37,570	6,894
200	745,479	702,096	43,382	5,812
…	…	…	…	…
1,900	2,297,719	2,164,006	133,714	1,771
1,950	2,327,756	2,192,295	135,462	1,748
2,000	2,357,410	2,220,223	137,187	1,726

The data (table 10.4) confirms, once again, that CS grows lexically at a greater pace than PS. A 50 million corpus of written collections in CS has around 22,000 more types than the same amount of similar texts in PS. This difference increases up to 137,000 types for a 2-billion-text collection.

Another interesting finding is that type-growth is not linear but plots a power trend line ($\sqrt{x}$, or $x^{0.5}$). This explains why the type-growth pace progressively decreases. This is obvious, as once we have a huge amount of text collections from a language variety, each time we add new texts to it, it becomes harder and harder to generate new types (types that have not appeared before). This phenomenon of nonlinear type-growth becomes evident in figure 10.2, which features the difference in type-growth rates between CS and PS (clearly in favor of CS).

These initial findings reveal that CS is lexically more prolific than PS, and probably also lexically more prone to innovation or less prescriptive, as it takes in more

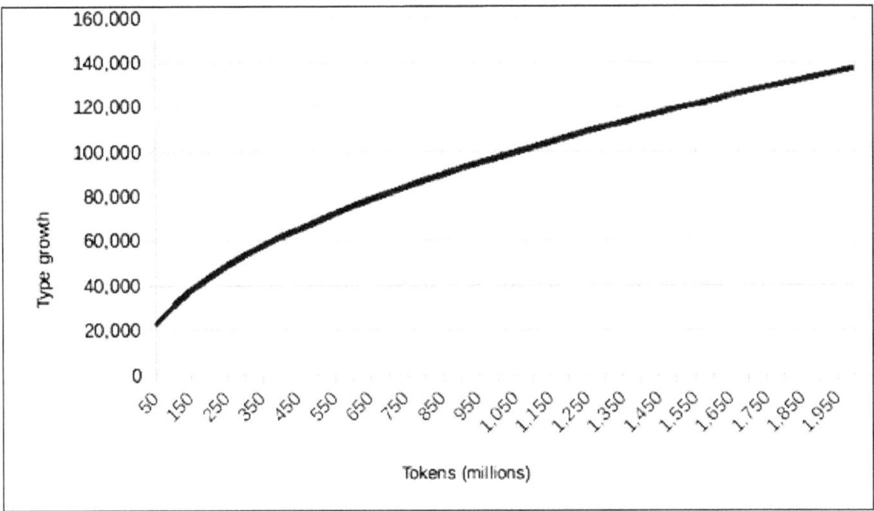

Figure 10.2. Type growth pace of Cuban Spanish with respect to Peninsular Spanish

new linguistic items to its lexical repertoire than PS; the higher *K*-value for CS supports this evidence ($K_{CS} = 52.71$ compared to $K_{PS} = 49.64$). A further consequence of these findings is that we can additionally model type-growth in both varieties. This should be taken with caution, as the language models for type-growth in CS and PS with the two *K*-values obtained above are only feasible if the hypothetical text samples have the same internal and compositional structures as the two corpora analyzed here (see table 10.4); any other corpus compositions, language varieties, texts, or genres, for example, would inevitably require the new calculation of their specific *K*-values.

In addition, we can also model the type-difference between both varieties for any given corpus size. This equation models the regression given in figure 10.4 and outputs the type-difference between CS and PS.

$$Type_{difference} CSvsPS = 21.691\sqrt{Tokens}$$

By simply instantiating the token size of any corpus or text collections, we obtain the type-difference; that is, how many more types CS has than PS.

The number of types does not equal the number of lemmas at all. Spanish is a highly inflected language, which allows us to conclude that the type-lemma ratio in Spanish will be different than the type-lemma ratio in less inflected languages, such as English. If the words (tokens) and the word forms (types) of a language relate to each other in a predictable way, we might also conclude that words and lemmas behave in a similar way (Sánchez and Cantos 1997).

$$Lemmas = K_L \sqrt{Tokens}$$

By using the lemmatized version of the two corpora, we obtained the following K_L-values for CS and PS:[19]

$$KL_{CS} = \frac{303,698}{121,166,000}\sqrt{121,166,000} = 27.54$$

$$KL_{PS} = \frac{286967}{121,166,000}\sqrt{121,166,000} = 26.07$$

Once again, this confirms that CS is more prolific and lexically richer than its Castilian counterpart. This facilitates the modeling of the lemma difference between both varieties for any given corpus size. The equation model regression that follows outputs the type-difference between CS and PS:

$$Lemma_{difference}CSvsPS = 1.52\sqrt{Tokens}$$

By simply instantiating the token size of any corpus or text collections, we obtain the lemma difference; that is, how many more lemmas CS has than PS.

With the type-token relation formula and the lemma-token relation formula, we can now solve the mathematical relationship between types and lemmas in CS and PS. So for CS we get:

$$Types = 51.71\sqrt{Tokens}$$

$$Tokens = \left(\frac{Types}{51.71}\right)^2$$

and

$$Lemmas = 27.54\sqrt{Tokens}$$

$$Tokens = \left(\frac{Lemmas}{27.54}\right)^2$$

giving

$$\left(\frac{Types}{51.71}\right)^2 = \left(\frac{Lemmas}{27.54}\right)^2$$

$$\frac{Types}{51.71} = \frac{Lemmas}{27.54}$$

$$Lemmas = \left(\frac{Types}{51.71}\right) * 27.54$$

$$Lemmas = 0.53 * Types$$

And for PS:

$$Lemmas = 0.52 * Types$$

This roughly means that on average, for every 100 types, we get 53 lemmas in CS and 52 in PS.

Frequency Bands and Distributions of Parts of Speech

In the section above, we discussed the distribution of types and lemmas in relationship to tokens, and the data evidenced a higher type-lemma density in CS compared to PS. However, there is little information on how these types are distributed in both Spanish varieties according to their usage: frequency. That is, how do highly used types and those used very rarely (hapax legomena[20]) conform structurally in the lexicon of PS and CS? Do both varieties exhibit similar frequency distribution patterns?

To grasp this issue, we distributed the types according to six different frequency bands (see Cantos and Sánchez 2011): (1) number of hapax legomena, (2) number of types with 2–5 occurrences, (3) number of types with 6–20 occurrences, (4) number of types with 21–100 occurrences, (5) number of types with 101–1,000 occurrences, and (6) number of types with more than 1,000 occurrences.

The data for frequency band type distributions (table 10.5) show evidence that CS is more prolific than PS in low-frequency types—frequency bands 1 and 2–5 with 2.93 percent more types—whereas PS has a greater number of higher-frequency types—frequency bands 6–20, 21–100, 101–1,000 and 1,000+ with 2.93 percent more types. There seems to be an inverse relationship regarding type frequency distributions in CS and PS: the lexicon of CS is more abundant in low-frequency types—that is, rare or less common types (with frequencies ranging from 1 to 5)—compared to PS, whose lexical repertoire accounts for more higher-frequency types

Table 10.5. Frequency distribution bands

Frequency bands	Peninsular Spanish		Cuban Spanish	
	Types	%	Types	%
1	219,630	40.19	247,532	42.66
2–5	138,969	25.43	150,225	25.89
6–20	109,132	19.97	110,885	19.11
21–100	52,517	9.61	47,406	8.17
101–1,000	22,187	4.06	20,541	3.54
1,001+	4,044	0.74	3,656	0.63
	546,478	100.00	580,244	100.00

(more than 5 occurrences). Once again, this supports and confirms our initial findings of higher type repetition rates in PS and a more prolific and innovative lexicon in CS.

As both corpora (*esTenTen11 [European, Freeling, v4]* and *esTenTen11 [American, Freeling, v4]*) are parts-of-speech tagged, we can go one step further and explore the distribution of types according to their morphological annotation (noun, verb, adjective, adverb, numeral, preposition, determiner, pronoun, conjunction, and interjection; see table 10.6).[21]

Table 10.6. POS distribution

POS	Cuban Spanish	Peninsular Spanish
Noun	305,412	301,442
Preposition	180,908	180,407
Determiner	152,801	146,721
Verb	135,131	144,681
Adjective	74,401	64,930
Conjunction	59,219	62,338
Pronoun	50,750	54,614
Adverb	35,904	39,481

A first approach is to quantify lexical types (nouns, verbs, adjectives, and adverbs) versus functional types (prepositions, determiners, pronouns, and conjunctions).[22] The distribution data on lexical and functional types in CS and PS show that they are virtually identical:[23] for lexical types, CS has 550,848 and PS has 550,534, and for functional types, CS has 443,678 and PS has 444,080.

To delve further into this issue, we needed a more fine-grained analysis that looks at the individual parts of speech to uncover other potential differences between CS and PS (figure 10.3). The major differences found are that CS overuses adjectives (14.59 percent), determiners (4.14 percent), and nouns (1.32 percent). For PS, the data shows overusage in adverbs (9.96 percent), pronouns (7.61 percent), verbs (7.06 percent), and conjunctions (5.26 percent).

These findings might also point toward important structural differences in CS compared to PS, not just in the lexicon, but probably also in their respective morphology and syntax. The instances of overuse of adjectives, determiners, and nouns might indicate that CS is more abundant in noun phrases formed with these three constituents, such as [determiner + noun], [determiner + noun + adjective], [noun + adjective], and probably also [determiner + adjective + noun] and [adjective + noun], due to the influence of the English language. In contrast, PS overuses verbs, adverbs, and conjunctions, which might be interpreted as PS being syntactically more abundant in verb phrase structures, such as [verb + adverb], and in coordinated or subordinated clauses. In addition, the overuse of pronouns in PS might be taken as potential evidence that PS resorts rhetorically more to referential patterns (anaphora and cataphora) than CS. Of course, these preliminary findings deserve a more exhaustive analysis.

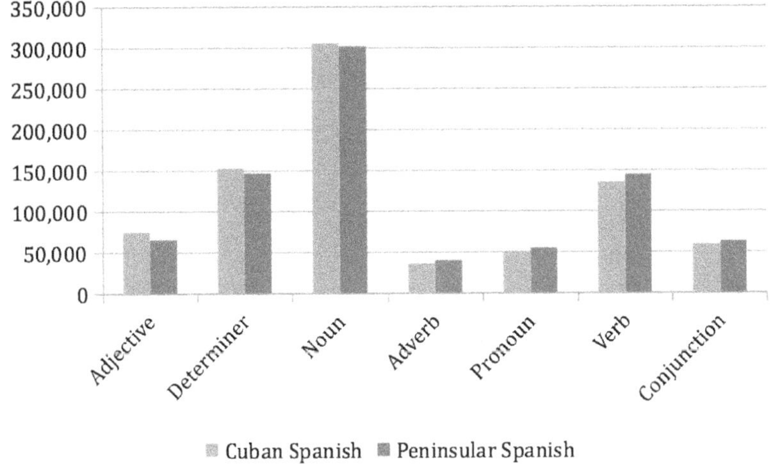

Figure 10.3. Comparing POS distributions

Distribution Trends of High-Frequency Types and Lemmas

So far in this analysis, we have relied solely on quantitative data, without contrasting the actual types and lemmas that occur in both language varieties. In what follows, we shall try to explore how the most frequent types and lemmas are distributed in CS and PS in order to find potential dissimilarities. Table 10.7 shows the thirty most frequent types in CS and PS.[24]

The data distribution is very similar in both varieties. CS and PS both exhibit a negative or decreasing power trend, or a hyperbolic function (figure 10.4):

$$CS_{Type-Frequency} = 20{,}000{,}000 * rank^{-1.242} = \frac{1}{rank^{1.242}}$$

$$PS_{Type-Frequency} = 20{,}000{,}000 * rank^{-1.25} = \frac{1}{rank^{1.25}}$$

An initial evaluation shows a perfect rank coincidence among the eleven most frequent types (*de*, *la*, *y*, *en*, *el*, *que*, *a*, *los*, *del*, *se*, and *las*) and minor rank dissimilarities among the types ranked twelve to twenty-six. All top twenty-six types are functional word forms. However, there are prominent frequency dissimilarities among these top twenty-six types (figures 10.5 and 10.6); these differences are not qualitative (types used) but quantitative (times each type is used). Particularly relevant discrepancies are found in the usage of *que*, *la*, *de*, *en*, *los*, *y*, *el*, *no*, *del*, and *a*.

Another salient difference is found in the type ranked 27 in CS: Cuba, which is ranked 3,041 in PS.[25] Other noteworthy differences are in *país* (ranked 47 in CS and 220 in PS), *cual* (74 in CS and 226 in PS), Estados Unidos (78 in CS and 461 in PS), Habana (79 in CS and 7,164 in PS), *pueblo* (80 in CS and 499 in PS), and *dijo* (84 in

Table 10.7. The 30 most frequent types in CS and PS

Rank	Cuban Spanish	Peninsular Spanish	Rank	Cuban Spanish	Peninsular Spanish
1	de	de	16	para	una
2	la	la	17	no	no
3	y	y	18	su	es
4	en	en	19	es	su
5	el	el	20	al	al
6	que	que	21	como	lo
7	a	a	22	lo	como
8	los	los	23	más	o
9	del	del	24	o	más
10	se	se	25	sus	ha
11	las	las	26	este	este
12	con	un	27	Cuba	sus
13	por	con	28	ha	me
14	un	por	29	entre	pero
15	una	para	30	esta	si

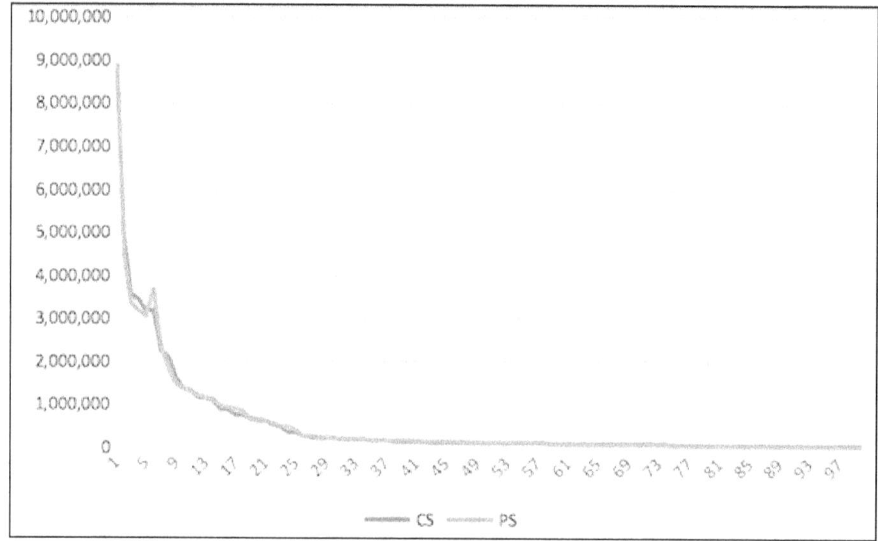

Figure 10.4. Frequency distribution of the 100 most frequent types

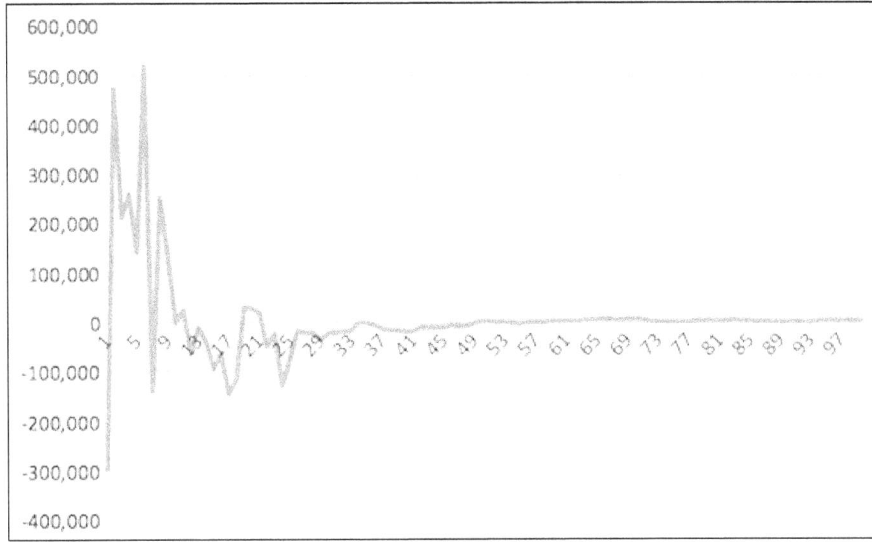

Figure 10.5. Type frequency dissimilarity between CS and PS (CS-PS)

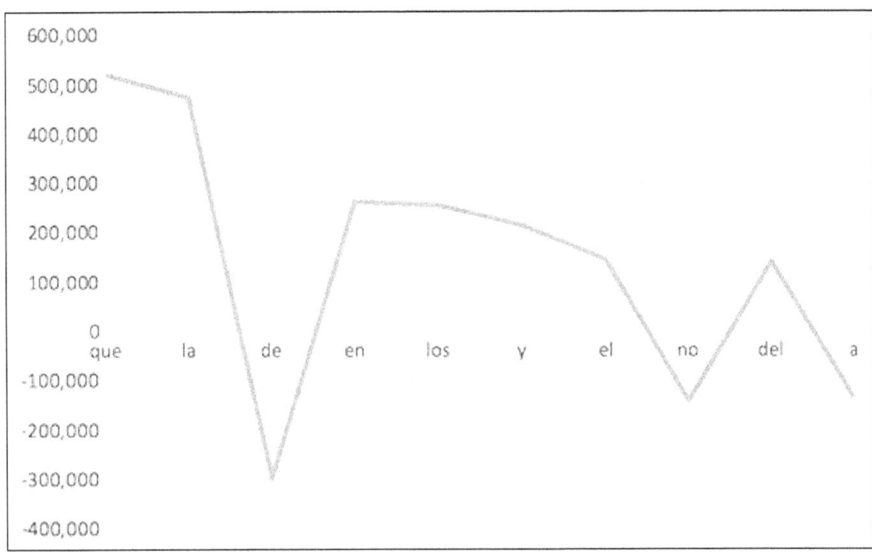

Figure 10.6. 10 most prominent frequency dissimilarities (CS-PS)

CS and 451 in PS). The most frequent lexical type in CS is Cuba (rank 27), whereas for PS we get *años* (rank 42). Curiously, in PS, España is ranked 77 and Madrid 117.

Comparing the one hundred most frequent types in both varieties, some types only occur in CS: *contra*, *cual*, Cuba, *cubano*, *desarrollo*, *dijo*, Estados Unidos, *era*, *esa*, *ese*, *eso*, *este*, *fueron*, Habana, *hoy*, *mayor*, *nuestro*, *otras*, *pacientes*, *país*, *pueblo*, and *solo*. There are also those that only occur in PS: *aunque*, *bien*, *caso*, *cuenta*, *día*, *eso*, España, *están*, *este*, *hacer*, *mejor*, *menos*, *mucho*, *nuevo*, *otro*, *persona*, *poco*, *sólo*, *te*, *tu*, *ver*, and *yo*. There also seem to be different semantic loadings among the top one hundred types in CS and PS. For CS we get more sociopolitically related types (Cuba, *cubano*, *pacientes*, *país*, *pueblo*, Habana, and Estados Unidos), but no such semantic clustering is found in PS: *caso*, *cuenta*, *día*, España, and *persona*.

As for the top thirty lemmas, the data are not too dissimilar from the top thirty types (table 10.8[26]):

$$CS_{Lemma-Frequency} = 20{,}000{,}000 * rank^{-1.2} = \frac{1}{rank^{1.2}}$$

$$PS_{Lemma-Frequency} = 20{,}000{,}000 * rank^{-1.214} = \frac{1}{rank^{1.214}}$$

There are strong rank similarities among the first thirty lemmas in both varieties. The most frequent top lemmas are, again, functional word forms, in both CS and PS. The most common lexical lemmas are auxiliary and modal verbs: *ser*, *haber*, *tener*, *poder*, *estar*, and *hacer.* Surprisingly, the most common noun in CS is not Cuba, but *año*, as in PS. We also find lemmas only occurring in CS: *conocer*, *contra*, *cual*, Cuba, *cubano*, *después*, Estados Unidos, *ellos*, *estudio*, *grupo*, Habana, *hoy*, *la*, *mayor*, *mundo*, *nacional*, *paciente*, *país*, *pueblo*, *quien*, *social*, and *solo*; and lemmas only present in PS: *así*, *aunque*, *bien*, *bueno*, *centro*, *crear*, *empresa*, España, *general*, *llevar*, *mejor*, *ni*, *poco*, *poner*, *público*, *querer*, *seguir*, *servicio*, *sólo*, *te*, *tu*,

Table 10.8. The 30 most frequent lemmas in CS and PS

Rank	Cuban Spanish	Peninsular Spanish	Rank	Cuban Spanish	Peninsular Spanish
1	el	el	16	este	su
2	de	de	17	haber	este
3	y	que	18	al	al
4	en	y	19	como	como
5	que	en	20	más	tener
6	a	a	21	tener	o
7	uno	uno	22	todo	más
8	ser	ser	23	poder	poder
9	del	del	24	ese	estar
10	se	se	25	estar	todo
11	por	por	26	o	lo
12	con	con	27	otro	hacer
13	su	haber	28	lo	pero
14	para	para	29	hacer	si
15	no	no	30	año	otro

último and *yo*. As for types, a significant amount of frequently used lemmas in CS are, again, related to sociopolitical concepts.

Despite the rank similarities mentioned, the differences between both varieties are very noticeable in the frequency of usage of the top twenty-six lemmas (figure 10.7).

Table 10.9 highlights the major differences among the one thousand most frequent lemmas (part-of-speech tagged) in both language variations.

Clearly, all or nearly all functional words are shared between both varieties. The divergences between both varieties become particularly patent in content words (adjectives, verbs, and nouns). Despite the high overlapping of lemmas in both varieties, there are nouns, adjectives, and verbs that occur only in one variety, where CS is again more prolific.[27] Once again, the CS lexicon is heavily dependent on its sociopolitical substratum, as seen in adjectives (*cubano*, *estadounidense*, *militar*, and *revolucionario*), verbs (*defender*, *enfrentar*, *impone*, and *luchar*), and nouns (*arma*, *asamblea*, *ataque*, *bloqueo*, Bush, Castro, *comandante*, *comité*, Cuba, *jefe*, *justicia*, *liberación*, *líder*, *lucha*, *manifestación*, Martí, Obama, *patria*, *paz*, *dólar*, *ejército*, Fidel, Granma, Guantánamo, *imperio*, *independiencia*, *presión*, Raúl, *república*, *resistencia*, *revolución*, *sangre*, *triunfo*, etc).

Lexical Profile of CS and PS

With all the quantitative evidence obtained on the lexical repertoires of CS and PS, we are now able to prompt an objective profile of both Spanish varieties.[28] So, for instance, two equally long (one hundred thousand token) texts, one for CS and

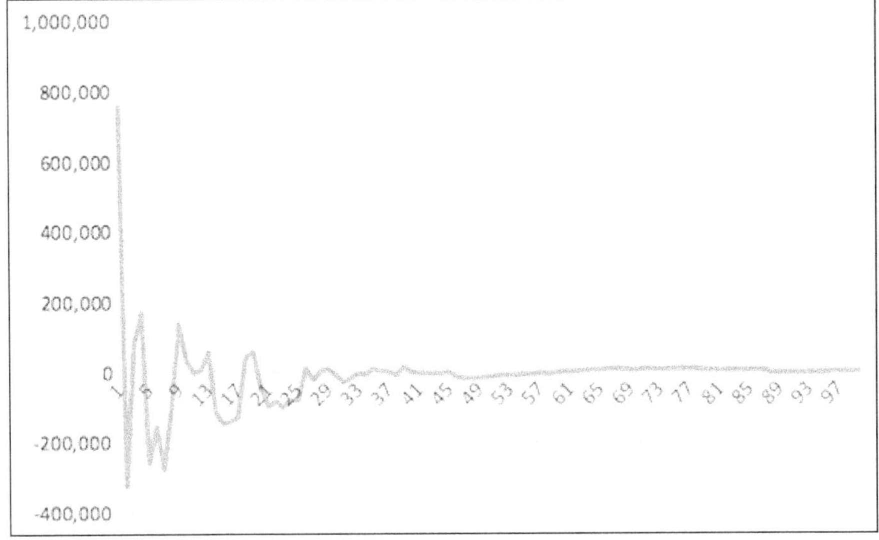

Figure 10.7. Lemma frequency dissimilarity between CS and PS (CS-PS)

Table 10.9. Distribution of POS-tagged lemmas used in CS and PS

	CS+PS	CS	PS	Totals
Conjunctions	14	0	0	14
Prepositions	19	0	0	19
Adjectives	74	26	22	122
Nouns	386	157	146	689
Pronouns	34	0	4	38
Adverbs	39	4	8	51
Verbs	179	41	33	253
Totals	745	228	213	1,186

another one for PS, are very likely to evidence the following lexical composition and features.[29]

Succinctly, the Cuban text is lexically more prolific than its Spanish counterpart. It accounts for more lemmas and types (approximately five hundred lemmas and one thousand types more), which is also evidenced by greater *K* and *KL* values. In addition, CS also has lower lemma- and type-repetition rates.

The frequency distributions of types also evidence different patterns in both varieties. Dissimilarities become particularly patent regarding low- and high-frequency bands: CS is more prolific in low-frequency words, whereas PS is more abundant in medium- to high-frequency types. That is, we are more likely to find rare words or hapax legomena in CS, whereas PS tends to repeat more commonly used types instead.

Regarding the grammatical nature or typology of types and parts of speech in CS and PS, no differences are found between functional and lexical types. However, a finer analysis shows that CS has a greater abundance of nouns, determiners, and adjectives, while PS is more fertile in verbs, adjectives, conjunctions, and pronouns.

Some Final Considerations

The approach adopted in the study has been predominantly of a quantitative nature, based on two equally sized subcorpora of written language (121,166,000 tokens); one for Cuban Spanish and one for Peninsular or Castilian Spanish. Each subcorpus was extracted from a larger corpus: the *esTenTen11 (European, Freeling, v4)* for PS and the *esTenTen11 (American, Freeling, v4)* for CS.

As all the data have been extracted from the two subcorpora mentioned, consequently all the findings and conclusions, necessarily, refer back to them. However, the large samples taken in both varieties somehow guarantee the feasibility and possibility of extrapolating the results to similar text samples or even, with caution, to the general written variety of CS and PS. Obviously, similar studies might differ from the one described here, but we are confident that most of the underlying lexical quantitative properties of CS and PS presented here will coincide with future findings.

Another consideration and limitation of this study is related to the content of the text samples. Most of the texts that compose both corpora are extracted from websites with an .es domain, that is, the top-level country code domain for Spain, and its equivalent .cu domain for Cuba. This means that most websites are official and government controlled. This applies particularly to Cuba and might partially explain the sociopolitical substratum found in its lexical repertoire. However, again, this does not, by any means, invalidate the findings obtained from the underlying lexical quantitative properties for CS.

We strongly believe, and this might be arguable, that the processing and analyzing of massive linguistic data (Sharoff 2006; Baroni et al. 2009; Kilgarriff 2012) using big data techniques can allow us to discover underlying lexical structures or other linguistic structures—independent of genre, register, etc.—that evidence the common core or the social cognition of a language or language variety (Goldberg 2006; Hoey 2009; Stubbs 2009). That is, we can uncover the idiosyncratic properties, linguistic traits, and linguistic DNA that make each language (variety) unique and different from the others.

This quantitative lexical contrastive approach has shed new light on Cuban Spanish and Peninsular or Castilian Spanish. The next step of this quantitative approach should be a new research agenda devoted to qualitatively interpreting and explaining the mathematical properties found here: exploring how frequency, rank distribution, and lexical clustering of types and lemmas conform and highlight specific concepts in differentiating the two language varieties. To what extent do these underlying quantitative properties explain linguistic and social differences between Cubans and Spaniards?

Notes

1. The data correspond to 2014 (see also Moreno Fernández 2014). http://eldiae.es/wp-content/uploads/2015/06/espanol_lengua-viva_20151.pdf.
2. The *native language skilled group* (GDN: Grupo de Dominio Nativo; Moreno Fernández and Otero Roth 2006)
3. The L2 learner group (GALE: Grupo de Aprendices de Lengua Extranjera; Moreno Fernández and Otero Roth 2006)
4. http://www.ethnologue.com/language/spa.
5. *The Internet World Stats*: http://www.internetworldstats.com.
6. *Internet Live Stats*: http://www.internetlivestats.com.
7. Note that the use of the Internet is tightly controlled in Cuba and .cu web pages are mainly governmental while contestation and literature in blogs strive to reach the public (see, for example, del Valle 2006; Calvo Peña 2010; O'Brien 2010; Oliva 2012; Human Rights Watch 2012; Suárez Sian 2012).
8. Real Academia Española: http://www.rae.es/recursos/diccionarios/drae.
9. This dictionary has been compiled using the *Cumbre Corpus*, a twenty-million-item corpus with oral and written materials (1950–95) from Castilian Spanish and all Latin American varieties.
10. *Lemma* is taken as a synonym for headword or dictionary entry.
11. We were unable to access any parallel or comparable corpora (Cuban Spanish–Peninsular Spanish) or any sufficiently large Cuban Spanish corpus; Mark Davies (Brigham Young University) pointed us to a forthcoming project (a massive Spanish corpus: twenty-one countries including Cuba); Adam Kilgarriff (Lexical Computing, Ltd) suggested using the Cuban part of the *esTenTen* (AmE) corpus (a 120-million-item subcorpus) and Roland Schäfer (Freie Universität Berlin) addressed us to the

ESCOW14 web corpus (with 62,725 documents, but not yet released). So the only available large Cuban Spanish corpus was, at that moment, the subcorpus of the *esTenTen* (AmE), accessible via Sketch Engine.

12. Both corpora are available on the Sketch Engine website as Open Corpora: http://www.sketchengine.co.uk; see also descriptions and contents for both corpora.
13. Objectively, the TTR of CS is greater than the one for PS and this evidences a lexical difference. However, the differences are too small to be considered significant and cannot be attributed straight on or only to geography; they could also be due to text type-differences or other potential factors, or simply just due to chance.
14. Note that these preliminary results might not be too revealing due to the dependence of the TTR on corpus size; the numerator (types) increases at a slower pace than the denomir (tokens); consequently, the bigger the corpus, the smaller its ratio. This results in the paradox that measures taken from the same corpus but with different sampling sizes output different TTRs. In addition, the type-increase given above applies to a 121-million-token corpus.
15. For other alternative size-independent measures see, for example, *Standardized Type Token Ratio* (Scott 1999) or those proposed by Tuldava (1995); Yang, Cantos, and Song (2000); Chipere et al. (2003).
16. Cantos (2000) experimented on the applicability of this index for automatic text discrimination.
17. The high *K*-values obtained clearly point out that the content of the two corpora is exclusively written material; oral samples evidence lower values, indicating a slower pace of incorporating new types due to a higher type repetition rate.
18. The online table 10.4-web includes the additional information that could not be included in print.
19. Note that *K* is the constant value that relates types to tokens and *KL* the one that relates lemmas to tokens.
20. Types that occur a single time.
21. The data has been normalized to one million tokens.
22. Numerals, interjections, and punctuations are not considered in this analysis.
23. Data is normalized to one million.
24. The online table 10.7-web includes the additional information that could not be included in print.
25. Some types are out of range in table 10.7. For a full type list for CS and PS contact the author.
26. The online table 10.8-web includes the additional information that could not be included in print.
27. The online table 10.10-web contains the differences in adjective, verbs, and adverbs among the top one hundred lemmas.
28. The online table 10.11-web contains the lexical profiles of CS and PS.
29. The online table 10.12-web contains a lexical profile samples of CS and PS.

References

Arias, S., and M. Meléndez. 2002. "Space and the Rhetorics of Power in Colonial Spanish America: An Introduction." In *Mapping Colonial Spanish America: Places and Commonplaces of Identity, Culture, and Experience*, edited by S. Arias, and M. Meléndez, 13–23. Cranbury, NJ: Rosemont Publishing and Printing Corp.

Asociación de Academias de la Lengua Española. 2010. *Diccionario de americanismos.* Madrid: Santillana.

Baroni, M., S. Bernardini, A. Ferraresi, and E. Zanchetta. 2009. "The WaCky Wide Web: A Collection of Very Large Linguistically Processed Web-Crawled Corpora." *Language Resources and Evaluation* 43 (3): 209–26.

Bernal, G. 1993. *Ethnic Identity: Formation and Transmission among Hispanics and Other Minorities.* New York: State University of New York Press.

Cabrera, L., and I. Castellanos. 2001. *Vocabulario congo: el bantú que se habla en Cuba: español-congo y congo-español.* Madrid: Ediciones Universal.

Calvo Peña, B., ed. 2010. *Buena Vista Social Blog.* Valencia, Esp.: Aduana Vieja.

Cantos, P. 2000. "Investigating Type-token Regression and its Potential for Automated Text Discrimination." *Cuadernos de Filología Inglesa* 9 (2): 71–91.

Cantos, P., and A. Sánchez. 2011. "El inglés y el español desde una perspectiva cuantitativa y distributiva: equivalencias y contrastes." *Estudios Ingleses de la Universidad Complutense* 19:15–44.

Cárdenas, G., A. M. Tristá, and R. Werner, coords. 2000. *Diccionario del español de Cuba. Español de Cuba – español de España.* Madrid: Gredos.

Castellanos, J., and I. Castellanos. 1988. *Cultura afrocubana.* Miami: Universal Miami.

Chipere, N., D. Malvern, B. Richards, and P. Duran. 2003. "Using a Corpus of School Children's Writing to Investigate the Development of Vocabulary Diversity." In *Proceedings of the Corpus Linguistics 2003 Conference*, edited by D. Archer, P. Rayson, A Wilson, and A. M. McEnery, 126–33. University Centre for Computer Corpus Research on Language Technical Papers 16 (Special Issue). Lancaster: University Centre for Computer Corpus Research on Language.

Davis, K. 1999. "The Sociopolitical Dynamics of Indigenous Language Maintenance and Loss: A Framework for Language Policy and Planning." In *Sociopolitical Perspectives on Language Policy and Planning in the U.S.A.*, edited by T. Huebner and K. Davis, 67–97. Amsterdam: John Benjamins Publishing Company.

del Valle, A. E. 2006. "Estados Unidos bloquea Internet en Cuba (I)." *Juventud Rebelde*, 2 de Noviembre del 2006. http://www.juventudrebelde.cu/cuba/2006-11-02/estados-unidos-bloquea-internet-en-cuba-l.

Fabelo, T. 1998. *Diccionario de la lengua conga residual en Cuba.* Santiago de Cuba: Casa del Caribe.

Firsova, N. 2007. *El español contemporáneo en España y países de América Latina.* Moscow: Vostok-Zapad.

Fishman, J. A. 1991. *Reversing Language Shift.* Clevedon, Eng.: Multilingual Matters Ltd.

Goldberg, A. 2006. *Constructions at Work: The Nature of Generalization in Language.* Oxford: Oxford University Press.

Haensch, G. 1991. "La lexicografía del español de América en el umbral del siglo XXI." In *Presencia y destino: El español de América hacia el siglo XXI*, Tomo 1, 43–77. Santafé de Bogotá, Col.: Instituto Caro y Cuervo.

Haensch, G., and C. Omeñaca. 2004. *Los diccionarios del español en el siglo XXI.* Salamanca, Esp.: Universidad de Salamanca.

Hanks, P. 2009. "The Impact of Corpora on Dictionaries." In *Contemporary Corpus Linguistics*, edited by P. Baker, 214–36. London: Continuum.

Hoey, Michael. 2009. "Corpus-Driven Approaches to Grammar: A Search for Common Ground." In Römer and Schulze, *Exploring the Lexis-Grammar Interface*, 32–48. Amsterdam: John Benjamins.

Hofland, K., and S. Johansson. 1982. *Word Frequencies in British and American English.* London: Longman.

Human Rights Watch. 2012. "Capítulo del Informe Mundial: Cuba." http://www.hrw.org/es/world-report-2012/cuba.

Instituto Cervantes. 2015. *El español: una lengua viva. Informe 2015.* Madrid: Instituto Cervantes.

Isbăşescu, C. 1968. *El español en Cuba: observaciones fonéticas y fonológicas.* Bucarest: Sociedad Rumana de Lingüística Romántica.

Kilgarriff, A. 2012. "Getting to Know Your Corpus." In *Text, Speech and Dialogue: 15th International Conference, TSD 2012, Brno, Czech Republic, September 3-7, 2012. Proceedings*, edited by P. Sojka, A. Horák, I. Kopecek, and K. Pala, 3–15. Lecture Notes in Computer Science 7499. Berlin: Springer.

Kilgarriff, A., and I. Renau. 2013. "esTenTen, a Vast Web Corpus of Peninsular and American Spanish." *Procedia – Social and Behavioral Sciences*, special issue, Corpus Resources for Descriptive and Applied Studies. Current Challenges and Future Directions: Selected Papers from the 5th International Conference on Corpus Linguistics, edited by C. Vargas-Sierra, 95:12–19.

Lipski, J. 1994. *Latin American Spanish.* London: Longman.

———. 2004a. "El español de América: los contactos bilingües." In *Historia de la lengua española*, edited by R. Cano, 1117–38. Barcelona: Ariel.

———. 2004b. "El español de América y los contactos bilingües recientes: apuntes microdialectológicos." *Revista Internacional de Lingüística iberoamericana* 4:89–103.

———. 2004c. "La lengua española en los Estados Unidos: avanza a la vez que retrocede." *Revista Española de Lingüística* 33:231–60.

López-Morales, H. 1971. *Estudios sobre el español de Cuba*. Madrid: Las Américas.
———. 1992. *El español del Caribe*. Madrid: Mapfre.
———. 1999. *Léxico Disponible de Puerto Rico*. Madrid: Arco/Libros.
———. 2003. *Los cubanos en Miami. Lengua y sociedad*. Miami: Ediciones Universal.
———. 2013. *Estudios sobre el español de América*. Valencia, Esp.: Vieja Editorial.
Moreno Fernández, F. 2014. "Fundamentos de demografía lingüística a propósito de la lengua española." *Revista Internacional de Lingüística Iberoamericana XII* 2 (24): 19–38.
Moreno Fernández, F., and J. Otero Roth. 2006. *Demografía de la lengua española*. Madrid: La Fundación Telefónica y el Instituto Complutense de Estudios Internacionales.
O'Brien, D. 2010. "The Malware Lockdown in Havana and Hanoi." Committee to Protect Journalists blog, June 8. http://cpj.org/blog/2010/06/the-malware-lockdown-in-havana-and-hanoi.php.
Oliva, P. 2012. "International Internet Connectivity (IIC) - Individual Country and Organization Experiences." Presentation given at the ITU Workshop on Apportionment of Revenues and International Internet Connectivity, Geneva, Switzerland, January 23–24. http://www.itu.int/ITU-D/finance/work-cost-tariffs/events/tariff-seminars/Geneva-IIC/pdf/Session4_P3_Oliva- sp.pdf.
Oliver, B. 1965. *Indoamericanismos léxicos en español*. Madrid: CSIC.
Penny, R. 2002. *A History of the Spanish Language*. Cambridge: Cambridge University Press.
Pomikalek, J. 2011. "Removing Boilerplate and Duplicate Content from Web Corpora." PhD thesis, Masaryk University.
Pomikalek, J., and V. Suchomel. 2012. "Efficient Web Crawling for Large Text Corpora." *Proceedings of the Seventh Web-as-Corpus Workshop*, edited by A. Kilgarriff and S. Sharoff, 39–43. Lyon: ACL.
Roca, A., and M. C. Colombi. 2003. *Mi lengua: Spanish as a Heritage Language in the United States, Research and Practice*. Washington, DC: Georgetown University Press.
Rojas-Arregocés, E. 2008. *El estereotipo: la comparación entre las definiciones del "Diccionario del español usual de México" y las de otros tres diccionarios redactados en España*. Alicante, Esp.: Biblioteca Virtual Miguel de Cervantes.
Römer, U., and R. Schulze, eds. 2009. *Exploring the Lexis-Grammar Interface*. Amsterdam: John Benjamins.
Sánchez, A., and P. Cantos. 1997a. "Predictability of Word Forms (Types) and Lemmas in Linguistic Corpora. A Case Study Based on the Analysis of the CUMBRE Corpus: An 8-Million-Word Corpus of Contemporary Spanish." *International Journal of Corpus Linguistics* 2 (2): 259–80.
———. 1997b. "El ritmo incremental de palabras nuevas en los repertorios de textos. Estudio experimental y comparativo basado en dos corpus lingüísticos equivalentes de cuatro millones de palabras, de las lenguas inglesa y española y en cinco autores de ambas lenguas." *Atlantis* XIX (2): 205–23.
Scott, M. 1999. *Wordsmith Tools Version 3*. Oxford: Oxford University Press.
Silva-Corvalán, C. 1997. "Variación sintáctica en el discurso oral: problemas metodológicos." *Trabajos de sociolingüística hispánica*: 115–136.
Sharoff, Serge. 2006. "Creating General-Purpose Corpora Using Automated Search Engine Queries." In *WaCky! Working Papers on the Web as Corpus*, edited by M. Baroni and S. Bernardini, 63–98. Bologna: Gedit.
Stubbs, M. 2009. "Technology and Phraseology: With Notes on the History of Corpus Linguistics." In Römer and Schulze, *Exploring the Lexis-Grammar Interface*, 15–32.
Suárez Sian, M. D. 2012. "Cuba: Internet, acceso y sociedad del conocimiento." *Razón y Palabra* 81. http://www.razonypalabra.org.mx/N/N81/M81/07_Suarez_M81.pdf.
Tuldava, J. 1995. *Methods in Quantitative Linguistics*. Trier, Deu.: Wissenschaftlicher Verlag Trier.
Valdés-Bernal, S. 1989. "Visión lingüística del Caribe." *Anales del Caribe* 9:269–78.
Varela, B., and S. Armistead. 1992. *El español cubano-americano*. New York: Senda Nueva de Ediciones.
Yang, D.-H. H., P. Cantos, and M. Song. 2000. "An Algorithm for Predicting the Relationship between Lemmas and Corpus Size." *International Journal of the Electronics and Telecommunications Research Institute (ETRI)* 22:20–31.

11

Lexical Influences and Perceptions of Cuban Spanish in Miami

ANTONI FERNÁNDEZ PARERA
University of Miami

FOR MANY PEOPLE IN the broader US context, the city of Miami is synonymous with Hispanic cultures and Spanish language use. According to the most recent census data, Hispanic people represent 65 percent of the total population of metropolitan Miami-Dade, and Cuban-origin population compose 34.3 percent of the total. Arriving in different migration waves since 1959, Miami Cubans have contributed to the creation of political, social, and economic structures that are beneficial for Spanish-English bilingualism in the area (Alfaraz 2002, 2014; López Morales 2003; Lynch 2000, 2009; Otheguy, García, and Roca 2000; Levine and Asís 2000). Cubans represent 3.6 percent of the total population of Hispanic origin in the United States and are the fourth largest group in the nation according to an estimate of the 2011 American Community Survey. However, if one compares the data from the 2000 census with the data from the 2010 census, the preponderance that Cubans had in Miami in previous years is being challenged by the rapid growth of other groups of Hispanic origin.

Even though Cuban Spanish is still the most commonly heard in South Florida, with concentrations of Cuban-origin speakers as high as 73 percent in some areas (e.g., Hialeah), the city is home to a substantial number of other Spanish-speaking groups such as Colombians, Ecuadorians, Nicaraguans, Salvadorans, Hondurans, and Dominicans, among others. With such a diverse environment, Miami provides one of the most suitable and unique contexts for the study of varieties of Spanish in contact in the US. Although the outcomes of dialect contact in English have been studied in works such as those of Trudgill (1986), Kerswill (2008) and Kerswill and Williams (2000), the situation of Spanish dialect contact in the US has not received much attention from scholars despite South Florida being very probably the most dialectally diverse Spanish-speaking region (Potowski 2011). Given the preponderance of Cuban Spanish speakers and the historical and political prevalence of Cubans in South Florida, the goal of the present study was to explore the extent of lexical influences of Cuban Spanish on other varieties of Spanish in Miami, as well as perceptions and attitudes toward Cuban Spanish in South Florida generally (cf. Alfaraz 2002, 2014). The analysis presents quantitative and qualitative perspectives based on questionnaire data from 129 participants with diverse backgrounds, as well as individual sociolinguistic interviews with 67 (of the 129) participants.

This chapter contributes to the study of varieties of Spanish in contact in the US, and intends to provide a deeper understanding of a sociolinguistic situation that many cities in the US will likely face in the future, especially given the rapidly growing number of Spanish heritage language speakers in this country. For Cuban dialectology specifically, this study is the first to explore empirically the extent of lexical influences of Cuban Spanish on other varieties of Spanish in the US.

Background Studies on Dialect Contact

Even though the US provides an optimal setting for the study of Spanish dialect contact, the amount of research conducted on the topic is limited and has not specifically focused on Cuban Spanish. The first analysis of Spanish dialect contact conducted in the US was that of Zentella (1990), who studied interdialectal contact and lexical leveling of Puerto Ricans, Dominicans, Colombians and Cubans in New York City. Zentella sought to find if "each group maintained it's [sic] country's regional lexicon, assimilated that of the largest Spanish group in the city or the most prestigious variety or produced another 'New Yorker Spanish lexicon.'" (1094). Zentella found that factors such as frequency, semantic weight, social barriers, and avoidance of homonyms that can produce misunderstandings were key. Furthermore, she found that there were social factors such as class, education, and race that shaped the attitudes that different groups had of each other as well as toward features of their linguistic codes.

Parodi and Santa Ana (2001) also examined Salvadorans in Los Angeles. They observed the emergence of a new koiné based on a combination of Mexican rural dialects, and noted that the Spanish spoken in Los Angeles—also known as Chicano Spanish—has features of rural Mexican Spanish in addition to borrowings from English. After interviewing 28 Salvadorans, focusing on uses of *tú* versus *vos*, lexical usage, and attitudes toward Chicano Spanish, they found that the most spoken variety was Chicano Spanish and that some of the speakers were not aware of the differences between Chicano Spanish and Salvadoran Spanish due to the process of accommodation that Salvadorans go through when they come into regular contact with Chicano Spanish speakers. Also examining dialect contact in Los Angeles, Villarreal focused on the major phonetic, lexical, and attitudinal characteristics of Spanish-speaking children in Los Angeles and examined how the classification of their home dialect and school neighborhood could influence such characteristics (2014, 3). Based on interviews with 160 Mexican and Central American Spanish-speaking fourth and fifth graders, the author notes that the majority of the subjects employed features of *tierras altas* Mexican Spanish. In addition to such features, the results from the attitude tests showed that children of Mexican and Central American origin have a preference for Mexican Spanish. She did not find any effect of dialect spoken at home or school neighborhood on the variety used by the participant. She predicts that the young participants will most probably speak a variety similar to that of the Mexican *tierras altas* as adults, since it appears to be the norm of the community.

Bayley, Cárdenas, Treviño Schouten, and Velez Salas studied variable subject personal pronoun (SPP) use among Puerto Rican and Mexican residents in San Antonio, Texas. Their results show that "Puerto Rican Spanish speakers with Mexican social networks use SPPs at a rate that is much closer to the rate of use by Mexican-background speakers than it is to the rate of Puerto Ricans in San Juan or New York City" (Bayley et al. 2012, 54). Otheguy, Zentella, and Livert (2007) also examined variable use of SPPs among 142 NYC speakers who belonged to six different national-origin groups (divided into Caribbean and Mainlander varieties of Spanish) and immigrant groups (recent arrivals, first generation, and second generation). Their results demonstrated that English language use had an influence on speakers from both regions, and they showed that speakers of Caribbean and Mainlander varieties were accommodating to one other by noting an increase in the occurrence rates of overt pronouns "with a slight tilt toward greater accommodation of Mainlanders to Caribbean" (Otheguy, Zentella, and Livert 2007, 796). They affirmed that language and dialect contact are giving birth to a particular variety of Spanish of New York City, constituting a New York Spanish speech community.

In Houston, Aaron and Hernández (2007) studied Mexican and Salvadoran speakers to determine if the Mexican Spanish spoken by 75 percent of the population in Houston had an influence on the normal tendency in Salvadoran Spanish to reduce final /s/. Qualitative data from their study show that Salvadorans are aware of the social stigmatization of final /s/ weakening among the Mexican population in Houston. They found that the factors that were statistically significant for /s/ reduction were age at arrival and surrounding phonological segment. Also examining Salvadoran Spanish in contact with Mexican Spanish, Hernández (2002) analyzed two variables: *voseo* and transitive *andar.* The author compared data from sociolinguistic interviews with Salvadorans living in Houston and in El Salvador. The results showed that there was a process of linguistic accommodation among Salvadoran Spanish speakers in Houston to Mexican Spanish norms. The author states that "while speakers in El Salvador showed a strong quantitative preference for the use of these two features, *voseo* and transitive *andar*, among Salvadorans in Houston the use of *tuteo* became almost categorical" (Hernández 2002, 108). Hernández also found that age of arrival was a factor that influenced the acquisition of new dialect features. Another study conducted in Houston by Schreffler (1994) analyzes the use of the second-person familiar pronoun *vos*, which is used in El Salvador. After analyzing a corpus of 60 interviews in which Salvadoran participants enacted role-plays, the author found a reduced use of the form *vos*, which is considered to be a result of the continuous contact with speakers of Mexican Spanish in that city.

Finally, studies based on Puerto Rican Spanish in contact with Mexican Spanish are those of Ghosh Johnson (2005), Ramos-Pellicia (2004), and Potowski (2008). Ghosh Johnson examines production of coda /s/ among Puerto Rican and Mexican students at a Chicago high school. Observing a strong social division between the two groups in the school, she found no accommodation in their speech. Ramos-Pellicia studied Mexican and Puerto Rican Spanish at the phonological level in a rural community in Lorain, Ohio. More specifically, she examined the raising of /e/ and /o/ and the realization of /dʒ/, /r/ and /b/ across three different generations in the Puerto Rican Spanish community. In the results, Lorain Puerto Rican Spanish (LPRS) showed continuity with Island Puerto Rican Spanish (IPRS) even though they diverged from each other to some extent. The author affirmed that "possibly in the future, due to the pressures of MAS (Mexican American Spanish) and AE (American English) on LPRS, this pattern will change and LPRS will become a dialect different from IPRS, if it survives at all" (Ramos-Pellicia 2004, 3). Potowski (2008) focuses on intra-familial dialect contact among participants who had one parent of Mexican origin and another of Puerto Rican origin. The aim was to find which dialectal features prevailed in the variety spoken by the participant. In 20 out of 27 cases examined, the Spanish spoken by participants was more similar to the variety spoken by the mother. Potowski notes that two factors intervened in this general pattern, however. First, one third of the participants presented hybridized dialects and, second, broader family influences outweighed those of the mother.

The Study

Purpose and Research Questions

The purpose of the present study is to contribute to the research on Spanish dialect contact in the US and more specifically, to provide deeper insight into the influence that Cuban Spanish in Miami exerts on other varieties of Spanish spoken in the city. It also aims to provide information about the attitudes and perceptions that Spanish heritage language speakers have of different varieties of Spanish, particularly varieties of Cuban Spanish and Cuban culture and communities in Miami. The research questions guiding the study are the following:

- To what extent do Miami Cubans, Non-Cubans, and Mixed-Ethnicity Cubans identify and use lexical items specific to the Cuban dialect?
- What is the general perception among study participants of the Cuban presence and Cuban culture in Miami?
- Do participants hold positive attitudes toward Cuban Spanish varieties as compared to other varieties of Spanish spoken in Miami? Do the participants in the study (Cubans, Non-Cubans and Mixed-Ethnicity Cubans) have different perceptions of two varieties of Cuban Spanish: the Spanish spoken by Cubans whose families arrived in Miami in the 1960s and '70s, and the Spanish spoken by Cubans whose families have arrived within the past ten years?

Method

In the present study, 129 participants with an average age of 21.5 years attending a private university in South Florida were surveyed. All were enrolled in basic or intermediate-level courses of Spanish as a heritage language. The origins of the participants were diverse: roughly half were of Cuban background (n = 56); another 27 were half Cuban, half other (n = 27);[1] there were 20 non-Cuban mixed-origin participants; the remainder hailed from several different countries—Argentina (1), Colombia (5), Dominican Republic (3), Ecuador (1), Honduras (1), Mexico (3), Nicaragua (4), Peru (2), Puerto Rico (4), and Venezuela (2). As Potowski and Matts (2008) state, "research on contact between members of United States Hispanic communities has tended to fall under one of two categories: (a) intergroup relationships and (b) linguistic outcomes" (138). The inclusion of the category Hispanics of mixed origins in the present study allows for another subcategory within the study of intergroup relationships in US Hispanic communities.

Questionnaires were written in English and individual interviews with the researcher were conducted in Spanish. The questionnaire contained four sections, and was administered during a regular class session. In the first section, participants provided personal information about themselves (age, birthplace, birthdate, years in Miami, country of origin of the parents, and age of parents upon arrival in the US). The second section contained twelve items that required students to self-rate their own and their parents' abilities to speak and write in Spanish, as well as questions about the extent of their daily use of Spanish and English. Section three contained fourteen affirmations about varieties of Spanish to which participants responded on a five-point Likert scale (1 = 'I totally disagree' and 5 = 'I totally agree'). Finally, the fourth section contained a table with fourteen different varieties of Spanish that participants rated based on two qualities ('correct' and 'pleasant'), following the method used by Alfaraz (2002, 2014). The rating system was again based on a Likert scale from 1 to 7, where 1 corresponded to 'Not at all' and 7 corresponded to 'Very much so.' Once the questionnaires were collected, all data was coded and entered into SPSS version 22 (Statistical Package for the Social Sciences) to obtain descriptive statistics and one-way ANOVAS to discover statistical correlations.

The questionnaire contained three specific questions about Cuban Spanish that were motivated by the studies of Alfaraz (2002, 2014), who sought to analyze the perceptions of varieties of Spanish in Miami, and to "examine Miami Cubans' perceptions at two different points in time, before and after 1959, in order to explore the effects of differences in political ideology on the perception of dialect boundaries" (2002, 2). Alfaraz (2002) and Lynch (2009) both note that Miami Cubans make a distinction "between the sociolects of pre-Castro Spanish spoken by early immigrants in the 1960s and 1970s and those spoken by later arrivals (particularly post-1980) who were born and grew up in communist Cuba" (Lynch 2009, 774). Characteristics of Cuba 1 and Cuba 2 varieties were outlined by Alfaraz (2002) and Lynch (2009). On the attitudes and perceptions level, Alfaraz (2002) shows how Cuba 2 variety was downgraded and entailed negative meanings as compared to Cuba 1. This was interpreted as an effort to differentiate the first Miami Cubans who came to the city in the '60s from the Cubans from the island who grew up under the communist regime and came later. On the phonological level, Lynch (2009) found that younger generations of Miami Cubans had higher rates of sibilant retention and inferred that one of the contributing factors could be "a heightened sense of personal investment in Cuban exile politics through relationships with their fathers and grandfathers" who spoke the Cuba 1 variety (785). Making this same distinction in the present study allows us to determine if speakers of different national origins (Cubans, non-Cubans, and mixed-ethnicity Cubans) hold different attitudes and perceptions of two different varieties of Cuban Spanish: the Spanish spoken by Cubans whose families arrived in Miami in the 1960s and '70s (labeled Cuba 1), and the Spanish spoken by Cubans whose families have arrived within the past ten years (labeled Cuba 2).

Complementary sources of data were obtained from individual interviews conducted with 67 of the 129 participants. Of those interviewed, 24 had Cuban origins, 12 had mixed-ethnicity origins, and 31 had non-Cuban origins. During the interview, participants responded to questions regarding lexical usage, and also completed a lexical naming task to gauge their knowledge and use of Cuban-specific variants, methodologically similar to those used by Potowski (2008) and Zentella (1990). Participants were shown a total of 69 images and were asked to provide a name for each. Of the 69 images, 10 could be named using a word specific to the Cuban variety of Spanish: *fruta bomba* (papaya), *guagua* (bus), *fajarse* (to fight), *guajiro* (farmer, peasant), *trusa* (swimsuit), *cake* (cake), *saya* (skirt), *pila* (faucet), *jimaguas* (twins), and *pullover* (t-shirt). All of the Cuban-specific words selected for the study are documented as commonly in use on the island according to lexicographic studies conducted there. Participants were asked to offer as many words as they knew for the given image. Once the participants could not provide any further words, if they had not mentioned the Cuban-specific term, they were told the Cuban term and were asked if it sounded familiar to them or if they had heard it before.

Based upon their responses to the picture-naming task, a scale of use and awareness of Cuban lexicon was created.[2] Participants received four points if they provided a Cuban Spanish word first; three points if they provided a Cuban Spanish word after they had already offered another term for the given image; two points if they offered a Cuban term third, perhaps following some further questioning by the researcher (i.e., "Do you know any other words for this?"); and one point if they stated that the Cuban-specific term was familiar to them when the interviewer subsequently asked them if they had ever heard it. In the case that participants neither knew nor found familiar the Cuban-specific word, they received zero points for that image. For example, if a participant provided *gemelos* as a first word when seeing the image of twins and afterward provided *jimaguas* as a second choice, she received three points. However, if she did not provide *jimaguas* in any of the positions nor recognize that word when being told it by the researcher, she received zero points. In this way, the calculated score reflected the strength of the influence of Cuban Spanish in participants' lexical knowledge; the higher the score, the stronger the influence of Cuban Spanish lexicon.

The data was divided into three different subgroups according to the participants' origins. These groupings provided deeper insight into the results only from Cubans (C), from mixed-ethnicity Cubans when either the mother or the father was from Cuba (MEC), and from all those who had non-Cuban national origins (NC).

Results and Discussion

Image-Naming Task

Table 11.1 reflects the percentage of participants in each group who provided each Cuban-specific lexical item in first, second, or third place, or were at least familiar with those items. The total number of points that each group obtained per word (i.e., the sum of points that participants of each group obtained according to the devised scale) appears in parentheses. The maximum score that each group could obtain was if all of the participants of that group provided a Cuban word as a first option and thus received 4 points. Cubans (C) could obtain a maximum of 96 points (i.e., twenty-four participants × 4 points), mixed-ethnicity Cubans (MEC) 48 points, and non-Cubans (NC) 124 points. The overall results show that the majority of Cubans retained specific vocabulary features of their home variety despite having been raised in Miami, and lend support to the claim that it is more probable that through social networks (Milroy and Gordon 2003) speakers of other varieties of Spanish are exposed to Cuban lexicon when in regular contact with Cuban Spanish speakers.

Table 11.1. Results from the image-naming task for the three groups of study

WORD	C (N = 24)	MEC (N = 12)	NC (N = 31)
FRUTA BOMBA	79% (60)	58% (19)	13% (5)
GUAGUA	99% (83)	100% (43)	61% (40)
FAJANDO	99% (83)	67% (23)	16% (9)
GUAJIRO	71% (50)	42% (8)	16% (5)
TRUSA	100% (94)	83% (25)	10% (3)
SAYA	75% (68)	58% (19)	16% (10)
CAKE	92% (88)	92% (38)	51% (16)
PILA	79% (72)	8% (4)	3% (1)
PULLOVER	46% (64)	33% (9)	13% (6)
JIMAGUAS	46% (64)	33% (6)	3% (1)

Notes: C = Cubans, MEC = Mixed-ethnicity Cubans, and NC = Non-Cubans.

Participants of Cuban origin reflect knowledge and use of most of the words from the list, with percentages up to nearly 100 percent in some cases (e.g., *guagua*, *fajando*, *trusa*, and *cake*). MECs demonstrate less robust knowledge of the same items, with the exception of words like *guagua* and *cake*. The NC group demonstrates minimal knowledge of Cuban-specific words, again with the exception of *guagua* and *cake*. Results of one-way ANOVA tests confirm that there are significant differences between the groups ($p > 0.001$). There is a statistically significant correlation between group and points obtained in the image-naming task.

Two extracts from interviews account for the prevalence of knowledge of food-related items among NC participants. Other Cuban-specific words known by non-Cuban participants are also probably acquired through face-to-face interaction (cf. Trudgill 1999). This pattern can be confirmed by GR, a twenty-year-old, second-generation male whose parents are from Honduras and who has grown up in Miami and lived in the city all his life (example 11.1), and RK, a nineteen-year-old, second-generation Venezuelan female who has also lived all her life in Miami (example 11.2). When asked if they used Cuban Spanish words they answered with the following.

Example 11.1. GR response to using Cuban Spanish words

"*Sí, bueno, yo lo hago para vacilar, para jugar, con amigos, oye* ***asere***, ***consorte***, *cosas así como, no, que como que yo tengo amigos cubanos, entonces, como uso cosas de comida como quiero una* ***ropa vieja***, ***cafecito***, ***una tostada***, ***croquetas***, *bastante comida pero también uso palabras solo jugando con amigos. Ahora mismo no recuerdo pero se me salen porque llevo tanto tiempo que he vivido aquí que ya están como memorizadas.*" (GR)

"Yes, well, I do it to tease, to play, with friends *oye* ***asere***, ***consorte*** as if like, as I have Cuban friends, then like I use things of food as such as I want a ***ropa vieja***, ***cafecito***, a ***tostada***, ***croquetas*** quite a bit of food but I also use words only when playing with my friends. Now I do not remember but they come from inside because I have been living here so much time that they are like memorized." (GR)

Example 11.2. RK response to using Cuban Spanish words

"*Yo uso* ***papaya*** *pero la gente dice* ***fruta bomba***. *Lo utilizo como si... me gusta comprar el batido de* ***papaya*** *pero si voy a comprarlo yo le digo* ***papaya*** *y me dicen, '¿****papaya****?' Entonces veo el menú y dice* ***fruta bomba*** *y digo* ***fruta bomba*** *en los restaurantes.*" (RK)

"I use ***papaya*** but people say ***fruta bomba***. I use it if I'd like to buy the ***papaya*** shake but if I am going to buy it and I say ***papaya*** and they say to me '***papaya***?' Then I look at the menu and it says ***fruta bomba*** and I say ***fruta bomba*** at restaurants." (RK)

These personal observations make evident the process of linguistic accommodation that non-Cubans who live in Miami sometimes experience.[3] RK accommodates (Giles 1973) to Cuban Spanish and uses *fruta bomba* to foster clarity in face-to-face interactions. RK's comment also shows that the motivation to use *fruta bomba* instead of papaya is instrumental (Siegel 116). In addition to that, GR's comment suggests that Cuban forms of greeting such as *asere* and *consorte* are also acquired but in more informal contexts.[4] He says that he uses Cuban words with his friends to tease them and as a consequence of having lived for such a long time in Miami interacting with Cubans. Other common Cuban expressions showing familiarity were provided by JP, a second-generation male whose Venezuelan and Colombian parents brought him to Miami from Barranquilla when he was ten years old. He provided *¿qué bolada* or *el mío* during the interview when asked if he knew Cuban words or expressions (example 11.3).

Example 11.3. JP's response to question about Cuban words or expressions

> "*El que ellos dicen mucho es el* ***¿Qué bolá?*** *que suena muy feo pero tienen muchos– yo no sé ahorita, déjame pensar... Como que ellos le dicen a un amigo en lugar de decirle* **mi hermano** *ellos dicen* ***el mío, dímelo el mío*** *como que tú sabes* **mi amigo**, *también dicen* consorte *para decirle* **mi amigo**, *muchas muchas palabras.*" (JP)
>
> "What they say a lot is ***¿Qué bolá?*** That sounds ugly but they have a lot- I don't know right now, let me think... Like they call a friend instead of saying **brother** they say ***el mío***, tell me ***el mío*** like you know **my friend**, they also say ***consorte*** to say **my friend**, lots and lots of words." (JP)

JP has spent his entire life in Miami, specifically in Hialeah where the majority of the population is of Cuban origin, and has knowledge of several Cuban words and expressions such as *¿qué bolá/bolada?*, *el mío*, and *consorte*.[5] The fact that JP and GR provide Cuban words for familiarity also shows how people notice certain linguistic features that are associated with the speech of a particular ethnic group. Labov refers to those features as 'markers' or 'stereotypes' (cf. Labov 1972, 2006). JP's example also supports Trudgill's claim that "lexical differences are highly salient, and are readily apparent to all speakers of the varieties concerned without any linguistic training or analysis. They are also (mostly) non-systematic, and susceptible to being learned one at a time. Crucially, they can also cause severe, and obvious, comprehension difficulties" (1986, 25).

There is a statistically significant correlation between the points obtained in the image-naming task and two affirmations from the attitudes and perceptions questionnaire. These affirmations are "Cuban culture makes Miami an interesting place" ($p > 0.002$) and "Miami is synonymous with Cuban culture" ($p > 0.05$). These results show how higher values on the affirmations about Cuban culture in Miami were significantly correlated with higher number of points on the lexical item scale.

Finally, the quantitative results obtained in tests of one-way ANOVA are further supported by qualitative evidence obtained from the interviews. Density and complexity of Cuban social networks and communities of practice in Miami have been previously noted (cf. López Morales 2003; Lynch 2000), and these facilitate the knowledge and acquisition of Cuban Spanish vocabulary. JP exemplifies this in one of his statements in the interview when asked if Miami is best characterized as Hispanic, Latino, or Cuban (example 11.4).

Example 11.4. JP's response to question about characterization of Miami

> "*Cubano porque por todos lados que tú vayas la gente es cubana o tiene algún familiar en su vida que lo trajo o que... tiene sangre cubana y también muchas de las cosas de la cultura en que uno está socializando todos los días es cubana, hay muchas cafeterías cubanas, muchos restaurantes cubanos.*" (JP)
>
> "Cuban because anywhere you go people are Cuban or have family in their lives who brought someone or who... have Cuban blood and also many of the things of the culture in which one is socializing every day is Cuban, there are many Cuban cafeterias, many Cuban restaurants." (JP)

Attitudes and Perceptions Regarding Varieties of Spanish

The statements included in the questionnaire attempt to capture the attitudes and perceptions of the Cuban presence, culture, and communities in the great social complex of Miami (cf. Aranda, Hughes, and Sabogal 2014; Lynch 2000; López Morales 2003). Overall, positive results confirm strong agreement with affirmations like "Cuban culture makes Miami an interesting place" and disagreement with affirmations like "Cubans control Miami" or "Cubans tend not to socialize with other Hispanic groups." As can be seen in table 11.2, Cuban presence in Miami is viewed positively and is not regarded as a threat by NC participants or by MECs. Even among NC participants, there is general agreement with the statement that "Cuban culture makes Miami an interesting place" (3.63), and disagreement with statements like "Cubans control Miami" and "Cubans tend not to socialize with other Hispanic groups" (2.65 and 2.60, respectively). It is important to emphasize that MECs as a group exhibited the strongest agreement with affirmations 1, 2, 3, and 4. At the same time, the same MEC group showed stronger disagreement with affirmations 5 and 6, which are the ones that are the most detrimental to the Cuban community. These disparate results can lead to interpret the group as one that has a different sense of cultural identity due to the unique transculturized backgrounds (cf. Aparicio and Chávez-Silverman 1997) of its members.

Table 11.2. Mean responses to statements regarding Cuban culture, presence, and community in Miami

STATEMENT	C	MEC	NC
1. Cubans control Miami.	2.12	2.69	2.65
2. Cuban culture makes Miami an interesting place.	4.35	4.53	3.63
3. For many people Miami is synonymous with Cuban culture.	4	4.15	3.7
4. When most Americans think of Latino Miami they think of the Cuban community.	4	4.11	4
5. Non-Cuban Hispanics do not have much of a voice in Miami.	2.12	1.65	2.3
6. Cubans tend not to socialize with other Hispanic groups.	2.26	1.88	2.6

Notes: 1= I totally disagree; 5= I totally agree

MECs are the personification of the mixture of the Cuban community with other Hispanic communities in Miami. One example of this mixture and of the influence of the Cuban presence on the identity of the MEC group can be seen in SP, a third-generation participant whose parents are from Cuba and Colombia (example 11.5).

Example 11.5. SP's response to question about which culture he most identifies with

> "*Me gusta más la cultura de los cubanos y yo puedo relacionar más con el abuelo de mi mamá y la familia de mi mamá.*" (SP)

> "I like more the culture of the Cubans and I can relate more with the grandfather from my mom and the family of my mom." (SP)

Even though the previous results from MECs and the extract from the interview display positive attitudes toward the Cuban presence and culture in Miami, questions about Cuban Spanish did not garner equally positive responses. Extracts from the interviews attested to this tendency, as can be seen in an excerpt from the interview with AC, a twenty-four-year-old NC participant whose parents were born in Nicaragua and who has lived all her life in Miami (example 11.6).

Example 11.6. Excerpt from AC's interview

> "*Lo escucho como más vulgar que cualquier otro español, no sé como más fuerte lo usan y demasiado rápido hablan, no sé, no me gusta mucho el español cubano. Además que no lo entiendo muy bien. Hablan demasiado rápido.*" (AC)
>
> "I hear it like more vulgar than any other Spanish, I don't know like they use it louder and they talk too fast, I don't know, I don't like Cuban Spanish very much. Moreover, I don't understand it very well. They talk too fast." (AC)

This excerpt from the interview with AC could provide an explanation for the low results from the 'pleasantness' and 'correctness' questionnaires obtained in the NC group.

In figure 11.1, the difference between the highest-rated varieties, Spain and Colombia, and the lowest-rated varieties, all the Caribbean ones, is significant. Moreover, NCs make a clear distinction between Caribbean varieties and non-Caribbean varieties, and they take into consideration the existence of at least two different varieties of Cuban Spanish. Ratings for Cuba 1, the variety spoken by

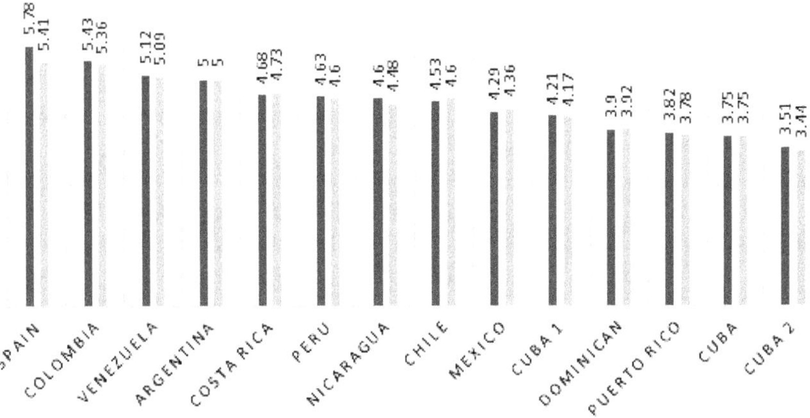

Figure 11.1. Non-Cuban participants' ratings of 'correctness' (dark grey) and 'pleasantness' (light grey) of diverse varieties of Spanish in Miami

those families who arrived in Miami in the 1960s and '70s, are significantly superior to ratings for Cuba, Dominican, Puerto Rican, or Cuba 2 Spanish, the variety spoken by those who have arrived within the past ten years.

Comments from individual interviews support these results. One example is that of MP, a second-generation twenty-two-year-old participant born in California. Her parents were from Ecuador and lived in California before moving to Miami when she was six years old. When asked if all Cubans speak the same kind of Spanish, MP gave the answer shown in example 11.7.

Example 11.7. MP's answer to question about varieties of Cuban Spanish

> "*Los cubanos no hablan igual el español. Yo me he dado cuenta que algunos cubanos hablan diferente. Los que son guajiros como dicen, hablan el español bien diferente, bien con palabras que casi no las entiendo, bien raras, bien rápido, diferente. Y me he dado cuenta que ellos [guajiros] son los que hablan el español más informal que ninguno de los otros. Los otros cubanos [no guajiros] suenan más formal. Yo creo que los que vienen recién, o sea, los que han pasado más tiempo aquí no hablan así tan- hablan más despacio, los que han crecido aquí hace 40 años o más.*" (MP)
>
> "Cubans don't speak Spanish the same way. I realized that some Cubans speak different. Those they call *guajiros* speak Spanish very different, with words that I barely understand, very weird, very fast, different. I realized that they [*guajiros*] are those who speak the most informal Spanish of all. Other Cubans [non-*guajiros*] sound more formal. I think that those who came, that is, those who have spent more time here speak like slower, those who grew up here forty years ago or more." (MP)

Having spent sixteen years in the city at the time of the interview, MP is a clear example of Miami Latinos of non-Cuban origin who perceive at least two varieties of Cuban Spanish in the city. For her, Cuba 2 is not as correct as Cuba 1 due to the differences in vocabulary, expressions, and tempo. At the same time, ratings obtained from Cubans and mixed-ethnicity Cubans provide further evidence of a distinction between Cuba 1 and Cuba 2 varieties, as can be seen in figures 11.2 and 11.3.

Cubans and MECs show a pattern similar to the one observed in the NC group; however, the distinction they make between Cuba 1 and Cuba 2 based on the ratings varies significantly. Cuban and MEC groups appear more concerned about this distinction than NCs, rating the Cuba 1 variety as much more pleasant and correct than Cuba or Cuba 2, or other Caribbean varieties. These results provide further support to Alfaraz's prior affirmation that "although Cubans are aware of and accept the stigmatization of other varieties of Caribbean Spanish, they do not recognize that their own variety belongs to that group, in spite of the fact that the linguistic features of Cuban Spanish are more like those of Puerto Rican and Dominican Spanish than those of Peninsular or Argentinean varieties" (2002, 5).

A clearer and more in-depth perspective of the aforementioned differences between groups is offered by the data in table 11.3. In this table, mean responses to the questionnaire statements about Cuban Spanish in relation to other varieties of

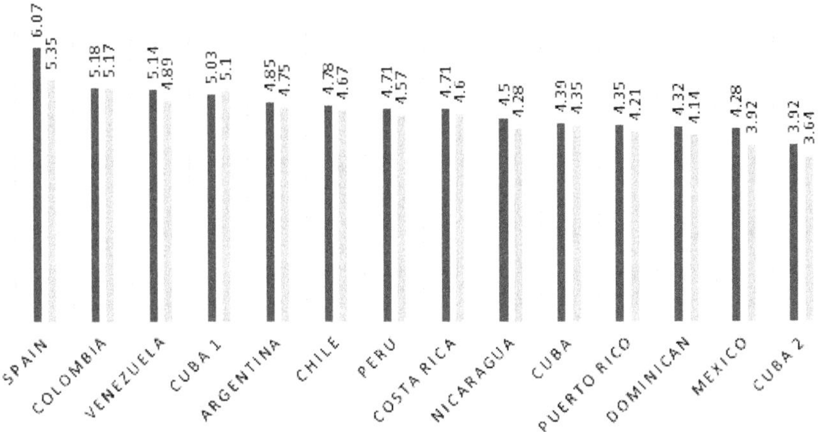

Figure 11.2. Cuban participants' ratings of 'correctness' (dark grey) and 'pleasantness' (light grey) of diverse varieties of Spanish in Miami

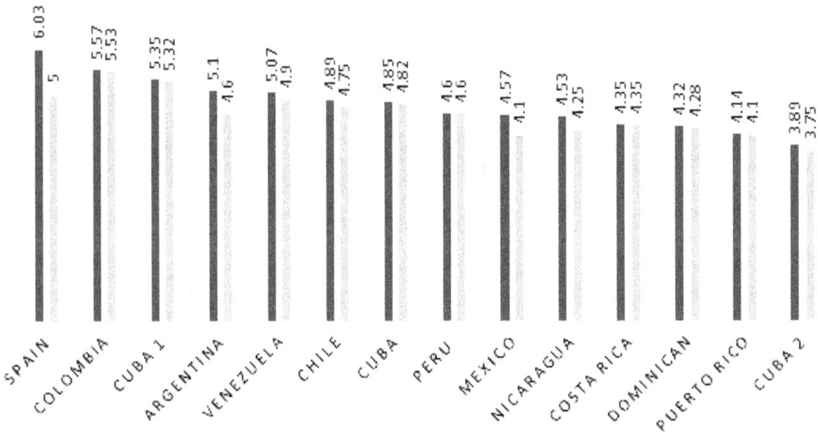

Figure 11.3. Mixed-ethnicity Cuban participants' ratings of 'correctness' (dark grey) and 'pleasantness' (light grey) of diverse varieties of Spanish in Miami

Spanish are displayed. Statements about the superiority of Colombian and Argentinian Spanish received the highest levels of agreement from NCs, and the second highest levels of agreement came from MECs. These responses suggest that MECs tend to distance themselves somewhat from the Cuban facet of their linguistic identity when asked to compare Cuban Spanish with other varieties of Spanish.

The mean responses to statements regarding varieties of Cuban Spanish reflect a similar tendency. Surprisingly, responses of the NC group suggest that their perception that 'not all Cubans speak the same kind of Spanish' is even stronger than that

Table 11.3. Mean responses to statements regarding Cuban Spanish in relation to other varieties of Spanish

STATEMENT	C	MEC	NC
1. Colombian Spanish is more proper than Cuban Spanish.	2.96	3.4	3.57
2. Colombians speak better Spanish than Cubans.	2.9	3.23	3.6
3. Nicaraguan Spanish sounds more formal than Cuban Spanish.	3.17	3.03	3.2
4. Argentinian Spanish sounds more educated than Cuban Spanish.	2.94	3.15	3.8
5. The Spanish spoken by Puerto Ricans and Cubans sounds almost the same.	2.7	2.9	2.8

Notes: 1 = I totally disagree; 5 = I totally agree

of Cubans and MECs, as can be seen in statement 1 in table 11.4. NC participants rate the previous statement with the highest score of 3.57, whereas Cuban and MEC participants provide mean responses of 3.37 and 3.4. However, Cubans and MECs appear to have a more acute perception of the differences between Cuba 1 and Cuba 2 varieties (statements 2 and 3). For statement 2, the mean for the Cuban group is 4.14, for the MEC group it is 3.57, and for the NC group it is 3.48. For statement 3 this difference remains similar, with means of 3.71 and 3.57 for the C and MEC groups respectively and 3.3 for the NC group.

In sum, the questionnaire data provide firm evidence that attitudes and perceptions of Cuban Spanish vary substantially—and in many aspects significantly—among second- and third-generation speakers of Cuban, MEC, and NC origins.

Conclusion

Data from the interview indicate that the Cuban Spanish lexicon is used not only by the Cuban Spanish group as was expected, but also by the mixed-ethnicity Cuban group and by the non-Cuban group. The attitudes toward and perceptions of different varieties of Spanish, and especially Cuban Spanish, are similar to those found by Alfaraz (2002, 2014). However, this study revealed two additional aspects not studied previously. First, mixed-ethnicity Cubans in Miami present substantially different attitudes and perceptions of Cuban Spanish than Cubans and non-Cubans, and their knowledge and use of Cuban-specific lexical items generally appears more restricted than among Cubans. Secondly, not only Cubans are aware of the existence of two different varieties of Cuban Spanish that coexist in Miami: non-Cubans also show that awareness, as exemplified by participants' statements in the interviews about the sociopolitical and ideological divisions among the Cuban-origin population (Lynch 2009, 774). Ratings of 'correctness' and 'pleasantness' of Cuba 1 and Cuba 2 varieties (following Alfaraz's [2002] methodology) also confirm this phenomenon. The results of the mixed-ethnicity Cuban group also differed from the other groups, especially in the section about Cuban culture, presence, and community. The

Table 11.4. Mean responses to statements regarding different varieties of Cuban Spanish

STATEMENTS	C	MEC	NC
1. Not all Cubans speak the same kind of Spanish.	3.37	3.4	3.57
2. The Spanish spoken by Cubans whose families arrived in Miami in the 1960s and '70s sounds more pleasant than the Spanish spoken by Cubans whose families have arrived within the past ten years.	4.14	3.57	3.48
3. The Spanish spoken by Cubans whose families arrived in Miami in the 1960s and '70s sounds more correct than the Spanish spoken by Cubans whose families have arrived within the past ten years.	3.71	3.57	3.3

Notes: 1 = I totally disagree; 5 = I totally agree

mixed-ethnicity Cuban group was the one that showed more positive attitudes toward the Cuban Spanish community, culture, and presence in Miami and at the same time it was the one that refused more firmly pejorative statements against the Cuban community in Miami. Overall, questionnaire results suggest that the Cuban community is perceived as making Miami a more interesting place and that, for many people, Miami is synonymous with Cuban culture.

To conclude, even though Cuban Spanish appears to exert a very limited influence on the varieties of Spanish spoken by non-Cubans, participants are aware of the Cuban Spanish lexicon. However, such influence is not as substantial as popular perception might suggest, which provides evidence that in reality Cuban culture in Miami might not enjoy the hegemonic status that it is perceived to have.

Notes

1. This means that one of the parents was of Cuban origin and the other was not (e.g., a Venezuelan mother and a Cuban father).
2. The creation of this scale was based on participant's comments and on Potowski's (2008) affirmation that "there is little evidence in the literature that the first word offered is the word that the participant tends to use more often, but several participants stated this was the case for them" (207).
3. Please note that in Cuba one can use both *papaya* and *fruta bomba*. While in the eastern part of the island *papaya* is the most commonly used word, in the western part of the country this word is obscene.
4. According to Sánchez-Boudy (1978), words such as "*asere, ambia, ecobio, consorte* y *cúmbila* se usan precedidos del adjetivo 'mi' para significar <<mi amigo, mi socio>>" (139).
5. *Consorte* is also used to refer to "my friend" as well as *el mío*.

References

Aaron, J. E., and J. E. Hernández. 2007. "Quantitative Evidence for Contact-Induced Accommodation." In *Spanish in Contact: Policy, Social and Linguistic Inquiries*, edited by K. Potowski and R. Cameron, 327–41. Philadelphia: John Benjamins North America.

Aranda, E. M., S. Hughes, and E. Sabogal. 2014. *Making a Life in Multiethnic Miami: Immigration and the Rise of a Global City*. Boulder: Lynne Rienner Publishers.

Alfaraz, G. 2002. "Miami Cuban Perceptions of Varieties of Spanish." In *Handbook of Perceptual Dialectology*, edited by D. R. Preston, 1–11. Philadelphia: John Benjamins North America.

———. 2014. "Dialect Perceptions in Real Time: A Restudy of Miami-Cuban Perceptions." *Journal of Linguistic Geography* 2:1–113.

Aparicio, F. R., and S. Chávez-Silverman. 1997. *Tropicalizations: Transcultural Representations of Latinidad*. Hanover, NH: University Press of New England.

Bayley, R., N. L. Cárdenas, B. Treviño Schouten, and C. M. Velez Salas. 2012. "Spanish Dialect Contact in San Antonio, Texas: An Exploratory Study." Paper presented at the 14th Hispanic Linguistics Symposium, Indiana University, October 14–17.

Ghosh Johnson, S. E. 2005. "Mexiqueño? Issues of Identity and Ideology in a Case Study of Dialect Contact." PhD diss., University of Pittsburgh.

Giles, H. 1973. "Accent Mobility: A Model and Some Data." *Anthropological Linguistics* 15:87–105.

Hernández, J. E. 2002. "Accommodation in a Dialect Contact Situation." *Revista de Filología y Lingüística de la Universidad de Costa Rica* 28 (2): 93–110.

Kerswill, P. 2008. "Koineization and Accommodation." In *The Handbook of Language Variation and Change*, edited by J. K. Chambers, P. Trudgill, and N. Schilling-Estes, 669–702. London: Blackwell Publishing.

Kerswill, P., and A. Williams. 2000. "Creating a New Town Koine: Children and Language Change in Milton Keynes." *Language in Society* 29 (1): 65–115.

Labov, W. 1972. *Sociolinguistic Patterns*. Philadelphia: University of Pennsylvania Press.

———. 2006. *The Social Stratification of English in New York City*. New York: Cambridge University Press.

Levine, R. M., and M. Asís. 2000. *Cuban Miami*. New Brunswick: Rutgers University Press.

López Morales, H. 2003. *Los Cubanos de Miami: Lengua y Sociedad*. Miami: Ediciones Universal.

Lynch, A. 2000. "Spanish-Speaking Miami in Sociolinguistic Perspective: Bilingualism, Recontact, and Language Maintenance among the Cuban-Origin Population." In *Research on Spanish in the United States*, edited by A. Roca, 271–83. Sommerville, MA: Cascadilla Press.

———. 2009. "A Sociolinguistic Analysis of Final /s/ in Miami Cuban Spanish." *Language Sciences* 31 (6): 766–90.

Milroy, L., and M. J. Gordon. 2003. *Sociolinguistics: Method and Interpretation*. Malden: Blackwell Pub.

Otheguy, R., O. García, and A. Roca. 2000. "Speaking in Cuban: The Language of Cuban Americans." In *New Immigrants in the United States. Readings for Second Language Educators*, edited by S. McKay and S.-L. C. Wong, 165–88. Cambridge: Cambridge University Press.

Otheguy, R., A. C. Zentella, and D. Livert. 2007. "Language and Dialect Contact in Spanish in New York: Toward the Formation of a Speech Community." *Language* 83 (4): 770–802.

Parodi, C., and O. Santa Ana. 2001. "The Los Angeles Spanish Koiné." Paper presented at La Primera Reunión de Pronombristas, City University of New York.

Potowski, K. 2008. "I Was Raised Talking like My Mom. The Influence of Mothers in the Development of MexiRicans' Phonological and Lexical Features." In *Bilingualism and Identity: Spanish at the Crossroads with other Languages*, edited by M. Niño-Murcia and J. Rothman, 201–20. Philadelphia: John Benjamins.

Potowski, K., and J. Matts. 2008. "MexiRicans: Interethnic Language and Identity." *Journal of Language, Identity, and Education* 7 (2): 137–60.

Potowski, K. 2011. "Intrafamilial Dialect Contact." In *The Handbook of Hispanic Sociolinguistics*, edited by M. Díaz-Campos, 579–97. Malden, MA: Blackwell Publishing.

Ramos-Pellicia, M. 2004. "Language Contact and Dialect Contact: Cross-Generational Phonological Variation in a Puerto Rican Community in the Midwest of the United States." PhD diss., Ohio State University.

Sánchez-Boudy, J. 1978. *Diccionario de cubanismos más usuales: como habla el cubano*. Miami: Ediciones Universal.

Santiesteban, A. 1985. *El habla popular cubana de hoy: una tonga de cubichismos que le oí a mi pueblo*. Habana: Editorial de Ciencias Sociales.

Schreffler, S. B. 1994. "Second-Person Singular Pronoun Options in the Speech of Salvadorans in Houston, TX." *Southwest Journal of Linguistics* 13 (1-2): 101–29.

Siegel, J. 2010. *Second Dialect Acquisition*. New York: Cambridge University Press.

Trudgill, P. 1999. "Dialect Contact, Dialectology and Sociolinguistics. Dialectos en contacto. Dialectología y sociolingüística." *Cuadernos de filología inglesa* 8 (1): 1–8.

———. 1986. *Dialects in Contact*. Oxford: Blackwell.

Villarreal, B. M. 2014. "Dialect Contact among Spanish-Speaking Children in Los Angeles." PhD diss., University of California, Los Angeles.

Zentella, A. C. 1990. "Lexical Leveling in Four New York City Spanish Dialects: Linguistic and Social Factors." *Hispania* 73 (4): 1094–105.

PART IV

HERITAGE LANGUAGE ACQUISITION

12

Pronominal Subject Expression with Inanimate Reference in Heritage Speakers of Cuban Spanish

ALEJANDRO CUZA
Purdue University

JOSÉ CAMACHO
Rutgers University

THE CURRENT STUDY EXAMINES the status of third-person pronominal subjects with inanimate reference in the grammar of heritage speakers of Cuban Spanish in the United States (US), an area of research so far unexplored.[1] Personal pronominal subjects in Spanish (henceforth PPSs) agree in gender and number with a linguistic (noun phrase, NP) or extralinguistic antecedent, and they can be omitted in subject position given the strong agreement features of a pro-drop language like Spanish (Camacho 2013; Jaeggli and Safir 1989; Rizzi 1982; Luján 1999). In contrast with Mainstream Spanish, PPSs in Cuban Spanish can co-refer with inanimate or nonhuman referents, as shown in example 12.1 below.

Example 12.1.

Question

¿Apagaste el horno?
Did you turn off the oven?

Response

*No, **él** se apaga solo.* (*él* meaning the oven)
No, **it** turns itself off.

In example 12.1, the pronominal subject *él* (he) refers to the oven, an inanimate object. Although no previous research to our knowledge has examined the status of this specific domain in Cuban Spanish, it has been attested in other varieties of Caribbean

Spanish, including Dominican Spanish (Bullock and Toribio 2009; Martínez-Sanz 2011) and Puerto Rican Spanish (Ávila-Jiménez 1996; Shin and Otheguy 2013). This structure is more common with inchoative verbs with the reflexive clitic *se*, as *arreglarse*, 'to fix' (*Él se arregló solo*, 'It fixed itself,' it meaning the TV). The subject in these cases undergoes the action of the verb. Speakers might emphasize the idea of the subject doing the action by explicitly producing it, as well as the adverb *solo* (itself). However, this phenomenon is not categorical, and a null subject or NP is often preferred, as in example 12.2 below.

Example 12.2.

Question

¿Qué le hiciste al carro?
What did you do to the car?

Response

Yo no le hice nada. (El carro, ∅) se rompió solo.
I did not do anything to it. The car broke down itself.

PPSs are uncommon with stative verbs in Cuban Spanish specifically, as in *Él está parqueado abajo* (It is parked downstairs, *él* 'it' meaning the car).[2] Thus, the use of the overt pronoun appears to be constrained by both pragmatic and lexical factors.

The present study addresses the extent to which heritage speakers of Cuban Spanish preserve this particular interface-related dialectal feature. Given the low frequency of the structure in the input, stemming from direct competition with null subjects and NPs, it is possible that this feature is not activated enough, leading to low patterns of use and acceptability; however, we might also find differences depending on the type of elicitation task, as documented in previous research (e.g., Cuza 2013; Frank and Toribio, this volume).

In what follows we provide a syntactic analysis of subject pronoun expression and distribution. We then discuss previous research on the L2 acquisition of this structure and postulate our research questions and hypotheses. The last part of the paper addresses the experiment, the results, discussion, and conclusions.

The Distribution of Subject Pronouns in Spanish

Mainstream Spanish is generally considered a null subject language in which subjects are licensed and identified through the information present in the inflectional endings of the verb, as seen in example 12.3.

Example 12.3.

a. *∅ Compr-é* *unas salchichas.*
bought-1SG some sausages
I bought sausages.

b. *∅ Compr-aron* *unas manzanas.*
bought-3PL some apples
They bought apples.

Formally, the null subject property of Spanish has been characterized as the result of having a nominal-like D-feature (i.e., a feature related to nominal reference) instantiated in Tense (T). This feature satisfies the requirement that clauses must have a subject (the so-called Extended Projection Principle, or EPP; e.g., Alexiadou and Anagnostopoulou 1998; Borer 1984; Jelinek 1984; Manzini and Savoia 2002; Ordóñez and Treviño 1999). The property of having a D-feature in T is indirectly related to the inflectionally rich morphological paradigm of Spanish, although a direct connection between the two properties cannot be generalized to other languages (e.g., Camacho 2013; Jaeggli and Safir 1989; Rizzi 1986; Taraldsen 1978).

As a result of having D in T (and rich inflectional morphology), pronominal subjects are optional and acquire different semantic values from null counterparts (notably, shifting the topic in discourse; e.g., Frascarelli 2007; Givón 1983). Most importantly for our purposes, overt subject pronouns do not refer to inanimate referents, as seen in example 12.4. In this example, the pronoun can only be used to refer to a human antecedent in Mainstream Spanish.

Example 12.4.

Ella solita suelta su agua. (*ella* meaning the beef)
It pours out its own juice by itself.

In most varieties of Mainstream Spanish, subject pronouns do not take an inanimate antecedent, as in example 12.4. However, in Cuban and other varieties of Caribbean Spanish, this is common, perhaps because PPSs have become weak pronouns in this variety.

In addition, Caribbean Spanish does not instantiate other properties relative to the expression and position of overt subjects characteristic of Mainstream Spanish. For example, there is no obligatory subject-verb inversion in interrogative sentences, and a *Wh-Subject-V* word order is the norm (*¿Qué María compró?* 'What did Mary buy'; e.g., Comínguez, forthcoming; Goodall 2011; Gutiérrez-Bravo 2008; Martínez-Sanz 2011; Ordóñez and Olarrea 2006; Suñer and Lizardi 1995). Furthermore, overt subjects are much more frequent in Caribbean Spanish, ranging from 30 percent to 60 percent across the different varieties of Caribbean Spanish, compared to 20 percent to 30 percent for other varieties of non-Caribbean Spanish (e.g., Cabrera 2008; Martínez-Sanz 2011). Although data on Cuban Spanish from the island is not readily available, Otheguy, Zentella, and Livert (2007) report 34 percent of overt subject use among recently arrived immigrants from Cuba in New York City, which is in line with data from Puerto Rican speakers.

Like other varieties with a higher incidence of overt subjects, Caribbean Spanish has relaxed the semantic restrictions on overt pronominal subjects. For example, overt pronouns with generic reference have been documented in Puerto Rican Spanish (Alva-Jiménez 1996), in Dominican Spanish (Bullock and Toribio 2009; Martínez-Sanz 2011), and in bilingual varieties of Caribbean Spanish in the US (Lapidus and Otheguy 2005). Bullock and Toribio (2009) document uses of overt PPSs with inanimate references, as illustrated in example 12.5, although in Martínez-Sanz's (2011) variationist study, inanimate reference strongly favored overt lexical subjects.

Example 12.5. Example from Martínez-Sanz's variationist study (2011, 29)

> *Pero yo no sé qué le pasó (a la camioneta) porque ella tiene gasolina y ella estaba caminando bien.*
> But I don't know what happened to it (the pickup), because she has gas and she was running fine.

Camacho (2016) proposes an account of how fully null subject varieties transition to partially null subject varieties like Caribbean Spanish or Brazilian Portuguese. He assumes that subjects in fully null subject languages can occupy at least two distinct positions that entail different discourse conditions: one closer to the Tense Phrase (TP), and one more peripheral. Formally, this distribution follows from an antilocality condition on agreement: when two categories agree (in this case the subject and tense), the target (the subject) cannot be in the specifier of the controller (Tense). As a result, overt subjects and pronouns are farther away, dislocated from T, whereas null subjects are encoded as the D feature in T in Mainstream Spanish. Overt subjects tend to be interpreted as focused, whereas null subjects indicate a continuing topic (see example 12.6 a and b respectively).

Example 12.6. Mainstream Spanish

a. Null subject

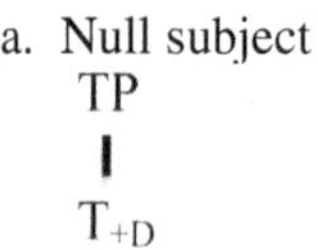

b. Overt subject

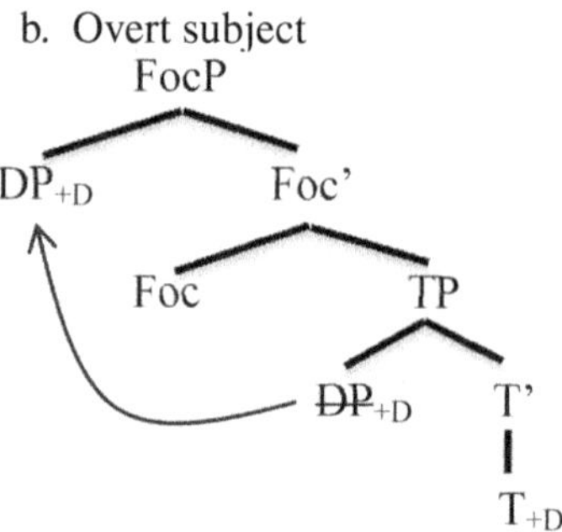

When overt PPSs increase their statistical frequency in Caribbean varieties, overt subjects no longer match the discourse conditions for focus. Specifically, many overt PPSs will not be compatible with a focus interpretation, so the correlation between a dislocated structural position and focus interpretation is weakened. Hence, PPSs can appear in the specifier of TP, violating the antilocality of agreement condition. As a result, T no longer reliably hosts a D feature, and an overt subject in its specifier will be able to agree and not violate the antilocality requirement (example 12.7).

Example 12.7. Cuban Spanish

a. Null subject

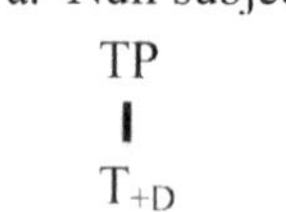

b. Overt subject

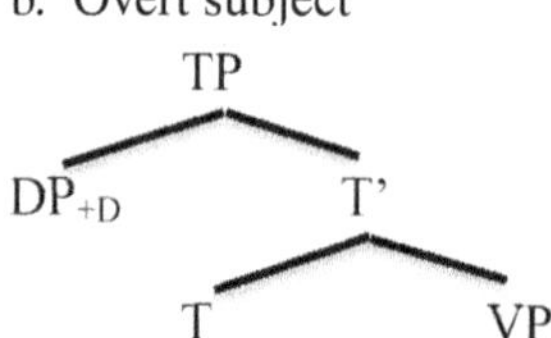

Arguably, this is the process that Cuban Spanish is undergoing: the overt or null semantic distinctions are no longer consistent with the context subjects appear in because of higher frequency.

Additionally, the shift from T^{+D} in Mainstream Spanish to T^{+D}/T in Cuban Spanish accounts for the emergence of inanimate referents for overt subject pronouns. As proposed by Cardinaletti and Starke (1999), strong pronouns typically refer to humans in consistent null subject languages like Mainstream Spanish. In Cuban Spanish, the structural shift from T^{+D} to T^{+D}/T implies that overt pronouns can incorporate to T and shift from strong to weak. Consequently, the restriction on animacy is relaxed. As noted above, however, PPSs with inanimate referents typically appear with *se* and with nonstative predicates, which further constrains their availability.

In sum, Mainstream and Cuban Spanish differ with respect to two syntactic properties: (1) whether overt subjects are required to appear dislocated or not and (2) whether overt pronouns are strong or weak and can refer to inanimate antecedents.

The Distribution and Acquisition of Pronominal Subjects in Spanish

The acquisition of pronominal subjects in Spanish is an area of research that has gathered quite some attention for more than three decades, crucially from a formal L2 acquisition perspective (e.g., Al-Kasey and Pérez-Leroux 1998; Camacho 2013; Isabelli 2004; Liceras 1989; Liceras and Díaz 1999; Montrul and Louro 2006; Phinney 1987; Quesada 2015; Rothman 2009). Most of previous research has examined this grammatical area as part of the set of properties argued to be part of the null subject parameter (NSP; e.g., Chomsky 1981; Rizzi 1982), and among speakers of non-pro-drop languages such as English or French. Researchers have also investigated the status of pronominal subjects in Spanish from a variationist perspective, shedding light on different lexical, phonological, and morphosyntactic variables constraining subject pronoun use (e.g., Abreu 2009; Alfaraz 2015; Cameron 1993; Erker, Ho-Hernández, Lapidus-Shin, and Otheguy, this volume; Ortiz, Dauphinais, and Aponte Alequín, this volume; Otheguy and Zentella 2012; Otheguy, Zentella, and Livert 2007; Lapidus and Otheguy 2005).

Liceras (1989) found no difficulties in the acquisition of null subjects in L2 Spanish by French and English native speakers, corroborating previous research (Phinney 1987). The learners consistently accepted null subjects and rejected overt expletives (**Ello hace mucho frío en Canada*, 'It is very cold in Canada') from early on and showed no specific patterns of crosslinguistic influence from English or French. However, on other properties of the NSP, such as *that*-trace effects, the results were mixed across all groups. Similar target behavior with the acquisition of null subjects was found by Al-Kasey and Pérez-Leroux (1998), who examined the comprehension and production of null subjects and null expletive subjects (i.e., *Llueve*, 'It rains') among English-speaking learners of Spanish. Although the authors found difficulties at early stages, with an overextension of overt subjects to generic contexts (expletive meaning), more proficient learners behaved native-like.

More recently, Montrul and Louro (2006) investigated the morphosyntactic and discourse-pragmatic properties of null subjects across English-speaking learners of Spanish of different proficiency levels. Results showed difficulties among the intermediate learners. They showed nontarget behavior with morphosyntactic aspects as well as with the pragmatic distribution of overt versus null subjects, evidenced in an overextension of overt subjects and illicit null subjects. These difficulties, however, were overcome at higher levels of proficiency, with the near-native speakers showing no difficulties in any front (Pérez-Leroux and Glass 1999). All in all, bilingual speakers appear to acquire the pro-drop property of the Spanish language. This is despite recent research arguing for linguistic optionality at the syntax-pragmatic interface (Serratrice, Sorace, and Paoli 2004; Sorace 2000; 2005; Tsimpli, Sorace, Heycock, and Filiaci 2004).

In regard to overt subject pronouns with inanimate reference, Martínez-Sanz (2011) and Toribio and Bullock (2009) found evidence of overt subjects with inanimate reference in Dominican Spanish (e.g., *Pero ella* [*la laguna*] *antes estaba llena*, 'But she [the lagoon] was full before'). They also document cases of overt expletives in impersonal constructions (e.g., *Ello tiene que haber otro paso*, 'There has to be another way'), where a null subject is categorically required in Mainstream Spanish. Lapidus and Otheguy (2005) also document cases of overt subject pronouns with nonspecific referent (e.g., *Ellos te llamaron del banco*, 'They called you from the bank') among Puerto Ricans in New York City. The authors argued that these third-person plural pronouns are quantitatively more frequent among Puerto Ricans in NYC, but already present in the precontact Spanish variety. They conclude that the contact variety of Spanish has quantitatively enhanced the strength of the pragmatic constraint regulating subject pronoun expression (an indirect transfer from English); however, this does not represent a case of qualitative change at the level of abstract syntactic values.

Research Questions and Predictions

Despite the extensive research on the expression and distribution of overt and null subjects in Spanish, the status of third-person subject pronouns with inanimate referents in Cuban Spanish remains unexplored, crucially among heritage speakers of Cuban Spanish living in the US. We aim to cover this gap in the literature by examining whether Cuban heritage speakers have knowledge of this specific dialectal feature. Specifically, we predict heritage speakers will show lower levels of use, acceptability, and preference of overt subjects with inanimate reference given the low frequency of this structure in day-to-day input; however, we do not discard the possibility of finding task effects stemming from prescriptive reasons in the use of an overt subject with inanimate referent.

The Study

Participants

Thirty-two (n = 32) participants of Cuban background living in the US participated in the study: twenty heritage speakers and twelve Cuban immigrants. Participants were recruited and interviewed in Miami and northeastern New Jersey. All of the participants completed a language-background questionnaire and an adapted version of the *Diplomas de Español como Lengua Extranjera* (DELE) proficiency test, as per previous research (e.g., Cuza, Pérez-Leroux, and Sánchez 2013; Montrul and Slabakova 2003). The language-background questionnaire included questions relative to participants' educational level, age of arrival in the US, length of residence, languages spoken during childhood, patterns of language use, and a language proficiency self-assessment section. This section measured the participant's knowledge of English and Spanish across all language skills.

The heritage speakers were either born in the US (n = 12; mean age at testing: 34; *SD* = 12.48; age range: 18–48) or had immigrated to the US during childhood (n = 8; mean age at testing, 42; *SD* = 16.88; age range, 19–59). Those who immigrated to the US had a mean age of arrival of eight years of age (range: 4–14) and a mean length of residence of thirty-six years (range: 10–53). Most of the participants were highly educated, with 80 percent reporting having a college degree and 20 percent reporting having a high school diploma. The majority of them reported feeling more comfortable in English (65 percent) or in both English and Spanish (25 percent). In regard to patterns of language use at home, 30 percent of the participants indicated speaking both Spanish and English, 20 percent indicated speaking mostly Spanish or Spanish only, and 15 percent indicated speaking slightly more Spanish. The rest of the participants indicated speaking English only or mostly English (25 percent) or slightly more English (10 percent). At work, 44 percent of the participants reported speaking English only or mostly English, 22 percent reported speaking slightly more English, and the rest reported speaking both (33 percent). In social situations, 45 percent reported to speak slightly more English and 35 percent English only or mostly English. Interestingly, a large number of the participants (80 percent, sixteen of the twenty) indicated speaking Spanish over the phone frequently or very frequent with family members. This shows very strong family ties and extended family orientation. Some participants also indicated chatting in Spanish frequently (35 percent, seven of the twenty). In regard to their language proficiency, results of the DELE proficiency test showed that 80 percent of the participants had high proficiency in Spanish, with an average score of 45 points out of 50. The rest of speakers (20 percent), were intermediate learners, with an average score of 30 points.

The immigrant group (n = 12) was formed of Cuban native speakers who immigrated to the US as adults (mean age at testing: 52; age range: 23–78). Their mean age of arrival in the US was thirty-seven years of age (range: 19–65) and their mean length of residence was fifteen years (range: 1–48). The majority of participants had a college degree (67 percent), and the rest had completed either primary school (17 percent) or high school (17 percent). Sixty-seven percent of the participants reported feeling more comfortable in Spanish, and 33 percent reported feeling more comfortable in both languages. In regard to patterns of language use, the large majority of the immigrants indicated speaking Spanish mostly or only Spanish at home (100 percent) and in social situations (67 percent). All of them had Spanish-speaking partners with whom they spoke Spanish very frequently. Except for one participant, they all reported speaking Spanish over the phone very frequently, and 83 percent reported texting in Spanish very frequently or frequently. The participants also reported watching TV in Spanish very frequently or frequently (83 percent). Regarding their bilingual proficiency, their self-assessment was not fluent in English (2.5/4), and excellent (3.9/4) in Spanish.

Tasks

Data collection included three tasks: an elicited production task (sentence completion task), an acceptability judgment task (AJT), and a preference task (Crain and Thornton 1998). The three tasks were completed in one sitting. The production task was completed first to avoid any priming effects in oral production.

Following previous research in heritage language bilingualism (Cuza and Miller 2015; Montrul 2009), the elicited production task consisted of a preamble followed by a sentence to be completed. The preamble depicted two characters and a situation where something had happened to an object, and one of the characters had to make it clear that they did not do anything using the verb in parenthesis and the photo provided (example 12.8).

Example 12.8. Elicited production task

Preamble

Esta mañana Juan conducía por la calle cuando su carro dejó de andar. Rosa le preguntó si él apagó el motor en el semáforo y Juan le dijo...

(*pararse*)

This morning John was driving along the street when his car stopped working. Rosa asked him if he turned the engine off at the traffic light and Juan told her…

(stop itself)

Prompt

Yo no hice nada...
I did not do anything…

Expected response

Él se paró solo.
It stopped itself.

There were a total of thirty-four tokens: sixteen test tokens, sixteen distracters, and two practice items. The test tokens included verbs with a reflexive meaning, as in example 12.9, and the distracters included inalienable pronoun use as part of a separate study.

The AJT was a paper and pencil task. It followed the same model as the production task in regard to the number of tokens and token type. The only difference was that a complete sentence was provided after the preamble, and the participant had to judge the sentence using a Likert scale ranging from 1 (completely odd) to 5 (completely fine). If the participant found the sentence odd or slightly odd, they were asked to explain why.

Example 12.9. Acceptability judgment task

Preamble

José hizo una fiesta en su casa y preparó un puerco asado riquísimo. Durante la fiesta, su amiga Susana le preguntó. "¿Te costó mucho trabajo preparar el puerco?" José le dijo: "Yo no hice nada..."
Jose had a party at his place and cooked a delicious pork. During the party, his friend Susana asked him: "Did it take too much work to cook the pork?" Jose told her: "I did not do anything…"

Test Token

Se cocinó solo.
It cooked itself.

I----------------------I--------------------I---------------------I----------------------I

(1)	(2)	(3)	(4)	(5)
completely odd	slightly odd	neither odd nor good	good	completely good

Reason if odd or slightly odd:____________________________________

Participants were asked not to judge the sentence based on pragmatic issues. There were a total of thirty-two sentences: eight with overt subjects, eight with null subjects, and sixteen distracters. All of the tokens were counterbalanced and randomized.

The forced preference task (e.g., Cuza and Frank 2015; Geeslin and Guijarro-Fuentes 2006) was the last task to be administered. The participants were presented with a preamble followed by two sentences, one with an overt pronoun, the other one with a null subject, and then required to choose the sentences they preferred the most based on the preamble. The goal of this task was to test the interpretation of the participants and find out if they had a preference toward the overt subject (example 12.10).

Example 12.10. Forced preference task

Preamble

Carlitos fue a calentar una taza de chocolate en el microondas pero el micro no funcionó. Llamó a su mamá y le dijo: "Mami el micro no funciona. Yo no le hice nada..."

a. *Se rompió solo.*
b. *Él se rompió solo.*

Carlitos was going to heat up a cup of hot chocolate but the microwave did not work. He called his mother and told her: "Mom, the microwave does not work. I did not do anything…"

a. It broke down itself.
b. It broke down itself.

Results

Elicited Production Task

Results from the production task showed a higher level of use of overt subjects among the immigrants (25 percent) compared to the heritage speakers (4 percent). Both groups, however, preferred to use a null element in most cases, which shows that this option is the preferred one in Spanish. Interestingly, the two groups behaved differently in their production of NPs. The heritage speakers used NPs much more than the immigrants (23 percent versus 0.06 percent respectively). This is represented in figure 12.1.

A univariate ANOVA analysis with the proportion of overt subjects realized as the dependent variable and group (heritage speakers, immigrants) as the independent variable revealed significant differences per group ($F(1, 28) = 13.87$, $p < 0.001$).[3] As predicted, the immigrants significantly outperformed the heritage speakers with a higher proportion of PPSs realized. Results also showed that both groups missed significance in their production of NPs, with the heritage speakers producing a higher number of NPs than the immigrants ($F(1, 28) = 3.64$, $p = 0.066$). There were no significant differences between groups in their proportions of null subjects ($F(1, 28) = 0.397$, $p = .534$) or other elements realized ($F(1, 28) = 0.632$, $p = 0.433$).

An individual analysis looking at the number of PPSs and NPs produced per participant confirmed the group results. Regarding overt subjects, five of the ten immigrants produced six to ten out of sixteen trials; two participants produced one and three respectively, and three participants produced none. This contrasts sharply with the heritage speakers: two participants produced three, one produced four, and two produced one to two subjects respectively. The rest of the participants (fifteen out of twenty) produced none. In regard to NPs, the heritage speakers produced many more cases than the immigrants, with eight participants producing six or more out of

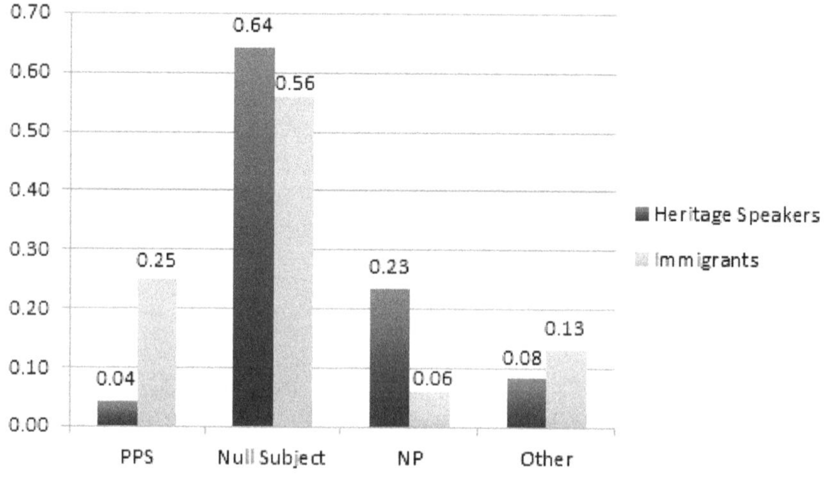

Figure 12.1. Proportion of PPS, null subjects, NPs, and Other realized by group

sixteen trials. The immigrants, however, showed very low production of NPs, with just two participants producing three and four respectively. This is represented in figure 12.2.

Acceptability Judgment Task

In contrast to what was expected, results from the AJT showed no significant differences between groups. The heritage speakers accepted overt subjects slightly more than the immigrants but not significantly so. Both groups showed almost ceiling performance in their intuition of null subjects (figure 12.3).

An ANOVA analysis showed no significant differences per group with their acceptability of either overt subjects ($F(1, 30) = 0.757$, $p = 0.391$) or null subjects ($F(1, 30) = 0.000$, $p = 0.986$). It seems as if the heritage speakers do not find PPSs to be completely ungrammatical, despite their lower level of use in the production task. Although both groups showed higher levels of acceptability of null subjects, this was not significantly different from their acceptability of overt subjects, either among the heritage speakers ($F(1, 38) = 2.820$, $p = 0.101$) or among the immigrants ($F(1, 22) = 2.881$, $p = 0.104$)

An individual analysis conducted on the participants' responses showed that 65 percent of the heritage speakers had a mean score across all of the PPSs between 4 and 4.9 out of 5 (fine or completely fine). Most of these participants (ten out of thirteen) also accepted the null subject sentences with mean scores between 4 and 5. One of the participants who rejected the null subject sentences preferred a PPSs instead, and the other two participants were somehow undecided in their responses. Regarding the immigrants, six of the twelve (50 percent) participants accepted the sentences with a PPS. Some explicitly stated disliking the overt pronoun for prescriptive reasons (e.g., an *él* with an accent is not needed there) while others indicated other reasons. In general, the immigrants accepted null subjects, although some of them rejected them for pragmatic reasons (e.g., a plane can't land by itself).

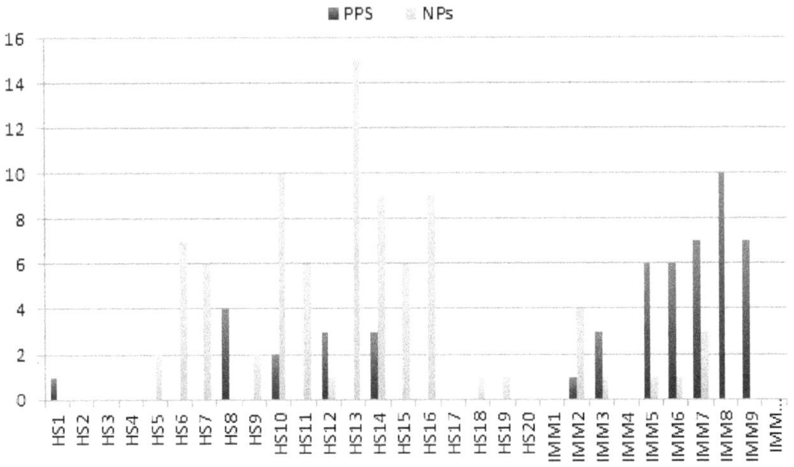

Figure 12.2. Individual analysis: Number of PPS and NPs realized per participant

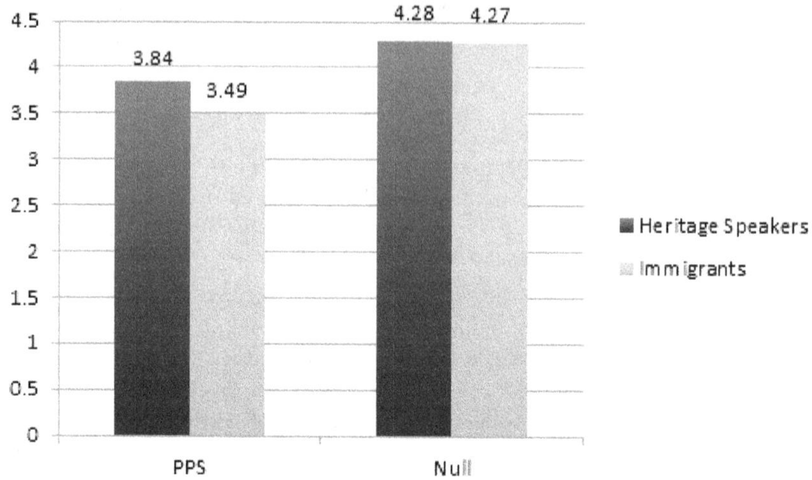

Figure 12.3. AJT results: Mean acceptability scores for PPS and null subjects by group

Forced Preference Task

In order to further test the knowledge that the heritage speakers have of this specific dialectal feature, we conducted a forced preference task, which examined the preference that the participants could have toward one structure versus the other. As in the AJT, the two groups did not behave any differently from each other ($F(1, 30) = 0.007$, $p = 0.933$) at the group level. About 70 percent of the participants preferred the null subject versus the overt option (figure 12.4).

An individual analysis performed on the number of overt subjects confirmed the group results. Regarding the heritage speakers, one participant preferred overt subjects 94 percent of the time, and four participants between 56 percent and 81 percent of the time. The rest of the heritage speakers (fifteen of the twenty) preferred null subjects most of the time. The immigrants behaved similarly, with one participant preferring overt subjects 81 percent of the time and another one 100 percent of the time. The rest of the participants showed a clear preference for null subjects. We did notice, however, item effects, crucially among the heritage speakers. A large number of heritage speakers preferred the overt pronoun with four items: (1) *Él se aterrizó solo* (It landed itself, *él* meaning the plane; nine of the twenty speakers); (2) *Él se cayó solo* (It fell itself, *él* meaning the tree; eight of the twenty speakers); (3) *Él se estropeó solo* (It broke down itself, *él* meaning the cell phone; eight of the twenty speakers); and (4) *Él se rompió solo* (It broke down itself, *él* meaning the microwave; eight of the twenty speakers). Regarding the immigrants, five of the twelve preferred the overt option with item 1, and six with item 2.

Discussion

The main goal of the present study was to examine the status of personal subject pronouns with inanimate reference in heritage speakers of Cuban Spanish. We expected

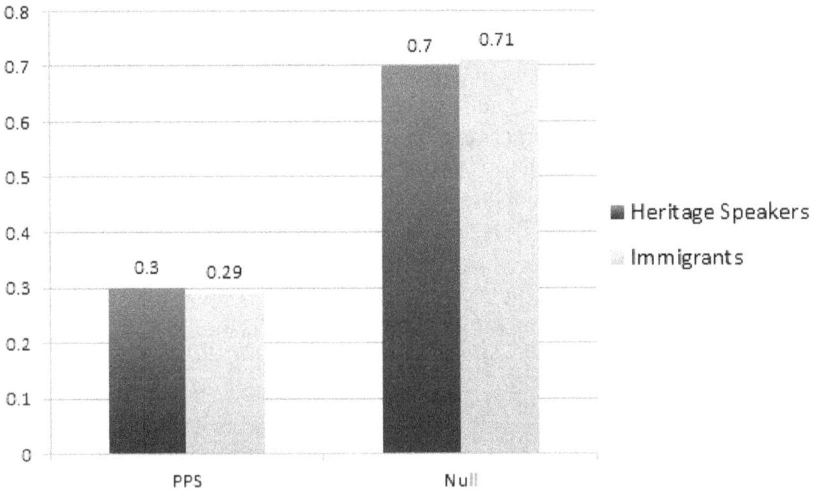

Figure 12.4. Preference task results: Mean preference scores for PPS and null subjects by group

heritage speakers to show lower levels of use, acceptability, and preference vis-á-vis adult immigrants to the US stemming from limited input and use of this specific dialectal feature in a language contact scenario.

Results from the elicited production task showed lower levels of PPSs use among the heritage speakers, as expected. The heritage speakers overwhelmingly preferred a null subject or an NP. Given their limited input to Spanish as a heritage language in a language contact scenario, heritage speakers might be more hesitant with the production of overt referential subjects in online production due to processing issues relative to gender features. Previous research on gender assignment and agreement among child (Cuza and Pérez-Tattam 2015) and adult heritage speakers of Spanish (Alarcón 2011; Montrul, Foote, and Perpiñán 2008) documents significant difficulties with DET/NOUN gender assignment. Thus, it is possible that heritage speakers find it easier to produce a null subject, or simply repeat the NP antecedent available in the preamble, than generate something from scratch.

Another explanation might be related to the lower frequency and activation of PPSs with inanimate reference in day-to-day oral speech (Ellis 2002; Paradis 2004; Yang 2002). Although this structure is possible, it is in direct competition with null subjects, and heritage speakers might not have been exposed to it sufficiently enough to be able to activate it more frequently in online production, along the lines of Michel Paradis's activation threshold hypothesis (Paradis 2004). Paradis (2004) argues that when an item in bilingual grammars does not receive a sufficient amount of neural impulses due to lack of stimulation, the activation threshold rises; therefore, the item becomes more difficult to activate over time (Paradis 2004, 28). This proposal has been discussed in the literature to account for cases of L1 attrition among long-term immigrants (see Gürel 2004), and more recently as an important component in heritage grammar's feature reassembly and reconfiguration (Cuza and Pérez-Tattam 2015; Putnam and Sánchez 2013).

In contrast with the production task, the results of the AJT did not reveal any significant differences between the two groups. In fact, 65 percent of the heritage speakers accepted PPSs with inanimate reference, and they did not, as a group, differentiate between overt and null subjects. This was also the case of the immigrants, who, despite having a slight preference toward null subjects, judged both types of sentences statistically similarly. Therefore, it appears that the heritage speakers have knowledge of the grammaticality of PPSs with an inanimate reference.

As in the case of the AJT, the heritage speakers did not behave significantly differently from the immigrants in the forced preference task. Both bilingual groups preferred null subjects about 70 percent of the time. As discussed earlier, we found an item effect among the heritage speakers: 40–45 percent of the participants preferred the PPS with four specific items. Thus, although the heritage speakers prefer null subjects, they are aware that their heritage language allows PPSs with inanimate reference. Furthermore, their preference for null subjects was on par with that of the immigrants. Therefore, no bilingualism effects can be attributed to their behavior.

Taking together the results of the three tasks, we can conclude that heritage speakers of Cuban Spanish have target knowledge of PPSs with inanimate reference, despite their low patterns of use in the elicited production measure. We have found clear task effects, with the acceptability judgment task and the forced preference task showing no significant differences between heritage speakers and immigrants, and significant differences between the two groups in the production task. This asymmetry between the tasks supports our view that the results of the production task stem from processing issues rather than lack of syntactic knowledge. This supports the importance of implementing different elicitation methods when studying the grammatical competence of heritage speakers in order to triangulate the data and avoid overgeneralizations.

An important factor to consider in discussing our data is the language dominance of our participants. As discussed earlier, 80 percent of the heritage speakers were highly proficient in Spanish, with a score of 40 points or more in the DELE test. This is, without a doubt, a key factor in the results, and something that must be taken into consideration before making any generalizations on heritage speakers' grammatical systems. In addition to language dominance, there is an important interrelated factor: community characteristics and the ethnolinguistic vitality of the Spanish language in Miami and northeastern New Jersey. Miami has the largest Cuban American community in the country, and is a region culturally, economically, and politically tied to the Spanish language and culture. This has profound implications on the day-to-day patterns of language exposure among Spanish heritage speakers and immigrants in Miami, creating more than ideal circumstances for minority language maintenance and transmission. This is also influenced by a strong sense of pride among Cuban Americans, given economic and geopolitical reasons, as well as strong family ties to their country of origin, and familism. Northeastern New Jersey has a large Hispanic population, many of them of Cuban origin, with similar community characteristics as Miami, and positive attitudes toward Spanish and bilingualism. Previous research documents strong correlation between these integrative variables and language maintenance and transmission among Hispanic families (e.g., Guardado and Becker 2014;

Pease-Álvarez, Hakuta, and Bayle 1996; Pérez-Leroux, Cuza, and Thomas 2011). The characteristics of these communities play a major role in the overall Spanish proficiency of the speakers vis-á-vis other areas of the country with a lower percentage of Spanish immigrants.

Conclusions

The present study has examined the knowledge that heritage speakers of Cuban background have of personal pronoun subjects with inanimate reference. Our data show that this particular feature of Cuban Spanish is part of the heritage speakers' grammatical system, despite previous research documenting linguistic variability in grammatical domains where the syntax interfaces with discourse, as is the case of subject pronoun realization and distribution (Serratrice, Sorace, and Paoli 2004; Sorace 2000, 2005). We have argued that these results are accounted for by considering the specific characteristics of the bilingual communities our speakers come from, and their specific patterns of language use and activation (Paradis 2004; Putnam and Sánchez 2013).

Heritage speakers are known to be highly heterogeneous in regard to their bilingual status. Future research would benefit from more in-depth consideration of the role of external factors in heritage language development and how they are closely intertwined with linguistic factors, including age of onset of bilingualism and language activation and use. This is determined by the ethnolinguistic vitality of the community, country of origin, geopolitical issues, and the extent to which these factors affect day-to-day patterns of language activation and use.

Notes

We would like to thank our research assistants Raúl Aguilar and Julio César López Otero for their assistance with data collection, and to Charlie Garrido and Ellen Thompson for their helpful support in recruiting participants in Miami. The study was partially funded by the generous support of the College of Liberal Arts at Purdue University. All errors remain our own.

1. For the purpose of our study, heritage speakers refer to second- and third-generation immigrants who were born and raised in the US, or who arrived in the US during childhood (Montrul 2008; Valdés 2001). We take the age of fourteen as the cut-off age to differentiate heritage speakers from adult immigrants following previous research on the role of age in heritage language development (Colantoni, Cuza, and Mazaro 2016).
2. English allows a similar construction with copula verbs when the speaker personifies an object in informal speech (e.g., She is a beauty, 'she' meaning the boat).
3. Two participants from the immigrant group did not complete this task.

References

Abreu, L. 2009. "Spanish Subject Personal Pronoun Use by Monolinguals, Bilinguals and Second Language Learners." PhD diss., University of Florida.

Alarcón, I. V. 2011. "Spanish Grammatical Gender under Complete and Incomplete Acquisition: Early and Late Bilinguals' Linguistic Behavior within the Noun Phrase." *Bilingualism: Language and Cognition* 14 (3): 332–50.

Alexiadou, A., and E. Anagnostopoulou. 1998. "Parametrizing AGR: Word Order, V-Movement, and EPP-Checking." *Natural Language and Linguistic Theory* 16:491–540.

Alfaraz, G. 2015. "Variation of Overt and Null Subject Pronouns in the Spanish of Santo Domingo." In *Subject Pronoun Expression in Spanish: A Cross-Dialectal Perspective*, edited by A. M. Carvalho, R. Orozco, and N. Lapidus Shin, 3–16. Washington, DC: Georgetown University Press.

Al-Kasey, T., and A. T. Pérez-Leroux. 1998. "Second Language Acquisition of Spanish Null Subjects." In *The Generative Study of Second Language Acquisition*, edited by S. Flynn, G. Martohardjono, and W. O'Neil, 161–83. Hillsdale, NJ: Lawrence Erlbaum.

Ávila-Jiménez, B. 1996. "Subject Pronoun Expression in Puerto Rican Spanish: A Sociolinguistic, Morphological and Discourse Analysis." PhD diss., Cornell University.

Borer, H. 1984. *Parametric Syntax. Case Studies in Semitic and Romance Languages*. Dordrecht, Nld.: Foris.

Bullock, B., and A. J. Toribio 2009. "Reconsidering Dominican Spanish: Data from the Rural Cibao." *Revista Internacional de Linguistica Iberoamericana* 7:49–73.

Cabrera, M. J. 2008. "Null Subject Patterns in Language Contact: The Case of Dominican Spanish." PhD diss., University Microfilm International.

Camacho, J. 2013. *Null Subjects*. Cambridge: Cambridge University Press.

———. 2016. "The Null Subject Parameter Revisited: The Evolution from Null Subject Spanish and Portuguese to Dominican Spanish and Brazilian Portuguese." In *Morphosyntax of Portuguese and Spanish in Latin America*, edited by M. Kato and F. Ordóñez, 27–48. Oxford: Oxford University Press.

Cameron, R. 1993. "Ambiguous Agreement, Functional Compensation, and Nonspecific *tú* in the Spanish of San Juan, Puerto Rico, and Madrid, Spain." *Language Variation and Change* 5 (3): 305–34.

Cardinaletti, A., and M. Starke. 1999. "The Typology of Structural Deficiency. A Case Study of the Three Classes of Pronouns." In *Clitics in the Languages of Europe*, edited by H. van Riemsdijk, 145–233. Berlin: De Gruyter.

Chomsky, N. 1981. *Lectures on Government and Binding*. Dordrecht, Nld.: Foris.

Colantoni, L., A. Cuza, and N. Mazzaro. 2016. "Task-Related Effects in the Prosody of Spanish Heritage Speakers and Long-Term Immigrants." In *Interdisciplinary Approaches to Intonational Grammar in Ibero-Romance Intonation*, edited by M. Armstrong, N. Henriksen, and M. del Mar Vanrell, 3–24. Amsterdam: John Benjamins.

Comínguez, J. Forthcoming. "The Syntax of Interrogative Wh-movement in Puerto Rican Spanish: Empirical Evidence and Theoretical Implications Interrogative." In *Current Research in Puerto Rican Linguistics*, edited by M. González-Rivera. London: Routledge.

Crain, S., and R. Thornton. 1998. *Investigations in Universal Grammar: A Guide to Experiments in the Acquisition of Syntax and Semantics*. Cambridge, MA: MIT Press.

Cuza, A. 2013. "Cross-Linguistic Influence at the Syntax Proper: Interrogative Subject-Verb Inversion in Heritage Spanish." *International Journal of Bilingualism* 17 (1): 71–96.

Cuza, A., and L. Miller. 2015. "The Protracted Acquisition of Past Tense Aspectual Values in Child Heritage Spanish." In *Hispanic Linguistics at the Crossroad: Theoretical Linguistics, Language Acquisition and Language Contact*, edited by R. Klassen, J. Liceras, and E. Valenzuela, 211–30. Amsterdam: John Benjamins.

Cuza, A., and J. Frank. 2015. "On the Role of Experience and Age-Related Effects: Evidence from the Spanish CP." *Second Language Research* 31:3–28.

Cuza, A., A. T. Pérez-Leroux, and L. Sánchez. 2013. "The Role of Semantic Transfer in Clitic-Drop among Simultaneous and Sequential Chinese-Spanish Bilinguals." *Studies in Second Language Acquisition* 35 (1): 93–125.

Cuza, A. and R. Pérez-Tattam. 2015. "Grammatical Gender Selection and Phrasal Word Order in Child Heritage Spanish: A Feature Reassembly Approach." *Bilingualism: Language and Cognition* 19:50–68.

Ellis, N. 2002. "Frequency Effects in Language Processing: A Review with Implications for Theories of Implicit and Explicit Language Acquisition." *Studies in Second Language Acquisition* 24:143–88.

Frascarelli, M. 2007. "Subjects, Topics and the Interpretation of *pro*: A New Approach to the Null Subject Parameter." *Natural Language and Linguistic Theory* 25:691–734.
Givón, T. 1983. *Topic Continuity in Discourse: A Quantitative Cross-Language Study.* Amsterdam: John Benjamins.
Goodall, G. 2011. "Syntactic Satiation and the Inversion Effect in English and Spanish *Wh*-questions." *Syntax* 14:29–47.
Guardado, M., and A. Becker. 2014. "Glued to the Family in Heritage Language Development Strategies." *Journal of Language, Culture and Curriculum* 27 (2): 1–19.
Geeslin, K., and P. Guijarro-Fuentes. 2006. "The Second Language Acquisition of Variable Structures in Spanish by Portuguese Speakers." *Language Learning* 56 (1): 53–107.
Gutiérrez-Bravo, R. 2008. "Topicalization and Preverbal Subjects in Spanish wh-interrogatives." In *Selected Proceedings of the 10th Hispanic Linguistics Symposium*, edited by J. Bruhn de Garavito and E. Valenzuela, 225–36. Somerville, MA: Cascadilla Proceedings Project.
Gürel, A. 2004. "Selectivity in L2-Induced L1 Attrition: A Psycholinguistic Account." *Journal of Neurolinguistics* 17:53–78.
Isabelli, C. 2004. "The Acquisition of the Null Subject Parameter Properties in SLA: Some Effects of Positive Evidence in a Naturalistic Learning Context." *Hispania* 87:150–62.
Jaeggli, O., and K. Safir. 1989. "The Null Subject Parameter and Parametric Theory." In *The Null Subject Parameter*, edited by O. Jaeggli and K. Safir, 1–44. Dordrecht, Nld.: Kluwer Academic Publishers.
Jelinek, E. 1984. "Empty Categories, Case, and Configurationality." *Natural Language and Linguistic Theory* 2:39–76.
Lapidus, N., and R. Otheguy. 2005. "Overt Nonspecific *ellos* in Spanish in New York." *Spanish in Context* 2:157–74.
Liceras, J. M. 1989. "On Some Properties of the Pro-drop Parameter: Looking for Missing Subjects in Non-native Spanish." In *Linguistic Perspectives on Second Language Acquisition*, edited by S. Gass and J. Schacter, 109–33. Dordrecht, Nld.: Foris.
Liceras, J., and L. Díaz. 1999. "Topic-Drop versus Pro-drop: Null Subjects and Pronominal Subjects in the Spanish of Chinese, English, French, German and Japanese Speakers." *Second Language Research* 15:1–40.
Luján, M. 1999. "Expresión y omisión del pronombre personal." In *Gramática descriptiva de la lengua española*, edited by I. Bosque and V. Demonte, 1277–315. Madrid: Espasa-Calpe.
Martínez-Sanz, C. 2011. "Null and Overt Subjects in a Variable System: The Case of Dominican Spanish." PhD thesis, University of Ottawa.
Manzini, M. R., and L. M. Savoia. 2002. "Parameters of Subject Inflection in Italian Dialects." In *Subjects, Expletives and the EPP*, edited by P. Svenonius, 157–99. Oxford: Oxford University Press.
Montrul, S. 2008. *Incomplete Acquisition in Bilingualism: Re-examining the Age Factor*. Amsterdam: John Benjamins.
———. 2009. "Incomplete Acquisition of Tense-Aspect and Mood in Spanish Heritage Speakers." *International Journal of Bilingualism* 13:239–69.
Montrul, S., and C. R. Louro. 2006. "Beyond the Syntax of the Null Subject Parameter: A Look at the Discourse-Pragmatic Distribution of Null and Overt Subjects by L2 Learners of Spanish." In *The Acquisition of Syntax in Romance Languages*, edited by V. Torrens and L. Escobar, 401–18. Amsterdam: John Benjamins.
Montrul, S., R. Foote, and S. Perpiñán 2008. "Gender Agreement in Adult Second Language Learners and Spanish Heritage Speakers: The Effects of Age and Context of Acquisition." *Language Learning* 58:503–53.
Montrul, S., and R. Slabakova 2003. "Competence Similarities between Natives and Near-Native Speakers: An Investigation of the Preterit/Imperfect Contrast in Spanish." *Studies in Second Language Acquisition* 25:351–98.
Ordóñez, F., and A. Olarrea. 2006. "Microvariation in Caribbean/Non Caribbean Spanish Interrogatives." *Probus: International Journal of Latin and Romance Linguistics* 18:59–96.

Ordóñez, F., and E. Treviño. 1999. "Left Dislocated Subjects and the Pro-drop Parameter: A Case Study of Spanish." *Lingua* 107:39–68.

Otheguy, R., A. C. Zentella, and D. Livert. 2007. "Language and Dialect Contact in Spanish in New York: Toward the Formation of a Speech Community." *Language* 83 (4): 770–802.

Otheguy, R., and A. C. Zentella. 2012. *Spanish in New York: Language Contact, Dialectal Leveling, and Structural Continuity*. New York: Oxford University Press.

Paradis, M. 2004. *A Neurolinguistic Theory of Bilingualism*. Amsterdam: John Benjamins.

Pease-Álvarez, L., K. Hakuta, and R. Bayley 1996. "Spanish Proficiency and Language Use in a California Mexicano Community." *Southwest Journal of Linguistics* 15:137–51.

Pérez-Leroux, A. T., A. Cuza, and D. Thomas. 2011. "From Parental Attitudes to Input Condition Spanish-English Bilingual Development in Toronto." In *Bilingual Youth: Spanish in English-Speaking Societies*, edited by K. Potowski and J. Rothman, 49–176. Amsterdam: John Benjamins.

Pérez-Leroux, A. T., and W. Glass. 1999. "Null Anaphora in Spanish Second Language Acquisition: Probabilistic versus Generative Approaches." *Second Language Research* 15 (2): 220–49.

Phinney, M. 1987. "The Pro-drop Parameter in Second Language Acquisition." In *Parameter Setting*, edited by T. Roeper and E. Williams, 221–38. Dordrecht, Nld.: Reidel.

Putnam, M., and L. Sánchez. 2013. "What's so Incomplete about Incomplete Acquisition? A Prolegomenon to Modeling Heritage Language Grammars." *Linguistic Approaches to Bilingualism* 3:478–508.

Quesada, M. 2015. *The L2 Acquisition of Spanish Subjects: Multiple Perspectives*. Berlin: De Gruyter.

Rizzi, L. 1982. *Issues in Italian Syntax*. Dordrecht, Nld.: Foris.

———. 1986. "Null Objects in Italian and the Theory of Pro." *Linguistic Inquiry* (17): 501–557.

Rothman, J. 2009. "Pragmatic Deficits with Syntactic Consequences: L2 Pronominal Subjects and the Syntax Pragmatics Interface." *Journal of Pragmatics* 41:951–73.

Serratrice, L., A. Sorace, and S. Paoli. 2004. "Subjects and Objects in Italian–English Bilingual and Monolingual Acquisition." *Bilingualism: Language and Cognition* 7 (3): 183–206.

Shin, N. L., and R. Otheguy. 2013. "Social Class and Gender Impacting Change in Bilingual Settings: Spanish Subject Pronoun Use in New York." *Language in Society* 42:429–45.

Sorace, A. 2000. "Syntactic Optionality in Non-native Grammars." *Second Language Research* 16 (2): 93–102.

———. 2004. "Native Language Attrition and Developmental Instability at the Syntax Discourse Interface: Data, Interpretations and Methods." *Bilingualism: Language and Cognition* 7:143–45.

———. 2005. "Syntactic Optionality at Interfaces." In *Syntax and Variation: Reconciling the Biological and the Social*, edited by L. Cornips and K. Corrigan, 46–111. Amsterdam: John Benjamins.

Suñer, M., and C. Lizardi. 1995. "Dialectal Variation in an Argumental/Non-argumental Asymmetry in Spanish." In *Contemporary Research in Romance Linguistics*, edited by J. Amastae, G. Goodall, M. Montalbetti, and M. Phinney, 187–91. Dordrecht, Nld.: Foris.

Taraldsen, T. 1978. "On the NIC, Vacuous Application and the *That*-Trace Filter." MS thesis, MIT.

Tsimpli, I. M., A. Sorace, C. Heycock, and F. Filiaci. 2004. "First Language Attrition and Syntactic Subjects: A Study of Greek and Italian Near-Native Speakers of English." *International Journal of Bilingualism* 8:257–77.

Valdés, G. 2001. "Heritage Language Students: Profiles and Possibilities." In *Heritage Languages in America: Preserving a National Resource*, edited by J. Peyton, J. Ranard, and S. McGinnis, 37–80. McHenry, IL: The Center for Applied Linguistics and Delta Systems.

Yang, C. 2002. *Knowledge and Learning in Natural Language*. Oxford: Oxford University Press.

13

Dative Experiencer Predicates in Child Heritage Speakers of Cuban Spanish

DIEGO PASCUAL Y CABO
Texas Tech University

INMACULADA GÓMEZ SOLER
University of Memphis

THE MAIN GOAL OF this chapter is to explore the acquisition and development of Spanish dative experiencer verbs (e.g., *gustar*-like) in Cuban and Cuban American children. To this end, we present production data elicited via a repetition task. Because, as a secondary goal, we are also interested in examining the sources of potential linguistic divergence (albeit indirectly), we compare and analyze the child data with those of two groups of Cuban adults, differing only in their degree of bilingualism (i.e., monolingual Cuban adults versus adult Cuban immigrants to the US) as well as place of residence (i.e., Cuba versus United States). Unlike typical monolingually raised individuals, all bilingual children examined herein grew up in Miami, Florida, a context where Spanish and English coexist, but where, given the unique sociolinguistic and sociopolitical realities of this region, and of the US more broadly, Spanish is considered a minority language (in the face of English, the majority language).

In the context of the US, those who grow up speaking or listening to a language at home (the minority language) other than English (the societal language) are generally referred to as heritage speakers (henceforth HSs; e.g., Valdés 2000, 2001). More specific definitions vary depending on the research questions being asked and the goals of the study. For some, the term HS simply highlights the connections between cultural and linguistic heritage in these individuals (e.g., Fishman 2001). From this perspective, linguistic competence in the heritage language (henceforth HL) is only marginally relevant. For others, actual linguistic and communicative competency in the HL is regarded as the principal criterion for inclusion or exclusion. For our purposes, since we are indeed interested in examining and addressing questions related to the HL linguistic system, we are adopting the narrow definition.

Under this view, most of the evidence provided to date indicates that HS linguistic competence is different from that displayed by monolingual speakers of the same language (e.g., Silva-Corvalán 1994, 2014; Montrul 2004, 2008, 2014). Although the area of morphosyntax stands out as being especially vulnerable (e.g., Cuza and Miller 2015; Cuza and Pérez-Tattam 2015; Montrul 2002, 2009, 2010; Bowles and Montrul 2009; Montrul and Sánchez-Walker 2013; Rothman 2009), vocabulary (e.g., Fairclough 2011), phonetics and phonology (e.g., Amengual 201–2; Henriksen 2015; Rao 2014; Ronquest 2012), and syntax (e.g., Cuza and Camacho, this volume; Cuza 2013; Pascual y Cabo and Gómez Soler 2015) have also been documented as loci for crosslinguistic influence. Said HS linguistic differences, however, do not seem to be uniform across individuals or grammatical domains. In fact, HL-unique developmental features are shaped by a series of factors and conditions that vary from individual to individual. These include but are not limited to (1) age of onset of bilingualism, (2) reduced access to HL input, (3) relative use of the HL (as compared to the societal majority language), (4) lack of formal education in the HL, and (5) attitudes toward the HL within the community, the family, or at the individual level.

HL linguistic competence has been analyzed from two main perspectives. The first of these perspectives, based mainly on linguistic attainment (i.e., incomplete acquisition [Montrul 2008] and L1 attrition [Polinsky 2011]), understand the HL to be the outcome of a process of language loss. From an incomplete acquisition position, the HL does not have the opportunity to develop like it would in a monolingual L1 grammar. That is, due to conditions mainly having to do with input reduction, part of the HL is never acquired. From an L1 attrition standpoint, HL erosion takes place after it had been previously acquired (and mastered). The onset of this process of language loss generally coincides with the onset of schooling, around age five or six.

On the other hand, the second of these perspectives maintains that the observed linguistic outcomes need not be a reflection of language loss or linguistic deficiencies, but rather a byproduct of the unique nature of the acquisition process HSs undergo (e.g., Cuza and Pérez-Tattam 2015; Pascual y Cabo and Rothman 2012; Pires and Rothman 2009; Putnam and Sánchez 2013). Under this approach, the differential nature of the input HSs receive is factored in and thus, the acquisition process is not regarded as interrupted, nor is the end result seen as deficient (Pascual y Cabo 2015).

As discussed, the goal of the present study is to continue down this path of research so as to try to describe and explain some differences in Cuban Spanish HS grammatical knowledge and use of their HL. Particularly, we are interested in Cuban child heritage speakers' production of dative experiencer verbs. We believe this is of interest to the research community for at least three reasons. First, we examine child HSs, an often-overlooked group yet one critical to our understanding of HS bilingual development. Second, we examine a somewhat understudied property in the HS literature in general (and HS children in particular), an illustrative domain of inquiry given the structural differences that exist between Spanish and English (e.g., Parodi-Lewin 1991). Third, we compare and contrast child HS Spanish to child and adult monolingual Spanish, as well as to first-generation immigrant Spanish while controlling for dialect. To this end, we build on previous findings that have shown this property to be vulnerable for crosslinguistic influence in Spanish-English bilingual HSs (e.g., Toribio and Nye 2006; Prada Pérez and Pascual y Cabo 2011; Pascual y Cabo 2013a, b) and discuss the results vis-à-vis accounts that seek to explain said divergence. Among the possibilities, we explore the notions of incomplete acquisition, L1 attrition, and the possibility that cross-generational attrition affects the quality of input that HSs receive (e.g., Montrul 2008; Pires and Rothman 2009; Polinsky 2011; Pascual y Cabo 2013a).[1] Foreshadowing, the data reveal significant variation across child HSs and to a lesser extent among the control groups. While the child HS group's accuracy in production of verbs other than *gustar* is high, they show significant differences in production of *gustar*-like verbs with respect to verb agreement configurations as well as the absence of the dative marker 'a' in obligatory contexts. As will be made clear in subsequent sections, we chose to study these two particular properties given *gustar* verbs' atypical reverse mapping of arguments to syntactic positions (e.g., Parodi-Lewin 1991) as well as the documented low perceptual salience of the case marker 'a' (Bowles and Montrul 2009). Interestingly, monolingual children show similar trends, but not as marked as the experimental group. Monolingual adults' accuracy is generally at ceiling across both verb types. Crucially for our purposes, adult first-generation immigrants (main HS input providers) exhibit some level of variation, but unlike their child counterparts, it is only in the production of the dative marker 'a'. Given these results, we will argue that the erosion of the dative marker in the input HSs receive is at least partially responsible for the HS linguistic outcomes observed. Considering this, we will also argue that the differences we observe are not a result of incomplete acquisition, but rather of variability in input received from immigrant–native speaker sources, which is testable in this domain.

Dative Experiencer Predicates

Experiencer predicates, also known as psychological verbs (or psych verbs), express either a mental state or an event. These verbs subcategorize for the arguments of an experiencer and a theme and are categorized into three classes according to the different types of mapping of these theta roles to syntactic positions (Belletti and Rizzi 1987; Parodi-Lewin 1991; Franco and Huidobro 2003, 2007). Class I represents a direct mapping since it includes transitive verbs that subcategorize for an experiencer subject and a theme object such as *odiar* (to hate; example 13.1).

Example 13.1. Class I verbs

Belén ***odia*** *las manzanas.*
Belén-NOM hate-3SG. apples-ACC
Belén **hates** apples.

On the other hand, class II represents a reversed mapping with respect to class I since the experiencer maps onto the object and the theme maps onto the subject position (example 13.2). Class II encodes predicates such as *asustar* (to scare) or *molestar* (to bother).

Example 13.2. Class II verbs

Paula ***asusta*** *a Carlos.*
Paula-NOM scare-3SG. to Carlos
Paula **scares** Carlos.

These verbs exhibit a hybrid behavior (Arad 1998; Landau 2010; Pesetsky 1995) since they can alternate between having an agentive or eventive or a stative interpretation. According to Arad (1998) a sentence like the one in example 13.2 can have an agentive reading if Paula intentionally did something to cause Carlos to be scared. On the other hand, the eventive reading could result from a situation in which Paula scared Carlos unintentionally. These two readings are indistinguishable in morphosyntactic terms. Additionally, class II can have a stative interpretation when there is neither an agent nor a change of state involved in the event. Rather, there is a perception by the experiencer that causes the experiencer to be in a specific mental state (Pylkkänen 1997; example 13.3). As can be seen below, the stative reading of class II overlaps morphosyntactically with class III.

Example 13.3. Stative reading of class II verbs

A Paula le ***asusta*** *Carlos.*
To Paula-DAT. le-DAT. scare-3SG. Carlos
Carlos **scares** Paula.

Class III includes verbs of unaccusative nature such as *gustar* (to like) or *encantar* (to love). These verbs subcategorize for a dative experiencer object and a nominative theme that controls verbal agreement and acts therefore as the structural subject. The dative experiencer, which functions as the logical subject of the sentence, is obligatorily doubled by a dative clitic and, when spelled out, it must also be preceded by the dative marker 'a' (example 13.4).

Example 13.4. Class III verbs

Los deportes le ***gustan*** *a Rosa.*
Rosa le* ***gustan* *los deportes.*
A Rosa le ***gustan*** *los deportes.*
To Rosa le like-3PL. the sports
Rosa **likes** sports. / Sports **are pleasing** to Rosa.

As can be seen in example 13.4a–c, class III (and stative class II) predicates present an additional peculiarity: their flexible word order configurations. While experiencer-verb-theme (13.4c) is the unmarked order, theme-verb-experiencer (13.4a) is also pragmatically appropriate depending on discourse conditions (Franco and Huidobro 2003, 2007; Gómez Soler 2012a, 2014)

To be clear, the present study focuses on class III and its overlap with class II. The learning puzzle resides in the noncanonical mapping of thematic roles to syntactic positions in these two groups of verbs, which also results in an unorthodox set of agreement relations in which the dative experiencer agrees with the dative clitic and the verb agrees with the theme. In English, on the other hand, verbal agreement is always controlled by the preverbal argument (example 13.5).[2]

Example 13.5.

> Carmen **likes** sweets.
> Carmen like-3SG. sweets

Additionally, English and Spanish also differ in the morphosyntactic spell-out of these verbs. English lacks dative experiencer subjects and dative clitics as well as the equivalent of the preposition 'a'. Finally, English, unlike Spanish, does not allow flexible word order configurations and always exhibits SVO order.

Previous Studies on the Acquisition of Dative Experiencer Verbs

Because the current study explores the grammars of monolingual and bilingual children as well as bilingual adults, we will review the literature on both child and adult acquisition of dative experiencer predicates in both monolingual and bilingual contexts.

Monolingual Acquisition

Most studies examining acquisition of *gustar*-like predicates have targeted monolingual speakers with some sort of pathological condition such as aphasias or Alzheimer (e.g., Beretta and Campbell 2001; Manovilidou 2008; Thompson and Lee 2009). Results from these and other related studies have consistently demonstrated that these verbs are problematic for these populations. Equivalent conclusions have been reported when testing monolingual children without any linguistic or cognitive impairment. For example, Lord (1979) and Figueira (1984) independently showed that both monolingual English and Portuguese child speakers produce a high rate of agreement errors.

In the particular case of Spanish, Gómez Soler (2011) reports that, in an analysis of spontaneous speech from the CHILDES database, children apparently start producing *gustar* constructions target-like at an early age (approximately at age 1;10). Although some errors related to agreement and choice (or absence) of the clitic are reported, these seem to dissipate by age 2;7. This pattern is confirmed by a comprehension study conducted with 3- and 4-year-old monolingual speakers of Peninsular Spanish in which children performed successfully in a truth-value judgment task (Gómez Soler 2012b). Alternatively, in an experimental study that analyzed children's responses to two comprehension tasks, Torrens, Escobar, and Wexler (2006) argue that it is not until much later (the age of 6;0 approximately) that Spanish monolingual children start having knowledge of this type of predicate. Although in general Gómez Soler (2011, 2012b) found high accuracy in *gustar*-like constructions at a very early age, it is not completely clear how productive a construction actually is. In other words, one cannot preclude some uses based on unanalyzed chunking. In spite of these conflicting claims, it is not unreasonable to believe that this is a later acquired property, certainly later than normal agentive-type predicates, which are fully productive very early in Spanish (as in other languages).

Bilingual Acquisition

In her study of the English-Spanish bilingual siblings Nico and Bresnan, Silva-Corvalán (2014) reports similar errors to the ones presented in Gómez Soler (2011) related to agreement and clitic misuse. Silva-Corvalán (2014) argues that the effect of English in this case causes a delay in bilingual children's target use of dative experiencer predicates, which start at age 3;9, later than monolingual children as reported in Gómez Soler (2011).

A number of studies have looked into adult heritage speaker acquisition of dative experiencer predicates. These studies attest that these predicates pose certain learnability problems for HSs, which are evidenced in several patterns not exhibited by monolingual speakers such as (1) omission of the preposition *a*, (2) use of an invariable clitic *le*, and (3) use of an invariable third-person singular verb (e.g., *gusta*). All these strategies converge on the same goal: a reversal toward a more transparent mapping of thematic roles to syntactic positions similar to class I verbs (e.g., *odiar*) and to English psych verbs (e.g., to like). Dvorak and Kirschner's (1982) study of Puerto Rican HSs in New York City found evidence for the use of invariable *le*. That is, speakers tended to use the singular clitic irrespective of the number of the experiencer. Additionally, there was evidence of omission of the case marker *a*, and a pattern of verbal agreement controlled by the experiencer instead of the theme. Toribio and Nye (2006) explored HSs' comprehension and production of dative experiencer verbs via a scalar grammaticality judgment task and an elicited written production task. Like Dvorak and Kirschner (1982), they also found evidence for the so-called invariable *le*, that is, a less categorical rejection of *le* with plural experiencers than *les* with singular experiencers. Toribio and Nye concluded that the HSs had mastered properties of the core grammar such as agreement and case but they still exhibited nontarget behavior in the properties that relate to interfaces, both the syntax-pragmatics interface (i.e., the constant preference for preverbal experiencers) and the syntax-lexicon interface (i.e., the restructuring of the argument structure toward a more transparent mapping: they mapped the animate argument to the structural subject position and the inanimate argument to the structural object position). Prada Pérez and Pascual y Cabo (2011) studied clitic and subject agreement in dative experiencer predicates through a scalar grammaticality judgment task. Unlike Toribio and Nye (2006), they did not find evidence for invariable *le* nor for a tendency to restructure the argument structure of these predicates. However, they found empirical support for invariable *gusta*, that is, the use of the third-person singular form regardless of the number of the experiencer. They ascribed this behavior to a process of morphological simplification of the verbal paradigm. Of particular interest to the present study are the findings of Pascual y Cabo (2013a) since, as is also the case herein, he examined Cuban HSs' knowledge and use of dative experiencer verbs and proposed that class III predicates have undergone a reanalysis in heritage grammars that allows them to alternate between agentive or eventive and stative readings in the same way class II predicates do.[3] Because one of the ways to test this distinction is by the availability of the passive with class II (as in example 13.6) but not with class III verbs (as in example 13.7), he predicts that HSs will accept passive constructions with class III verbs if, in fact, they can project an optional agentive syntax for class III psych verbs. In other words, this optionality emerges as a grammatical reflex of the abovementioned syntactic shift.

Example 13.6. Class II psych verb sample token

Nícola ***fue asustada*** *por Pau.*
Nícola **was scared** by Pau.

Example 13.7. Class III psych verb sample token

(*)*La película* ***fue gustada*** *por Teo.*
The movie **was liked** by Teo.

Pascual y Cabo's hypothesis found support in the results of a grammaticality judgment task that showed that HSs tend to accept passivization with class III predicates, a process categorically rejected by monolingual Spanish speakers of the same dialect. These results are taken to indicate that the classification of these predicates in HS grammars may be undergoing a process of restructuration.

Relatedly, Montrul (2016) examined the incipient loss of dative case in Mexican Spanish by contrasting lexical (e.g., dative experiencer verbs) and structural (e.g., indirect objects) dative case. She tested three groups of bilingual speakers in the US and two monolingual control groups. Her findings reveal high rates of erosion of the lexical dative case across all groups, as evidenced by the acceptance of ungrammatical sentences lacking the dative marker 'a,' probably due to its low phonological salience (e.g., Bowles and Montrul 2009). This nonstandard outcome was consistent with the following two nonexclusive explanations: input differences due to attrition in the first-generation immigrant group, and changes in progress in monolingual varieties accelerated in a language contact situation (Silva-Corvalán 1994).

Motivation and Research Questions

Broadly, this study attempts to refine our understanding of the linguistic mechanisms that underlie HS grammars and of the factors that shape HS language development. More specifically, we aim to shed light on the acquisition, development, and maintenance of *gustar*-like verbs among Cuban American (Spanish-English) bilingual children.

The research questions that guide our study are the following: Do child HSs and Spanish monolingual speakers exhibit differences with regard to their production of *gustar*-like verbs? And if so, what do their patterns of use look like for the specific cases of verbal agreement and obligatory use of dative marker 'a'?

According to previous findings (Pascual y Cabo 2013a, b; Prada Pérez and Pascual y Cabo, 2011; Toribio and Nye 2006), we hypothesize that bilingual children will show differences from monolingual norms for *gustar*-like verbs and for the properties associated with them. Specifically, we predict that bilingual children will have a tendency to analyze the sentence initial argument (experiencer) as the structural subject of the sentence yielding, therefore, nonstandard verb agreement uses whenever there is a subject-object number mismatch. Furthermore, bilingual HS children will also have a tendency to omit the dative marker 'a' in obligatory contexts. Considering recent findings in this particular domain (Montrul 2016), it is also possible that we will see innovation with *gustar*-like verbs in the production of monolingual adults as well as first-generation immigrants.

As we see it, the present experiment provides an advantage over most previous studies examining HS bilingual development in that, in addition to controlling for potential dialectal variation, we present novel data from monolingual children as well as child and adult HSs using the same task. We believe this allows us to explore in more detail the role that linguistic input plays in shaping heritage grammars. In the next section, we present the specific details of the current study.

The Study

Participants

Forty-eight participants completed the study. Participants were classified into four groups according to age and linguistic background: monolingual children, child HSs, monolingual adults, and adult immigrants. As discussed, we controlled for dialect so all our participants were either Cuban or of Cuban descent. That is, the monolingual participants were from Havana and its surrounding areas (Cuba) and reported having very minimal knowledge of a foreign language. The bilingual groups (adult immigrants and child HSs) were Cubans and Cuban Americans respectively.

In terms of age of acquisition of Spanish, all participants acquired Spanish from birth and reported using it on a daily basis in a wide variety of contexts. With regard to English, the group of adult bilinguals reported having been born and raised in Cuba (as monolingual Spanish speakers) and only coming into contact with English after they immigrated to the US after the age of 15. At the time of data collection, they had all resided in the US for at least 10 years (average 24;1 years). The child HSs, on the other hand, had all been exposed to Spanish and English from birth and were therefore simultaneous bilinguals. A standardized proficiency measure (i.e., a modified version of the DELE [*Diploma de español como lengua extranjera*, 'Certificate of Spanish as a Foreign Language']) was used to get an accurate proficiency score in Spanish for the two adult groups. This test consists of a vocabulary section and a grammar section and it is widely used in the fields of second and heritage language acquisition (see Montrul and Slabakova 2003). The monolingual adults (M = 46.9 (2.04)) performed slightly better than the adult immigrants (M = 44.8 (1.84)) but not significantly so. Additionally, we collected self-ratings of proficiency for all adult groups. In the case of the children groups, their parents or caretakers provided a rating for them. As was the case for the two adult groups, the monolingual children's overall score for Spanish was native-like. That said, Spanish proficiency for the child HSs was considerably lower ($M = 6.9$ (3.1)). With respect to English proficiency ratings, the monolingual adults reported very minimal or no knowledge of the language ($M = 1.87$ (1.78)) while the child HSs' ($M = 8.45$ (1.88)) and the immigrants' scores ($M = 7.3$ (2.66)) were much higher. Notice that for the child HSs, English was rated higher than Spanish while the opposite is true for the adult immigrants. For clarity, a summary of the background information is reported in table 13.1.

Table 13.1. Participants' profiles

	Monolingual children *n* = 9	**Child HSs** *n* = 11	**Monolingual adults** *n* = 16	**Adult immigrants** *n* = 13
Age	7–11 *(avg. 8.77)*	8–11 *(avg. 8.66)*	18–71 *(avg. 37.1)*	28–59 *(avg. 32.5)*
Age of onset				
Spanish	From birth	From birth	From birth	From birth
English	NA	From birth	NA	20.3
DELE score	NA	NA	46.9 (2.04)	44.8 (1.84)
Self-ratings				
Spanish (10 max.)	9.2 (0.41)	6.9 (3.1)	9.6 (0.56)	9.8 (0.31)
English (10 max.)	NA	8.45(1.88)	1.87 (1.78)	7.3 (2.66)

Methodology

To specifically test children's knowledge and use of dative experiencer verbs (though adults also completed this task) data were elicited using a semi-interactive puppet show in Spanish, which is essentially a repetition task (Austin, Blume, and Sánchez 2013). The idea behind a repetition task of this sort is, as Crain and Thornton put it, to see whether children can correctly repeat sentences presented to them, or whether they change the input sentences and reformulate them in some other way (1998, 71). Similar experimental protocols have proven to be critical in assessing language skills in children (Pérez-Leroux, Cuza, and Thomas 2011).

Prior to the completion of the task, informants were introduced to the three puppet characters (Mario, Ana, and *abuela* [Grandma]) and trained on the task at hand. Two of these puppets (Mario and Ana) appeared conversing on a computer screen. A third puppet (Grandma), an older adult with hearing problems, was responsible for engaging the informants in conversation. The adult puppet is watching the video recordings but has difficulties hearing and understanding what the other puppets are saying. Participants were asked to help the older adult by repeating what the young child puppet had said. The logic of the task is as follows: the ungrammatical instances provided by the puppets should be corrected for grammar when reported by the child, unless the structure is in fact not ungrammatical for them. In other words, if there are changes, these will be indicative of the underlying grammar (Crain and Thornton 1998). Hispanic bilingual children have been shown to do just this in the very same methodological design used by Austin, Blume, and Sánchez (2013) for a series of properties in ongoing work on child HS syntactic development. As was also the case in their experiment, in some cases, the HS children tested here provided more than one utterance as their answer. In such cases, all utterances were coded and analyzed.

In order to consistently show the same interaction across all participants, these conversations had been previously video recorded. The recording lasted a total of six minutes and nine seconds. The first thirty-five seconds were used for instructions. The remainder of the recording included a total of thirteen short conversations. Between one conversation and the next, there was a six-second pause, time used to engage the child in conversation. Of these thirteen conversations, eight included critical items and five were used as distracters. The eight conversations that included the critical items were distributed among two conditions, differing from each other regarding verb agreement configurations. First, participants were presented with six conversations that targeted prescriptively grammatical sentences with the verb *gustar*. Of these six conversations, three included a final sentence that contained a 1stSG experiencer-3rdSG theme (as in example 13.8 below) and three included a final sentence that contained a 1stSG experiencer-3rdPL theme (as in example 13.9 below).

Example 13.8.

MARIO: *Hola Ana, ¿cómo estás?*
Hi Ana, how are you?

ANA: *Estoy muy bien.*
I am very well.

MARIO: *¿Por qué? ¿qué pasó?*
How come?

ANA: *Hoy mi madre compró mucho chocolate y, ¿sabes qué? A mí me gusta el chocolate.*
Today my mother bought a lot of chocolate and you know what, I like chocolate.

GRANDMOTHER: *Ay, no lo escucho. ¿Qué dijo?*
Agh, I can't hear, what did she say?

CHILD: ___________________

Example 13.9.

ANA: *Hola Mario, ¿cómo estás?*
Hi Mario, how are you?

MARIO: *No estoy bien.*
I am not well.

ANA: *¿Por qué? ¿qué pasó?*
How come?

MARIO: *Hoy mi madre hizo empanadas para comer y, ¿sabes qué? a mí no me gustan las empanadas.*
Today my mother made empanadas for lunch and you know what, I do not like empanadas.

GRANDMOTHER: *Ay, no lo escucho. ¿Qué dijo?*
Agh, I can't hear, what did he say?

CHILD: ___________________

The remaining two conversations presented an ungrammatical use of *gustar* with a nominative preverbal experiencer and an invariable third-person form of the verb *gustar* with a plural theme. Consider example 13.10 below.

Example 13.10.

MARIO: *Hola Ana, ¿cómo estás?*
Hi Ana, how are you?

ANA: *No estoy bien.*
I am not well.

MARIO: *¿Por qué? ¿qué pasó?*
How come?

ANA: *Hoy mi madre me dijo que no podia jugar con las muñecas, ¿sabes qué? *yo me *gusta las muñecas.*
Today my mother told me that I could not play with my dolls and you know what, I like. 3rd SG my dolls.

GRANDMOTHER: *Ay, no lo escucho. ¿Qué dijo?*
Agh, I can't hear, what did she say?

CHILD: ___________________

The five remaining distracter items targeted ungrammatical tokens due to subject-verb agreement with verbs other than *gustar*. That is, these tokens tested whether the invariable third-person singular form attested with *gustar*-like verbs in Prada Pérez and Pascual y Cabo (2011) also expanded to other types of verbs. The verbs used in these conversations were *comer* (to eat), *correr* (to run), and *montar* (to ride). Example 13.11 below offers a representative example of a distracter item.

Example 13.11.

MARIO: *Hola Ana, ¿cómo estás?*
Hi Ana, how are you?

ANA: *Estoy regular, un poco triste.*
I am so-so, a little sad.

MARIO: *¿Por qué? ¿qué pasó?*
How come?

ANA: *Hoy mi madre me hizo un pastel y, ¿sabes qué? mis hermanos *come todo el pastel.*

Today my mother made me a cake, and you know what, my brothers *ate 3rd SG the whole cake.

GRANDMOTHER: *Ay, no lo escucho. ¿Qué dijo?*

Agh, I can't hear. What did she say?

CHILD: ________________

Results

Next, we report the data obtained via the elicited production task described above. Recall that participants were asked to repeat grammatical as well as ungrammatical sentences presented to them. In the case of the ungrammatical sentences, participants were expected to reformulate the input provided so as to make it grammatical. As discussed, we believe this experiment to be adequate to test production of *gustar*-like verbs, particularly with children, because we do not expect them to repeat the ungrammatical input, unless this in fact matches their mental representation. Also, the children's lack of metalinguistic knowledge of the property being examined adds credence to this statement.

We explored three main variables. The first one, accuracy, refers to whether a sentence was grammatical or ungrammatical. Then we examined two more-specific variables dealing with the particular difficulties participants could face while completing the task: verb agreement, which refers to standard or nonstandard verbal agreement, and dative marker, which examined the absence or presence of the dative marker 'a' in obligatory contexts. We ran three different analyses to explore these three variables. We will start by analyzing accuracy and then proceed to the description and analysis of the other two.

Figure 13.1 below illustrates average percentage of accuracy for each of the four groups examined, which from left to right are: monolingual adults, monolingual children, bilingual heritage children, and bilingual immigrant adults. The columns in grey represent the percentage of accuracy in production of *gustar*-like verbs. The columns in black represent the percentage of accuracy with regard to verbs other than *gustar*. Often times our participants produced a combination of noncanonical uses of *gustar*-like verbs within the same sentence (e.g., **y ella le gusta las muñecas*, 'And she likes the dolls'). For our purpose, those cases were only tallied once in the calculations we present here.

Next, to better understand these results, we present a detailed description of the statistical analysis conducted for accuracy. We ran a 4 (group) × 2 (verb type) mixed-design ANOVA with group (monolingual adults, immigrant adults, child monolinguals, child heritage speakers) as the between-subjects variable and verb type (*gustar*-like or verbs other than *gustar*) as the within-subjects variable. The dependent variable tested was accuracy. The results revealed a main effect for group ($F(3, 45) = 16.030$, $p < 0.001$), verb type ($F(1, 45) = 67.198$, $p < 0.001$), and an interaction between verb type and group ($F(3, 45) = 10.360$, $p < 0.001$).

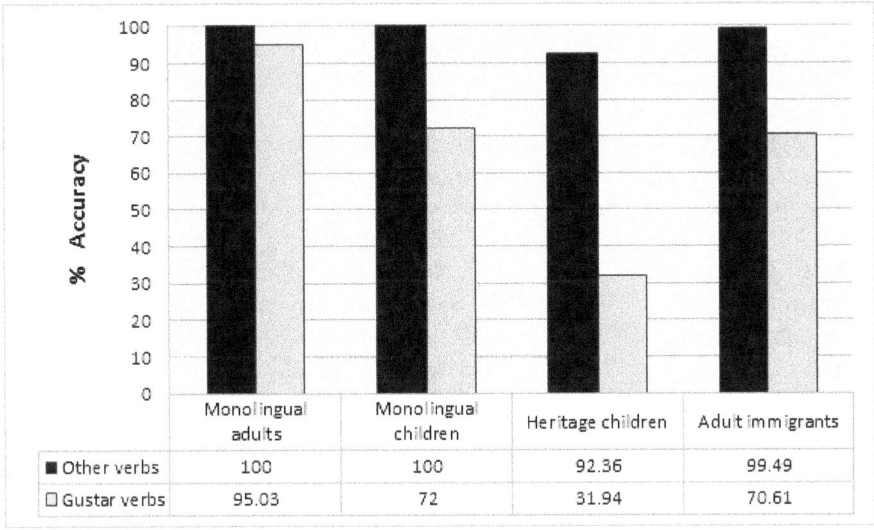

Figure 13.1. Percentage of accurate uses of gustar vs. other verbs

As can be seen in the two black columns in the middle of figure 13.1, both the monolingual child group and the heritage child group produced finite clauses with verbs other than *gustar* very accurately, 100 percent and 92.36 percent respectively. These results are of utmost importance for the present study as they clearly show that the children do not just repeat the ungrammatical properties presented to them, but rather reformulate them and make them grammatical.[4]

Elevated accuracy percentages are also observed in the columns on the far right (first-generation immigrant adults) and far left (monolingual adults), 99.49 percent and 100 percent respectively. The high accuracy exhibited by all groups for this specific condition is taken to indicate that, in general, all groups share similar full-fledged grammars, at least as it pertains to this particular group of predicates (i.e., canonical agentive predicates). On the other hand, performance accuracy for *gustar*-like verbs is visibly lower for all groups. That said, this drop in accuracy is not as marked for the monolingual adult group (whose overall percentage decreases from 100 percent to 95.03 percent, which is not significant [$p = 0.440$]) as compared to the other groups (monolingual children $p = 0.002$; child HSs $p < 0.001$; adult immigrants $p < 0.001$).

Pairwise comparisons examining the variable of group with *gustar* verbs indicate that the heritage child group stands out as different from all other groups to a level of significant difference (monolingual adult, mean difference = –0.631, $p < 0.001$, 95 percent CI –0.828, –0.434, $d = 2.42$; adult immigrant, mean difference = –0.387, $p < 0.001$, 95 percent CI –0.593, –0.180, $d = 1.26$; monolingual child, mean difference = –0.401, $p = 0.001$, 95 percent CI –0.627, –0.174, $d = 1.2$). Monolingual children, on the other hand, differ from monolingual adults (mean difference = –0.230, $p = 0.032$, 95 percent CI –0.440, –0.020, $d = 1.05$) and from heritage children (mean difference = –0.401, $p = 0.001$, 95 percent CI –0.627, –0.174, $d = 1.2$) but not from the immigrant group (mean difference = 0.014, p = 0.898, 95 percent CI –0.204, 0.232, d = 0.05). Crucially, in addition to being different from both child groups, monolingual adults differ from the immigrant group (mean difference = –0.244, p = 0.012, 95 percent CI –0.432, –0.056, d = 1.38)

With regard to accuracy in production of verbs other than *gustar*, only the heritage child group was found to differ from the other three groups to a statistically significant degree (monolingual adult, mean difference = –0.076, p = 0.005, 95 percent CI –0.128, –0.025; adult immigrant, mean difference = –0.071, p = 0.011, 95 percent CI –0.25, –0.017; monolingual child, mean difference = –0.076, p = 0.012, 95 percent CI –0.135, –0.017). That said, it should be noted that HS children are still showing 94.02 percent accuracy. With regard to accuracy of production of *gustar*-like verbs, we observe much greater differences between the groups.

Next, we move on to examining the specific factors that we believe contribute to these accuracy rates. For this purpose, in table 13.2 we present the descriptive statistics for verb agreement both with *gustar* and with verbs other than *gustar* as well as for dative marker. This will illustrate more clearly where the differences in accuracy lay between the groups and how the difficulties related to agreement and the dative marker are distributed within each group. The data are presented by group, which from top to bottom are: monolingual adults, monolingual children, immigrant adults, and heritage children.

Table 13.2. Descriptive statistics for verb agreement and dative marker

	Verb agreement				Dative marker	
	Other		Gustar			
	Mean	SD	Mean	SD	Mean	SD
Monolingual adult	100	0	96.96	5.4	91.67	26
Monolingual child	99.47	1.5	97.73	11	76.59	27
Adult immigrant	100	0	94.34	7.5	70.84	28
Heritage child	92.36	13	66.33	31	44.16	50

As can be seen, verb agreement does not seem to constitute a problem with verbs other than *gustar* since all groups, HS children included, reveal over 90 percent accuracy ratings. With respect to *gustar* verbs, the monolingual adult group performs at 96.96 percent in terms of accuracy of verb agreement and shows some omissions of the dative marker (91.67 percent). The monolingual children and the adult immigrants generally pattern together: their verb agreement accuracy rate is fairly high (97.73 percent and 94.34 percent respectively) and, interestingly, most of their errors corresponded to the omission of dative marker ‘a’ in obligatory contexts (76.59 percent and 70.84 percent respectively). Examples of this pattern of use include the following: **Ella no le gusta el pescado* (She does not like fish) and * *Él no le gusta el pastel* (he does not like cake). Like monolingual children and immigrant adults, HS children omitted the dative marker 'a' in obligatory contexts but in an even more systematic fashion (44.16 percent). Unlike any of the other three groups, however, they also revealed having problems producing verb agreement accurately (66.33 percent), especially in instances in which the theme was plural but the experiencer was singular. In other words, HS children have a tendency to produce a singular form of the verb even when the subject is plural (i.e., invariable *gusta*), a finding already documented in Spanish HL acquisition (e.g., Prada Pérez and Pascual y Cabo 2011).

Next, in order to explore verb agreement, we ran another 4 × 2 mixed-design ANOVA with group as the between-subjects variable, verb type as the within-subjects variable, and verb agreement as the dependent variable. The results revealed a main effect for group ($F(3, 45) = 15.34$, $p < 0.001$) and verb type ($F(1, 45) = 14.22$, $p < 0.001$), and an interaction between verb type and group ($F(3, 45) = 3.49$, $p = 0.023$).

Pairwise comparisons indicate that, in terms of agreement, the child HSs performed significantly differently from all groups with verbs other than *gustar* (monolingual adult, mean difference = –0.076, p = 0.004, 95 percent CI –0.128, 0.025; monolingual children, mean difference = –0.071, p = 0.019, 95 percent CI –0.130, –0.012; immigrant adult, mean difference = –0.076, p = 0.006, 95 percent CI –0.130, –0.023). The two adult groups did not differ from each other (4.649E–16, p = 1, 95 percent CI –0.049, 0.049) or from the monolingual child group (monolingual adult, mean difference = 0.005, p = 0.846, 95 percent CI –0.049, –0.060; adult immigrant, mean difference = 0.005, p = 0.852, 95 percent CI –0.051, 0.062). The pattern of comparisons for the agreement of *gustar* verbs is exactly the same as the one for verbs other than *gustar*, with child HSs differing from all groups (monolingual adult, mean difference = –0.306, p < 0.001, 95 percent CI –0.435, –0.178, d = 1.36; monolingual children, mean difference = –0.254, p = 0.001, 95 percent CI –0.402, –0.106, d = 1.08; immigrant adult, mean difference = –0.280, p < 0.001, 95 percent CI 0.415, –0.146, d = 1.23). The monolingual adults and the adult immigrants (mean difference = 0.026, p = 0.669, 95 percent CI –0.096,0.149, d = 0.4) as well as the monolingual children and the adult groups (monolingual adult, mean difference = 0.052, p = 0.445, 95 percent CI –0.082, –0.189, d = 0.6; adult immigrant, mean difference = –0.026, p = 0.714, 95 percent CI –0.168, 0.116, d = 0.28), showed the same use of agreement relations.

Finally, we explored the variable dative marker. The outcome of a within-subjects one-way ANOVA examining accuracy in production of the dative marker 'a' indicates that there was a main effect for dative marker ($F(1, 46) = 15.95$, $p < 0.001$). Additionally, we found an effect across groups ($F(3, 43) = 3.987$, $p = 0.014$). Child HSs differed significantly from both monolingual children (mean difference = –0.32431, p = 0.042, 95 percent CI –0.6360, –0.0126, d = 0.79) and adults (mean difference = –0.47511, p = 0.001, 95 percent CI –0.7545, –0.1957, d = 1.17) but, crucially, not from the adult immigrant group (mean difference = –0.26686, p = 0.065, 95 percent CI –0.5510, 0.0172, d = 0.65). Additionally, as will be further discussed in the next section, the large effect-size values observed particularly between the two adult groups (d = 0.76) are of importance to the present study as they reveal robust differences with regard to accuracy in production of dative marker 'a' in obligatory contexts (e.g., Plonsky 2015).

We next present in figures 13.2–13.5 below the individual performance averages by group and sentence type. The average ratings for *gustar*-like sentences are marked with a black circle. The average ratings for sentences including verbs other than *gustar* are marked with a grey square.

At the individual level, all participants performed similarly with verbs other than *gustar*: their accuracy was generally at ceiling and they exhibited very little to no variation. However, the four groups presented very different patterns of individual variation with regard to their use of *gustar*-like verbs. On the one hand, all monolingual adults performed above the 80 percent accuracy rate with ten out of sixteen (that is, 62.5 percent of the monolingual adults) reaching the 100 percent accuracy level. On the other hand, we see a higher rate of individual variation in the other three groups. For example, the monolingual children's individual scores are scattered across the whole scale, with three children performing at 100 percent accuracy, four children scoring between 50 and 90 percent, and two performing below the 30 percent rate. With respect to the immigrant group, almost half of the participants (46 percent) were 100 percent accurate with *gustar*, five were above the 70 percent level, and only two fell below the 40 percent level of accuracy. Finally, heritage children showed the highest rate of variation with only one subject performing at ceiling, six of them (60 percent of the participants in this group) scoring below 20 percent accuracy, and only three subjects scoring between 50 and 80 percent accuracy.

To sum up, in this section we have shown that all groups were more accurate with verbs that do not belong to the *gustar* category (although this difference is not significant for the monolingual adults). With respect to their uses of *gustar*, we identify three main patterns: (1) monolingual adults were highly accurate and only exhibited minimal deviations from the expected behavior, (2) immigrant adults and monolingual children had more difficulties than the monolingual adults and their performance errors were mostly related to the absence of the preposition 'a' in obligatory contexts (although some agreement errors were also present in their data), and (3) heritage speaker children had the lowest accuracy rates as well as the highest

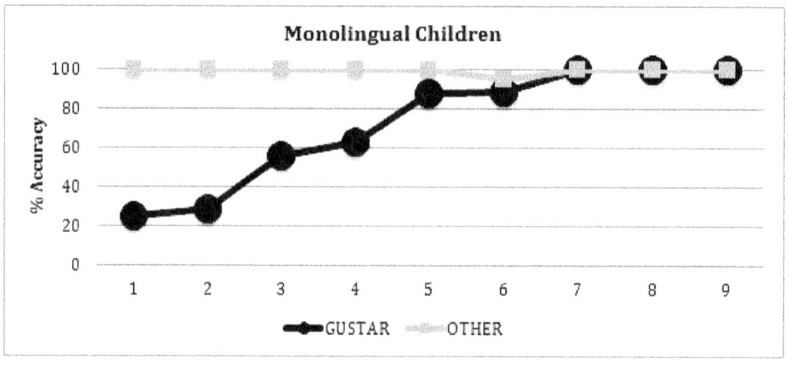

Figure 13.2. Monolingual children's individual results

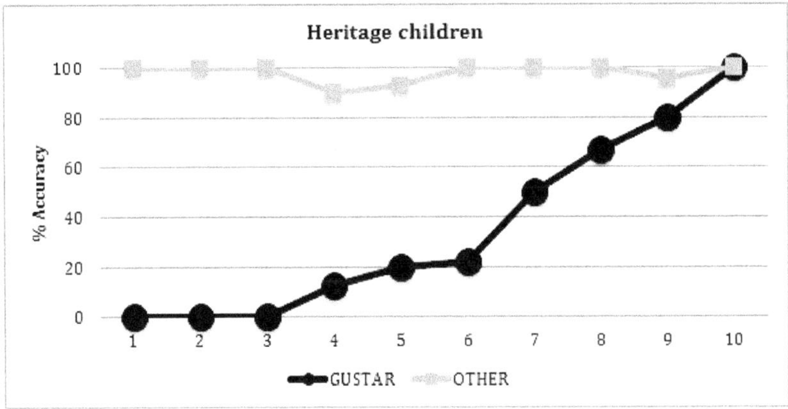

Figure 13.3. Heritage children's individual results

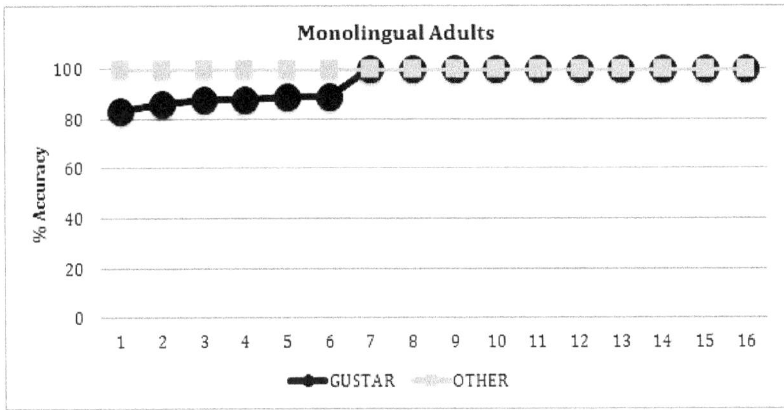

Figure 13.4. Monolingual adults' individual results

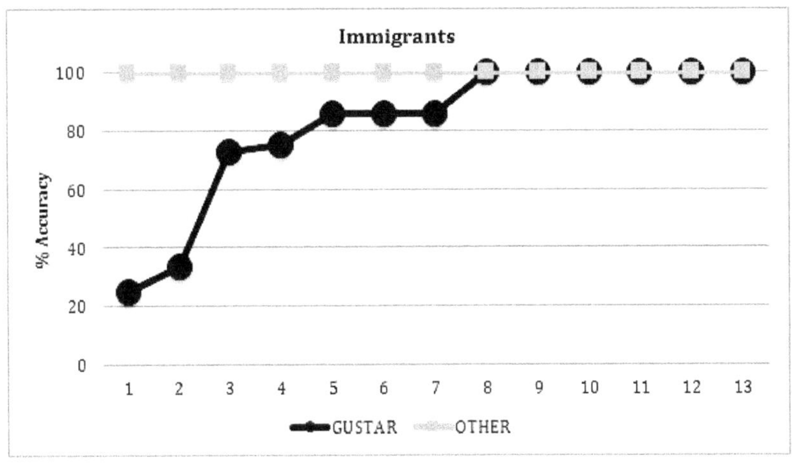

Figure 13.5. Immigrants' individual results

rate of interspeaker variation. Furthermore, in addition to exhibiting significantly higher rates of omission of 'a' in obligatory contexts (much more marked than the other groups), they also experienced more problems with verb agreement. Next, we proceed to provide a detailed analysis of the data.

Discussion and Conclusion

In this study, we set out to investigate how Cuban children and Cuban child heritage speakers use dative experiencer verbs. To this end, we created an experiment that elicited production of *gustar*-like verbs in different contexts and forms. A total of forty-eight participants distributed into four groups (monolingual adults, monolingual children, bilingual immigrant adults, and bilingual heritage children) completed this task and produced a total of 1,169 sentences. The ensuing dataset was submitted to statistical analysis to determine differences within and across groups.

The main research question we explored was whether Cuban child heritage speakers and Cuban Spanish monolingual children (as well as the two adult control groups) differed in their production of *gustar*-like verbs. We predicted that bilingual children would show differences from monolingual norms for *gustar*-like verbs and for the properties associated with them. As described in the previous section, this prediction has found support in the data. More generally, the analysis of accuracy between *gustar*-like verbs and verbs other than *gustar* shows some interesting differences among the participant groups: all groups performed more accurately with the non-*gustar* verbs than with *gustar*-like verbs, including the two monolingual groups. This difference, however, was not significant for the monolingual adults. Particularly, child HSs' productions of sentences with *gustar*- and non-*gustar* verbs revealed the most extreme differences (31.94 percent versus 92.36 percent). This is not surprising given that *gustar*-like verbs are inherently complex because of their noncanonical thematic and agreement relations, and that they have been documented to pose challenges to various populations of speakers such as L1 learners (e.g., Torrens, Escobar, and Wexler 2006), L2 learners (e.g., White et al. 1999), HSs (e.g., Pascual y Cabo 2013a), and speakers with pathological conditions (e.g., Thompson and Lee 2009). Note that although we also see some divergent uses of *gustar* among monolingual children, their accuracy rate is much higher than that of the child HS group (72 percent versus 31.94 percent respectively). Furthermore, the divergent uses of *gustar* shown by these speakers have also been reported in the L1 literature (Gómez Soler 2011) as developmental errors. That said, given their context of acquisition, there is no reason to believe these children will not overcome these developmental difficulties. Adult immigrants showed a production pattern that was similar to that of the monolingual children. Unlike the monolingual adults, first-generation immigrants' production was not at ceiling across conditions, which could be indicative of some early signs of L1 attrition within this group.

Our second goal was to further understand the nature of these differences as they relate to verb agreement and to the presence or absence of dative marker 'a'. For the former, we hypothesized that child HSs would experience more problems with verb agreement relations than the other groups. As described, we found empirical support for this hypothesis, particularly when the two arguments mismatched in number (e.g., theme is plural and experiencer is singular). This is consistent with so-called invariable *gusta*, attested in previous studies (e.g., Prada Pérez and Pascual y Cabo 2011), which could indicate a simplification of the verbal paradigm. With regard to accuracy with use of the dative marker 'a,' we predicted that HS children would show higher rates of omission in obligatory contexts, which is exactly what our data show. Furthermore, while monolingual adults' use of dative marker 'a' and verb agreement is mostly consistent with the descriptions found in the theoretical literature (e.g., Parodi-Lewin 1991), adult immigrants and monolingual children patterned together not only in having a similar rate of accuracy but also in terms of the distribution of their nontarget uses. In particular, most of the differences documented had to do with the lack of the dative marker 'a,' although there were also a few noncanonical verb agreement relations.

So, considering the evidence provided herein, the next logical question is about the source of these differences. The first option we consider is that child HSs' production of *gustar*-like verbs has not had a chance to reach age-appropriate levels of accuracy (Montrul 2008). This is a possibility given that child HSs show marked differences compared to all other groups, specifically with regard to the (age-matched) monolingual group. Not only did they show higher rates of omission of the dative marker 'a' in obligatory contexts, but they also produced a substantial number of sentences with noncanonical verb agreement. Furthermore, unlike the case of the monolingual children, we cannot simply predict that with time these child HSs will develop a full-fledged grammar, as evidenced by the triangulation of our two monolingual groups. Although this interpretation of the child HL outcomes is a possibility, it is not completely satisfactory as it leaves out important features that are at play here. Particularly, this approach does not take into consideration other important factors that contribute to the acquisition of the HL, specifically that of the input, which, in the spirit of Pires and Rothman (2009) or Pascual y Cabo and Rothman (2012), is not only important but also essential to our search for a better understanding of HL acquisition. Consequently, if we consider the production trends observed among the monolingual adults and the adult immigrants, it stands to reason that input differences must be (at least in part) responsible for the trends observed. In other words, we believe this is the case based on the large effect-size values observed between the two groups for production of dative marker 'a' in obligatory contexts (e.g., Plonsky 2015). Recall that, regardless of verb type, monolingual adult production was always on target and always consistent with the descriptions found in the theoretical literature. Similarly, the immigrant adult group produced mostly on-target sentences. Interestingly, however, their accuracy in production of this obligatory marker dropped drastically. This is not completely unexpected since the dative marker has been shown to be an element with low perceptual salience as well as little communicative value, whose absence does not really interfere with communication (Bowles and Montrul 2009). Without the dative case preceding the experiencer, this sentence initial argument can be taken to be in nominative case, which is the canonical case assigned to subjects in Spanish regular agentive sentences. If that is the case, the ambiguity of the input HSs are exposed to forces their grammars to make sense by means of reanalysis (Lightfoot 2010). This is consistent with Pascual y Cabo's findings (2013a), which point in the direction of an incipient change in heritage Spanish in the area of psychological predicates whereas in HS Spanish, class III psych verbs (verbs like *gustar*) are being reanalyzed as class II psych verbs (verbs like *asustar*). In other words, according to Pascual y Cabo (2013), in HS Spanish, class II and III verbs merge, which means that *gustar* allows both an agentive or eventive and a stative interpretation. Because of this restructuring, class III verbs start showing properties of agentive or eventive predicates such as agreement relations driven by the experiencer instead of the theme and the presence of sentence-initial nominative case instead of dative. We believe the results obtained in this study provide further support for said reanalysis.

Relatedly, another option we entertain here is the possibility that the dative marker 'a' is already in the process of being lost in monolingual grammars (as part of a more general diachronic process of loss of the dative case [e.g., Montrul 2016]), and so, when in contact with English (i.e., bilingual context) said process is accelerated and changes become more noticeable (Silva-Corvalán 1994). As previously discussed, this could be an option as it has already been attested in other dialects of Spanish, specifically in Mexican Spanish (Montrul 2016). However, our monolingual adults show a high rate of accuracy with respect to dative markers. So, if there is a change in progress in monolingual Cuban Spanish, why is it that our monolingual adults' accuracy is still at ceiling? Shouldn't their production already show some evidence of this diachronic change? At this point in time, at least for the particular monolingual adult speakers tested, the data is not supportive of such change. However, it is possible that these monolingual speakers are able to conceal this loss because of the metalinguistic knowledge they acquired via formal education. That said, given its propensity to undergo deletion, it would not be completely unexpected that this element be lost in a bilingual environment, as we see happening to an extent among adult immigrants. Future research and additional data are needed to confirm these hypotheses. Additionally, future research exploring knowledge and use of dative experiencer predicates in the populations tested herein should attempt to overcome the limitations encountered in this study by increasing the number of tokens per condition as well as the number of participants per group. Additionally, we believe that controlling for working memory capacity in the repetition task (especially those working with children) would not only enhance the validity of the findings, it would also allow to make more generalizable claims and observations.

To conclude, in this study we have examined production of *gustar*-like verbs in child HS Spanish. As discussed throughout, our child experimental group has exhibited important differences with respect to the other groups in terms of accuracy, particularly as it pertains to verb agreement and absence of the dative marker. Based on the evidence provided, we believe that the target-divergent results documented in the child HS group are due to differences in the input triggered by cross-generational attrition (as evidenced by speech of the adult immigrant group).

Notes

1. In the spirit of Pires and Rothman (2009) and others, we use the term cross-generational attrition to mean that HSs receive input that has been affected to some degree by L1 attrition or other language contact consequences.
2. Although English certainly has a few predicates that exhibit this noncanonical alignment (e.g., to please), they are indeed very infrequent and a product of a formal register that native speakers do not tend to use.
3. As mentioned earlier, the difference between class II and class III psych verbs hinges on the fact that while class II predicates present a hybrid nature (they can alternate between an agentive or eventive reading and a stative one), class III predicates are unaccusative predicates restricted to a stative interpretation in monolingual varieties of Spanish.
4. The reader should recall that all distracter items (i.e., verbs other than *gustar*) presented to our participants included noncanonical verb agreement configurations.

References

Amengual, M. 2012. "Interlingual Influence in Bilingual Speech: Cognate Status Effect in a Continuum of Bilingualism." *Bilingualism: Language and Cognition* 15 (3): 517–30.

Arad, M. 1998. "VP-Structure and the Syntax-Lexicon Interface." PhD diss., University College London.

Austin, J., M. Blume, and L. Sánchez. 2013. "Morphosyntactic Attrition in the L1 of Spanish-English Bilingual Children." *Hispania* 96 (3): 542–61.

Belletti, A., and L. Rizzi. 1987. "Psych-Verbs and Θ-Theory." *Natural Language and Linguistic Theory* 6 (3): 291–352.

Beretta, A., and C. Campbell. 2001. "Psychological Verbs and the Double-Dependency Hypothesis." *Brain and Cognition* 46 (1/2): 42–46.

Bowles, M., and S. Montrul. 2009. "Instructed L2 Acquisition of Differential Object Marking in Spanish." In *Little Words: Their History, Phonology, Syntax, Semantics, Pragmatics and Acquisition*, edited by R. Leow, H. Campos, D. Lardiere, 199–210. Washington, DC: Georgetown University Press.

Cuza, A. 2013. "Crosslinguistic Influence at the Syntax Proper: Interrogative Subject–Verb Inversion in Heritage Spanish." *International Journal of Bilingualism* 17 (1): 71–96.

Cuza, A., and L. Miller. 2015. "The Protracted Acquisition of Past Tense Aspectual Values in Child Heritage Spanish." In *Hispanic Linguistics at the Crossroad: Theoretical Linguistics, Language Acquisition, and Language Contact*, edited by R. Klassen, J. Liceras, and E. Valenzuela, 211–30. Amsterdam: John Benjamins.

Cuza, A., and R. Pérez-Tattam. 2015. "Grammatical Gender Selection and Phrasal Word Order in Child Heritage Spanish: A Feature Reassembly Approach." *Bilingualism: Language and Cognition* 19 (1): 50–68.

Crain, S., and R. Thornton. 1998. *Investigations in Universal Grammar: A Guide to Experiments on the Acquisition of Syntax.* Cambridge, MA: MIT Press.

Dvorak, T., and C. Kirschner. 1982. "Mary Likes Fishes: Reverse Psychological Phenomena in New York Puerto Rican Spanish." *Bilingual Review* 9 (1): 59–65.

Fairclough, M. 2011. "Testing the Lexical Recognition Task with Spanish/English Bilinguals in the United States." *Language Testing* 28 (2): 273–97.

Figueira, R. 1984. "On the Development of the Expression of Causativity: A Syntactic Hypothesis." *Journal of Child Language* 11:109–27.

Franco, J., and S. Huidobro. 2003. "Psych Verbs in Spanish Leísta Dialects." In *Linguistic Theory and Language Development in Hispanic Languages*, edited by S. Montrul and F. Ordóñez, 138–57. Somerville, MA: Cascadilla Press.

Fishman, J. A. 2001. "300-Plus Years of Heritage Language Education in the United States." In *Heritage Languages in America: Preserving a National Resource*, edited by J. K. Peyton, D. A. Ranard, and S. McGinnis, 81–99. Washington, DC: Center for Applied Linguistics and Delta Systems.

Franco, J., & Huidobro, S. 2007. "Topicalization, word order and the bare noun Constraint in psych constructions." *Papers from the 39th Chicago Linguistic Society Meeting: Main Session*, 179-192. Bloomington, IN: Author House Publications.

Gómez Soler, I. 2011. "The L1 Acquisition of Gustar: Evidence against Maturation." In *Selected Proceedings of the 4th Conference on Generative Approaches to Language Acquisition North America*, edited by M. Pirvulescu, M. C. Cuervo, A. T. Pérez-Leroux, J. Steele, and N. Strik, 51–65. Somerville, MA: Cascadilla Proceedings Project.

———. 2012a. "Acquiring Spanish at the Interfaces: An Integrative Approach to the L2 Acquisition of Psych-Verbs." PhD diss., University of North Carolina at Chapel Hill.

———. 2012b. "Acquiring Spanish Psych-Verbs: Maturation or Continuity?" In *Proceedings of the 36th Boston University Conference on Language Development*, edited by A. Biller, E. Chung, and A. Kimball. Somerville, MA: Cascadilla Proceedings Project.

———. 2014. "Beyond Interfaces: Pragmatic Development vs. Syntactic Deficiencies in the L2 Acquisition of Reverse Psychological Predicates." *Linguistic Approaches to Bilingualism* 4 (4): 494–525.

Henriksen, N. C. 2015. "Acoustic Analysis of the Rhotic Contrast in Chicagoland Spanish: An Intergenerational Study." *Linguistic Approaches to Bilingualism* 5 (3): 285–321.

Landau, I. 2010. *The Locative Syntax of Experiencers*. Cambridge, MA: MIT Press.

Lightfoot, D. 2010. "Language Acquisition and Language Change." *Wiley Interdisciplinary Reviews: Cognitive Science* 1 (5): 677–84.

Lord, C. 1979. "Don't You Fall Me Down: Children's Generalizations Regarding Cause and Transitivity." *Papers and Reports on Child Language Development* 17:81–89.

Lynch, A. 1999. "The Subjunctive in Miami Cuban Spanish: Bilingualism, Contact, and Language Variability." PhD diss., University of Minnesota.

Manouilidou, C. 2008. "Thematic Roles in Alzheimer's Disease: Hierarchy Violations in Psychological Predicates." *Journal of Neurolinguistics* 22 (2): 167–86.

Montrul. S. 2002. "Incomplete Acquisition and Attrition of Spanish Tense/Aspect Distinctions in Adult Bilinguals." *Bilingualism: Language and Cognition* 5:39–68.

———. 2004. "Subject and Object Expression in Spanish Heritage Speakers: A Case of Morpho-syntactic Convergence." *Bilingualism: Language and Cognition* 7:1–18.

———. 2008. *Incomplete Acquisition in Bilingualism. Re-examining the Age Factor.* Amsterdam: John Benjamins.

———. 2009. "Knowledge of Tense-Aspect and Mood in Spanish Heritage Speakers." *International Journal of Bilingualism* 13 (2): 239–69.

———. 2010. "Current Issues in Heritage Language Acquisition." *Annual Review of Applied Linguistics* 30:3–23.

———. 2014. "Structural Changes in Spanish in the United States: Differential Object Marking in Spanish Heritage Speakers across Generations." *Lingua* 151:177–96.

———. 2016. "Losing Your Case? Dative Experiencers in Mexican Spanish and Heritage Speakers in the United States." In *Advances in Spanish as a Heritage Language*, edited by D. Pascual y Cabo, 99–123. Amsterdam: John Benjamins.

Montrul, S., and M. Bowles. 2009. "Back to Basics: Incomplete Knowledge of Differential Object Marking in Spanish Heritage Speakers." *Bilingualism: Language and Cognition* 12 (3): 363–83.

Montrul, S., and N. Sánchez-Walker. 2013. "Differential Object Marking in Child and Adult Spanish Heritage Speakers." *Language Acquisition* 20:1–24.

Montrul, S., and R. Slabakova. 2003. "Competence Similarities between Native and Near-Native Speakers: An Investigation of the Preterite/Imperfect Contrast in Spanish." *Studies in Second Language Acquisition* 25 (3): 351–98.

Parodi-Lewin, C. 1991. "Aspects in the Syntax of Spanish Psych-Verbs." PhD diss., University of California, Los Angeles.

Pascual y Cabo, D. 2013a. "Agreement Reflexes of Emerging Optionality in Heritage Speaker Spanish." PhD diss., University of Florida.

———. 2013b. "Knowledge of *gustar*-Like Verbs in Spanish Heritage Speakers." In *Proceedings of the 12th Generative Approaches to Second Language Acquisition Conference*, edited by J. Cabrelli Amaro, T. Judy, and D. Pascual y Cabo, 162–69. Somerville, MA: Cascadilla Proceedings Project.

———. 2015. "Issues in Spanish Heritage Morphosyntax." *Studies in Hispanic and Lusophone Linguistics* 8 (2): 389–401.

Pascual y Cabo, D., and I. Gómez Soler. 2015. "Preposition Stranding in Spanish as a Heritage Language." *Heritage Language Journal* 12 (2): 186–209.

Pascual y Cabo, D., and J. Rothman. 2012. "The (Il)logical Problem of Heritage Speaker Bilingualism and Incomplete Acquisition." *Applied Linguistics* 33 (4): 1–7.

Pérez-Leroux, A. T., A. Cuza, and D. Thomas. 2011. "From Parental Attitudes to Input Conditions: Spanish–English Bilingual Development in Toronto." In *Bilingual Youth: Spanish in English-Speaking Societies*, edited by K. Potowski and J. Rothman, 149–76. Amsterdam: John Benjamins.

Pesetsky, D. 1995. *Zero Syntax: Experiencers and Cascades*. Cambridge, MA: MIT Press.

Pires, A., and J. Rothman. 2009. "Disentangling Sources of Incomplete Acquisition: An Explanation for Competence Divergence across Heritage Grammar." *International Journal of Bilingualism* 13 (2): 1 28.

Plonsky, L. 2015. "Statistical Power, *P* Values, Descriptive Statistics, and Effect Sizes: A "Back-to-Basics" Approach to Advancing Quantitative Methods in L2 Research." In *Advancing Quantitative Methods in Second Language Research*, edited by L. Plonsky, 23–45. New York: Routledge.

Polinsky, M. 2011. "Reanalysis in Adult Heritage Language: A Case for Attrition." *Studies in Second Language Acquisition* 33:305–28.

Prada Pérez, A. de, and D. Pascual y Cabo. 2011. "Invariable gusta in the Spanish of Heritage Speakers in the US." In *Proceedings of the 11th Generative Approaches to Second Language Acquisition*, edited by J. Hershenschon and D. Tanner, 110–20. Somerville, MA: Cascadilla Proceedings Project.

Putnam, M., and L. Sánchez. 2013. "What's So Incomplete about Incomplete Acquisition: A Prolegomenon to Modeling Heritage Language Grammars." *Linguistic Approaches to Bilingualism* 3 (4): 476–506.

Pylkkänen, L. 1997. "Finnish Psych Verbs." Paper presented at the Workshop on Events in Grammar, LSA Summer Institute, Cornell University.

Rao, R. 2014. "On the Status of the Phoneme /b/ in Heritage Speakers of Spanish." *Sintagma: revista de lingüística* 26:37–54.

Ronquest, R. 2012. "An Acoustic Analysis of Heritage Spanish Vowels." PhD diss., Indiana University.

Rothman, J. 2009. "Understanding the Nature and Outcomes of Early Bilingualism: Romance Languages as Heritage Languages." *International Journal of Bilingualism* 13 (2): 155–65.

Silva-Corvalán, C. 1994. *Language Contact and Change: Spanish in Los Angeles*. Oxford: Oxford University Press.

———. 2014. *Bilingual Language Acquisition. Spanish and English in the First Six Years*. Cambridge: Cambridge University Press.

Thompson, C., and M. Lee. 2009. "Psych Verb Production and Comprehension in Agrammatic Broca's Aphasia." *Journal of Neurolinguistics* 22:354–69.

Toribio, A. J., and C. Nye. 2006. "Restructuring of Reverse Psychological Predicates." In *New Perspectives on Romance Linguistics*, edited by J. Montreuil and C. Nishida, 263–77. Amsterdam: John Benjamins.

Torrens, V., L. Escobar, and K. Wexler. 2006. "The Acquisition of Experiencers in Spanish L1 and the External Argument Requirement Hypothesis." In *Acquisition of Syntax in Romance Languages*, edited by V. Torrens and L. Escobar, 183–202. Philadelphia: John Benjamins

Valdés, G. 2000. Introduction in *Spanish for Native Speakers*, vol. 1 of AATSP Professional Development Series Handbook for Teachers K-16. New York: Harcourt College.

———.2001. "Bilingual Individuals and Language-Based Discrimination: Advancing the State of the Law on Language Rights." In *Language Ideologies: Critical Perspectives on the Official English Movement*, edited by R. Dueñas González and I. Melis, vol. 2, *History, Theory, and Policy*, 140–70. Mahway, NJ, and Urbana, IL: Erlbaum and National Council of Teachers of English.

White L., C. Brown, J. Bruhn-Garavito, D. Chen, M. Hirakawa, and S. Montrul. 1999. "Psych Verbs in Second Language Acquisition." In *The Development of Second Language Grammars: A Generative Approach*, edited by E. Klein and G. Martohardjono, 173–99. Amsterdam: John Benjamins.

14

Examining Code-Switching Performance Theories: Copula Choice in Spanish among Cuban Heritage Speakers

ANA DE PRADA PÉREZ
University of Florida

ANDREA HERNÁNDEZ
University of Florida

THE STUDY OF THE Spanish copulas has received significant attention in both monolingual and bilingual populations. From a theoretical perspective, there are a variety of proposals that have aimed to explain the difference between the copulas: aspect (Bosque 1990; Camacho 2012), individual versus class frames (Falk 1979), and individual-level versus stage-level predicates (Carlson 1989; Fernández Leborans 1999; Leonetti 1994), among others (Luján 1981; Maienborn 2005; Roby 2009). For instance, regarding frame of reference (Falk 1979), *ser* identifies the subject as something that belongs to a class (example 14.1a) while *estar* marks the subject as belonging to an individual frame, where there is a comparison of the subject to a previous experience or time (example 14.1b; Cortés-Torres 2004).

Example 14.1.

a. *A mí me gusta mucho beber jugo pero el de limón no me gusta. Ese jugo es amargo.*
   I like drinking juice a lot but I don't like lemon juice. That juice is bitter.
b. *Me encanta el jugo de naranja de Florida pero éste se ha estropeado. Este jugo está amargo.*
   I love drinking Florida orange juice but this one has gone bad. This juice is bitter.

In example 14.1a, the juice is being compared to other juices while in example 14.1b the juice is being described as being bitter now and not in the past.

In the variationist literature, these definitions are included as variables in the analyses of monolingual and bilingual data, assuming that not a single variable can explain the data (Brown and Cortés-Torres 2012). Previous research from this perspective has identified an innovative use of *estar* in contexts where the use of *ser* used to be categorical (class frame of reference). These changes have been thoroughly studied in a variety of contexts (for Cuban Spanish in Miami: Alfaraz 2012; for Venezuela: De Jonge 1993; Díaz-Campos and Geeslin 2011; Díaz-Campos, Galarza, and Delgado-Díaz, this volume; Malaver 2000; for Mexico: Cortés-Torres 2004; De Jonge 1993; Gutiérrez 1992, 1994, 2003; López-González 2010; for Spain: Guijarro-Fuentes and Geeslin 2008). To expand on this literature, the present study examines the effect of code-switching (CS) on copula selection across four adjective classes well studied in the literature (adapted from Alfaraz 2012).

For bilingual communities, there are several explanations for the increased extension of *estar*. The prolonged interaction of two languages, according to Gutiérrez (1992) and Silva-Corvalán (1986), accelerates the ongoing change in Spanish. Additionally, Silva-Corvalán (1994) points out differences with English, which only has one copula, and processes of simplification to alleviate the cognitive load of processing two languages, as possible explanations for the increased use of innovative *estar* in bilingual communities in the US.

To the best of our knowledge, there is only one previous study where the use of CS is examined with respect to copula selection in Spanish. Salazar (2007) coded whether copulas occurred near CS or not and included that variable in the analysis. She reported a higher use of *estar* in CS contexts than in non-CS contexts. Since her data came from the New Mexico–Colorado corpus, where CS was not frequent, only seven instances appeared in local CS (that is, CS within the sentence). Thus, she was unable to draw strong conclusions from her data, given the scarcity of CS contexts as well as the possible different CS junctures within the sentence (criteria she used to define local CS). Examining the effects of CS on variable phenomena is a recent approach to CS that has exclusively been applied to subject expression (Prada Pérez 2015a; Prada Pérez and Toribio, under review; Toribio 2004; Torres Cacoullos and Travis 2011). Therefore, the current project aims to expand on this literature by examining the effect of CS on copula choice with adjectival predicates among Cuban bilingual speakers. In particular, it examines acceptability judgment task (AJT) data from three speaker modes (Spanish-only, CS with English adjectives, and CS with Spanish adjectives) to improve our understanding of the variability of copula choice and of the morphosyntactic consequences of CS.

The chapter is organized as follows. First, we offer a review of previous studies regarding copula choice in monolingual and bilingual communities, as well as previous literature on CS and variable phenomena. Next, we present our research questions and hypotheses and a description of the methods. Subsequently the results are presented and discussed. Lastly, we offer some conclusions.

Previous Literature

Copula choice in Spanish, specifically between the two copulas *ser* and *estar*, has received extant attention both in monolingual and bilingual Spanish.

Monolingual Copula Distribution in Spanish

Silva-Corvalán's (1986) seminal work on copula choice among bilinguals in LA raised the question of the stability of the copulas in monolingual Spanish and, thus, generated an interest on the possible linguistic change in the copulative verbs in monolingual Spanish. Several research projects have analyzed monolingual copula distribution in different Spanish-speaking countries, also reporting a semantic extension of *estar* in the [copula + adjective] construction (Alfaraz 2012; Cortés-Torres 2004; De Jonge 1993; Díaz-Campos and Geeslin 2011; Guijarro-Fuentes and Geeslin 2008; Gutiérrez 1992, 1994, 2003; López-González 2010; Malaver 2000). For instance, in Morelia, Mexico, Gutiérrez (1992) reports a 12.5 percent usage of innovative *estar* with some but not all adjectives. With respect to the nature of the linguistic change, the author notes that the innovation is being used largely by younger generations within Morelia. Also in Mexico, Cortés-Torres (2004) examined the monolingual copula distribution in the Spanish of Cuernavaca. Similarly to Gutiérrez, she found an extension of *estar* 23 percent of the time.

In a similar vein, Díaz-Campos and Geeslin (2011) examined copula use in Caracas. Their analysis focused mainly on sociolinguistic variables, which were included to better understand the nature of the linguistic change attested across varieties of Spanish. Although they found evidence of stabilization, the data is consistent with an ongoing change in the use of the copulas in the community. Expanding on this project, Díaz-Campos, Galarza, and Delgado-Díaz (this volume) examined copula choice in Cuban Spanish, using similar coding and methods, and compared the results to previous results from Caracas, Puerto Rico, and Mexico. They show that the direction of effect was the same across studies for those variables selected as significant. This comparison is interpreted as indicative of a stable stage in the grammaticalization of the Spanish copulas.

Lastly, Alfaraz (2012) also examined the nature of the linguistic change in Cuban Spanish. Although the data was collected in Miami, she did not carry out an analysis of contact effects, as the fifty participants were recent arrivals. The analysis was both real-time (comparisons of data from the 1960s with participants in their thirties and the 1990s with participants in their sixties) and apparent time (comparisons of two age groups in the 1990s corpus).There was evidence of innovative *estar* across generations as well as real time (1960s versus 1990s) but some interesting trends were evident in the data. The data from the 1960s did not differ from the older generation in the 1990s, which is interpreted to mean that speakers maintained their use of the copulas throughout their lifetime. There were, however, significant differences with the younger 1990s generation, who used innovative *estar* with more frequency. Alfaraz (2012) concludes, then, that this ongoing change in Cuban Spanish is similar to that attested in other monolingual communities.

In summary, there is a significant body of research on monolingual copula distribution, including Alfaraz (2012), Cortés-Torres (2004), Díaz-Campos and Geeslin (2004), and Gutiérrez (1992), among others, that reports an ongoing linguistic change in the copulative verbs in Spanish. In the following section, we review the literature that examines contact effects on copula distribution in Spanish.

Bilingual Copula Distribution

In bilingual communities, similarly, there have been studies that corroborate findings from monolingual communities of an extension of *estar* with certain adjectival classes.

In a pioneering study, Silva-Corvalán (1986) examined the recordings of interviews she carried out with twenty-seven Mexican American bilinguals in eastern Los Angeles. From these recordings she extracted 1,178 tokens of *ser* and *estar*, 344 of which were cases of innovative *estar*. She coded uses of *estar* within a class reference frame as cases of innovative *estar*, as seen in example 14.2.

Example 14.2.

> **R:** *Está alta. Mide seis diez. Está muy alta la muchacha.* (C: *¿Cuánto mides tú?*)
> **R:** *Seis uno.* (C: *¡Ella es más alta que tú!*) *No. Yo estoy seis uno y ella cinco; quiero decir cinco diez, no seis.*
> **R:** She's tall. She is 6.10. This girl is very tall. (C: How tall are you?)
> **R:** 6.1. (C: She is taller than you!). No. I am 6.1 and she is 5, I meant, 5.10, not 6.

Within this excerpt, we can observe that the participant is using *estar* in an innovative fashion with a size adjective, *alto*. While in this example, the participant alternates between both copulas to compare the speaker's height to the addressee, they are using the copulas within a class frame context and, as a consequence, the use of *estar* is innovative in this context.

Once she coded all innovative uses of *estar*, she examined several factors that correlated with this use. A notable factor that seemed to favor innovative *estar* was adjective class, with results similar to those found in monolingual communities. In this paper she also examines the role of language contact in the use of the Spanish copulas, concluding that the innovative use of *estar* was more prevalent with speakers who had more contact with English. The specific outcome of this contact situation is interpreted by Silva Corvalán (1986) as an acceleration of the ongoing change in the Spanish copulas, as the trends are similar to those encountered in the monolingual community, with a larger rate of use of innovative *estar* in bilinguals. This change, where *estar* is losing semantic content, is considered a case of simplification of the system (with the semantic bleaching characteristic of the grammaticalization of verbs into auxiliaries). Additionally, she indicates that there are other language-external factors at play in this situation: the intense and prolonged contact situation where Spanish is the minority language and the lack of access to a formal standard of Spanish. These hypotheses have generated subsequent research on the effect of language contact on copula choice in Spanish in other communities.

Still within the mainland United States, Gutiérrez (2003) and Salazar (2007) carried out variationist analyses of bilingual data from Houston and New Mexico–Colorado, respectively. Gutiérrez (2003) compared data from twenty-six one-hour interviews with monolingual Spanish speakers from the city of Morelia, Mexico, with existing data from Houston (Balestra and Ayres, p.c., cited in Gutiérrez 2003) and LA (Silva-Corvalán 1986). He interprets the higher frequency of innovative *estar* and the extension to other adjective classes in bilingual communities as an acceleration of linguistic change in contact situations. Salazar (2007) also carried out a variationist analysis of copula selection in bilingual Spanish, in this case without comparison to monolingual data. She analyzed twenty interviews from the New Mexico–Colorado Spanish Survey (Bills and Vigil 1999), which yielded 307 tokens. The results indicated that adjective type was the highest ranked variable, followed by time adverbial, CS, and presence or absence of an intensifier. Of interest to this section is the effect of adjective type (the effect of CS is further discussed below) on the use of the copula *estar*, where the data showed a favoring effect for other (physical description, states of being) and age adjectives and a disfavoring effect for evaluation adjectives while description adjectives did not have a favoring or a disfavoring effect. It is important to note, though, that these were general copula uses and not necessarily examples of innovative uses of *estar*.

In summary, the different studies on language contact in the mainland US report similar results. The trends found in monolingual Spanish, where there is an attested extension of *estar* to contexts with a class frame of reference, are also present in the speech of bilinguals in the US. There is, nonetheless, a contact effect on the data in terms of a quantitative difference, where the instances of innovative *estar* are more numerous in bilingual than in monolingual data. This contact effect has been interpreted in this literature as an example of the acceleration of a simplification change already occurring in the monolingual grammar (grammaticalization of the copula *estar*) due to differences with the contact language (English only has one copula) and the lack of access to formal Spanish in the communities studied. Some of these conclusions have invited further research in contexts other than the mainland US.

Ortiz López (2000), for example, examines Spanish in Puerto Rico, where, in contrast with eastern LA, access to formal Spanish can be teased apart from language contact, as speakers with access to formal Spanish can be monolingual or bilingual. Consistent with previous research, Ortiz López reports that the use of innovative *estar* is not the same across adjective classes. Further analysis of the questionnaire data, where speaker proficiency information was available, revealed that contact with English was not a relevant factor in these data. Thus, Ortiz López concludes that contact with English is not a sufficient factor for an increased use of innovative *estar* and that access to formal Spanish seems to be a more relevant factor. In line with Ortiz López's research, Guijarro-Fuentes and Geeslin (2008) examined the choice of copula in a language contact environment different from the mainland US context where the contact language was not English (Spain). Results indicated similar patterns across speaker groups, with some differences in rates across groups. The authors concluded that simplification did not take place in all language contact situations.

Research on Spanish copula choice in bilingual communities indicates differences across communities. In communities where Spanish is in contact with English and where access to formal Spanish is limited there is evidence of an increased use of innovative *estar*, as compared to monolingual communities. This effect has been interpreted as the acceleration of a simplification change in situations of contact where the minority language status does not provide speakers with access to formal Spanish. In communities where Spanish is in contact with English but where there is access to formal Spanish (Puerto Rico) and in communities where Spanish is in contact with languages other than English (Spain) there is no evidence of a contact effect on the use of the Spanish copulas. There are, nonetheless, Spanish heritage speakers (HSs) in the US, where Spanish is the minority language, who are taking Spanish for HS courses and, therefore, have access to formal Spanish. Examining this type of speaker (which we do here) may further elucidate the roles of language contact situation and access to formal Spanish in the use of innovative *estar* in Spanish. Additionally, although there has been great interest in the result of language contact in copula use in bilinguals when they are in Spanish monolingual mode, little is known about their use when they are code-switching.

Code-Switching and Copulative Distribution

While the study of *ser* and *estar* among bilinguals has been researched heavily, to date, the area of study that pertains to this research in terms of CS and the Spanish copulas is minimal. Salazar (2007) carried out a variationist analysis of data from the New Mexico–Colorado Spanish Survey (Bills and Vigil 1999). The analysis of twenty interviews yielded 307 tokens (157 of which were included in the final analysis), which were coded for the copula used, whether it was innovative or not (not included in the analysis), TAM, lexical entry, presence or absence of an intensifier, presence or absence of a time adverbial, and CS. Tokens occurring near CS were coded as having CS (46 tokens, 23 percent of the data). The results indicate that adjective type was the highest ranked variable, followed by time adverbial, CS, and intensifier. Crucially, in contexts of CS, the probability of using *estar* was higher. Salazar (2007) indicates that further research is needed. With the low number of tokens and without knowing if those tokens were cases of regular or innovative uses of *estar*, the effect of CS needs further examination.

There is a longstanding interest in better understanding CS. Only recently, though, have researchers focused on the effects of CS on the morphosyntax of the languages involved. To date, research under this approach has focused on subject expression. Previous studies on Spanish-English CS in the US report a higher rate of overt pronominal use in Spanish when bilinguals are code-switching than when they are in monolingual Spanish mode (Prada Pérez and Toribio, under review; Toribio 2004; Torres Cacoullos and Travis 2011). Toribio (2004), for instance, examines subject expression in the extended discourse of two Mexican-American Spanish-English bilingual speakers in a monolingual and a bilingual mode condition. Toribio reports pragmatically odd overt pronominal subjects in the code-switching condition.

Torres Cacoullos and Travis (2011) examine New Mexican Spanish-English bilingual speakers' expression of *yo* in the absence or presence of CS and found that the trend to use more overt pronominal subjects in CS did not reach significance. Nonetheless, the authors further examined if there was a crosslinguistic priming effect that could possibly explain the higher use of overt pronominal subjects. They concluded that priming affects the higher expression of *yo* during CS.

In order to address the confounding effect of priming and convergence in the English-Spanish CS data, Prada Pérez and Toribio (under review) examined the effect of language mode and syntactic priming on subject expression across speaker modes. Crucially, participants used more overt pronominal subjects in CS than in monolingual Spanish even with a null prime, which cannot be interpreted as a result due to priming. The authors hypothesize that the result is due to either convergence or simplification, since overt pronominal subjects are easier to process than nulls.

Lastly, Prada Pérez (2015a) examined the effects of CS on subject expression in Spanish in contact with another null subject language, Catalan, in Menorca. The bilinguals used significantly more overt subjects (albeit lexical and not pronominal) in the CS condition than in the monolingual mode condition. This result cannot be ascribed to convergence, given that both Spanish and Catalan are null subject languages with similar subject expression (i.e., with similar overt pronominal subject rates as well as the same significant variables and direction of effect; Prada Pérez 2015b). Thus, the author's interpretation is that in CS speakers may resort to less cognitively costly options (e.g., overt subjects in this study).

Bearing in mind the results from Salazar (2007), it is possible that the effects of CS constitute not only a simplification but also an acceleration of linguistic change, that is, the extension of *estar* present in monolingual data and enhanced in bilingual Spanish may be further intensified in CS. In this chapter, we present new data regarding copula selection in monolingual versus bilingual mode conditions in order to better understand the consequences that CS has on this morphosyntactic feature of Spanish.

In summary, there is previous research providing ample evidence from monolingual and bilingual communities that the [copula + adjective] context is variable and susceptible to crosslinguistic influence. Additionally, CS also seems to be a predictor of copula choice. The current study expands on previous research by examining copula choice in Cuban Spanish second-generation HSs in Florida, who are literate in Spanish, through a contextualized AJT, which allows for the examination of manipulated conditions that might otherwise not occur in spontaneous data. Crucially, it compares the same group of speakers' judgments in a Spanish-only condition and a CS condition. Thus, this design allows us to isolate CS effects and to contribute to the recent literature, which examines these effects only in subject expression.

The Present Study

Research Questions and Hypotheses

The current investigation examines the effect that code switching has on Cuban HSs' copula choice. Thus, the main research question addressed in this study is the following:

- Do Cuban HSs exhibit different patterns of copula choice in monolingual than in bilingual mode conditions?

While there is limited literature on CS and copula choice, previous research on bilinguals extending one of the copulas with certain adjectival classes in Spanish-only modes has discussed that this change can be derived from language contact and simplification, but that is not always the case with different bilingual contact situations, as previously mentioned (Silva-Corvalán 1986; Guijarro-Fuentes and Geeslin 2008). It is also proposed that individuals whose families have settled in the US for a long time are most affected by the linguistic simplification of the Spanish copulas (Silva-Corvalán 1986). Such explanation of an extension of one particular Spanish copula is not yet concrete, but has been thought to be due to a loss of semantic distinction (Silva-Corvalán 1986), where the copula *estar* has been extended to overlap with *ser* with a gradual loss of the individual frame of reference and susceptibility to change. Given that these results have been reported in different English-Spanish communities in the US, we expect to find evidence of an extension of *estar* in our data, even in monolingual mode. Regarding CS, Salazar (2007) reports a CS effect, manifested as an increased use of innovative *estar* in CS contexts. Recall, however, that the corpus she used only had seven instances of local CS (i.e., within the [copula + adjective] predicate), and that she coded a token as CS if CS took place during the interchange on the topic where the copulative verb that was included in the analysis appeared. With this antecedent research in mind, we anticipate that the changes in copula selection will be more pronounced in CS than in monolingual mode.

If this CS effect is attested in our data, it could be interpreted as an example of linguistic simplification or an intensification of convergence with English in CS. Thus, this paper also aims to answer the following question:

- If there is a CS effect on copula choice, can it be interpreted as a simplification?

Previous literature on the effects of CS on morphosyntactic phenomena indicates that bilinguals resort to simpler options (Prada Pérez and Toribio, under review) or converge with English (Toribio 2004) more in CS than in monolingual mode conditions. Following Prada Pérez and Toribio (under review), we anticipate our participants will exhibit evidence of simplification in the bilingual mode conditions. In particular, we expect to find evidence that the loss of distinction between the copulas in favor of one of the copulas will be enhanced (if already present in the monolingual mode condition) in the CS conditions. Since the copulative verb *ser* is syntactically less complex than *estar* (Camacho 2012), an overuse of the copula *ser* would be expected, although in the previous literature an acceleration of the ongoing change in Spanish toward an extension of *estar* has been attested in CS (Salazar 2007). If this result is also attested in our data, it would indicate that CS intensifies language change already present in the Spanish monolingual mode of bilinguals.

In order to address these questions, we collected data from HSs of Cuban heritage in Florida.

Method

A total of sixty-two Cuban participants took part in the study. Since the nature of the study consisted of several sessions on separate days, there was participant attrition in addition to the participants who did not qualify after completing the language background questionnaire. To qualify, participants had to report that they regularly engaged in CS, that they were of Cuban descent, and that they were second-generation HSs, which was defined as either those born and raised in the US or those who moved to the US before age nine (Montrul 2008). After exclusion of participants who did not qualify or finish both sessions, a total of twenty-three Cuban second-generation HSs who reported they regularly engaged in CS were included in the analysis. Results from the DELE-based proficiency test indicated that twelve participants were advanced, seven intermediate, and four low proficiency. Their proficiency in English was not tested but they all reported being English-dominant. Participants were either born in the US (second generation, n = 15) or migrated to the US by the age of eight (1.5 generation, n = 8).[1] The data were collected in Gainesville, Florida, and Miami, Florida, via an online survey program, Qualtrics.

All participants completed a language background questionnaire (LBQ) and a proficiency test for participant selection and profiling. In terms of the experimental tasks, there were three contextualized four-point Likert scale AJTs. The first task was the monolingual Spanish-only mode (example 14.3; target items n = 32), and the second task and third tasks dealt with two code-switching conditions: one with English adjectives (example 14.4; target items n = 32) and one with Spanish adjectives (example 14.5; target items n = 32).

Example 14.3. Monolingual Spanish task

Roberto y Pepe van a jugar baloncesto. Es la primera vez que Pepe juega y nunca ha visto una pelota de baloncesto y le pide a Roberto que describa la pelota. Roberto le contesta:

a. *La pelota* ***es*** *redonda.*
b. *La pelota* ***está*** *redonda.*

Roberto and Pepe are going to play basketball. It is the first time that Pepe plays and he has never seen a basketball and asks Roberto to describe the ball. Roberto answers:

a. The ball is round. (*ser*)
b. The ball is round. (*estar*)

Example 14.4. English adjectives task

Roberto y Pepe are going to play *baloncesto*. It's the first time that Pepe plays *y nunca ha visto una pelota de baloncesto* and he asks Roberto to describe *la pelota. Roberto le contesta:*

a. *La pelota* ***es*** round.
b. *La pelota* ***está*** round.

Example 14.5. Spanish adjectives task

Roberto y Pepe are going to play *baloncesto*. It's the first time that Pepe plays *y nunca ha visto una pelota de baloncesto* and he asks Roberto to describe *la pelota. Roberto le contesta:*

a. The ball ***es*** *redonda.*
b. The ball ***está*** *redonda.*

As can be seen from the preceding examples,[2] participants rated each of the responses related to the contexts. For all of the tasks, four adjectival classes were chosen: physical property, value, age, and dimension, following Alfaraz (2012). For each adjectival class, there were four adjectives chosen.

On all three of the tasks, the context was manipulated so that half of the experimental items (n = 16) favored *estar* (i.e., individual frame of reference; example 14.6) and half favored *ser* (i.e., class frame of reference; example 14.7), while the rest of the forty-nine questions consisted of fillers. Each experimental item had two answer choices, one with *ser* and one with *estar*, which participants rated on a four-point Likert scale where 1 was completely unacceptable and 4 was completely acceptable, with a 'not applicable/not sure' option placed outside of the scale.[3] Additionally, all items were controlled for person, number, and TAM (third-person singular present indicative).

Example 14.6.

Juan works *en una cafetería* making *café. Aunque tiene experiencia*, today *el café le quedó bitter*. Jessica, a client, buys *una taza del café que* Juan made *y le tiene que echar* sugar. *Ahora*,

a. The coffee ***es*** *dulce*. (*ser*)
b. The coffee ***está*** *dulce*. (*estar*)

Juan works at a coffee shop making coffee. Although he has experience, today he made the coffee bitter. Jessica, a client, buys a coffee cup that Juan made and put some sugar in it. Now,

a. The coffee is sweet. (*ser*)
b. The coffee is sweet. (*estar*)

Example 14.7.

Luisa es diabetic y su médico told her *que no puede comer tantos* sweets. *Cuando ella va al* grocery store, *no puede comprar* ice cream *porque*

a. *El* ice cream ***es** dulce. (ser)*
b. *El* ice cream ***está** dulce. (estar)*

Luisa is diabetic and her doctor told her not to eat so many sweets. When she went to the grocery store, she couldn't buy ice cream because

a. Ice cream is sweet. (*ser*)
b. Ice cream is sweet. (*estar*)

In summary, the experimental design included the following variables: rating of sentence on a four-point scale (dependent variable), copula (*ser* or *estar*), context (favoring *ser* or favoring *estar*), adjective type (physical property, age, dimension, and value) and speaker mode (monolingual, CSE, and CSS).

Participants completed each task on a different day: the Spanish-only task on the first day, CSE task on day two, and CSS task on day three.

Results

Participants were asked to rate two responses, one with *ser* and one with *estar*, for each context (half favoring *ser* and half favoring *estar*), with four different adjective types (physical property, value, age, and dimension) and in three speaker modes (monolingual, CS with an English adjective, and CS with a Spanish adjective). The data was organized by condition and submitted to analysis with SPSS, v.23. As shown in table 14.1, participants rated the favored copula higher than the nonfavored copula in all monolingual mode conditions except with dimension adjectives in contexts favoring *estar*, where the preference for *estar* did not reach significance ($p > 0.05$).

An interesting trend found in the data is the different treatment of physical property and value adjectives on the one hand and dimension and age adjectives on the other. With the first two types of adjectives, participants rate the favored copula very high on the acceptance range (consistently above 3) while the other copula is not within the acceptance range (with ratings of 2 or below 2), showing that, with these two adjectives, copula distribution is largely regulated by the context. With age adjectives, although the preference exists and it reaches significance, the difference is smaller (only 0.6 points with contexts favoring *ser* and 0.5 points with those favoring *estar*). Lastly, with dimension adjectives, there seems to be an extension of *ser* to contexts favoring *estar* since there is no significant preference for *estar*.

The distribution is rather similar in CS with English adjectives, as can be observed in table 14.2. The only difference is that the lack of preference for *estar* with contexts favoring *estar* occurs not only with dimension adjectives but also with age adjectives ($p > 0.05$).

Table 14.1. Monolingual mode copula choice preferences

Adjective type	Context	Response	Mean rating	N	Std. Deviation	Paired-samples t-tests
Physical property	SER	ser	3.7609	23	0.32402	t(22) = 11.47; p = 0.000
		estar	1.8478	23	0.56779	
	ESTAR	ser	2.0652	23	0.67089	t(22) = –8.169; p = 0.000
		estar	3.7717	23	0.45172	
Value	SER	ser	3.7717	23	0.37623	t(22) = 12.473; p = 0.000
		estar	1.7283	23	0.53785	
	ESTAR	ser	2.0761	23	0.67181	t(22) = –8.287; p = 0.000
		estar	3.6522	23	0.40409	
Age	SER	ser	3.2826	23	0.48444	t(22) = 2.919; p = 0.008
		estar	2.6522	23	0.68149	
	ESTAR	ser	2.7174	23	0.57556	t(22) = –3.43; p = 0.002
		estar	3.2609	23	0.48546	
Dimension	SER	ser	3.6413	23	0.4636	t(22) = 5.865; p = 0.000
		estar	2.1957	23	0.88535	
	ESTAR	ser	2.837	23	0.60588	t(22) = –1.149; p = 0.263
		estar	3.0761	23	0.57621	

Table 14.2. CSE mode copula choice preferences

Adjective type	Context	Response	Mean rating	N	Std. Deviation	Paired-samples t-tests
Physical property	SER	ser	3.1522	23	0.61579	t(22) = 5.809; p = 0.00
		estar	1.9457	23	0.73452	
	ESTAR	ser	2.0543	23	0.71492	t(22) = –4.532; p = 0.000
		estar	3.1848	23	0.79493	
Value	SER	ser	3.3478	23	0.5826	t(22) = 8.28; p = 0.000
		estar	1.75	23	0.65279	
	ESTAR	ser	2.1739	23	0.7325	t(22) = –4.842; p = 0.000
		estar	3.2283	23	0.77207	
Age	SER	ser	2.9022	23	0.46306	t(22) = 3.427; p = 0.002
		estar	2.413	23	0.62436	
	ESTAR	ser	2.8696	23	0.71059	t(22) = –0.575; p = 0.571
		estar	2.9783	23	0.67804	
Dimension	SER	ser	3.2174	23	0.59019	t(22) = 4.305; p = 0.000
		estar	2.3152	23	0.86674	
	ESTAR	ser	2.8478	23	0.64288	t(22) = 0.848; p = 0.406
		estar	2.6739	23	0.70079	

Lastly, in CS with a Spanish adjective (table 14.3), the preference for the favored copula is again significant in all conditions except for those with contexts favoring *estar* with dimension and age adjectives ($p > 0.05$).

Thus, the data indicate similar preferences across speaker modes with physical property and value adjectives, where a preference for the favored copula was attested. With dimension adjectives, too, participants responded similarly across modes, albeit with no significant preference for *estar* in contexts favoring *estar*. Lastly, the small yet significant preference for *estar* in contexts favoring *estar* with age adjectives present in the monolingual mode condition is not present in both CS mode conditions. To further examine these trends, the data were submitted to statistical analysis on SPSS v. 22.

The difference between the *ser* and the *estar* rating was computed, creating a new variable for the preference for *ser* or *estar*. In all *ser*-favoring contexts (class frame of reference) the *ser* response was rated higher than the *estar* response, resulting in positive values for the preference variable. In all *estar*-favoring contexts (individual frame of reference) the *estar* response was rated higher than the *ser* response, also resulting in positive values, with the exception of dimension adjectives in both CS conditions. In order to examine copula preference across speaker modes, a 2 (context: favoring *ser* or favoring *estar*) × 4 (adjective type: physical property, value, age, and dimension) × 3 (speaker mode: monolingual, CSE, CSS) repeated-measures ANOVA was run. The analysis revealed a main effect for context ($F(1) = 20.872$, $p = 0.000$, partial $\eta^2 = 0.487$), a main effect for adjective type ($F(2) = 8.920$, $p = 0.001$, partial

Table 14.3. CSS mode copula choice preferences

Adjective type	Context	Response	Mean rating	N	Std. Deviation	Paired-samples t-tests
Physical property	SER	ser	3.3261	23	0.62357	t(22) = 7.426; p = 0.000
		estar	1.9457	23	0.60751	
	ESTAR	ser	2.3587	23	0.6022	t(22) = –3.789; p = 0.001
		estar	3.1848	23	0.70798	
Value	SER	ser	3.3804	23	0.52152	t(22) = 7.494; p = 0.000
		estar	1.8587	23	0.67767	
	ESTAR	ser	2.337	23	0.46226	t(22) = –4.466; p = 0.000
		estar	3.1196	23	0.59767	
Age	SER	ser	3.2391	23	0.51389	t(22) = 5.057; p = 0.000
		estar	2.5	23	0.63514	
	ESTAR	ser	2.8587	23	0.66498	t(22) = –1.072; p = 0.296
		estar	3.0543	23	0.72283	
Dimension	SER	ser	3.25	23	0.56408	t(22) = 4.113; p = 0.000
		estar	2.5652	23	0.65807	
	ESTAR	ser	3.0435	23	0.60138	t(22) = 1.72; p = 0.100
		estar	2.7609	23	0.77047	

$\eta^2 = 0.288$), and a main effect for speaker mode ($F(3) = 59.893$, $p = 0.000$, partial $\eta^2 = 0.731$). Additionally, two interactions were found: a context by adjective type interaction ($F(3) = 7.294$, $p = 0.000$, partial $\eta^2 = 0.249$) and a speaker mode by adjective type interaction ($F(6) = 2.549$, $p = 0.023$, partial $\eta^2 = 0.104$). No speaker mode by context interaction ($F(2) = 0.571$, $p = 0.569$, partial $\eta^2 = 0.025$) or speaker mode by context by adjective type interaction ($F(6) = 1.005$, $p = 0.425$, $\eta^2 = 0.249$) were found. These results were examined further through Bonferroni post hoc analyses. Across modes, the preference for *ser* in contexts favoring *ser* was significantly higher than the preference for *estar* in contexts favoring *estar*, which can be interpreted as evidence of an extension of *ser*. Given the differences found across adjectives, the effect of CS was examined separately for each of the adjectives.

With physical property adjectives, a 2 (context) × 3 (speaker mode) repeated-measures ANOVA revealed a main effect for speaker mode ($F(2, 44) = 7.883$, $p = 0.001$, partial $\eta^2 = 0.264$) and no main effect for context ($F(1, 22) = 2.759$, $p = 0.111$, partial $\eta^2 = 0.111$) or context by speaker mode interaction ($F(2, 44) = 2.137$, $p = 0.120$, partial $\eta^2 = 0.089$). In particular, participants rated the monolingual condition significantly higher than the two bilingual mode conditions.

With value adjectives, a 2 (context) × 3 (speaker mode) repeated-measures ANOVA returned a main effect for context ($F(1, 22) = 20.800$, $p = 0.000$, partial $\eta^2 = 0.486$), a main effect for speaker mode ($F(2, 44) = 6.898$, $p = 0.002$, partial $\eta^2 = 0.239$), and no context by speaker mode interaction ($F(2, 44) = 0.843$, $p = 0.437$, partial $\eta^2 = 0.037$). In particular, participants' preference for the copula *ser* in conditions favoring *ser* was significantly higher than participants' preference for the copula *estar* in conditions favoring *estar*. As was the case with physical property adjectives, the copula preference was stronger in monolingual conditions than in both bilingual conditions. These results can be interpreted as indicating a slight extension of *ser* to contexts favoring *estar* and a slight weakening in copula preference in bilingual modes.

With age adjectives, a 2 (context) × 3 (speaker mode) repeated-measures ANOVA returned a main effect for context ($F(1, 22) = 4.583$, $p = 0.044$, partial $\eta^2 = 0.172$) and no main effect for speaker mode ($F(2, 44) = 1.627$, $p = 0.208$, partial $\eta^2 = 0.069$) or context by speaker mode interaction ($F(2, 44) = 0.904$, $p = 0.412$, partial $\eta^2 = 0.039$). The preference for the copula *ser* in contexts favoring *ser* is higher than the preference for *estar* in contexts favoring *estar* across modes. As shown above, the preference for *estar* only reached significance in monolingual mode.

With dimension adjectives, a 2 (context) × 3 (speaker mode) repeated-measures ANOVA returned a main effect for context ($F(1, 22) = 24.308$, $p = 0.000$, partial $\eta^2 = 0.525$), a main effect for speaker mode ($F(2, 44) = 8.550$, $p = 0.001$, partial $\eta^2 = 0.280$), and no context by speaker mode interaction ($F(2, 44) = 0.189$, $p = 0.829$, partial $\eta^2 = 0.009$). In particular, the copula *ser* was preferred across contexts, although significantly more in contexts favoring *ser*, a result that can be interpreted as indicative of an extension of *ser*. In the monolingual condition the copula preference was significantly stronger than in the CSS condition but not the CSE condition. The copula preference in CSE, though, was not significantly greater than in CSS.

Overall, thus, there is a speaker mode effect (except with age adjectives), where copula preference is significantly more marked in monolingual mode than in the bilingual modes. This code-switching effect is not present with age adjectives, which already have a smaller preference for the copula favored in the context in the monolingual mode. Nonetheless, there is a qualitative difference between the monolingual and the two bilingual modes with contexts favoring *estar*; participants rated *estar* significantly higher than *ser* only in the monolingual mode. Regarding the role of the context, there is evidence of an extension of *ser* in contexts where the copula *estar* was favored, except for with physical property adjectives. The preference for the copula *ser* in contexts where it was favored was significantly higher than the preference for the copula *estar* in contexts where *estar* was favored with value, age, and dimension adjectives. Crucially, no context by speaker mode interaction was found, indicating that the difference in strength in copula preference between the two contexts was similar in monolingual and bilingual modes. The following section discusses these results in order to answer the research questions posed.

Discussion

The aim of this chapter is to examine Cuban HS copula choice in monolingual versus bilingual modes to determine if there is a CS effect and if so, if this effect would constitute an example of simplification. We anticipated a CS effect resulting in simplification of the copular verbs in Spanish. In this section we evaluate these hypotheses in light of the results.

From the results, it is evident that Cuban heritage speakers have a rather determinate knowledge of the distribution of *ser* and *estar* in Spanish in our data. Participants rated sentences with *ser* significantly higher than sentences with *estar* in contexts where *ser* was favored. More variation, however, was encountered with contexts favoring *estar*, where the rating of sentences with *estar* was not always significantly higher than with *ser*. This was particularly evident with dimension adjectives in monolingual mode and dimension and age adjectives in both bilingual mode conditions. Thus, in general, there was a preference for the favored copula in our data but there was also some variability. This variability, we will argue in what follows, is better interpreted as a loss of copular distinction in our data than as an extension of one of the copulas.

At first, the preference for the favored copula might seem contrary to the extension of *estar* widely reported in the literature. However, our results are in line with previous studies when we consider that the previous research reports an innovative *estar* in only around 20 percent of the data. While our data does not allow for direct comparisons with rates of use of *estar* in contexts favoring *ser* in variationist studies, it is worth pointing out that the rejections of *estar* in those contexts were not categorical in our data either. In the monolingual mode condition, with contexts favoring *ser*, where previous research reports an extension of *estar*, there is general rejection of responses with *estar* with physical property, value, and dimension adjectives (ratings below 2.5) but the mean ratings for age adjectives are within the acceptance rate (above 2.5). Without a monolingual control group to compare our bilingual speakers to and bearing in mind the variable nature of the copula distribution in Spanish, it is hard to interpret these data in terms of an extension of *estar*. What our data show, nonetheless, are cases where there is no significant preference for *ser* in cases favoring it, which is consistent with an interpretation of an extension of *estar*. Less clear are the cases where there is a significant preference for *ser* but where the sentences with *estar* are barely below the rejection range, although these cases are also consistent with an extension of *estar*. Thus, as in previous literature, these data show evidence of maintenance of copula distinction in Spanish, as in the prevalent preference for the favored copula, but also of extension of *estar* in *ser* contexts, as the ratings for *estar* sentences are not always below the acceptance range. This interpretation, however, needs to be revisited in light of the data from contexts favoring *estar*, where the variability in the ratings is more prevalent in Cuban Spanish–English second-generation HSs. With contexts favoring *estar*, there is a general rejection of sentences with *ser* with physical property and value adjectives but the mean ratings for dimension and age adjectives are within the acceptance rate. Therefore, our data are better explained by different degrees of copula distinction maintenance. In some cases, there is a clear preference for the favored copula while in others this distinction is being lost. These data do not indicate that this loss of distinction is in favor of *estar* since both copulas were rated the same in certain contexts. There are several reasons why our results might differ from the previous research where the results were interpreted as indicative of an extension of *estar*.

Previous research largely focused on contexts favoring *ser*, to the exclusion of contexts favoring *estar* from analysis (e.g., Alfaraz 2012). Thus, it is possible that variability might also be encountered in contexts favoring *estar* in data from previous studies. Our results, though, indicate the need to examine both contexts favoring *ser* and those favoring *estar*. Regardless, as was the case with previous research, there was evidence of variation with some but not all of the adjective classes examined in our data. In particular, our data indicate the loss of distinction between the copulas with dimension and age adjectives. With those adjectives the preference for a copula in a given context was not clear in either context. Thus, more than stipulating an extension of *estar* or *ser*, we interpret these data as indicative of neutralization of the copulas with certain adjective types.

Another difference between this study and previous research is the methodology employed. Our contextualized AJT task allowed us to control for variation by constructing contexts where the frame of reference, susceptibility to change, and other factors were manipulated such that they were all favoring the same copula in each context. We acknowledge, though, that this methodology is rather artificial and that triangulation with other tasks is necessary. We took measures to make the task less artificial by making the content relatable to our participants' daily lives and having them written by a member of the community of study. Although these measures may not have yielded data comparable to spontaneous production, to examine the specific contexts in the three different speaker modes, an interview would not have yielded enough instances of CSS and CSE involving copulas. The present data, however, call for further research using an elicited production task. In previous work on the effects of CS, we have successfully elicited specific forms (e.g. subject expression, the vowel /a/, clitic climbing) across speaker modes using a reading and retelling task as well as short answer questions. Future research should compare the results of this study with more naturally occurring uses of the copulas.

Reflecting on the research questions of this study, there is evidence of CS effects in our data. The variable speaker mode was significant with all adjectives with the exception of age adjectives, where the preference for the favored copula was stronger in monolingual than in bilingual modes. We interpret this effect as a weakening in preferences in bilingual modes. This effect was attested across contexts (there was no speaker mode by context interactions), indicating that the effects were in the same direction and of similar magnitude in contexts favoring *ser* and in contexts favoring *estar* (against the interpretation of the extension of *estar*). In fact, there is evidence that the strength of the preference for *ser* in contexts favoring *ser* is larger than the preference for *estar* in contexts favoring *estar* in our data (the variable context was significant with all adjective types except for physical property). In particular, both in the monolingual and in the bilingual mode conditions, contexts favoring *ser* had a significant preference for *ser* while some of the contexts favoring *estar* did not have a significant preference for *estar*. This extension of *ser* was more evident in the bilingual mode conditions. Since *estar* requires aspectual specifications, *ser* can be considered simpler. Thus, we interpret the effect attested in our data as an example of simplification. Although our results differ from those of Salazar (2007), who reports that CS had an effect on copula selection in favor of the innovative use of *estar*, there are many differences between the two studies that have to be considered. Salazar's (2007) data only included seven examples of local CS that would be comparable to our data. As stated above, the comparison of our data with more naturalistic elicited production data is necessary. Overall, our results are consistent with those in previous research on CS effects on variable phenomena (Prada Pérez and Toribio, under review; Prada Pérez 2015a; Toribio 2004; Torres Cacoullos and Travis 2010) in that a CS effect that can be interpreted as a simplification is attested. While Toribio (2004) attributed the increase in overt pronominal subjects in Spanish-English CS to convergence, Torres Cacoullos and Travis (2010) attributed it to priming from English. In the current study, priming was controlled for in the methodology; no copula was used in any of the contexts. Thus, priming from English cannot explain our data. While convergence with English is a possible interpretation here (*es* is rather similar to 'is'), so is a simplification interpretation. These two accounts would make different predictions for copula selection data in other tenses. Other research projects seem to indicate that simplification is a better account for CS effects (Prada Pérez 2015a), an interpretation that we posit here. This simplification effect can be ascribed to the demanding processing of simultaneously activating both languages as in CS.

Conclusion

In conclusion, the present study sought to examine the effect of code-switching among Cuban heritage speakers in regard to copula choice across different adjective classes. The data indicate robust knowledge of copula distribution with certain adjective classes while other classes admitted more variation. The variation attested in our data we argued was better interpreted as loss of distinction between the copulas than as the extension of one of the copulas. This loss of distinction, though, was more prevalent in contexts favoring *estar* than in contexts favoring *ser*, where the preference for *ser* was stronger.

Finally, the present chapter contributes to the field of Hispanic linguistics in that it presents findings of a dual extension of the copulas within code-switching modes. Many theories have presented themselves within this field to try to answer questions about how exactly code-switching mechanisms function, if and how bilinguals balance both language systems when code-switching, and if there is a grammar the bilingual chooses more than the other when activating these systems simultaneously. This study's results, in particular, align with the theory of simplification, where bilingual speakers resort to less complex or cognitively costly forms, in this case *ser* (Clements 2006). This at least would explain why these participants lose the copula distinction with some adjectives.

Notes

We would like to thank Alexa Pérez, Charlotte Park, and Jarret Lane for their help piloting the study, Susana Braylan and Phillip Carter for their help during the data collection, and the two anonymous reviewers and the editor of this volume for their useful comments. Any mistakes remain our own.

1. We do not anticipate differences across proficiency and generational groups with respect to the effects of CS. Thus, they were not included in the statistical analysis.
2. Note that no translation is offered for examples 14.4 and 14.5 as they are equivalent to example 14.3.
3. An even number scale was used to avoid the use of the middle point as an uncertain response instead of an intermediate judgment of the sentence. Additionally, the option to indicate uncertainty was given separate from the scale with an 'N/A, not sure' option.

References

Alfaraz, G. 2012. "The Status of the Extension of estar in Cuban Spanish." *Studies in Hispanic and Lusophone Linguistics* 5 (1): 3–25.

Bills, G. D. and Vigil, N. 1999. *New Mexico Colorado Spanish Survey*. Albuquerque: University of New Mexico.

Bosque, I. 1990. "Sobre el aspecto en los adjetivos y en los participios." In *Tiempo y aspecto en Español*, edited by I. Bosque, 177–211. Madrid: Cátedra.

Brown, E. and M. Cortés-Torres. 2012. "Syntactic and Pragmatic Usage of the [estar + Adjective] Construction in Puerto Rican Spanish: ¡Está brutal!" In *Selected Proceedings of the 14th Hispanic Linguistics Symposium*, edited by K. Geeslin and M. Díaz-Campos, 61–74. Somerville, MA: Cascadilla Proceedings Project.

Camacho, J. 2012. "Ser and Estar: The Individual/Stage-level Distinction and Aspectual Predication." In *The Handbook of Hispanic Linguistics*, edited by J. I. Hualde, A. Olarrea, and E. O'Rourke, 453–76. Chichester, Eng.: Wiley-Blackwell.

Carlson, G. 1989. "On the Semantic Composition of English Generic Sentences." In *Properties, Types and Meaning*, vol. 2, *Semantic Issues*, edited by G. Chierchia, B. H. Partee, and R. Turner, 167–92. Dordrecht, Nld.: Kluwer.

Clements, J. C. 2006. "Ser-estar in the Predicate Adjective Construction." In *Functional Approaches to Spanish Syntax: Lexical Semantics, Discourse, and Transitivity*, edited by J. C. Clements and J. Yoon, 161–202. London: Palgrave MacMillan.

Cortés-Torres, M. 2004. "¿Ser o estar? la variación lingüística y social de estar más adjetivo en el español de Cuernavaca, México." *Hispania* 87 (4): 788–95.

de Jonge, B. 1993. "(Dis)Continuity in Language Change: "Ser" and "estar" + Age in Latin American Spanish." In *Linguistics in the Netherlands*, edited by F. Drijkoningen and K. Hengeveld, 69–80. Amsterdam: John Benjamins.

Díaz-Campos, M., and K. L. Geeslin. 2011. "Copula Use in the Spanish of Venezuela: Is the Pattern Indicative of Stable Variation or an Ongoing Change?" *Spanish in Context* 8 (1): 73–94.

Falk, J. 1979. *Ser y estar con atributos adjetivales*. Uppsala, Swe.: Alqvist and Wiksell.

Fernández Leborans, M. J. 1999. "La predicación: Las oraciones copulativas." In *Gramática descriptiva de la lengua española*, edited by I. Bosque and V. Demonte, 2354–460. Madrid: Espasa.

Guijarro-Fuentes, P., and K. L. Geeslin. 2008. "Introduction to Language Acquisition, Bilingualism and Copula Choice in Spanish." *Bilingualism: Language and Cognition* 11 (Special Issue 3): 273–75.

Gutiérrez, M. J. 1992. "The Extension of estar: A Linguistic Change in Progress in the Spanish of Morelia, Mexico." *Hispanic Linguistics* 5 (1-2): 109–41.

———. 1994. *Ser y estar en el habla de Michoacán, México*. Distrito Federal, Méx.: Universidad Autónoma de México.

———. 2003. "Simplification and Innovation in US Spanish." *Multilingua* 22:169–84.

Leonetti, M. 1994. "'Ser' y 'estar': Estado de la cuestión." *Barataria* 1:182–205.

López-González, M. 2010. "Ser and Estar: Their Syntax, Semantics, Pragmatics, and Acquistion in Mexican Spanish." PhD diss., Johns Hopkins University.

Luján, M. 1981. "The Spanish Copulas as Aspectual Indicators." *Lingua* 54 (2): 165–210.

Maienborn, C. 2005. "A Discourse-Based Account of Spanish ser/estar." *Linguistics* 43 (1): 155–80.

Malaver, I. 2000. "'Cuando estábamos chiquitos': 'Ser' y 'estar' en expresiones adjetivales de edad. Un fenómeno americano." *Boletin de Lingüística* 16:44–65.

Ortiz López, L. A. 2000. "Extensión de estar en contextos de ser en el español de Puerto Rico: ¿evaluación interna y/o contacto de lenguas?" *Boletín de la Academia Puertorriqueña de la Lengua Española*, 98–118.

Prada Pérez, A. de. 2015a. "Code-Switching Effects: Evidence from Variable Subject Pronoun Expression in Spanish-Catalan Bilinguals." Paper presented at the Hispanic Linguistics Symposium, Urbana-Champaign, Illinois, September 24–27.

———. 2015b. "First Person Singular Subject Pronoun Expression in Spanish in Contact with Catalan." In *Subject Pronoun Expression in Spanish: A Cross-Dialectal Perspective*, edited by A. M. Carvalho, R. Orozco, and N. L. Shin, 121–43. Washington, DC: Georgetown University Press.

Prada Pérez, A. de, and A. J. Toribio. Under review. "The Effects of Syntactic Priming and Language Mode in Bilingual Spanish."

Roby, D. B. 2009. *Aspect and the Categorization of States: The Case of ser and estar in Spanish*. Amsterdam: John Benjamins

Salazar, M. L. 2007. "*Está muy diferente a como era antes*: 'Ser' and 'estar' + Adjective in New Mexico Spanish." In *Spanish in Contact: Policy, Social and Linguistic Inquiries*, edited by K. Potowski and R. Cameron, 343–53. Amsterdam: John Benjamins.

Silva-Corvalán, C. 1986. "Bilingualism and Language Change: The Extension of estar in Los Angeles Spanish." *Language* 62 (3): 587–608.

———. 1994. *Language Contact and Change: Spanish in Los Angeles*. Oxford: Clarendon Press.

Toribio, A. J. 2004. "Convergence as an Optimization Strategy in Bilingual Speech: Evidence from Code-Switching." *Bilingualism: Language and Cognition* 7 (2): 165–73.

Torres Cacoullos, R., and C. E. Travis. 2011. "Testing Convergence via Code-Switching: Priming and the Structure of Variable Subject Expression." *International Journal of Bilingualism* 15 (3): 241–67.

Contributors

Gabriela G. Alfaraz is an associate professor in the Department of Romance and Classical Studies at Michigan State University. Her research interests include language variation and change, language attitudes, bilingualism, and Cuban Spanish dialectology.

Scott M. Alvord is an associate professor of Hispanic linguistics at Brigham Young University. His main research interests are in Spanish phonetics and phonology, especially in language contact or learning environments.

Ann Aly is a member of the Center for Assessment, Research, and Development at the American Council on the Teaching of Foreign Languages (ACTFL). She received her PhD in linguistics from UCLA, where her research areas included phonetics, bilingualism, and intonation. Ann's current research involves code-switching, language education, and prosody.

Héctor Aponte Alequín is an adjunct professor in the School of Communication and in the Graduate Programs of Linguistics and Translation at the University of Puerto Rico, Río Piedras. His research focuses on syntax, variation, and applied linguistics, with Caribbean Spanish as the target language.

José Camacho is a full professor of Spanish linguistics at Rutgers University and specializes in theoretical syntax.

Pascual Cantos Gómez is a full professor of English linguistics at the University of Murcia (Spain). His main research interests are in corpus linguistics, quantitative linguistics, and computational lexicography. He is the head of the LACELL (Applied Computational Linguistics, Second Language Learning and Lexicography) Research Group and president of the Spanish Association of Corpus Linguistics (AELINCO).

Kristin M. Carlson is an assistant professor of languages and chair of the Department of Languages at Thiel College. Her research interests include phonetics and phonology, acoustic and articulatory phonetics, general and theoretical Spanish linguistics, and Caribbean Spanish dialectology.

Alejandro Cuza is a full professor of Spanish and director of linguistics at Purdue University. His research addresses formal approaches to the acquisition of Spanish morphosyntax and semantics, heritage language acquisition, and child bilingual development.

Ashlee Dauphinais is a PhD candidate in Hispanic linguistics at Ohio State University. Her areas of focus currently include phonetics, sociocultural linguistics, and linguistic variation, particularly in the Caribbean and Brazil.

Gibran Delgado-Díaz is a PhD candidate at Indiana University, Bloomington. His research focuses on sociolinguistic variation in Caribbean Spanish. He is particularly interested in tense and aspect variation in L1 Spanish as well as sociophonetic variation.

Manuel Díaz-Campos is a full professor of Hispanic sociolinguistics at Indiana University, Bloomington. He has published on phonological and morphosyntactic variation, the acquisition of sociolinguistic variables in L1, including phonological and morphosyntactic variation, acquisition of second language phonology, and topics in Spanish laboratory phonology.

Daniel Erker is an assistant professor of Spanish and linguistics at Boston University. His primary interests are linguistic variation and the intersection of language and society, especially as these topics relate to Spanish in the United States.

Antoni Fernández Parera is a PhD candidate in Hispanic linguistics at the University of Miami. His research interests are second and heritage language acquisition through the lens of sociocultural theory, sociolinguistics, and Cuban Spanish.

Josh Frank is a PhD candidate at the University of Texas at Austin. His research considers representational- and processing-based accounts to language acquisition and usage, with specific reference to morphosyntactic properties in bilingual populations.

Iraida Galarza is a PhD candidate at Indiana University, Bloomington. Her dissertation focuses on the acquisition of mood and modality in L2 Spanish. Her research interests include the acquisition of variation in L2 Spanish, the production, perception, and linguistic attitudes toward sociophonetic variables.

Inmaculada Gómez Soler is an assistant professor of Spanish and director of the Basic Spanish Program at University of Memphis. Her research interests focus on second language acquisition and heritage speaker bilingualism, especially as they pertain to the syntax-semantics and syntax-pragmatics interfaces.

Robert M. Hammond is emeritus professor of linguistics and Romance languages at Purdue University. His principal areas of research are Caribbean Spanish phonetics, phonology and dialectology, experimental phonetics, and psychoacoustics. Prior to his twenty-five years at Purdue University, he held full-time professorial positions at the Universidad Interamericana in Puerto Rico, the University of Florida, Boston University, Miami-Dade College, and the Catholic University of America. Two of his books, *Introducción a la historia de la lengua Española*, 2011 (with Melvyn C. Resnick) and *The Sounds of Spanish: Analysis and Application*, 2001, are widely used in universities across the US.

Andrea Hernández studied Spanish at the University of Florida and graduated with her bachelor of arts in 2014. She is currently finishing her master's in education and specialist education degree in mental health counseling also at the University of Florida.

Eduardo Ho-Fernández is a PhD candidate in Hispanic linguistics at the Graduate Center, CUNY. His primary interests are in the areas of functional linguistics, language contact, and language change.

Andrew Lynch is an associate professor of Spanish and Latin American studies at the University of Miami. He has published numerous studies and essays on the sociolinguistic situation of Spanish in the United States and, specifically, bilingualism among the Cuban-origin population in Miami.

Luis A. Ortiz López is a full professor of Hispanic linguistics and linguistics at the University of Puerto Rico, Rio Piedras Campus. His research areas include sociolinguistics, language contact and change, morphosyntactic variation, second language acquisition, and Afro Hispanic linguistics.

Ricardo Otheguy is emeritus professor of linguistics at the Graduate Center, CUNY. His work in theoretical linguistics is in the areas of sociolinguistics, language contact, functional-semiotic approaches to grammar, and the study of Spanish of the United States. In applied linguistics, his publications are in the areas of bilingual education and the teaching and assessment of the language of Latinos in the United States.

Diego Pascual y Cabo is an assistant professor of Hispanic linguistics and the director of the Spanish Heritage Language Program at Texas Tech University. His primary research interests are heritage speaker bilingualism and second language acquisition.

Ana de Prada Pérez is an assistant professor of Hispanic linguistics in the Department of Spanish and Portuguese studies at the University of Florida. Her research focuses on language contact outcomes of Spanish-English and Spanish-Catalan bilingualism.

Brandon M. A. Rogers is an assistant professor of Spanish linguistics and language at Ball State University. His primary research interests are phonetics and phonology, particularly sociophonetics, prosody, and language contact and change.

Naomi Lapidus Shin is an associate professor of linguistics and Hispanic linguistics at the University of New Mexico. Her primary interests include bilingualism, language contact, child language acquisition, and morphosyntactic variation.

Almeida Jacqueline Toribio is a full professor of linguistics in the Department of Spanish and Portuguese at the University of Texas at Austin. Her areas of scholarship include language variation and a trajectory from theoretical to more empirically based approaches, as she examines the ways in which the facts of rural and contact varieties can be brought to bear on issues central to structural linguistics and sociolinguistics.

Index

Figures and tables are denoted by the letters *t* and *f* following the page number.

www.ingramcontent.com/pod-product-compliance
Lightning Source LLC
LaVergne TN
LVHW010352080826
844660LV00004B/252

* 9 7 8 1 6 2 6 1 6 5 0 9 0 *